Tax Systems and Tax Reforms in Latin America

This book provides a comprehensive analysis of tax systems and tax reforms in a number of Latin American countries since the early 1990s, including Argentina and Brazil, Costa Rica and Mexico, Paraguay, Colombia, Chile and Uruguay.

The authors present and discuss tax systems from a broad quantitative and historical perspective and describe the main taxes existing in each country, presenting the details of their institutional features. The existing interactions between the economic structure, the corporate tax system and the attraction of FDI inflows are of paramount importance and these issues are deeply analyzed in the book. A characteristic trait of the area is the proliferation of tax havens, particularly located in the Caribbean and in some other small islands, and the book provides an analysis of these havens and the counteractions adopted by the OECD countries. Finally, the book investigates the political economy of Latin America's taxation, exploring why many of these countries have experienced a democratic transition but poor economic performances.

The book presents an impressive array of hitherto difficult to source information which can be followed by the non-specialist reader. It is highly relevant to postgraduate courses concerning taxation, both at an empirical and a theoretical level, and will also be useful for international economic organizations, tax research centers, tax planning agencies and consultants.

Luigi Bernardi is Professor of Public Finance at the University of Pavia, Italy. **Alberto Barreix** is Senior Fiscal Economist at the Inter-American Development Bank, Washington, DC, USA. **Anna Marenzi** is Professor of Public Economics at the University of Insubria, Varese, Italy. **Paola Profeta** is Professor of Public Economics at Bocconi University, Milan, Italy.

Routledge international studies in money and banking

Tax Systems and Tax Reforms in Latin America

**Edited by Luigi Bernardi,
Alberto Barreix, Anna Marenzi
and Paola Profeta**

Introduction by Vito Tanzi

Routledge
Taylor & Francis Group

LONDON AND NEW YORK

First published 2008
by Routledge
2 Park Square, Milton Park, Abingdon, Oxon OX14 4RN

Simultaneously published in the USA and Canada
by Routledge
270 Madison Ave, New York, NY 10016

Routledge is an imprint of the Taylor & Francis Group, an informa business

© 2008 Editorial matter and selection, Luigi Bernardi, Alberto Barreix, Anna Marenzi and Paola Profeta; individual chapters, the contributors

Typeset in Times by Wearset Ltd, Boldon, Tyne and Wear

British Library Cataloguing in Publication Data
A catalogue record for this book is available from the British Library

Library of Congress Cataloging in Publication Data
A catalog record for this book has been requested

ISBN10: 0-415-44336-9 (hbk)
ISBN10: 0-203-48139-9 (ebk)

ISBN13: 978-0-415-44336-4 (hbk)
ISBN13: 978-0-203-48139-4 (ebk)

Contents

PART II
Country studies of tax systems and tax reforms in Latin America

Illustrations

Figures

Tables

Contributors

José Roberto Afonso, Economist, National Bank for Economic and Social Development – BNDES and University of Campinas – UNICAMP, Avenida Chile 100/1405, Rio de Janeiro, 20031–917, Brazil.

Daniel Alvarez, Advisor to the Revenue Policy Unit, Ministry of Finance and Public Credit of Mexico, Hidalgo 77, Col. Guerrero, 06300 Mexico, DF, Mexico.

Alberto Barreix, Senior Fiscal Economist, Inter-American Development Bank, 1300 New York Av. NW, Washington, DC, 20577, USA.

Rafael Barroso, Senior Adviser to the Secretary, San Paolo State Secretariat of Finance, Rua Ouro Branco, 75/21B, San Paolo 01425–080, Brazil.

Luigi Bernardi, Professor of Public Finance, Department of Public and Environmental Economics, University of Pavia, Strada Nuova 65, 27100 Pavia, Italy.

Martin Bès, Fiscal Economist, Inter-American Development Bank, 1300 New York Av. NW, Washington, DC, 20577, USA.

Matteo Cominetta, Ph.D. student, Department of Economics, University of Sussex, Falmer, Brighton, BN1 9SN, UK.

Jorge Cornick, Economist, Executive Director EurekaRed Comunicación Centroamericana and independent consultant, San José, Costa Rica. P.O. Box 707–1005.

Caterina Ferrario, Assistant Professor of Public Finance, University of Ferrara and Econpubblica – Università Bocconi, University of Ferrara, Via Voltapaletto 11, 44100 Ferrara, Italy.

Francesco Figari, Research Fellow, University of Genova, Department of Economic and Financial Sciences – DISEFIN, Largo Zecca 8–14, 16124 Genova, Italy and Institute for Social and Economic Research, University of Essex, Colchester, CO4 3SQ, UK.

Elena Fumagalli, Ph.D. Student, Department of Economics, University of Venice, S. Giobbe, 873–30121 Venice, Italy.

Laura Fumagalli, Ph.D. Student, Institute for Social and Economic Research, University of Essex, Colchester CO4 3SQ, UK and Department of Public and Environmental Economics, University of Pavia, Strada Nuova 65, 27100 Pavia, Italy.

Luca Gandullia, Professor of Public Economics, Department of Economic and Financial Sciences – DISEFIN, University of Genova, Largo Zecca 8–14, 16124 Genova, Italy.

Juan C. Gómez Sabaini, Professor of Tax Policy, Universidad Nacional de Buenos Aires, Independent Consultant, Esmeralda 847, piso 12, 1007 Buenos Aires, Argentina.

Giorgia Maffini, Research Fellow, Department of Public and Environmental Economics. University of Pavia, Strada Nuova 65, 27100 Pavia, Italy, Ph.D. Student in Economics, University of Warwick, UK.

Anna Marenzi, Professor of Public Economics, Department of Economics, University of Insubria, Via Monte Generoso 71, 21100 Varese, Italy.

Ricardo Martner, Chief, Area of Budgeting and Public Management, ECLAC, United Nations, Avenida Dag Hammarskjold 3477, Santiago, Chile.

Jeffrey Owens, Director, Centre for Tax Policy and Administration, Organization for Economic Co-operation and Development, 2 rue André-Pascal, 75775 Paris Cedex 16, France.

Paola Profeta, Professor of Public Economics, Università Bocconi and Research Fellow at Econpubblica, Università Bocconi, Via Gobbi, 5, 20136 Milano, Italy.

Jerónimo Roca, Researcher, Department of Quantitative Economics (Economic Analysis II), Universidad Complutense of Madrid and Independent Consultant, Valle del Roncal 7, 1ero. C. 28230, Las Rozas, Madrid, Spain.

Alessandra Sanelli, Economist, Fiscal Department, Bank of Italy, Via Pastrengo, 14, 00185 Rome, Italy.

Simona Scabrosetti, Assistant Professor of Public Economics, Department of Public and Environmental Economics. University of Pavia, Strada Nuova 65, 27100 Pavia, Italy.

Vito Tanzi, Senior consultant Inter-American Development Bank, 5912 Walhonding Road, Bethesda MD 20816, USA.

Eric Thompson, Tax Partner Facio & Cañas, Tax Consultant and Litigator, Barrio Tournon, San José, Costa Rica, P.O. Box 5173–1000.

Adrian Torrealba, Tax Partner Facio & Cañas, Professor of Tax Law, Universidad para la Cooperación Internacional, Universidad de Costa Rica, Barrio Tournon, San José, Costa Rica, P.O. Box 5173–1000.

Preface

To present a book on taxation in Latin America is not an easy task. Countries largely differ for their dimension, economic structure and wealth, historical heritage, political and administrative institutions. Other features contribute to this complex picture: the presence of many custom unions, the tight political relationship with the US – which shapes political choices in many countries – the particular surveillance of fiscal policies by the IMF and other international organizations through binding agreements. All these factors make it difficult to find a large number of common features among Latin American countries' tax systems. The neat Musgrave's distinction between "early period" and "modern" tax systems cannot encompass the articulate scattering of Latin American tax systems. Nor this task can be performed using uni-dimensional criteria for classifying tax systems, such as for instance the level of fiscal pressure, taxation structure, intensity of recent tax reforms, "modernity" of main single taxes. Each of these criteria in fact would deliver a different evaluation of Latin American tax systems. However a multidimensional classification criterion is not easy to found – perhaps it does not exist.

To deal with this complex picture, we present more country chapters and a deeper analysis for each of them with respect to the previous companion volumes of the same Routledge series (2004: EU 15; 2005: EU NMS; 2006: South and East Asia, all still available in electronic format). The book gives to the interested reader – in a friendly user format, distilled from many not easily accessible sources – comprehensive descriptions and analyses of tax systems and tax reforms in a large sample of representative Latin American countries. The book discusses three larger countries (Argentina and Brazil in South America and Mexico in North America), an example of a small Central American economy (Costa Rica), two Andean countries (Chile and Colombia), a Mediterranean economy (Paraguay), and one small country which made relevant tax reforms in the last year (Uruguay). The countries' studies follow a similar layout. They begin with an introduction which gives some reference data for the country, such as its main economic, institutional and public budget features. In a second section, the tax system is presented and discussed in a broad quantitative and historical perspective and in a comparative view. The third section describes the main taxes of each country and presents the details of their institutional features.

The fourth section discusses the main debated tax policy issues. Finally, the last section examines the recent undertaken or planned tax reforms, and sketches out authors' recommendations to improve the country's tax system.

The aim of this book is not only to inform the interested reader with descriptive materials on Latin American tax systems. We also want to equip the reader with a series of cross-country critical analyses – supported by taxation's multifaceted theory – on the main tax policy issues which arise across the selected countries. To begin with, Tanzi's introduction aims at providing the reader with a broad perspective on Latin American tax systems and on the historical, geographic and structural forces that have influenced and shaped them during the past 50 years. Historical factors, such as cultural links with Europe and the United States combined with structural factors, such as the openness of the countries economies, their degrees of informality, their dependence on the export of natural resources, and the allocation of national income between labor and capital all played major roles in shaping the Latin American tax systems. Tanzi also discusses the role that the United States played, or attempted to play, through various international organizations (especially in the 1950s and 1960s) in making the tax systems of Latin American countries more elastic and progressive. Coming to the major taxes, Tanzi provides an explanation of why the personal income tax has not grown into a major source of revenue in Latin America. The main reasons are:

1   the large share of national income that does *not* go to wages and salaries;
2   the high levels of personal exemptions (as compared to per capita incomes) and of deductions;
3   the fear that higher taxes on incomes from capital sources could lead to capital flight, especially towards the United States.

The United States' treatment of interest payments to "non resident aliens" gives substance to this fear. Latin American countries were among the first to introduce value added taxes and have been quite successful in the use of this tax. Several such countries collect from these taxes as large a share of their GDPs from these taxes as industrial countries. However, there is a large dispersion in the revenue productivity of these taxes among the various countries. Zero rating for some categories of goods and services and the use of multiple rates are major reasons for this dispersion in productivity. Tanzi also discusses issues related to the taxation of enterprise profits and especially problems raised by the use of transfer prices, and by the fluctuation in the prices of products from natural resources. An interesting aspect of the Latin American taxation of enterprises is the taxation of small enterprises. There has been a lot of experimentation related to the taxation of these enterprises. Various reforms have replaced taxes based on accounting with taxes based on presumptive criteria. Finally, attention is called to the growth of tax levels in the past two decades and to the continuing search for new taxes (taxes on assets, taxes on financial transaction, taxes on net wealth, etc.) that could provide revenue in a less painful way. This search for an

Eldorado of the tax world seems to be a Latin American characteristic that is likely to persist.

One of the main goals of taxation is to finance goods and to services government expenditures, as we are reminded by Gómez Sabaini and Martner (Chapter 1). Thus, the choice of the level of taxation indicates, in the medium run, the level of public expenditures. A way to evaluate if the levels of taxation and the tax structures are "appropriate" is to compare the relation between taxes and GDP for a large number of countries. A simple evaluation shows that the fiscal pressure in OECD is 2.2 times the fiscal pressure of Latin America and the Caribbean. In OECD countries, direct taxes and social security contributions are relatively more important, while the tax system of Latin America and the Caribbean is mainly based on indirect taxation. Despite the general growth of the average fiscal pressure in all countries (with the exception of Mexico), which started in the early 1990s and accelerated in the last two years, there still exist potential space to further increase fiscal pressure (Brazil is the big exception). The effective fiscal pressure is below the expected or potential level given the per capita income, a gap that can be estimated between 10 percent and 20 percent. Furthermore, in the majority of Latin American countries, the distribution of revenues *ex post* is more concentrated than *ex ante*, meaning that the overall effect of the tax system is regressive. Unfortunately this happens in one of the most unequal areas of the world. In this sense, the extension of inequality of revenues in the region has affected the design and implementation of the tax system. Indeed, VAT and excises accounts for more than 70 percent of tax revenues and, strikingly, personal income taxation rarely reached 2 percent of GDP in spite of fact that in all Latin American countries more than 50 percent of total income belongs to the richest 20 percent of the population. From the political perspective, social inequality may be explained by the supremacy of "élite groups," who try to minimize their relative fiscal burden by controlling the legislative process. This generates a vicious circle of inequality of revenues and tax regressivity, instead of a virtuous circle which may correct the large disequilibrium of revenue through the tax system. Hence, the current country tax systems have been the result of a series of compromising decisions adopted under different circumstances.

Beginning in the 1980s, and until the mid-1990s, Latin American countries began to implement a set of tax reforms that fiscally supported the trade and financial liberalizations switching from the import substitution developing model to an export promotion strategy. These reforms, based on the structural adjustment approach that followed the debt crises of the early 1980s, were focused on revenue enhancing and neutrality. According to Figari and Gandullia (Chapter 2), these reforms have been influenced by exogenous determinants, such as the urgency to consolidate public finances and the external constraints deriving from trade and capital liberalization. The general goal of tax reforms was to enhance revenue collections and provide more stability in the revenue systems. In this context tax reforms have tended to include the following elements: implementation of broad-based and uniform VAT systems; reduction in the highest statutory tax rates; reduction in preferential tax treatments for specific sources of corporate income and specific economic sectors; modernization and strengthening of the institutions involved in tax administration. Although not fully implemented, these reforms have generally increased the efficiency of tax systems and their revenue-raising capacity. However, they have come at a price: other issues have been driven off the tax policy agenda. Figari and Gandullia agree with Gómez Sabaini and Martner that the excluded issues include considerations of tax equity and redistribution and the financing of social security programs. With few exceptions Latin American countries continue to be "allergic" to taxing incomes and collecting social security contributions. Thus revenues from income taxes continue to be low compared with international levels. On the contrary, Latin American countries rely heavily on indirect taxes, mainly VAT and excise duties, but also foreign trade taxes. At present, after two decades of tax reforms, there is still the issue of raising more tax revenue, but the main challenges for next years seem to be: broadening tax bases and enlarging the number of taxpayers, especially in the field of direct taxes; reducing reliance on the more distorting taxes, such as those on financial transactions, exports, and enterprise turnover and payroll; and improving tax administration.

Each country chapter in the book devotes a section to the analysis of the structure of the levels of government and the intra-layers financing. We here provide some general comment on this issue. The main characteristic of the fiscal decentralization process in Latin America is that in many countries it occurred in the last three decades, together with democratization. Fiscal decentralization, both as an economic and a political process, has failed to smooth growth disparities, to enlarge service provision, and to increase fiscal efficiency, or equity. Actually, the region displays both serious "vertical" imbalances – shortfalls due to insufficient revenues to cover expenditures – and "horizontal" imbalances – generated for the heterogeneous fiscal capacity of sub-national governments in both the federal republics (i.e. Argentina, Brazil, Mexico and Venezuela) and the more unitary regimes. With the exception of Uruguay and Chile – which collect close to 2 percent on GPD at municipal level – in the unitary regimes, revenues from property taxes (including levies on vehicles) are particularly weak. They account for less than 0.4 percent of GDP. Due to the lack of political will for improving institutional capacity, most of the countries had no updated cadastral information or reliable registry of property. Moreover, limited borrowing autonomy makes municipalities dependent on government transfers, and on discretionary programs of the executive power.[1] In the past, large Latin American countries had serious problems in the decentralization process with enormous difficulties on transfers distribution and the control of sub-national expenditure. This triggered a wave of fiscal responsibility laws that succeeded in curbing deficits but not on improving fiscal sustainability and/or efficiency of sub-national jurisdictions. Although increasing revenue sources to sub-national governments were approved by the congress, Mexico's sub-national governments barely collect 0.8 percent of GDP, municipal property taxes are less than 0.3 percent and a similar figure is collected on payroll taxes. Argentina faces a significant challenge as well: sub-national levels of government collect close to 5 percent of GDP (provincial around 4 percent and municipal 1 percent) but spend about 11 percent of GDP. Moreover, provincial taxation includes a sales tax (2.5 percent of GDP) that is collected in addition to the national VAT with significant cumulative effect. In Brazil, on the other hand, states and municipalities collect almost 12 percent of GDP and spend around 14 percent. The two main revenue sources, ICMS (state tax on consumption and other revenues) and ISS (municipal tax on services), which collect almost 10 percent of GDP, present serious cumulative effects. Colombia is a particular case; since the 1991 Constitutional Reform, it started to assign greater control over welfare expenditure to the municipalities. Actually, revenue share – especially on excises – produced a sharp rise in the flow of resources from central to the lower governments, which are added to sub-national taxes (above 2.5 percent of GDP), thus making Colombian municipalities financially stronger than the rest of Latin America's. Finally, it is worth noting that Peru and Venezuela have started a decentralization process. Small steps have been undertaken on sub-national taxation, while the emphasis was on transfer mechanisms to finance social and infrastructure spending.

The political economy of Latin America's taxation is a crucial issue, as analyzed in Profeta and Scabrosetti's chapter (Chapter 3). In the last decades many Latin American countries have experienced a democratic transition, but poor economic performances. Despite the democratic transition, fiscal pressure has remained low in most countries, contrary to the predictions of the prevailing political economy literature on democracy and economic development, and the median voter's theories. Moreover, the tax structure turns out to be dominated by indirect taxes, with a low weight of income and capital taxes. Thus, while political economy theories predict an increase of redistributive taxation associated with democratic institutions, in many Latin American countries taxation is almost regressive, and the very high *ex ante* income inequality is even larger *ex post*. This is especially surprising in countries, such as Latin American ones, where the support for democracies largely relies on economic issues. After assessing this puzzling evidence, the authors try to reconcile it with political explanations, by including specific elements which characterize politics in Latin America and may have played a role in keeping the fiscal pressure low despite the democratic transition. Their arguments can be grouped as follows:

1 the quality of many Latin American democracies suffers from low levels of representation, while vested interests, or lobbying and interest groups, play a crucial role, leading to economic outcomes rather different than median voter's choices.
2 Financial institutions, which are crucial for tax enforcement, have typically provided a low value added to Latin American firms which use them, generating a high degree of "disintermediation."

3   the economic policies suffer from the heritage of "populism," which in previous political regimes was keeping taxation very low in order to maintain the support of the mass, even at a cost of increasing debt.

All these arguments have a role in this complex evidence and the best explanation has to be thought of as a combination of them.

As in all developing and transition countries, a very important tax policy issue in Latin America concerns the effects of the corporation income tax (CIT) and fiscal incentives on foreign direct investment (FDI). This issue is discussed in Maffini and Marenzi's chapter (Chapter 4). The CIT affects both the marginal and inframarginal return to investment through the effective marginal and the effective average tax rate. Hence, together with tax incentives, it is an important factor in determining the cross-country distribution of FDI. After the restrictive policies of the 1970s and the debt crisis of the 1980s, FDI in Latin America became a key factor for fostering growth and development. The liberalization of the economy and the deregulation and privatization of services have largely contributed to the FDI inflows in the region since the 1990s. Fiscal incentives to the booming FDIs were generally granted in the form of tax-free free-trade zones. In the same years, many countries in the region tried to reorganize their fiscal systems more efficiently, mainly following the "low-rate broad-based" (LRBB) approach. As a result, nowadays Latin America has relatively low statutory corporate tax rates although there are still differentials in the tax rates and in the maturity of the CIT system. Nonetheless, the benefits from tax competition are not equally distributed among the countries of our selected sample. Today, Latin America seems to lose headway to East Asian competitors, especially in attracting high value-added FDIs. Globalization in the form of increased trade and foreign investment has put fiscal systems under even more pressure. Developing countries all around the world have to attract investment in a more competitive environment and therefore they still have to make use of fiscal incentives. At the same time, it is important to maintain an adequate stream of revenues for financing projects (e.g. education of the labor force, infrastructures) aimed at making the location more attractive, especially for those FDIs more likely to have positive spillovers in the local economy. Latin American fiscal administrations started adopting measures to protect their tax base internationally. They endorsed transfer-pricing, thin capitalization rules and Controlled Foreign Corporation legislation. They developed a network of tax treaties against double taxation, as well. This is a further step in the direction of a more efficient and modern fiscal system. The reforms were not implemented by all countries of the region, though. Furthermore, complex rules such as those regulating transfer-pricing are sometimes not enforced as the administrations still lack the expertise to apply them.

A specific feature of taxation in the area is a concentration of fiscal havens, especially in the Caribbean region. This topic is discussed by Owens and Sanelli (Chapter 5). The authors examine the role of Caribbean tax havens and review them in the light of the OECD's *Harmful Tax Practices* initiative. Over the last

30 years, with the growth of international capital flows fostered by improved communications and liberalization of financial markets, individuals and companies have made an increasing use of offshore financial centers for tax evasion and avoidance. The resulting concerns over the potential adverse consequences on the economies of non-haven countries led the OECD to launch in 1998 the *Harmful Tax Practices* initiative, which put a great emphasis on information exchange between national tax authorities. Consistently with the theoretical finding, many Caribbean jurisdictions have found in the offshore financial center sector a viable alternative for their economic development as other traditional sectors, such as agriculture, declined. Offshore financial services required a modest initial investment and the colonial heritage and proximity to or links with major onshore financial centers (such as the US and the UK) gave these territories important competitive advantages, which have been strengthened through the adoption of favorable tax rules. The move has been quite successful for some jurisdictions (the Bahamas, the Cayman Islands, the British Virgin Islands, Bermuda), which have become leading OFCs. Others, particularly some of the late arrivals, had little success, because they have not been able to offer any advantage over the more established centers. Overall, available indicators show that the size of the Caribbean tax havens varies significantly from one jurisdiction to another, and that there is a wide range of specialization across the region. The specific features of each Caribbean offshore center affect their response to the OECD *Harmful Tax Practices* initiative. Although 35 jurisdictions have made commitments to the international standards on transparency and exchange of information, effective compliance varies across the region. The more established centers, which had already developed extensive regulatory frameworks and thus have been able to introduce the additional measures without substantial costs, are well ahead in the process. Nevertheless, some of the smaller Caribbean centers still lag behind.

To sum up and conclude, it seems that Latin American tax systems share at least one common feature. They all represent (perhaps with the exception of Chile, which is a relatively "modern" system) transition tax systems. Our general suggestion – to improve selected countries' tax systems – translates into different specific recommendations. Some countries have to raise their fiscal pressure under the need of financing public expenditure at a level required by a full democratic society. Almost all countries must reconsider the regressiveness of their tax-basket, imbalanced towards indirect taxation and with low income taxation and/or low social contributions (as well as other mandatory contributions to finance public/private welfare transfers, such as health and social security). This requires broadening the bases of direct taxes and an enlargement of the number of taxpayers subject to the personal income tax. Many authors in this book suggest that here the obstacle to overcome is mainly a political one. The inter-layers fiscal relations have to be reformed in many countries, both unitary and federal. The enlargement of intermediate and low governments' tax autonomy must take the first place in this reforming process. The modernization of the tax structure is also urgent under the internationalization of Latin American economies, especially with respect to corporate and financial capital taxation, both internally and externally sourced. Tax administrations must be strengthened almost everywhere to better fight against tax evasion and the informal economy and widespread corruption must be dealt with. We are aware that these are not easy tasks. They require time and, most of all, a strong political will.

This book ends a successful Routledge series, which began in 2004 and was devoted to critically inform the interested academic or professional reader about the current status and recent developments of tax systems and tax reforms in several economic areas of the world: EU 15, EU NMS, South and East Asia, and now Latin America. The core of the research team, made up by V. Tanzi, L. Bernardi, P. Profeta and S. Scabrosetti, together with the editors and authors of the other books in the series, passionately worked to find out and present the main institutional features, the evolutionary trends, and the most recent reforms of taxation around the world and to provide their recommendations for improving the current status quo. What did we learn?

Let us sketch out a few points. First, we learned that economic and political forces may drive the evolution of tax systems more than previously predicted by theories (see Tanzi, Gómez Sabaini and Martner, and Profeta and Scabrosetti's chapters in this book). As an example, the attempt to concretely apply the optimal taxation specific prescriptions (and not just its flavor of efficiency) to the reform of indirect taxation in India, recommended by Ahmad and Stern in the 1980s, remained an isolated (and not implemented) proposal. Kaldor and Meade's expenditure tax was not applied by almost any country. Followers of supply-side view must comply with empirical evidence about the (low) magnitude of marginal tax disincentives and with equity's concerns. Equitable taxation's supporters cannot deny the widespread erosion of comprehensive personal income taxes' bases, especially as capital incomes are concerned. Under the pressure of globalization, a sort of – explicit or implicit – Nordic Dual Income Taxation is emerging in many countries. It may be efficient and equitable, when the effective core rates (on labor: employed and self-employed: capital: corporate and financial; and consumption) do not diverge too much. It is neither efficient, nor equitable, when they do so (see Barreix and Roca, Chapter 13). Global personal taxes pale, being substituted for – legally or de facto – special income taxes. Capital income taxation went down almost everywhere, especially for foreign taxpayers. In EU NMS, Asian and Latin American countries indirect taxation still prevails over direct taxation. Thus, equity reasons seem take second place to other goals, such as efficiency, easiness of administration, political willingness of the forces in office. Among indirect taxes, custom duties drop down and excises duties concentrate on few demerit goods. VAT emerges almost everywhere as the main indirect tax, except for the US, the only great country in the world which did not introduce a VAT system. Neutrality and simplification continue to be the buzzwords of tax reforms. A general effort is underway to strengthen tax administration. But preferential treatments are not easy to remove, while their effects seem barely to improve or even to reduce both efficiency and equity (see Chapters 2 and 4). On the other hand, reducing preferential treatments may stimulate activities and capitals' location in the fiscal heavens (see Chapter 5).

We wonder whether some of our conclusions in the previous volumes have become obsolete after these few years. EU 15 countries tried, albeit marginally, to reduce their – too high – tax wedges on both corporate capital and employed work, sometimes by enlarging the room of consumption taxes (e.g. Germany). Most EU NMS countries dramatically cut their late 1990s total fiscal pressure (e.g. the Baltic states) and raised a strong tax competition among them and against EU 15 countries. Asian countries must still comply with an unavoidable pressure to raise taxes in order to finance at least some basic welfare provisions.

Finally, we wish to remember that the views expressed in the volumes do not necessarily reflect a common agreement – ideological, theoretical and technical – among all the authors and all the editors but, as in all free democracies, they may contain different opinions.

Luigi Bernardi, Alberto Barreix, Anna Marenzi and Paola Profeta

Note

1 Except for Argentina, Bolivia, Brazil, Colombia and Venezuela the share of sub-national expenditures on total public expenses is lower than 18 percent.

Acknowledgments

This book has benefited from a grant by the Fondazione Cassa di Risparmio delle Provincie Lombarde (*Foundation of the Saving Bank of Lombardy's Counties*), which is gratefully acknowledged. The editors are grateful to S. Scabrosetti, who, in addition to her own chapter, provided excellent research assistance during the whole project, and to S. Rizzo, who efficiently contributed to the editing of the manuscript. Thanks are also due to IBFD of Amsterdam and to ILPES-CEPAL of Santiago (Chile) for various help received.

Introduction

Tax systems and tax reforms in Latin America

Vito Tanzi

Introduction

Latin America is a huge region containing enormous diversity in culture, natural and human resources, ethnic backgrounds, per capita incomes, and general economic development. This is a region where the populations of all continents converged. Over the past century the Latin American countries have reflected the cultural influence of two outside areas: the United States and Europe. These two areas have exercised strong pulls that have, in part, reflected the backgrounds of the countries' populations and the distance from the two outside areas. Broadly, the more to the south and the east are the countries, the stronger has been the pull coming from Europe. The more to the north and the west, the greater has been the influence of the United States. Naturally, in several of the countries of the region these two outside influences have competed with domestic traditions linked to pre-Columbian cultures that have remained strong in particular countries.

The cultural differences mentioned above have inevitably influenced the role that the governments of the Latin American countries are playing in the economies. Naturally the tax systems are a major instrument, and an important expression, of that role. An aspect that surprises is the very large difference in tax burdens – i.e., in the share of tax revenue into the countries' gross domestic products – between, say, Brazil, where the tax burden is now at European levels (close to 40 percent of GDP) and countries such as Guatemala and Haiti, where it is still close to 10 percent of GDP, or about the levels that prevailed a century ago in the now-developed countries. Tax structures also reflect big differences among the countries, again differences that are bigger than those found among European countries.

Historical and regional factors

The structure of the economies of the various countries has inevitably influenced their tax systems by making certain tax bases more useable while creating difficulties in the use of other tax bases.

For a long time foreign trade taxes, and especially taxes on imports, played a significant role, especially for countries that had important foreign trade.

This trade provided the countries with an easy "tax handle." The ideological attraction for import substitution policies (policies advocated by Raul Prebisch in the 1950s), especially in the three decades after World War II, encouraged the use of these taxes. However, as predicted by the so-called "theory of tax structure change," with the passing of time, these taxes lost their appeal and their importance. Today, import duties retain some importance predominantly in the island countries of the Caribbean, where imports are often as large as their GDPs (see Tanzi 1987).

Export taxes had been of some importance especially in the decades immediately after World War II. At that time policymakers believed that these taxes could be exported, in the sense that they would be borne by the citizens of the countries that imported the commodities from the major Latin American countries. These taxes were used by Argentina and Uruguay, on the export of grain and meat; by Brazil, Colombia, and Haiti, on the export of coffee; by Ecuador, on the export of bananas; and by some other countries. Export taxes almost disappeared in the last two decades of the twentieth century but they have reappeared in recent years in Argentina. An export tax, imposed at a given rate of x, is conceptually equivalent to a tax rate of x on the production of the exported commodity, combined with a subsidy of x for the domestic consumption of that commodity. Thus, export taxes discourage production while they stimulate the domestic use of the commodity, by lowering its domestic price. The net effect for the countries that impose them is a loss of foreign exchange earnings (see Tanzi 1976).

In some cases export taxes have been imposed on the assumption that they would stimulate an increase in the value added of the exported product, by forcing some domestic transformation of the commodity into a more elaborate or refined product. For example Brazil had taxed the export of coffee beans under the assumption that this taxation would stimulate the export of (more valuable) instant coffee. South Africa has recently introduced export taxes on raw, unpolished diamonds under the assumption that these taxes will stimulate the domestic polishing and cutting of raw diamonds, thus increasing the value of exports. There is no evidence to suggest that these policies work.

The theory of tax structure change predicted that, with the passing of time, foreign trade taxes would be replaced by domestic taxes and especially by domestic indirect taxes. This replacement role has been assumed largely by the value added tax. Latin America was an early user of this European idea. Brazil introduced it in 1967 and Uruguay in 1968. The VAT spread quickly in the region and became a major producer of tax revenue. It was introduced in Peru and Bolivia in 1973; in Argentina, Chile, Colombia, Costa Rica, and Nicaragua, in 1975; in Honduras in 1976; and in Panama in 1977 (see Ebrill *et al.* 2001). In later years it was introduced in the remaining countries. With the exception of a few Caribbean island countries, all Latin American countries now have a value added tax. In several of these countries the revenue from this tax is at a level comparable to that of advanced industrial countries. This tax has become the workhorse of Latin American tax systems.

Latin America is a major producer of commodities, both agricultural and mineral products. Some countries (Venezuela, Mexico, Ecuador, Trinidad and Tobago) export petroleum while others (Bolivia, Chile, Colombia, Brazil, Peru, Jamaica) export other mineral products or agricultural products. The export of commodities has provided governments with large public revenues that, to some extent, have reduced the need to impose taxes on citizens. This is certainly the case in Mexico, Chile, Bolivia, Ecuador, and some other countries. Two issues are raised by this non-tax government revenue. First, what to do when, as in Mexico and Ecuador, the revenue from petroleum exports are expected to fall in the not too distant future because of the exhaustion of the resources? Second, what to do about so-called commodity cycles that push the prices of exported commodities up and down thus creating significant year-to-year instability in public revenue?

The first situation (the Mexican one) calls for the creation of tax systems that are elastic and broad-based and that lend themselves to rate increases that can be enacted when the time comes to replace the falling revenue from the mineral exports with domestic taxes. The second calls for policies, such as the establishment of stabilization funds, that attempt to provide the government with a kind of permanent income in the face of fluctuating foreign earnings. Chile has established such a fund, to stabilize the share from copper export earnings that the government is able to spend each year. When the price of copper is high, the fund accumulates resources that can be drawn when the prices fall. Fluctuations in commodity prices have major implications for tax revenue and for tax systems. They make it more difficult to determine the kind of tax system that a country should have. It is politically difficult for the government to resist the temptation to spend all the revenue during good times and to convince the citizens or the legislatures that the tax system must be reformed to make it more flexible to deal with bad times (see Davis *et al.* 2003).

The structure of the economy also has implications for income taxes. Mineral resources make it easier for countries to impose taxes on the income of enterprises, especially when these are foreign-owned. In Latin America, the revenue from the taxation of the profit of enterprises has been, on average, at a level at least comparable to that of industrial countries. However, taxes on personal incomes have been relatively unproductive. Personal income is the tax base that remains the most unexploited in Latin America. The reasons for this will be discussed more fully later. At this point it should be mentioned that tax experts have often followed Richard Goode's position, argued five decades ago (1965), that maintained that elements necessary for the successful use of personal income taxes are missing in Latin American countries. Some believe that, because many of these economies are characterized by a large informal sector (that often exceeds 50 percent of the economically active individuals), it contributes substantially to the underutilization of personal income taxes. Goode had specifically mentioned the existence of reliable accounting records. Other explanations for the low productivity of the personal income tax will be suggested later.

In the 1950s and 1960s there were various attempts to reform the Latin American tax systems in order to introduce modern income taxes in Latin American countries. Some of these attempts had the strong sponsorship of the American government, at a time when the United States had a lot of leverage in the region and the global income tax was still very popular and generally considered the best tax by tax experts. During the Kennedy Administration, a program called "Alliance for Progress" was created within the Organization of American States, the political international institutions that include all the countries of the Americas. The program continued during the Johnson Administration and the first years of the Nixon Administration. This program, largely financed by the American government, was endowed with significant financial resources. Its main task was to bring better economic policy in Latin America. A part of this program, the "Joint Tax Program," jointly supported by the OAS, the Inter-American Development Bank and the United Nations, had the explicit goal of promoting tax reform in Latin America in order to raise more revenue, make taxes more progressive, and make them more efficient and of easier administration. Many tax missions and advisors were sent to Latin American countries and several books came out of these missions. Two major conferences were held in Quito and in Mexico City. It is difficult to assess how much real success these activities had in establishing modern tax systems in Latin American countries. One area in which they were definitely not successful was in making the personal income tax productive and progressive. There was a continuous process of rejection of this tax on the part of many Latin American countries.

Before moving to the next section, a few words should be added about property taxes and about tax incentives. Especially in earlier decades the Latin American economies were still heavily dependent on agricultural activities. This, together with the fact that in most Latin American countries land ownership was and still is highly concentrated, created pressures to redistribute land through land reform and impose taxes on the potential income of land, or alternatively high property taxes that would force the landowners to use it productively or, alternatively, to sell it. The capitalization of the tax was expected to reduce the market value of land.

There were attempts in some countries at land reform and attempts to establish cadastral values for the land in order to facilitate the imposition of property taxes. However, the fact that many of these countries were experiencing high rates of inflation, and that it takes a long time to establish good cadastral values, especially in places were land records were not kept in an easily accessible way, made this task difficult. Political oppositions from the powerful landowners also played a role. The bottom line is that success in this area has been limited so that property taxation continues to play a very limited role in Latin America. It has not been possible to use property taxes as alternatives to personal income taxes.

In the 1950s there was great confidence in the ability of governments to promote growth. There was also a firm belief, based on work by Harrod, Domar, Rostow and other economists, that investment was the main factor that could contribute to growth. Investment can, of course, be public or private. Public investment could be promoted by increasing the level of taxation while controlling the level of current spending. This led to the great interest in the level of taxation and in its determinants. There were many studies that tried to determine the potential level of tax revenue for developing countries (see Tanzi 1987). Countries were praised by outside experts for maintaining or achieving high tax levels. See, for example, the report of the Musgrave's Commission in Colombia.

While public investment could be promoted by raising the tax level of countries, private investment could be stimulated through the use of tax incentives. At the time these incentives were supported by many experts, and Latin American governments responded to the prevailing view by introducing incentives for promoting investment for "essential" or "necessary" activities. These incentives became important tools for industrial policy together with the import-substitution policies. With the passing of time the experts' enthusiasm for tax incentives began to fade, but countries have continued to have them. Experts now tend to believe that:

1 tax incentives have limited effects;
2 they complicate the administration of taxes;
3 they are often associated with corruption.

Some of these incentives, in Argentina, Brazil, Chile, Peru and other countries have been aimed at regional development. The evaluations of them have generally given negative results.

We shall discuss below some important, specific taxes.

Income taxes

Personal income taxes

As already mentioned and as shown by the chapters in this book taxes on personal incomes have been remarkably unproductive in most Latin American countries. This is definitely the area where the differences in revenue from industrial countries are greatest. In this section we provide some reasons why this is so. These reasons are somewhat different from those often suggested.

As mentioned earlier, the normal explanation for this result is the importance of the informal sector in Latin America and its impact on tax evasion. To this it is often added that tax administrations are weak and so they tolerate large tax evasion on the part of taxpayers. Additionally some rely on sociological explanations, such as the presumed dislike on the part of the citizens of many of these countries for income taxes.

Latin American countries are characterized by very uneven income distributions. The Gini coefficients that are estimated for the countries of this region are the highest in the world, at times approaching 0.60. When income distributions are as uneven as that, and governments are chosen through democratic elections, as is now the case in most Latin American countries, one would expect that those with incomes below the mean income for the country, being in the majority, would elect individuals who would support progressive income taxes because these taxes would fall more heavily on the relatively few, rich citizens. The fact that this has not happened in Latin America is puzzling. Economists from DeViti De Marco to James Buchanan feared that in these circumstances very progressive income taxes would prevail thus reducing personal incentives and growth rates. Evidence indicates that their fear was misplaced.

In Latin America the share of total national income that compensates workers employed in official economic activities is remarkably low. For example in Mexico it is only 28 percent. In many places it is less than 30 percent compared to more than 70 percent in many industrial countries. Evidence from industrial countries suggests that revenue from personal income taxes is heavily dependent on the wages received by the employees of especially larger establishments, such as the government and enterprises. These employees are taxed at the source (i.e. their taxes are withheld) so that they would find it difficult to evade paying taxes. The low share of wages and salaries in the national incomes of Latin American countries begins to provide some explanation to the revenue puzzle. In order to collect tax revenue as high as in industrial countries, Latin American countries should:

1   tax adequately those who receive wages and salaries as dependent workers;
2   tax adequately the 70 or so percent of national income received as non-wage income.

Latin American countries have failed on both counts: wages and salaries have not been taxed as adequately as they should have; and non-wage and salary incomes have been hardly taxed.

An interesting aspect of the taxation of incomes from dependent work (wages and salaries) has been the relatively high level of personal exemptions, accorded by the countries' tax laws to working individuals and families. These levels are especially high when compared to the level of per capita incomes of these countries. In many Latin American countries the level of legally exempted income has been so high, as to wipe out a large part of the income from wages and salaries. Furthermore, the relatively low marginal tax rates are applied at such high income levels that few individuals are ever exposed to them. A few countries (Brazil, Chile and, recently, Argentina) have managed to get some revenue from personal incomes but the revenue obtained is still very low when compared with that obtained in industrial countries. The prevailing view that higher tax rates would discourage effort and damage economic growth has helped keep these rates down.

While the high level of personal exemptions (combined with the low tax rates and, possibly, the high tax evasion) has reduced the tax revenue that could have been received from wages and salaries, the weakness of the personal income tax, as a source of revenue, owes much more to the low taxation of non-wage incomes which, as indicated earlier, often account for at least 70 percent of the total personal income. The taxation, or better the non-taxation, of these incomes provides a large part of the explanation of why personal income taxes produce so little revenue in Lain America. These non-wage incomes are for the most part returns to capital (rents, interest, dividends, capital gains, profits) and, to a much lesser part, earnings by individuals engaged in informal activities. Given the information on income distributions, it is safe to assume that the share of personal income going to those engaged in non-official and informal activities is low so that their exclusion from taxation cannot be of great consequence for revenue.

Most Latin American countries have been reluctant to tax income from capital sources in part because of the fear that, being mobile, these incomes would emigrate toward that immense black hole that is the US economy. In spite of the low tax rates imposed by the Latin American countries on incomes from capital sources the US economy exercises a kind of fatal suction for Latin American taxpayers who have transferred hundred of billions of dollars toward that economy and toward tax havens. Being classified as "non-resident aliens" by the US tax authorities they have enjoyed a tax-free status in the United States. Because of limited or non-existent exchange of information between countries, or because of the territorial nature of several Latin American tax systems, taxpayers have not reported these incomes to the tax authorities of their own countries. The net result has been the low revenue from personal income taxes and the low progressivity of tax systems.

It is not clear how much truth there is in the assertion that an increase in the taxation of dividends, interest incomes, rents, capital gains and profits would lead to a (greater) emigration of capital. However, the non-taxation of this capital in the places where it goes (tax havens and the United States) does provide a strong incentive to its exodus. This incentive becomes particularly strong in periods when there is economic and political instability in the Latin American countries. This was the case during the "lost decade" of the 1980s, when huge capital flight from Latin American countries took place. The United States could help by taxing fully these incomes or by providing information to the tax authorities of the countries from which this capital originates. However, neither of these two alternatives is likely. The attempt to reduce the role that tax havens play in tax evasion started a few years ago. It remains to be seen how far it will go. It is also an open question whether the elites of the Latin American countries, who are often overrepresented in the governments of these countries, would allow a fuller taxation of personal income. In conclusion, personal income taxes can become productive only if the governments concentrate their efforts on the top 10–20 percent of the population that absorbs much of these countries taxable income (see Tanzi 1966).

Taxes on enterprise income

As far as the taxation of enterprises is concerned, the issues in Latin America are largely the same as those of industrial countries. Also the rates are broadly similar. These rates have fallen significantly in the past two decades as in the rest of the world. Until the mid-1990s high inflation had created particular difficulties in measuring real profits. Inflation had distorted the measurement of depreciation allowances and, often, the cost of inputs. Also, by sharply increasing nominal interest rates, it had created strong incentives for enterprises to replace equity with debt. Many enterprises had taken advantage of this possibility. Problems of "thin capitalization" had become significant and because of the deductibility of large nominal interest payments, enterprises had routinely shown losses in their accounts. Several countries (Brazil, Chile, Mexico) had taken steps to index various aspects of the tax system for inflation. Some (Argentina, Mexico, Peru, Colombia, Costa Rica) had also introduced taxes on gross assets or on net worth in order to force enterprises to contribute something to tax revenue. Some of these taxes continue to be imposed today and some countries continue to index the accounts of enterprises for inflation. Mexico, for example, continues to tax only (and to allow a deduction for only) inflation-adjusted interest incomes and payments. These adjustments for inflation introduce administrative complications and raise the cost of compliance for taxpayers. Given the now prevailing low rates of inflation in Latin American countries, it is a valid question whether these inflation adjustments are still justified.

As in other countries in the world, the issue of how to value inputs purchased from abroad – the issue of "transfer prices" – is receiving a lot of attention by Latin American tax administrators. In recent years various countries have introduced legislation to establish criteria to deal with this issue. The prevailing principle in this legislation is that of "arm's length," that is the price that the input would command in a competitive market where buyers and sellers were not related. This is a good principle but often it is not sufficient for dealing with the problem, especially when:

1   the inputs may be purchased from related companies, that is from foreign subsidiaries or branches of the same multinational enterprise;
2   the input are specific to a final product, so that they do not have a market price that can be observed;
3   the inputs may be trade marks, copyrights, patents, or the output of research done at the headquarters of a multinational company.

However, these are not issues strictly limited to Latin America. They worry the tax administrators of other countries as well (see Mercader 2007).

Other Latin American issues related to the taxation of enterprises are:

1   tax incentives;
2   the treatment of foreign enterprises engaged in the extraction of natural resources;
3   the taxation of small enterprises.

We have already commented on the problems created by tax incentives so there is no need to repeat them. However, a typically Latin American aspect, and one that has acquired importance especially in Central America, is what could be called the process of "tax incentive shopping" on the part of foreign companies. These companies often rely on the competition among countries of the same area (say, Central America) to get the best possible deals. For fear of losing an important investment to a neighboring country, that may be willing to offer better tax deals, countries compete in offering incentives that at times are not in their best interest. Countries should be encouraged to coordinate their actions in order to be able to resist requests that essentially pit one country against the others and that are not in the countries' interest (see Bird 2007).

The sharp increase in the prices of mineral products (oil, copper, tin, iron, etc.) in recent years has brought strong political reactions in some countries (especially Bolivia and Venezuela) against contracts that foreign companies had negotiated in the past, when commodity prices were low. When the prices rose these contracts became very profitable for some companies. Furthermore, there have been reports that some of these foreign companies, exploiting fully the possibilities offered by transfer prices, have paid nothing for years to the countries. As a consequence, royalty taxation has become an important topic in Latin America. Royalty taxation would make companies pay some taxes (in relation to the physical extraction of natural resources) even when the reported profits of the companies are reported to be zero. These royalty taxes can be justified on grounds that the extraction of natural resources by a foreign company makes a country poorer in some basic sense and that this kind of production always causes some environmental damage. It is likely that this aspect of taxation will become more important in future years in Latin America if environmental concerns keep growing.

In Latin America there are many small enterprises. These enterprises have difficulties dealing with complex aspects of income taxes, value added taxes, social security taxes, net wealth taxes, local taxes, and so on. It is very costly for them to acquire the expertise to comply with the tax requirements and to keep the accounts in the way required by the tax authorities. At the same time the tax administrations have had difficulties in verifying the tax declarations presented by these small enterprises. There has thus been a movement, in several Latin American countries, toward tax simplification for the small enterprises (see Gonzales 2006). The aim of this simplification is that of combining, in a single and simple tax, all the payments that the enterprise would make to meet the various legal obligations as reflected in the existing taxes. In some way this movement replaces taxes based on formal accounting data with taxes that are, in effect, presumptive taxes.

This movement toward simplification has been pursued by:

- Argentina, that in 1998 introduced a Régimen Simplificado para Pequeños Contribuyentes, or "monotributo," a system applied to enterprises with a turnover lower than a well-defined minimum.
- Bolivia, that introduced a Régimen Tributario Simplificado, a Sistema Tributario Integrado, and a Regimen Agropecuario Unificado. These three systems apply to three different areas of the economy.

- Brazil, that in 1997 introduced a "simples" system that replaced, for small enterprises, various taxes with a single tax. More recently the "simples" tax has been replaced by a "supersimples" tax that has extended further the scope of the taxes that are replaced by the "simples tax."
- Costa Rica, that has introduced a Régimen de Tributacion Simplificada that has replaced, for small enterprises, the income tax and the value added tax.
- Mexico, that has introduced a Régimen de Pequeños Contribuyentes ("REPECOS") that has replaced various national and local taxes with a single and simple payment.
- Peru, that has introduced a Nuevo Règimen Unico Simplificado (RUS) to replace the income and the value added taxes.
- Uruguay, that has introduced a special tax on small enterprises (IPE) and a monotributo. Both of these aim at simplifying the taxation of small and unipersonal enterprises.

The above reforms have been accompanied by administrative charges that in several countries have created so called "Large Taxpayers Units." These are special units within the tax administrations that follow closely and intimately large enterprises or important individual taxpayers. These large taxpayers, while often small in number, often account for as much as 80 or even 90 percent of all income and value added taxes paid. The Latin American countries have realized that small and large enterprises and small and large individual taxpayers cannot be treated in identical ways and cannot be subjected to the same rules. Larger taxpayers require more attention. While large enterprises are expected to report incomes and sales based on modern and formal accounting rules, small enterprises are being subjected more and more to modern versions of presumptive taxes that had been predominant in the past. This is an important conceptual change that can be expected to have a major impact on the tax systems and the tax administrations of Latin American countries.

Value added taxes

As indicated earlier, value added taxes are now very important in the tax system of Latin American countries. In some of them (Brazil, Uruguay, and Chile), they raise more than 8 percent of GDP in revenue. This puts them among the top countries in the world in terms of tax revenue from value added taxes. Several other countries (Argentina, Bolivia, Colombia, Ecuador, El Salvador, Honduras, and Nicaragua) collect more than 6 percent of GDP, even above the Italian level. There is thus no question that the introduction of the VAT has been a remarkable achievement in the fiscal development of Latin American tax systems.

A VAT imposed with a broad base and with a single rate can be a very effective instrument of economic policy. It is essentially a flat tax on income defined as consumption. Thus, it is a version of an expenditure tax often recommended in the past by Mill, Kaldor, Einaudi and others. By not taxing income saved, it is growth friendly. Because it is collected with a short lag (generally not much more than one month passed between the taxable event and the receipt of the tax payment by the government) it is relatively insensitive to moderate rates of inflation. The revenue impact of a rate change is almost immediate and it is easy to calculate with small margins of error. It does not lend itself easily to social engineering, as happens with income taxes. Furthermore, it can be a useful tool for stabilization policy because it is easy to estimate the impact of a rate change and to explain the change to members of parliament. A single-rate, broad-based value added tax is also much easier to administer. All these are remarkable characteristics.

Many of these virtues disappear, however, or become attenuated, when VATs are not applied with one rate on broad bases. One of the more contentious issues in Latin American taxation has been whether the VAT should in fact be levied on a broad base and with a single rate. In spite of overwhelming evidence to the contrary, provided by many economists, the politicians of several countries continue to support VATs with much reduced tax bases because of the exclusion or the zero rating of various categories of consumption. Furthermore, in the illusory pursuit of tax equity many countries continue to adopt value added taxes with more than one rate. The reduced rate or rates tax more lightly consumer goods that are presumably more important for families in lower income groups.

Inefficient VATs now exist in Mexico, Colombia, Venezuela, Peru, Jamaica, Argentina and a few other countries. The concept often used to measure the productivity of the value added taxes is the relationship between revenue and rate. Productivity is measured as the revenue share in GDP produced by a unit rate of VAT. In Latin American countries, this index of revenue productivity in 2004 ranged from a low of 24.6 in Mexico and between 26–7 in Haiti and Trinidad and Tobago to a high of about 52 in Ecuador and Honduras. Given a high productivity index, a country can raise more revenue without the need to impose a high tax rate. For example, Ecuador and Honduras could raise the same share of GDP in revenue from the VAT with a rate half that of Mexico, Haiti, and Trinidad and Tobago. Thus a high productivity of the VAT does not automatically implies that the country collects large revenue from the VAT because the revenue collected depends on both the productivity of the tax and the rate (or rates) used.

In some countries, legislatures continue to resist the widening of the base and the elimination of multiple rates, to replace them with a single rate. This has been a particularly lively issue in Mexico that, being a member of the OECD, finds itself in the uncomfortable place of having the least productive VAT in Latin America.

Value added taxes exempt exports and tax imports. In Latin America, imports have been a large part of the tax base often providing as much as half of total VAT revenue. When exporters export products, they often present claims for taxes that have been included in the products that they bought and exported. Two issues have been associated with this process. The first, common in all countries that use VATs, is the possibility that exporters will fake exports and present claims that are not legitimate. The second has been the long delay in getting the rebates. In periods of fiscal stress, countries may tend to slow down the payment of the tax rebates, thus getting a cheap loan from the exporters. In Latin America this second aspect has occasionally become a significant issue.

In particular countries and in particular periods, the faking of invoices to evade tax payments has been a problem. Another has been the sale of services without the payment of the VAT. At times, the users of the services have been given discounts to agree to pay for a service (professional services or services related to construction) without a receipt and without a VAT payment. Naturally these problems are not limited to Latin America but they seem to be more widespread there than in European countries.

Other issues

During the past two decades the level of taxation in Latin America has increased considerably especially in countries such as Brazil, Argentina, Bolivia, Colombia, Nicaragua and a few others (see Table 0.1).

These tax increases have reflected both policy changes introduced by tax reforms as well as improvements in the tax administrations that have accompanied the introduction, and subsequently the better use of computers. With the passing of time tax administrators have learned to utilize computers to get more and better information than previously and to be able to follow more closely the compliance of the larger taxpayers. Large taxpayers are now controlled by so-called "Large Taxpayers Units." The increase in tax revenue has been accompanied, in the more recent years, and for some countries, by larger revenue from government owned natural resources, reflecting the boom in commodity prices. Venezuela, Bolivia, Chile, Mexico and a few other countries have been large beneficiary of this boom. At the same time several Latin American countries have got rid of many small taxes that had created administrative difficulties while contributing little to total revenue.

Over the years there has been a lot of experimentation with new taxes promoted, first, by the countries' revenue needs and, second, by a continuing search for simple solutions to the revenue needs. This in fact has been an interesting characteristic of the policymakers of these countries: the search for the magic solution. In some circumstances, instead of pursuing well-traveled roads toward better revenue performance, policymakers have tried novel ways and novel taxes.

Some of these ways have included taxes on gross assets, to replace traditional taxes on enterprises, or to establish minimum taxes. This was a tax first proposed by Maurice Allais, the French Nobel Prize winner in economics. Mexico, Argentina, Peru and some other countries tried this route. Another experiment has been the tax on financial transactions and, especially, on the use of checks. Variations of this tax now exist in Argentina, Brazil, Colombia, Peru, and a few other places. This tax is defended on the grounds that it provides easy revenue as well as useful information on taxpayers to the tax administrations. However, it may, in time, discourage the use of the financial instruments subject to taxation and, indirectly, stimulate underground economic activities.

Table 0.1 Latin America and the Caribbean general government fiscal revenues (as % of GDP), 1990–2005 (including social security and excluding petroleum and natural resource revenues)

	1990	1991	1992	1993	1994	1995	1996	1997	1998	1999	2000	2001	2002	2003	2004	2005
Argentina[1]	16.1	18.4	21.5	21.6	21.5	20.3	19.7	20.6	21.0	21.2	21.5	20.9	19.9	23.4	26.3	26.7
Bolivia[2]	8.4	8.9	10.7	18.1	18.4	18.7	20.0	20.0	21.3	20.6	20.4	19.9	19.9	20.7	24.1	25.2
Brazil[3]	28.8	23.3	24.5	25.0	29.1	29.0	28.1	29.0	29.7	31.7	32.6	34.0	35.6	34.9	35.9	37.4
Chile[1]	16.7	18.5	19.1	19.6	18.7	18.0	19.3	19.0	19.3	18.7	19.3	19.8	19.7	18.9	18.5	18.8
Colombia[4]	12.4	13.9	14.0	15.1	15.7	16.7	17.8	18.7	19.2	19.1	18.9	21.0	21.2	21.6	22.3	17.6
Costa Rica[1]	16.5	16.7	17.3	17.7	17.5	17.7	18.2	18.4	18.3	17.6	18.2	19.2	19.4	19.4	19.4	20.5
Dom. Republic[1,9]	10.5	11.9	13.9	14.9	14.1	13.9	13.2	14.8	15.1	15.6	15.0	15.9	15.9	14.8	15.3	16.7
Ecuador[1]	10.2	10.8	10.3	10.1	10.2	11.0	9.4	10.5	11.0	11.0	13.2	14.3	15.2	14.3	13.4	14.9
El Salvador[5]	9.0	10.1	10.8	11.5	12.5	13.7	13.2	12.9	13.2	13.2	13.2	13.0	13.8	12.4	13.2	14.2
Guatemala[6,9]	6.9	7.3	8.4	7.8	6.8	7.9	8.7	8.8	8.7	9.9	10.0	9.7	10.6	10.3	10.3	9.8
Haiti[6,9]	7.3	7.6	5.5	4.8	2.8	5.9	6.7	8.5	8.1	8.5	8.1	7.6	8.3	9.0	8.9	9.7
Honduras[1,9]	15.3	16.3	15.8	16.4	15.6	16.9	14.8	14.2	17.2	18.3	17.0	16.9	17.1	17.6	18.2	18.3
Mexico[7]	12.6	n.a.	n.a.	n.a.	n.a.	11.3	10.9	11.6	12.0	12.9	12.1	12.9	13.2	12.6	11.4	11.0
Nicaragua[1,9]	9.0	12.4	13.6	13.0	13.7	14.2	14.2	15.7	17.2	17.1	17.4	16.9	16.8	18.4	18.9	21.5
Panama[8,9]	14.7	15.3	19.8	18.4	18.6	19.9	19.3	19.2	16.2	16.7	15.0	14.7	14.4	14.7	14.9	14.2
Paraguay[1,9]	9.9	9.8	9.9	10.2	12.0	13.6	12.7	12.7	12.6	11.8	12.0	12.0	11.2	11.2	12.9	13.0

continued

Table 0.1 continued

	1990	1991	1992	1993	1994	1995	1996	1997	1998	1999	2000	2001	2002	2003	2004	2005
Peru[1,9]	11.6	13.1	14.1	14.3	14.9	15.4	15.8	16.0	15.6	14.4	14.0	14.2	13.8	14.7	14.9	15.4
Uruguay[5]	29.5	32.6	32.2	31.1	30.8	32.2	33.6	34.0	32.9	32.5	31.9	32.3	31.7	28.2	29.9	32.2
Venezuela[1,9]	4.4	4.8	5.9	7.1	9.4	8.9	8.2	10.1	11.6	11.6	9.4	9.6	10.3	10.4	11.8	12.6

Source: International Monetary Fund, Country Reports. ECLAC-ILPES. IDB studies. Country governments. 2005 data from Martner, R. (2007) "La política fiscal en tiempos de abundancia," Documento XIX seminario regional de política fiscal. Elaboration: IDB, INT/ITD.

Notes
1 Source: ECLAC-ILPES, database: Estadísticas de las Finanzas Públicas de América Latina.
2 Source: IMF data, 1994–2004, includes hydrocarbons revenue. Data ECLAC 1990–2, and 2005 excludes hydrocarbons. Social security data from ECLAC.
3 Source: 1990 Receita Federal; Revenues 1991–2004: SRF – Estudos Tributários/Carga Tributária – elaboration: Amir Khair.
4 Government data, includes taxes from petroleum revenue (except 2005). Dirección de Impuestos y Aduanas Nacionales (DIAN); Oficina de Estudios Económicos DIAN.
5 Data from IDB studies and consultancies. El Salvador 2005 data is from ECLAC. Uruguay 2004–5 data is from the IMF.
6 IMF, Country Reports. Guatemala and Haiti 2005 data is from ECLAC. Haiti data excludes social security.
7 Data from Martner, R. (2007) "La política fiscal en tiempos de abundancia," Documento XIX seminario regional de política fiscal.
8 IMF, 1992–2002, ECLAC 1990–1 and 2003–5.
9 Central government data.

Hopefully, the reintroduction of export taxes by Argentina will not spread to other countries. Like the tax on checks the tax on exports is easy to administer. In periods of high prices for exports, or after large devaluations, it can have some short term logic. But, in time, it can become a very damaging instrument.

Another issue that continues to affect the tax systems of Latin America is fiscal federalism. Countries such as Argentina, Brazil, Bolivia, Colombia, Mexico and some others have constitutional or other legal arrangements that give significant spending powers to sub-national governments or entities. These arrangements have often a large impact on tax systems because they restrict the degrees of freedom that national governments have in reforming their tax systems. For example, in Argentina, foreign trade taxes are not shared with the provinces; therefore they are preferred by the national government even though they are inefficient taxes. In Brazil it has been impossible to reform the badly structured VAT because this tax is the responsibility of the states and not of the national government. In Brazil taxes are such a controversial and constitutional issue that a tax lawyer is essentially a constitutional lawyer. Similar difficulties exist in Mexico where more than 90 percent of all the cases that go to the Supreme Court are tax cases. Clearly, regardless of the merits of fiscal federalism and of fiscal decentralization, they do complicate tax policy and often force on countries tax options that are not the most desirable. This is most evident in Latin America.

What can be called institutional externalities are also clearly in evidence in Latin American countries. By institutional externalities it is meant the impact that a public institution can have on another institution. A good tax administration needs a good educational system, to provide the qualified personnel that it will hire. It also needs an efficient justice system that pursues and punishes tax-payers that do not comply with the legal tax requirements. When a tax administration depends on the justice system to punish tax evaders but the justice system is too inefficient or too corrupt to do this rapidly or efficiently, tax compliance suffers and the blame should not be placed only on the tax administrations.

Finally, tax administrations need to be monitored to assure that they remain efficient and objective. However, in several Latin American countries, controls can become political interference when highly placed individuals, within both the executive and the legislative branches, are able to influence administrative decisions for political ends. In some Latin American countries this still happens more than, perhaps, it should.

Concluding remarks

There has been a gradual and continuous evolution of the tax systems of Latin American countries. Over the years levels of taxation have risen and the quality of the tax administration has improved considerably. The constraints that remain are partly structural, partly administrative, and partly political. This brief foreword has mentioned a few political obstacles that continue to prevent the tax systems from acquiring a more modern look. However, progress has been made and continues to be made. Part of this progress has been the elimination of many unproductive and nuisance taxes that had been expensive to administer and that yielded little revenue.

Selected references

Bird, R. (2007) "Tax Incentives for Foreign Investment in Latin America and the Caribbean: Do They Need to be Harmonized?," in Tanzi, V., Villela, L. and Barreix, A. (eds) *Taxation and Latin American Integration*, Washington, DC: IDB.

Davis, J. M., Ossowski, R. and Fedelino, A. (2003) *Fiscal Policy Formulation and Implementation in Oil-Producing Countries*, Washington, DC: IMF.

Ebrill, L., Keen, M., Bodin, J. P. and Summers, V. (2001) *The Modern VAT*, Washington DC: IMF.

Gonzales, D. (2006) "Regimenes Especiales de Tribulación Para Pequeños Contribuyentes en America Latina," mimeo, Washington, DC: IDB.

Goode, R. (1972) "Personal Income Tax in Latin America," in Joint Tax Program, OAS/IDB/ECLA, *Fiscal Policy for Economic Growth in Latin America*, Baltimore: Johns Hopkins Press, pp. 157–71.

Mercader, A. (2007) "Transfer Pricing and Latin American Integration: Current Practices and Future Problems," in Tanzi, V., Villela, L. and Barreix, A. (eds) *Taxation and Latin American Integration*, Washington, DC: IDB.

Tanzi, V. (1966) "Personal Income Taxation in Latin America: Obstacles and Possibilities," *National Tax Journal*, vol. XIX, n. 2.

—— (1976) "Export Taxation in Developing Countries: Taxation of Coffee in Haiti," *Social and Economic Studies*.

—— (1987) "Quantitative Characteristics of the Tax Systems of Developing Countries," in Newbery, D. and Stern, N. (eds) *The Theory of Taxation for Developing Countries*, New York: Oxford University Press.

—— (2000) "Taxation and Economic Structure," in Perry, G., Whalley, J. and McMahon, G. (eds) *Fiscal Reform and Structural Change in Developing Countries*, UK: Macmillan Press.

—— (2003) "Taxation Reform in Latin America in the Last Decade," in Gonzales, J. A., Corbo, V., Krueger, A. O. and Tornell, A. (eds) *Latin American Macroeconomic Reform: The Second Stage*, Chicago: The University of Chicago Press.

Part I

A general picture of tax systems and tax reforms in Latin America

1 Taxation structure and main tax policy issues

Juan Carlos Gómez Sabaini and Ricardo Martner

The regional features and the level of taxation[1]

Latin American countries are strongly characterized by different economic and social indicators within the area, a fact that is crucial for the analysis of their tax systems. Total population is about 540 million citizens in 2005 for 19 countries,[2] from Brazil with more than 187 million and Mexico with 106 million, to Panama and Uruguay, with more than three million inhabitants each. Similarly, the level of development differs in the region. The average GDP per capita is estimated at about $3,750 in 2005, with, on one hand, countries such as Mexico (about $6,800 per capita) and Chile ($5,200), and, on the other hand, Bolivia ($960), Nicaragua ($830) and Haiti ($400).

The World Bank's Atlas method, which classifies countries according to their income per capita, identifies four groups of countries: in 2005, countries with less than $875 per year are low income, up to $3,465 per year low-medium income, up to $10,725 medium-high income, more than $10,726 high income. Applying this classification to Latin America we find three low-income countries (Bolivia, Haiti and Nicaragua), ten low-medium income countries (Brazil, Colombia, Dominican Republic, Ecuador, El Salvador, Guatemala, Honduras, Jamaica, Paraguay and Peru) and seven medium-high income countries (Argentina, Chile, Costa Rica, Mexico, Panama, Uruguay and Venezuela).

The three largest countries have, however, a larger share, while the three smallest ones contribute only a small amount to the production of the GDP of the area. Argentina, Brazil and Mexico contribute for more than 70 percent of the total, while Bolivia, Haiti and Nicaragua all together contribute less than 1 percent of the total. Latin America has an area of more than 20 million km², of which 42 percent is occupied by Brazil, 14 percent by Argentina and 9 percent by Mexico, while on the other extreme, El Salvador and Haiti occupy only 0.1 percent.

Latin America is also characterized by different sub-area features. Countries have developed their own type of integrations. Argentina, Brazil, Paraguay and Uruguay belong to MERCOSUR (Mercado Común del Sur). Venezuela has recently joined as a full member, while Bolivia and Chile are associate members. On the other side, the Andean Community (CAN) is constituted by

Bolivia, Colombia, Ecuador and Peru. The Central American Common Market (MCCA) groups Costa Rica, Guatemala, Honduras, El Salvador and Nicaragua and, for some specific issues, the Dominican Republic.

As we already noticed, differences are enormous. As a consequence, performing a global analysis of the different tax features of the countries is a quite difficult task, which may produce ambiguous conclusions.

The analysis of the tax situation during the last decades can be conducted using two methods: the first one would compile all the statistical and institutional information of each country in order to analyze the evolution and the results of the changes that occurred in each circumstance. This valuable and rigorous method is developed through a series of specific analyses for each country in the second part of this book. The second method, which will be followed in this chapter, is more oriented towards stylized facts, exemplified cases, and provides material for the analyses in the next chapters, taking into account the possibility of making mistakes of interpretation or generalizations beyond the necessary.

To build series of data comparable over time and across countries is a difficult task which may lead to mistakes. In particular, we should be very careful in expressing numbers on "fiscal pressure," a well-known concept among economists. A first issue concerns the levels of government which we consider. Most of the Latin American countries are unified: the central government collects the majority of revenue, while municipalities less than 10 percent of it. However in some cases there exist federal governments, such as Argentina, Brazil, Mexico and Venezuela, with their own tax authorities, which may provide, such as in Brazil, significant revenue. Note that fiscal pressure in 2005 in Argentina was 81 percent in the central government, 14 percent in the provinces and 5 percent in municipalities (estimated values). For Brazil, the importance of decentralized governments is substantially higher, amounting to about 30 percent of fiscal pressure.

A part of revenue, in turn, derives from levels, or organizations that have to transfer part or all their revenue to other levels of government without disposing totally of it. This happens, for instance, with the tax or social funds sharing.

Moreover, although the majority of countries have privatized their manufacturing firms in the last decades, public firms are very important especially in countries which export natural resources (Chile with copper, Venezuela and Ecuador with petroleum, Bolivia with gas) or take advantage of their geographical position (Panama with payments linked to the canal). In these cases revenues are considered as non-tax revenues, but they may be very high.

Moreover, since one of the functions of the government is to guarantee a social coverage through different instruments, we should also take into account social security revenue. The total or partial privatization of them in some countries in the last decades, however, poses serious problems on the comparisons of the different levels of this kind of revenue in these countries. Some countries, such as Chile, have a private system with no public revenue. Some other countries, such as Argentina and Uruguay, have a mixed system, so that the government receives lower revenue than the years before the privatization, since part of the current revenue goes to the private sector to finance the current debt, left as a government responsibility. The case of Brazil is again relevant: taxes and contributions to finance social security in 2005 amount to 15.4 percent of GDP, i.e. almost 41 percent of the total tax revenue has been assigned to finance these provisions.

Finally, there are non-tax revenues, such as the inflation tax, the most used complementary instrument during the 1980s. Although the growth of price levels has been reduced during the 1990s, the inflation tax is still relevant when we compare the evolution of the levels of revenue over time in many countries and we analyze countries, such as Argentina, Brazil, Uruguay and the Dominican Republic, that had a significant inflation in recent years. The application of different types of exchange rates is also another source of revenue which makes it difficult to compare only tax revenue across countries and over time.

Figure 1.1 shows the level (in percentage of GDP) and the composition of government (central or general, depending on the cases) tax revenues in 2005. In several countries (Argentina, Brazil, Colombia, Costa Rica, Guatemala, Haiti, Honduras and Uruguay) tax revenues are the only source of current revenues of central governments. In others (Bolivia, Chile, Ecuador, Mexico, Peru and Venezuela) they are complemented by other current revenues originating from natural resources (hydrocarbon and mines). In Nicaragua and, to a much lesser extent, in El Salvador and the Dominican Republic, bilateral and multilateral donations contribute to raise current revenues with respect to tax revenues. In Panama current revenues from services also complement central government tax revenues.

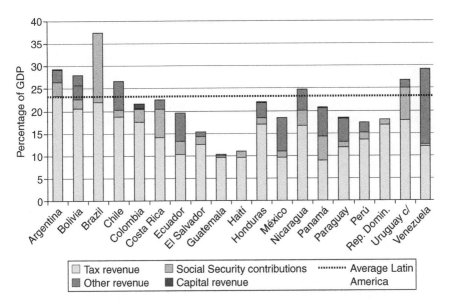

Figure 1.1 Fiscal burden in Latin America and the Caribbean (% of GDP, 2005) (source: official numbers of ILPES, CEPAL).

To find a classification criterion which, as such, is arbitrary, it seems appropriate to group countries according to the average level of fiscal pressure. We assume that countries with a fiscal pressure of at least 2 percentage points of GDP more than the average of 2005 (18 percent) have a high fiscal pressure. As a result, we have a group of five countries with a high fiscal pressure (Argentina, Bolivia, Brazil, Chile, Uruguay), higher than 20 percent of GDP, another five countries with a fiscal pressure close to the average 18 percent and another five of low fiscal charge (Paraguay, Ecuador, Venezuela, Guatemala, Haiti), with a fiscal pressure lower than 10 percent of GDP.

The evolution of fiscal burden (including social security) between 1990 and 2005 (see Table 1.1) shows that fiscal pressure has, on average, strongly grown in the region from 12.6 percent in the 1990s to 18 percent in 2005. Taking the average during this period as a criterion, we can classify countries depending on whether they overcome by three or more percentage points the regional average or not. As a result, Argentina, Brazil, Chile, Costa Rica and Uruguay show higher levels than the average, while Paraguay, Ecuador, Venezuela, Guatemala and Haiti have lower fiscal pressure.

Argentina and Brazil have significantly raised their taxes, from an initial relatively high level of taxes with respect to the regional average. Starting with a low fiscal pressure, Bolivia, Costa Rica, Colombia, the Dominican Republic and Venezuela show a strong increase. Tax revenue significantly increases from 2005 in these countries and in Chile, with an elasticity higher than one, following administrative improvements and full returns of the new taxes. Mexico is the only country where the tax revenue has remained very low, close to 12 percent of GDP.

In the 1990s, the higher growth rates push for a higher tax burden. In general, the elasticity of the tax collection is higher than one (see Martner and Traubeu 2004). In the growing phases, this is due to the fact that growth produces an increase of the formal economy and generates an increase more than proportional of imports and associated taxes. On the contrary, during recessions, revenues decrease more than proportionally, due to the opposite direction of the above relations and to the significant increase in tax evasion. The relation between inflation and tax revenue is also strong. First, this is because inflation decreases the real value of tax revenues due to delays between tax generation and collection. Second, since inflation reduces real revenues, families and firms will try to maintain their disposable real revenue through a lower tax payment. Thus, macroeconomic stability, i.e. high growth combined with low inflation, is the main condition for more tax revenues. In a recession phase with growing inflation, any tax system faces difficulties to avoid the loss of revenues.

One of the main goals of taxation is to finance the expenditure of government goods and services. Thus, the choice of the level of taxation indicates, in the medium run, the level of public expenditures. Beyond the traditional recommendations of avoiding taxes that may distort resources allocation, the economic theory provides a very limited guide with respect to the decision on the level of

Table 1.1 Central government: fiscal revenue (with social security contributions, % of GDP)

	1990	2000	2005p	Average 1990–2005
GROUP 1	**20.7**	**23.2**	**26.0**	**22.8**
Brazil[1]	30.5	32.5	37.4	31.0
Uruguay	22.4	23.6	25.2	23.6
Argentina[1]	16.1	21.5	26.7	21.3
Chile[1]	17.4	19.3	20.2	19.4
Costa Rica[1]	16.9	18.9	20.5	18.7
GROUP 2	**11.3**	**15.0**	**17.0**	**14.6**
Honduras	15.3	17.0	18.3	16.6
Colombia[1,2]	10.5	16.8	20.4	16.1
Panamá	14.7	16.0	14.2	15.7
Nicaragua	9.0	17.5	20.1	15.6
R. Dominicana	10.5	15.0	16.8	14.5
Perú	11.6	14.0	15.2	14.5
Bolivia	8.2	14.0	22.6	13.2
México	12.6	12.1	11.0	12.4
El Salvador	8.9	13.0	14.2	12.4
GROUP 3	**7.7**	**10.1**	**11.7**	**9.6**
Paraguay	9.9	12.0	13.0	11.7
Ecuador	10.1	11.6	13.4	11.0
Venezuela	4.4	9.4	12.6	9.1
Guatemala	6.9	9.7	9.9	9.0
Haití	7.3	7.9	9.7	7.2
Simple average	**12.8**	**15.9**	**18.0**	**15.4**

Notes
1 It corresponds to the central government. In other countries the information may be different from other sources on the social security contributions, such as for Uruguay.
2 Data correspond to 2004.

tax burden and tax structure. Some studies find a negative relation between fiscal pressure, or public expenditures, and economic unemployment. To this respect however a final conclusion can not be reached: some countries have grown with a high level of taxation and others have a poor macroeconomic performance with a low fiscal pressure. Causality may even be reversed: as long as countries grow, the tax base enlarges and the system becomes more progressive, creating a virtuous circle between growth, public expenditure, level of taxation and progressivity of the system.

A way to evaluate if the levels of taxation and the tax structures are "appropriate" is to compare the relation between taxes and GDP for a large number of countries. The simple comparison between Latin America and the Caribbean and the other world areas is very insightful (Figure 1.2). In 2005 the fiscal pressure in OECD was 2.2 times the fiscal pressure of Latin America and the Caribbean. In OECD countries, direct taxes and social security contributions are relatively more important, while the tax system of Latin America and the Caribbean is based on indirect taxation. The levels of fiscal

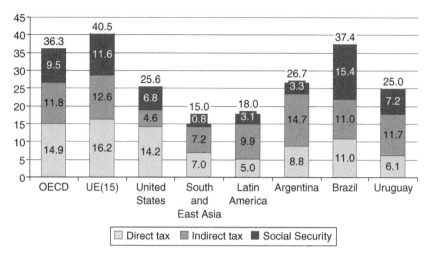

Figure 1.2 International comparisons of the fiscal burden (2005) (source: authors calculations on official data of each country).

pressure in Latin America and the Caribbean are similar to the ones of East
Asia, although the composition is very different. Asian countries show a
higher level of direct taxes (especially corporate taxes) and very low social
security contributions.

Using panel regressions, some authors estimate the "fiscal capacity" of each
country (see for instance Agosin *et al.* 2005 for Central American countries),
which can be compared to the effective taxation. This type of analysis is beyond
of the scope of this chapter. We show, however, the relation between fiscal and
tax revenue in Latin America and the Caribbean and the level of per capita
revenue in Figures 1.3a and 1.3b.

To conclude, in spite of the general growth of the average fiscal pressure in
the last decades in all countries (with the exception of Mexico), in the current
situation there still exists potential space (Brazil is the big exception). The level
of effective fiscal pressure is below the expected or potential level given the per
capita income of the countries and the concentration coefficient of incomes (see
Agosin *et al.* 2004; Perry *et al.* 2006). This loss of fiscal revenue is about three
or four points of GDP which implies that, given the level of fiscal pressure of
17 percent in 2005, there exists a loss of revenue which can be estimated
between 15 percent and 25 percent of the current level.

Main features of the evolution of tax systems in Latin America

The composition of the tax structures shows significant changes during the
period 1990–2005, following a series of stylized facts which we summarize as
follows:

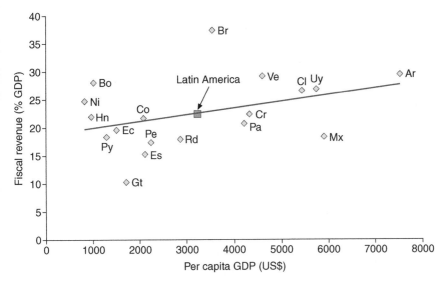

Figure 1.3a Fiscal revenue and per capita GDP (2005) (source: CEPAL).

1　First, we observe a lower participation of revenues from external commerce on the total level of tax revenues, in part as a consequence of the abolition of taxes on exports in the area,[3] and especially for the substantial reduction of the nominal and effective tariffs on the imports. This trend originates in the 1980s and it is complemented with the process of generalization and growth of VAT in all regions, which became the main source of revenue, doubling its value with respect to GDP during the period 1990–2005, as shown in Table 1.2.

2　Second, the weight of taxes on income is also increasing in the same period, but at a lower rate, although in the last years the weight of corporate taxation seems to be larger. To this respect, notice that the information about corporate taxation and taxes on natural or physical persons are insufficient for the majority of countries. In Figure 1.4 we also observe a decreasing trend of top tax rates, both for personal taxes (from 40 percent/60 percent in the middle of 1980s to 25 percent/35 percent now) and for corporate taxes (44 percent on average in 1986 and 26 percent in 2004);

3　Third, the VAT tax base has been progressively rising, especially through the inclusion of services. The average level of this tax is also growing, from 11 percent to 15 percent with a maximum level of 23 percent (Uruguay). Although its adoption has been general, VAT shows important differences from one country to another, both in terms of the tax base and of the tax rates (variety and levels) applied in each country. Concerning the first issue, in some countries VAT is generally applied to goods and services, while in others only to goods and some services and, in very few ones, only to goods. Regarding the tax rates, a first difference is between

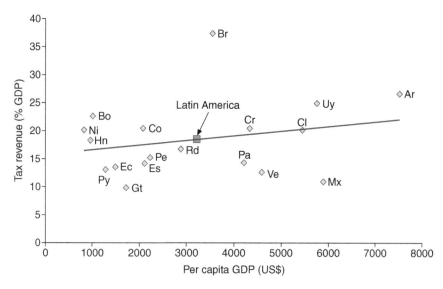

Figure 1.3b Tax revenue and per capita GDP (2005) (source: CEPAL).

countries with multiple tax rates (applied to different types of consumption) and countries with a unique generally applied tax rate. Argentina, Colombia, Costa Rica, Honduras, Mexico, Nicaragua and Panama use a system of multiple tax rates, while the other countries apply a unique, uniform tax rate.

Tax rates in turn show two basic features. On one side there is a general trend to growth, since between 1994 and 2004 the average VAT revenue

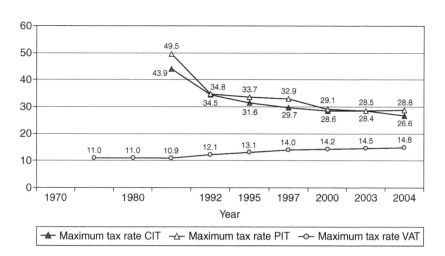

Figure 1.4 Evolution of average CIT, PIT and VAT in Latin America.

Table 1.2 Structure of fiscal revenue in Latin America (% of GDP)

	1990	1995	2000	2005(p)
Total tax revenue	10.5	12.2	13.0	15.0
Direct tax revenue	2.9	3.5	3.9	5.0
Rent and capital gain	2.1	2.8	3.1	3.9
Property	0.6	0.6	0.7	0.9
Other direct	0.1	0.1	0.1	0.2
Indirect tax revenue	7.6	8.7	9.0	10.0
General on goods and services	2.9	4.4	5.1	6.0
Specific on goods and service	1.9	1.9	2.0	1.8
Commerce and international transactions	2.0	2.0	1.6	1.5
Other indirect	0.7	0.4	0.4	0.7
Social security	2.4	2.9	2.9	3.0
Total	12.9	15.1	15.9	18.0

Source: CEPAL, United Nations.

in the area rose by almost three percentage points of GDP. On the other side, there are remarkable differences across countries with respect to the size of the tax rates (see Table 1.3). Argentina, Brazil, Chile, Peru and Uruguay apply tax rates higher than or close to 20 percent, while Bolivia, Costa Rica, Ecuador, El Salvador, Guatemala, Haiti, Honduras, Panama and Paraguay have adopted tax rates no higher than 13 percent, thus lower than the average 14.8 percent. In comparative terms, in 2004 the simple average of VAT tax rates applied in Latin America and the Caribbean was almost five percentage points below the average of the European Union (14.6 percent and 19.6 percent respectively). The differentiation across countries was lower in the European Union than in Latin America and the Caribbean (standard deviation of three in the former case and 4.5 in the latter).

Moreover, the VAT productivity (defined as revenue in percentage of GDP divided by the general tax) is comparatively low in the region, since it reached a 40 percent in 2005 (notice that the average productivity in developed countries is higher than 60 percent). Even in this case there are important differences across countries, as shown by Figure 1.5. Five countries (Haiti, Mexico, Peru, Panama and Dominican Republic) show a revenue efficacy much lower than the average of the area.

This indicator does not, of course, necessarily reflect administrative efficiency, but the dispersion of tax rates around the general tax. For instance, in Mexico, exemptions for food make the dispersion larger. Thus, Figure 1.5 only shows the distance with respect to a potential collector in case there would be no exemptions. In a context with growing difficulties to introduce new taxes or higher tax rates, the abolition of exemptions and the limits to tax deductions emerge as significant sources of fiscal revenues in the future.

Table 1.3 Latin America and the Caribbean: tax rates of VAT

	1994	*2000*	*2005*
Argentina	18.00	21.00	21.00
Bolivia	14.92	14.92	13.00
Brazil	20.48	20.48	20.48
Chile	18.00	18.00	19.00
Colombia	14.00	15.00	16.00
Costa Rica	8.00	13.00	13.00
Ecuador	10.00	12.00	12.00
El Salvador	10.00	13.00	13.00
Guatemala	7.00	10.00	12.00
Haití	10.00	10.00	10.00
Honduras	7.00	12.00	12.00
México	10.00	15.00	15.00
Nicaragua	10.00	15.00	15.00
Panamá	5.00	5.00	5.00
Paraguay	10.00	10.00	10.00
Peru	18.00	18.00	19.00
R. Dominicana	6.00	8.00	16.00
Uruguay	22.00	23.00	23.00
Venezuela	10.00	15.50	15.00
Average Latin America	11.70	14.20	14.80
Standard deviation Latin America	5.10	4.60	4.40

Source: CEPAL, on the official numbers of each country.

4   Fourth, there is a raising degree of informality of markets, especially in the labor field and in small firms, which induces the majority of countries to implement several tax measures to adapt to these circumstances: some have adopted alternative systems to integrally treat these groups of taxpayers, some others to exempt taxpayers considered less remunerative for the tax administration or, in other cases, countries have opted for living with the problem and not complying with the rules.

Of the 17 countries analyzed in Latin America, 14 have adopted a special regime of taxation of small taxpayers, and only three did not (El Salvador, Panama, Venezuela). Nevertheless these three countries apply an exemption of VAT according to the amount of sales. In the majority of countries special regimes are adopted on voluntary basis. Seven countries apply more than one regime. Chile applies four general regimes and some of them admit sub-regimes with specific features according to the economic activity of the taxpayers.[4] Argentina applies a regime denominated "*monotributo impositivo*" which is a substitute for the income tax, social security contributions and VAT.[5] Brazil has adopted a regime called "*simples*" which is also a way to capture the informal economy through a simplified system.

5   Fifth, "tax expenditure" is a term largely used to refer to exemptions, deductions, credits, delays and returns of taxes. In a wider sense, tax expenditure

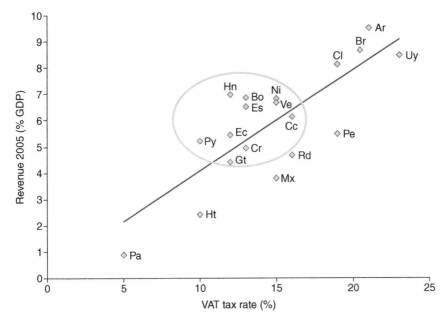

Figure 1.5 VAT productivity (2005) (source: CEPAL).

is the revenue which is left uncollected, due to franchises or special tax regimes, aiming at favoring or stimulating specific sectors, activities, regions or agents of the economy.

In Latin America and the Caribbean, an increasing number of countries provide information on tax expenditure. The amounts are very significant in all cases, with a minimum of 1.4 percent of GDP for Brazil and a maximum of 7.4 percent of GDP for Colombia. Concerning the taxes coming from the tax expenditure, notice that in Argentina, Ecuador, Peru and Uruguay incentives related to indirect taxes prevailed, especially VAT, while in Chile the incentives focused more on the income tax. Regarding the destination, in Argentina 80 percent of tax expenditure (2.4 percent of GDP) corresponded to treatments established by the laws of the respective taxes and the other part to benefits given to the different regimes of economic, regional and sectoral promotion. In Chile, the tax expenditure (4.2 percent of GDP) is mainly directed to the financial sector (61.3 percent), housing (12.6 percent) and education (7.4 percent).

6   Finally, we notice two additional facts: on one side the significant reduction of the number of taxes, especially selective taxes, which has been limited to non-elastic goods and services, such as tobacco, alcoholic beverages, telecommunications, on the other side the emergence of taxes applied to extraordinary bases such as bank debts or credits, tax on financial services and other "heterodox" charges, aiming at establishing a minimum weight of direct taxes.

Perspectives of the main taxes

The reduction of taxes on external commerce, which started in the past decades, does not seem to be completed, since the current process induced by both the multilateral treatments of commerce (TLC with the European Union and other bilateral treaties of free commerce) and the different areas of regional integration will necessarily have impact on the collection of the import rights. The agreement of the DR-CAFTA for instance, which is a convention of Central American countries, the US and the Dominican Republic, establishes a loss of collection for tariffs (see Agosin *et al.* 2005).

This situation highlights that it will be necessary to recollect resources which will be lost, in order on one side to avoid stopping the process of openness and on the other side to avoid fiscal losses which may affect the country's level of fiscal sustainability, the equity of the tax system and its productive structure. As noticed by Baunsgaard and Keen (2005):

> an informal revision of the information also suggests that the countries which successfully recollected the lost revenues of external commerce did it not only with resources coming from consumption tax – a standard recipe – but also with a heavier income tax. This may be somehow due to the fact that the increase of income tax helps to overcome the political economy

Table 1.4 Tax expenditures in selected Latin American and OECD countries

Country	Year	Total fiscal pressure (% GDP)	Total (% GDP)	Tax expenditure		Total tax expenditure/ total fiscal pressure (%)
				Direct taxes (% of total)	Indirect taxes (% of total)	
Latin America						
Argentina	2004	22.6	2.4	27.4	72.6	10.5
Brazil	2004	16.5	1.4	68.6	31.4	8.5
Chile	2002	18.1	4.2	74.0	26.0	23.2
Colombia	1998	14.4	7.4	35.0	65.0	51.4
Ecuador	2000	11.6	4.9	47.0	53.0	42.1
Guatemala	2000	9.7	7.3	28.0	72.0	75.2
México	2003	12.6	6.3	–	–	50.0
Peru	2003	14.7	2.5	34.0	66.0	17.0
Uruguay	2000	23.6	5.3	11.0	89.0	22.3
OECD						
Australia	1999–2002	24.2	4.3			17.8
Canada	1999–2002	17.6	7.9			44.9
US	2001–4	18.5	7.5			40.5
Netherlands	2002	39.2	2.4			6.1

Source: Gómez Sabaini (2005).

difficulties concerning a greater weight of the consumption tax, which are perceived (correctly or not) as regressive.

The evolution of tax structure in Latin America however did not follow that direction. It was instead focused on raising consumption taxes, and when these were not sufficient, on heterodox or distortionary resources to strengthen the collection, which is an issue for the future of the tax income.

Regarding tax income, the reduction of marginal taxes of personal and corporate income followed a general international trend, as long as the majority of medium and small countries have adopted competitive measures aimed at stopping the charge of the effects of commercial and financial liberalization of the last two decades.

The strong participation of the society in the total collection of taxes and the high mobility of tax bases under the globalization process make it urgent to include changes in this field in order to avoid a growing delay in the increase of collection of income taxes. To this respect, many countries still apply tax rules more appropriate to closed economies with controlled financial markets, which is the opposite of the real world.

Many practices are still frequent: the use of the source principle instead of the world income; the absence of rules to control the excessive deductions of interests; the lack of explicit rules to determine transfer prices between international firms; the absence of connection across tax administrations in the field of exchange information; and many other rules aimed at enlarging and strengthening the potential base of charge and avoiding the effects of a dangerous tax competition, through rules frequently used in developed countries and recommended by the OECD. The generous and not always effective systems of incentives to investments, and the favorable treatments of financial incomes also limit tax collection.

Other progressive taxes, such as taxes on the personal wealth, complementary to the income tax, are used in very few countries (for instance Argentina and Uruguay). They do not have the desired impact, however, due to serious administrative problems, especially of control.

To sum up, we still need a debate on the role of the personal income tax in Latin America, in particular we wonder about the treatment of revenues from any kind of financial assets, both private and public, the role of capital gains, and the best way to effectively control the application of the tax. Given the different goals of personal income tax, on one side, and corporate income tax, on the other side, it is convenient to separately analyze the perspectives of both taxes on equity and investments.

Additionally, as we have noticed, "the diffusion of VAT has been the tax event of the last 50 years, since from being a largely unknown tax outside France, in the 1950s it became adopted by 136 countries, where it usually represents a fourth of the tax collection."[6] VAT is a continuously developing tax as shown in the agreements of the Andean Pact. The design of the Andean Pact can be summarized as follows:

1   credit method for invoicing with consumption base under the destination principle;
2   possible adoption in the long run of a common list of exempted goods and services, mainly the sensible services – education, health and internal transport of travelers, except flight – and the financial services;
3   the reduction, in case of existence of multiple tax rates, to a maximum of two, being the general tax rate equal or lower than 19 percent, while the minimum tax rate can not be lower than 30 percent of the general tax, to ease the VAT administration.

The timing of adoption of these regulations varies according to the type of measure, with a maximum of ten years.

Countries have invested a large amount of money to improve tax compliance. There exists a trend toward a reduction of tax evasion, although very few studies analyze this phenomenon. Also, a process of learning and cooperation has started, not only among the countries of the region, but also in relation with the rules followed by the industrialized countries, up to the extent that the rules established by the Sixth European Directive are frequently used in all countries of the region. This is in contrast with the evolution of the tax income.

Despite these improvements, there are still questions on the effects of the tax, especially relative to its distributive impact. The best way to address this problem is still a debated issue in these countries. The process of enlarging the tax base however provides alternatives under different grounds, for instance, the treatment of merit goods or goods involving large externalities, the case of financial instruments, electronic commerce, the destination principle in relation with the process of integration at regional level.

On the technical point, there is consensus that the use of a zero tax should be reserved only for exports. However this has not been the case in several countries, which have instead applied the same tax to domestic activities to try to limit the effect of taxation on the lower levels of income. These mechanisms are certainly not recommended and their use should be discouraged. This opens the question if it is necessary to give some progressivity to this tax or if it has to be as more neutral as possible – enlarging totally the bases – while the progressivity should be left to the income and wealth tax.

As we already noticed and has been remarked upon by the final document of the VAT Commission:

> the choice between a VAT with a unique tax rate or a VAT with multiple tax rates depends mainly on administrative considerations: the application of a unique tax rate is usually preferred when other instruments are available, which are considered more appropriate for distributive goals and whose absence tends to favor a greater differentiation.

There exists a necessary interrelation between the VAT treatment and the consumption selective taxes on goods and services. These taxes have been focused almost exclusively on the "vicious" – tobacco and alcoholic beverages. In other words, they have a mere collecting role, with a regressive substantial impact, since these consumptions represent a major proportion of revenue of the sectors with lower resources. On the contrary, although differential VAT tax rates are not recommended with respect to the application of tax rates higher than the general one, a combination with a selective taxation could be a better option.

To sum up, the role of selective taxes has been decreasing during the last decades. It is thus worthwhile to wonder about a global analysis of selective taxation in the framework of consumption tax and about its role.

The effects of taxes in Latin America: equity and efficiency

Many industrialized countries show high *ex ante* (before the public intervention of taxes and transfers) income concentration coefficients and better concentration indexes *ex post*. On the contrary, in the majority of Latin American countries, as shown by the evolution of the Gini Index in Figure 1.6, the distribution of revenues *ex post* is more concentrated than *ex ante*, meaning that the effect of the tax system is regressive. Unfortunately this happens in one of the extremely unequal areas of the world.

Although it is frequently to mention that the most effective state action takes place through public expenditure, there is still a question on the role of taxes on distributive issues, i.e. if both instruments – taxes and expenditures – should be considered as alternative or complementary ways to reach in the long run more efficiency with more equity. To this respect, in many cases tax rules affect the

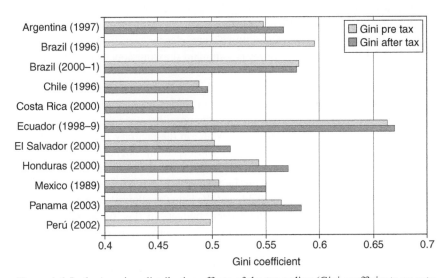

Figure 1.6 Latin America: distributive effects of the tax policy (Gini coefficients ex ante and ex post) (source: Gómez Sabaini 2005).

distributive results, bearing differently on people under the same circumstances, affecting the essential principle of horizontal equity. The doubt should not only be on how to improve vertical equity but, in particular, on how to avoid horizontal inequities. Although the general level of taxation in the region has increased during the last decades, the importance of personal income tax did not grow, while at the same time the degree of regional inequality has increased.

This situation points out the necessity of rethinking the role of each tax in the general context of the tax structure of the countries and, as suggested by Bird *et al.* (2004), to look in detail at the directions of ongoing reforms, more than at the past situations. The studies on distributive incidence show, even with methodological and informative limits, that the distributive effect of tax systems is, in a large amount of cases, regressive, since the tax structure is dominated by the indirect taxes, with a smaller weight for taxes on capital and wealth.

In this sense we wonder about the degrees of advance and efficiency of the tax administration since, as far as they are weak and they can not reach an acceptable outcome, a substantial tax evasion is facilitated, which creates a significative wedge between the legal and effective tax rates. Due to this, the expected goals may not be reached. At the same time, corruption and the low degree of the government institutions also establish a limit to the effectiveness of redistributive measures.

It is difficult to disentangle the importance of the tax incentives by the changes occurred in each time to the degree of commercial openness, since in many countries these tax benefits were either part of the measures to stimulate direct foreign investments and strengthen the process of substitute imports, or they were aimed to build free areas of exports.

The results obtained are not clear, due to the absence of specific analysis, the difficulties of information, or possibly the lack of interest in knowing the actors of this process. The quantification effectuated, following the different alternatives to estimate the "tax expenditures" are clearly significant, although the methodological alternatives do not recommend drawing conclusions from comparisons across countries.

Nevertheless some conclusions may be drawn. First, we observe that developed countries largely used instruments to sustain tax income, instead of external commerce and consumption. Second, the benefits provided were more automatic and contained in the general rules of taxes, while on the contrary in the Latin American region they were more discretional and based on independent texts of law referred to special sectors or activities. Third, countries such as in the EU and Canada have a significant weight in the field of tax expenditure, which indicates an active role of the state in this field, and the benefits allowed are made transparent through their inclusion in the federal budget. In this sense, the available information does not clarify the role of taxes in the process of moving savings and investments, since, although currently one can have information on fiscal costs, the results obtained are not clear. This opens a series of questions not only relative to the objectives of promoting investments, but also to the better instruments and the capacity of the state in their administrative and managing process.

The political economy of the tax reforms in Latin America

It is clear that, for different reasons, the majority of reforms required to raise the level of taxation, to eliminate the problems which make taxes not economically neutral and the effects of inequity on the distribution of tax charge have not been implemented yet.

We may identify some reasons for that: on one side, several elements intrinsic to the political reality of the countries which condition their economic decisions; on the other side, the weakness of the institutional development of tax administrations required to apply measures which need a high degree of efficiency and managing capacity. The two elements are not independent and it is not by chance that the countries where the "élites" are stronger the tax administrations are weaker.

First, it is widely accepted that Latin America is the area with the highest degree of inequality of revenues, a fact that has been accentuated during recent years, although the region is showing a growing GDP per capita and a decreasing index of poverty.[7] In this sense some authors have developed the thesis that the extension of inequality of revenues in the region has affected the design and implementation of the tax system. This generates a vicious circle of inequality of revenues and tax regressivity, instead of a virtuous circle which may correct the large disequilibrium of revenue through the tax system.

From the political perspective, social inequality may result in the generation of "élite groups," which try to minimize their relative fiscal burden, by controlling the legislative process or inducing tax laws with these effects, in order to translate a major percentage of the fiscal burden to sectors with fewer resources. It is also feasible to expect a raise in pressures for the same "élite groups" to control the process of implementation and fiscal rules, and also to design administrative rules which would have a more beneficial effect for them, such as laundering, moratorium and other similar measures. Under these circumstances, the design of a progressive fiscal structure is more difficult.

Similarly, in economies with a large poor class it is feasible to find high levels of informality both in labor and in goods markets and under these circumstances the design of tax systems with a certain degree of equality is not simple, since the informal economy makes it difficult to have an efficient administration of tax instruments.

To sum up, the absence of a substantial middle class is a critical limit for the development of a personal income tax which would account for at least 20 percent of the main revenues, and would make it in a large and general way with respect to any type of rent.

It has also been observed that while developed countries have enlarged and extended the tax bases having as a consequence an increase of the tax collection, the joint or simultaneous movement of reduction of taxes and enlargement of bases had not an equivalent correspondent in Latin America taxation. The expansion of tax bases, eliminating exemptions, special deductions and preferred treatments in fact did not happen in the majority of these countries.[8]

In this sense we should notice, once again, the preferential treatment received in the past and also currently by the rents generated by the financial sector in the majority of countries, due to legal rules which have protected them, and due to inefficient control mechanisms, which render a large part of these financial rents in practice not taxed.

The debate on the openness and mobility of the financial market in all countries of the region, and the fact that a good percentage of the personal saving portfolios and of the firm benefits are collocated outside – both in developed countries which are not available to apply retention mechanisms of taxes at the source and in fiscal heavens – has as effect that, in the majority of cases, the financial rents escape all types of taxation, both at the source and at the taxpayer residence.

The insufficient development of tax administration did not have the success which was desirable to reach the sectors "hard to tax," such as informal sectors, agricultural sector, professional sectors and small firms. These economies have also experienced a substantial growth of services, which delivers new and more difficulties for an efficient control of the tax administration.

As a consequence, the design of tax policy in developing countries should especially consider the administrative issue, without implying that the political economy objectives would be subject to a certain level of administration, while using other mechanisms to improve this level. In this sense, the objective would be to reach an adequate balance between a better distributive equity, the reduction of economic distortions and the consideration of the tax administration, in each particular circumstance. It seems that in the last decades in Latin America the "adequate balance" has not been like that, while the directives in the tax field have been largely influenced by efficiency goals with a lower weight for distributive issues.

As noted by Sokoloff and Zolt (2005) the evidence suggests that the large history of inequality in the region is a central element to understand the distinctive features of tax systems in Latin America, and at the same time that the élite groups have benefited from a light tax burden over the years.

All together these factors indicate the enormous problems which oppose changes of the tax system. An appropriate "political environment" seems necessary to complete the required changes and adopt the required measures.

On one hand, in recent years there has been a significant improvement in the knowledge and transparency of the information about the beneficiaries of the differential incentives allowed by the system. This information was not available in the past. The efforts employed in realizing a better transparency pushed by the international climate set the issue in various countries of the region at a legislative level. The publication of the complete and ordered texts of the law, the diffusion of the "tax expenditures" which quantify the amount of benefits allowed, the public knowledge of the name of the main fiscal debtors, the elimination of the financial and stock market secrets in almost all countries, the diffusion of the failures of the fiscal and stock market courts, all these are factors which contribute to the change. On the other hand, it is evident that the current technological level allows the tax administration, if correctly applied, to convert into a tool of enormous value which was not available before. Currently, through the computers it is possible to manage large external databases on the behavior of the taxpayers which allow the tax administration to make the declaration on behalf of them, as it is happening in some countries of the region, such as for example Chile.

Equally, the systems of source retention may be currently generalized without big difficulties for the tax administration, which receives the information from those who have retained the tax at the source without more complexity, while this mechanism – widely used in developed countries – had an serious problem of information. This allows to capture data in real time and to know in a general way the transactions between different economic sectors.

Similarly, the countries have found it convenient to agree on exchanging information, which shows a cooperation effort among them since, through it, it is possible to increase their own efforts and the possibility of applying these taxes.

To sum up, the experience shows that three elements are essential to improve the efficiency of tax administration in each country:

1   the political will of effectively implement the tax rules voted by the policy-makers;
2   an administrative strategy clearly defined and continuous during the time in order to reach all the proposed objectives;
3   a flexible endowment of resources, personal and financial, which are necessary to reach these objectives.

The observed experience in the countries turns out to be ambiguous in this field, since while the objectives are changing, the strategies followed by the tax administrations are also constantly changing in each of the directions in which they develop, and there is a systematic insufficiency of resources to comply with the proposed goals. However it should also be mentioned that the existence of "political interferences" in the fiscal management often conditions their activity.

Some features which may help the implementation of tax reforms in Latin America

Mahon (1997) analyzes some circumstances related to the reforms in the Latin American tax structure and considers four possible events which make reform possible:

1   as a result of situations of economic crisis;
2   as the action of governments recently elected;
3   as a consequence of the existence of authoritarian regimes;
4   as a result of international pressures, either due to the external context or to existent conditions.

Additionally, as a fifth determinant operating on the tax structure of recent decades, we may mention the weakness of tax administration, an issue that we have discussed in the previous section. To strengthen this is a central element for the application of the tax reforms.

1   The more substantial changes in the structure of countries are usually possible during the period of crisis, since in these circumstances it is feasible to overcome the political opposition and the administrative inertia which usually stop the relevant changes. In this sense, there are many examples of crisis in Latin America which have facilitated the application of deep reforms, both in the tax field and in other public policies. An example are the economic emergency laws in Argentina in 2002, which made it possible to approve tax measures which were rejected by law not many years before. This is especially important when tax changes have to be implemented with serious redistributive implications, which would be strongly rejected if proposed in situation out of crisis. Again, various reforms contained in the laws approved in Argentina in December 1999, especially for personal income taxation, have found support in this situation.

2   Similarly, electoral cycles can also be considered as a vehicle which facilitate the adoption of significative changes. In many countries tax reforms take place in the first months of a new government, when it enjoys the support of the citizens which voted for it. Many reforms took place in the first year of government, and then the debate around them takes place over a longer period.

3   Last, we should mention the external pressure exerted as consequence of economic programs subject to conditions of political economy, as well as the pressure exerted by the external trends in the field. In the tax field, as in few other economic ones, the effect of "keeping up with the neighbors" is significant and so the tax systems of the region have been subject to many trends, one of the major ones being the application of a generalized VAT in all countries.

4   As we already noticed, the weakness of tax administration has also affected the directions of many tax changes in some countries in recent years. These changes had the purpose of translating part of the responsibilities of an efficient tax administration on the taxpayers themselves, using systems considered as "imperfect substitutes" to the design of an appropriate tax system. We refer to taxes such as the tax on "active entrepreneurs" or "tax on financial activities," as well as other proposals that put the financial sector at the centre of the tax collection.

5   Given the legal and administrative difficulties to raise tax collection on corporate rents, it is a general fact in the region to adopt different methods of determination, complementary or substitute, to improve the obtained results. They have been based on the application of a tax which determined the "presumed base" in order to determine a minimum amount of tax, much beyond the effective result which would be obtained as a consequence of the tax on the "net rent" of firms. Some countries use for this purpose as a presumed tax base the active value, or, in other cases and more recently, the

amount of the gross sales, or revenues, before deducing costs and expenditures. The so determined taxation is considered a minimum amount to pay. When the determination of the tax amount taking into account the net rent leads to higher amounts, the taxpayer should pay the exceeding amount. In the opposite case the tax on actives or on gross sales remains as a ceiling under which it is impossible to go. In facts, the application of these taxes is the result of the limits of the countries, from both a legal and an administrative point of view, to apply a tax structure in which the nominal or legal taxes used would correspond to the effective taxes. These systems would however de facto lead to the elimination of corporate income tax, and would convert the taxation in non-tax revenues with cumulative effect, worsening the problems of economic efficiency.

6 The use of taxes on bank debts and credits basically replied to the urgencies of obtaining fast collections, translating the responsibility of its revenue to the financial institutions, taking into account the weakness of tax administration, which assumes a smaller role in its capture. Although they were introduced with the specific purpose of improving resources in the short run under emergency, more than as an instrument to remain in the tax structure, they have been so successful in some countries that it is difficult to replace them without affecting the level of revenue. The evidence shows that they have proved effective in obtaining revenue in the short run while, at the same time, as indicated by Coelho *et al.* (2001), the reaction of the market to the tax impact shows that there exist adverse effects, including in particular a significant degree of financial disintermediation. Baca-Campodónico *et al.* (2006) however confirm this trend and indicate that this source of revenue may not be too sure in the long run.

To sum up, the current tax systems have been the result of a series of compromising decisions adopted under different circumstances, going from the possibility of a crisis, to the limits of the institutional capacity of collecting taxes. These limits, in one or another scenario, were not equal in all countries and the results observed for the tax structure of each country are the consequence of specific facts which have to be evaluated analyzing each specific case.

Notes

1 We thank Alberto Barreix for useful comments and Lic. Maximiliano Geffner and Maria Victoria Espada for research assistance.
2 In this analysis we will not include Cuba, since tax information is not available, as well as English speaking countries, which are not comparable, due to their tax systems, substantially different from the other Latin American countries.
3 The recent case of Argentina with respect to the withholding of exports since 2002 is an exception to the general rule.
4 González (2006).
5 Gómez Sabaini and Geffner (2006).
6 International Tax Dialogue (2005), Conclusions Conference VAT.

7 Sokoloff and Zolt (2005).
8 To this respect see the analysis by Keen and Simon (2004).

References

Agosin, M., Machado, R. and Nazal, P. (2004) *Pequeñas economías, grandes desafíos*, Interamerican Development Bank (IABD), Washington, DC: IADB.

Agosin, M., Barreix, A., Gómez Sabaini, J. C. and Machado, R. (2005) "Reforma tributaria para el desarrollo humano en Centroamérica," *Revista de la CEPAL*, Santiago de Chile: CEPAL.

Baca-Campodónico, J., de Mello, L. and Kirilenko, A. (2006) "The Rates and Revenue of Bank Transaction Taxes," Working Paper 494, Paris: OECD.

Baunsgaard, T. and Keen, M. (2005) "Tax Revenue and (or?) Trade Liberalization," IMF Working Paper 05/112, Washington, DC: IMF.

Bird, R., Martínez-Vázquez, J. and Torgler, B. (2004) "Societal Institutions and Tax Effort in Developing Countries," International Studies Program, Working Paper 04/06, Atlanta, Andrew Young School of Policy Studies, Georgia State University.

Coelho, I., Ebrill, L. and Summers, V. (2001) "Bank Debit Taxes in Latin America: An Analysis of Recent Trends," Working Paper 01/67, Washington, DC: IMF.

Gómez Sabaini, J. C. (2005), *Evolución y situación tributaria actual en América Latina: una serie de temas para la discusión*, Santiago de Chile: CEPAL.

Gómez Sabaini, J. C. and Geffner, M. (2006) *Efectos de las políticas tributarias sobre la informalidad*, Buenos Aires and Washington, DC: World Bank.

González, D. (2006) *Regímenes especiales de tributación para pequeños contribuyentes en América Latina,* Interamerican Development Bank (IABD), Washington, DC: IADB.

International Tax Dialogue (2005) "El Impuesto sobre el Valor Añadido. Experiencias y Problemática," Conferencia sobre el IVA organizada por el Diálogo Fiscal Internacional VAT, Roma, 15 and 16 March, Washington, DC: IMF.

Keen, M. and Simon, A. (2004) "Tax Policy in Developing Countries: Some Lessons from the 1990, and Some Challenges Ahead," in Gupta, S., Clements, B. and Inchauste, G. (eds) *Helping Countries Develop: The Role of Fiscal Policy*, Washington, DC: IMF.

Mahon, J. (1997) "Tax Reform and its Determinants in Latin America, 1974–94: Implications for Theories of State Development," Latin America Studies Association, Guadalajara, Mexico, Williamstown, MA.

Martner, R. and Tromben, V. (2004) "Reform and Fiscal Stabilization in Latin American Countries," *Serie Gestión Pública* n. 45, Santiago de Chile: CEPAL.

Perry, G., Arias, O., Lopez, J., Maloney, W. and Serven, L. (2006) *Poverty Reduction and Growth: Virtuous and Vicious Circles*, Washington, DC: World Bank.

Sokoloff, K. and Zolt, E. (2005) "Inequality and the Evolution of Institutions of Taxation: Evidence from the Economic History of the Americas," University of California LA.

2 An outline of tax systems and tax reforms

Francesco Figari and Luca Gandullia

Introduction and main conclusions[1]

In the mid-1970s and until the mid-1990s Latin American countries began to implement a set of tax reforms, involving the simplification of tax structures and the removal of exemptions and special privileges, the replacement of trade taxes by value-added taxes and an emphasis on improved tax administration (Shome 1992, 1995, 1999; Tanzi 2000; Lledo *et al.* 2004). Reforms were significantly influenced by foreign experts and by international financial institutions that promoted a fairly homogeneous set of tax changes, often in the context of macroeconomic stabilization programs. The first goal of these reforms has been to enhance revenue collection and provide more stability in the revenue systems (OECD 2006a).

A number of exogenous determinants influenced tax reforms (Tanzi 2000). A first set of determinants concerned the precarious macroeconomic situations of many countries and the inflationary context that compelled many countries to look for short-term tax measures and to rely more heavily on indirect taxes over direct taxes. A second set of determinants came from trade and capital liberalization; the consequences, similar to what has been experimented elsewhere in the world (Bernardi 2004; Bernardi *et al.* 2006), have been twofold: a reduction in revenues from foreign trade taxes and its compensation with other revenue sources (broad-based consumptions taxes and partly also direct taxes); second, a rapid reduction in personal income tax rates and in corporate income tax rates. In this context during the 1980s and 1990s all the Latin American countries (following Brazil where valued added taxation started in 1967) introduced the VAT which represents the most important innovation in Latin America's taxation during recent decades.

Although not fully implemented, these reforms have generally increased the efficiency of tax systems and their revenue-raising capacity (Shome 1995, 1999). However, they have come at a price: other issues have been driven and kept off the tax policy agenda. One of the main excluded issues deals with considerations of tax equity and redistribution and the financing of social security programs. With few exceptions Latin American countries continue to be allergic to taxing incomes and collecting social security contributions. Thus revenues from income taxes continue to be low compared with international levels. Many reasons combine to explain this (Tanzi 2000): very large personal exemptions and deductions; reluctance to tax financial incomes; falling in tax rates; low efficiency in tax administration. At present, after two decades of tax reforms, there is still the issue of raising more tax revenue (OECD 2006a), but the main challenges for next years seem to be: broadening tax bases, especially in the field of direct taxes; reducing reliance on the more distorting taxes, such as those on financial transactions, foreign trade and enterprise turnover and payroll; and improving tax administration (OECD 2006a).

The chapter is organized as follows. The next section discusses the main issues in tax reforms enacted in the last decade and the main perspectives for the future. We then present some indicators of the macro structure and evolution of the tax systems over the last decade, focusing on tax ratios by legal categories. The following section gives an overview of the main institutional features of the present tax systems in Latin American countries, focusing on personal income taxes, corporate income tax and consumption taxes.

Tax reforms during the last decade: main issues and perspectives

Over the past two decades, tax reforms in Latin American countries have been significantly influenced by foreign experts and by international financial institutions that have promoted a fairly homogenous set of tax reforms, often as a prerequisite for the disbursement of loans and in concert with structural adjustment programs (Shome 1992; Tanzi 2000). The reforms have been intended in particular to increase the tax-to-GDP ratio, to make tax systems more neutral and compatible with market economy, international trade integration and financial liberalization (Lledo *et al.* 2004; Perry and Herrera 1994; IDB 1996; CEPAL 1998; Shome 1999).To provide more stability in the revenue systems (Jenkins 1995) a greater reliance has been placed on value-added type taxes and on a reduction in the top statutory income tax rates for individual and corporation income taxes. A necessary, even if not sufficient, condition, to achieve macroeconomic stability had been to build a tax system that could be administered and yield an adequate level of revenue to the public sector. This has been the focus of the main tax reforms in most of the countries in the Latin American region during the last two decades (OECD 2006a). Thanks to these reforms since the early 1990s many countries in the region had made substantial progress in consolidating their public finances adversely affected by the financial crises at the end of 1990s. Fiscal adjustment has taken place against a background of volatile growth, continued disinflation and strengthening external positions, facilitated by improvements in the terms of trade in some cases. At the same time, given that in the last two decades many Latin American countries were facing a precarious fiscal situation, policymakers were often deterred from pursuing comprehensive tax reforms in the face of uncertainty about revenues in the short and medium run (IDB 2006; OECD 2006a).

Based on these goals, tax reform proposals in the region have tended to include the following elements (Jenkins 1995):

1   Implementation of broad-based and uniform VAT systems to replace taxes on foreign trade and cascading turnover taxes;
2   Reduction of the highest statutory tax rates and simplification of the personal income tax system;
3   elimination of preferential treatment for particular sources of corporate income and particular economic sectors;
4   modernization and strengthening of the institutions involved in tax administration.

The reforms in tax administration that were promoted and supported by international organizations have been implemented more consistently than other reforms (Lledo *et al.* 2004). A proliferation of programs included staff training, introducing modern information technology, and revising procedures and internal organization. Collection of taxes through banks was adopted everywhere, as well as internal organization by functions instead of the traditional tax base by tax base approach (IDB 1997).

In other areas successful reforms were implemented: the reform of foreign trade taxation and the reduction in high marginal income tax rates. During 1980s tax reforms also reflected development policy strategies; the policy of import substituting industrialization, that was common until the early 1980s, implied high tariffs and tax incentives for selected growth-promoting sectors. The latter narrowed the corporate tax base and led to the creation of multiple corporate income tax rates (Perry and Herrera 1994). From the mid-1970s taxes on foreign trade have been replaced by domestic broad-base consumption taxes. In this context all the Latin American countries (following Brazil) introduced the VAT which represents the most important innovation in Latin America's taxation during recent decades. In the same years the rate of decline in highest marginal PIT rates and corporate income tax rates has been more rapid than in the OECD countries (Shome 1999). Some areas of tax reform in the Latin American region represent interesting examples and experimentations in tax policy and tax institutions (Tanzi 2000). For instance, during the 1990s several countries in the region introduced business taxes on gross assets that performed well in the inflationary environment (Tanzi 2000). Such a tax was first adopted in Mexico in 1988 and subsequently introduced in Argentina, Colombia, Costa Rica, Paraguay and Uruguay (Shome 1999). The business asset tax has been used as a minimum income tax or sometimes as a complement to it. At present Mexico continues to operate the gross assets tax as a minimum income tax. A second example of experimentation is in the field of small business taxation. Almost all Latin American countries have introduced simplified taxation schemes for small firms. The aim has been twofold: reducing the administrative burdens and increasing tax compliance. A third example of tax experimentation is the tax on banking transactions, mainly on debits, that was originally introduced in

Argentina in 1983; it was reintroduced there in 1988 and 2001, and implemented in many other countries (for instance in Brazil in 1994 and 1997, in Colombia in 1998). As was the case with other tax policy innovations, governments' urgent revenue needs have been the major reason for the adoption of BDTs in Latin America. The tax has also proved to be very popular and easy to administer given the consolidated and satisfactory role of banks as collection agents (Tanzi 2000). Bank debits are still taxed in Brazil, as well as in several other countries in the region, discouraging financial intermediation in most cases.

At present, after two decades of tax reforms, there is still the issue of raising more tax revenue (OECD 2006a). Brazil's tax-to-GDP ratio is already closer to the OECD average than that of the other Latin American countries. But in some countries, such Mexico and Paraguay, government revenue is much lower. This reflects the inability of the governments to bring the more dynamic sectors of the economy into the tax net. Other than increasing tax revenues, the main challenges for the future seem to be: broadening tax bases; reducing reliance on the more distorting taxes, such as those on financial transactions, foreign trade, enterprise turnover and payroll; and improving tax administration in many countries (OECD 2006a). The reform of foreign trade taxes and their gradual elimination has still to be completed along the progress in regional and international integration (Martner and Tromben 2004); the lost revenues of external commerce have to be recollected with resources mainly from consumption taxes and income taxes. Latin American countries need to vastly improve the system of personal income taxation and social contributions. The present pay-as-you-go social security systems in Latin America are basically bankrupt. The high payroll taxes used to finance these schemes create a major distortion in the labor market and are subject to a high degree of evasion. With a few notable exceptions, the income tax has performed badly in Latin America during the last two decades. Income taxes, both personal and corporate, suffer from a large erosion of tax bases, mainly as a consequence of generous incentives for investments, favorable treatments of capital income (Shome 1999) and large tax exemptions. The main challenge is thus to broaden tax bases (Tanzi 2000; OECD 2006a), especially in the field of personal income taxation, but also in field of business taxation. Tax evasion in the field of direct taxes shows a decreasing trend in more recent years, even if additional measures seem essential for the effective collection of the income tax.

An additional area that is likely to see increased tax policy activity is the use of taxes to control pollution. Moreover, the property tax that has been implemented by some local governments is a source of revenue that Latin American countries should consider carefully as a way to finance the maintenance costs of their urban infrastructure. Finally, in the field of banking transactions, there is consensus that despite their revenue-raising capacity bank debts taxes have to be reformed because of their inefficiencies: the cumulative and cascading nature of their base; and their potential to cause disarticulation in the banking system, reduce market liquidity, and generate economic distortions (Tanzi 2000).

Tax systems: structure and developments

Historically Latin American tax systems have been characterized by:

1 a low tax-to-GDP ratio;
2 a tax structure weighted towards indirect taxes with narrow tax bases, multiple rates and many exemptions;
3 under-taxation of income, wealth and property;
4 a limited tax administration capacity;
5 a mild redistributive impact;
6 a highly centralized tax assignment with tax revenues transferred to subnational governments in the form of ad hoc negotiated block grants (Lledo *et al.* 2004; Bird and Oldman 1990; Shome 1992, 1995, 1999; CEPAL 1998).

Based on data made available by ILPES-CEPAL (2006), Table 2.1 provides information on tax revenues as shares of GDP for eight Latin American countries in the last decade (1995–2005). Table 2.1 gives also some information about the way these countries provide arrangements between the central and the sub-central levels of government. Broadly speaking there are large differences in tax ratios between Latin American countries and the OECD or EU countries. In Latin American countries there is considerable diversity in the size and the scope of governments which are typically much smaller than in the OECD or EU area (OECD 2006a). The total fiscal pressure in Latin American countries is less than half than in the OECD countries and even lower than in the EU countries (OECD 2006a and b; Bernardi 2004; Gandullia 2004). Also the composition of tax revenues shows very different approaches, where OECD countries collect a larger share from direct taxes and from social security contributions. In terms of total taxation, but not of revenue composition, Latin American countries show patterns similar to those of the countries in the South and East Asian area (Bernardi *et al.* 2006).

A number of factors help explain the level and structure of Latin American tax systems: for instance, colonial heritage, political institutions and regimes, economic structure and income inequality (Lledo *et al.* 2004). In particular, historically the region shows a number of characteristics of transition or developing countries: a larger share of agriculture in total output and employment; a large informal sector; and limited technical capacity of the tax administration reduce the feasibility of direct taxes as reliable sources of revenue, and limit the total tax revenues (Tanzi 1993). In Latin America in particular, high income inequality concentrates both political and economic power, and undermines tax capacity and the political feasibility of direct taxation (Lledo *et al.* 2004; IDB 1998). During the 1990s the limited capacity of Latin American tax agencies was reflected in a large tax gap – the difference between what revenue authorities would collect if everyone paid the tax legally due and what is actually collected. The gap can be attributed to avoidance, evasion, and tax expenditures (CEPAL

Table 2.1 Structure and development of fiscal revenue in selected countries as % of GDP (1995–2005)

	1995							
	AR	BR	CL	CO	CR	MXc	PYc	UY
Direct taxes, of which:	*3.9*	*8.6*	*5.7*	*4.7*	*2.4*	*4.2*	*2.5*	*5.3*
Income	2.5	4.8	3.9	4.0	2.2	4.0	2.5	1.8
Personal income	–	3.4	1.0	0.2	–	2.0	–	–
Corporate income	–	1.4	2.9	3.8	–	2.0	2.5	1.8
Property	1.4	1.5	1.8	0.6	0.2	0.2	0.0	3.5
Others	0.0	2.3	–	0.1	0.0	0.0	0.0	–
Indirect taxes, of which:	*11.6*	*11.2*	*12.8*	*7.1*	*9.6*	*5.1*	*9.9*	*11.5*
VAT	8.8	7.8	8.2	4.1	4.6	2.8	4.9	7.7
Excise duties	1.8	2.1	1.9	1.7	1.9	1.4	1.3	3.1
Import and export duties	0.4	0.8	2.1	1.0	3.0	0.6	3.1	0.5
Others	0.6	0.5	0.6	0.3	0.1	0.3	0.6	0.2
Total tax revenue	15.5	19.8	18.5	11.8	12.0	9.3	12.4	16.8
Social contributions	*4.7*	*9.9*	*1.3*	*3.7*	*5.9*	*2.0*	*1.1*	*8.5*
Total fiscal revenue	20.2	29.7	19.8	15.5	17.9	11.3	13.5	25.3
Administrative level								
Central government	12.9	20.5	18.4	13.4	12.3	11.3	13.5	23.1
State – local government	7.4	9.3	1.4	2.1	5.7	–	–	2.2

	2000							
	AR	BR	CL	CO	CR	MX	PY	UY
Direct taxes, of which:	*5.7*	*9.0*	*6.0*	*5.9*	*3.3*	*4.9*	*2.0*	*6.2*
Income	4.0	5.4	4.1	4.3	2.7	4.7	2.0	2.3
Personal income	–	3.9	1.2	–	–	1.9	–	–
Corporate income	–	1.5	2.8	–	–	2.8	2.0	2.3
Property	1.7	1.3	1.9	1.2	0.5	0.2	0.0	3.9
Others	0.0	2.3	–	0.4	0.1	0.0	0.0	–
Indirect taxes, of which:	*12.4*	*11.0*	*12.0*	*8.0*	*9.2*	*5.8*	*8.9*	*11.4*
VAT	8.8	8.0	7.9	4.8	4.9	3.5	4.7	7.9
Excise duties	2.5	1.7	2.3	1.9	3.2	1.6	1.8	3.2
Import and export duties	0.5	0.8	1.4	1.0	1.0	0.6	2.0	0.2
Others	0.6	0.5	0.4	0.3	0.1	0.1	0.4	0.1
Total tax revenue	18.1	20.0	18.0	13.9	12.5	10.7	10.9	17.6
Social contributions	*3.4*	*12.5*	*1.4*	*2.9*	*6.3*	*1.5*	*1.2*	*8.4*
Total fiscal revenue	21.5	32.5	19.4	16.8	18.8	12.2	12.1	26.0
Administrative level								
Central government	13.1	23.0	17.8	14.1	12.3	12.2	12.1	23.6
State – local government	8.3	9.5	1.5	2.7	6.6	–	–	2.4

	2005p							
	AR	BR(2004)	CL	CO(2004)	CR	MXc	PYc	UYc
Direct taxes, of which:	*8.8*	*10.4*	*7.2*	*8.4*	*4.1*	*4.8*	*2.1*	*4.7*
Income	5.5	6.2	5.3	6.0	3.4	4.6	2.1	2.9

continued

Table 2.1 continued

Personal income	–	4.1	–	–	–	–	–	–
Corporate income	–	2.1	–	–	–	–	2.1	2.9
Property	3.3	1.5	1.9	2.0	0.7	0.2	0.0	1.8
Others	0.0	2.7	–	0.4	0.0	0.0	0.0	–
Indirect taxes, of which:	*14.6*	*10.7*	*11.5*	*9.2*	*10.1*	*4.9*	*9.8*	*13.1*
VAT	9.5	8.4	8.2	5.9	5.5	3.8	5.2	8.5
Excise duties	2.0	1.3	1.9	2.0	3.3	0.7	2.2	2.6
Import and export duties	2.7	0.5	0.4	0.9	1.2	0.3	1.8	1.4
Others	0.4	0.5	1.0	0.4	0.1	0.1	0.6	0.6
Total tax revenue	23.4	21.1	18.7	17.6	14.2	9.7	11.9	17.8
Social contributions	*3.3*	*14.8*	*1.4*	*2.8*	*6.4*	*1.3*	*1.2*	*5.7*
Total fiscal revenue	26.7	35.9	20.1	20.4	20.6	11.0	13.1	23.5
Administrative level								
Central government	17.1	25.8	18.8	17.3	13.7	11.0	13.1	23.5
State – local government	9.6	10.0	1.4	3.1	6.9	–	–	–

Source: ILPES-CEPAL (2006).

Notes
p preliminar.
c central government.

1998). During the 1990s the share of tax revenues to GDP increased significantly in Latin American countries (Tanzi 2000) as a consequence of economic growth and of the design of more efficient tax systems (Martner and Tromben 2004). Also in more recent years (2000–5) the tax-to-GDP ration of the region continued to increase on average, by about 1.5 percent of GDP, reaching the average level of 21.4 percent.

In the last decade the increase in the tax ratio of the eight selected countries reached 2.3 percent of GDP. The expansion was particularly high in the last few years, when the strengthening of revenues seems to have contributed to significant improvements in the whole fiscal position of the Latin American region (Clements *et al.* 2007). This results from different patterns of individual countries. On the one hand, in some countries (Argentina, Brazil, Costa Rica and Colombia) the tax burden has increased significantly (6.2 percentage points in Brazil and 6.5 percentage points in Argentina). On the other hand, in other countries (Chile, Mexico and Paraguay) it has remained quite stable. Uruguay is the only country that in the last decade has registered a decrease (from 25.3 to 23.5 percent) in the tax-to-GDP ratio. These patterns can be explained by different factors. In Argentina and Colombia the increase in the tax burden has been caused by the expansion of tax revenues (both direct and indirect taxes), partly offset by the reduction in revenues from social security contributions. On the contrary in Brazil the increase in the tax burden is mainly explained by the expansion of social security contributions and to a less extent by direct taxes. In general the increase in the tax burden of the region as a whole is mainly explained by the expansion of direct taxes and to less extent of indirect taxes and value added taxes, while social security contributions has remained stable on average.

Both at the beginning and at the end of the period Latin American countries show the considerable range in these tax ratios with Brazil collecting around 36 percent of GDP while Chile and Colombia collected only around 20 percent.[2] Taking into consideration only taxes collected by the central government, the highest fiscal pressure is found in Brazil and Uruguay (around 23–6 percent) and the lowest in Mexico, Paraguay and Costa Rica (around 11–13.6 percent). Argentina, Chile and Colombia occupy an intermediate position (around 17–19 percent). At the end of the observed period (2005) the difference between the high fiscal pressure countries (Brazil and Uruguay) and the low fiscal pressure countries (Mexico, Costa Rica and Paraguay) is larger than in the middle of the 1990s. Among the Latin American countries the share of individual taxes in GDP shows large differences. The lower tax burden that can be found in the Latin American countries compared with the international standards is due to the lower incidence of both tax revenues and social security contributions. With the exception of Brazil, which collects from social security contributions a level of revenues as a percentage of GDP comparable with the EU average, in general social security contributions generate less than 6 percent of GDP and in several countries much less than that (1.2–1.4 percent in Chile, Mexico and Paraguay).

Also, the composition of fiscal revenues differs across Latin American countries and in comparison with the OECD area. The tax structure by legal categories, measured as the distribution of tax revenue among major taxes (direct taxes, indirect taxes and social security contributions) has changed over time (see Table 2.2). In Latin American countries the tax mix shows a general preference for indirect taxes over direct taxes and social security contributions. With the exception of Brazil, that gives the same weight to direct and indirect taxes, about half or more of total fiscal revenues comes from indirect taxes in most Latin American countries (Argentina, Chile, Costa Rica, Paraguay and Uruguay). Social security contributions account on average for around 18.9 percent of total revenues, with Brazil and Costa Rica much over the average (41.2 and 31.1 percent respectively). During the last decade the tax mix has changed between taxes and social security contributions. In all these countries, with the exception of Brazil and Uruguay, the importance of social contributions has decreased in favor of taxes. In the same period the role of direct taxes has increased, while the incidence of indirect taxes has decreased mainly as a consequence of the reduction in the revenues from import and export duties.

In 1995 the broad fiscal structure of Latin American countries was composed by social security contributions (22.5 percent), indirect taxes (52.8 percent) and direct taxes (24.7 percent). At the end of the period (2005) the tax mix changed as an effect of the reduction in indirect taxes (1.4 percent) and social security contributions (3.6 percent), compensated by the increase in the share of direct taxes (5 percent). The decrease in indirect taxes is due to the large reduction in import and export duties (2.8 percent), partly offset by the increase in revenues from the VAT (1.4 percent). Among individual countries the tax structure is

Table 2.2 Tax mix in selected countries as % of total taxation (1995–2005)

	1995							
	AR	BR	CL	CO	CR	MXc	PYc	UY
Direct taxes, of which:	*19.5*	*29.0*	*28.6*	*30.2*	*13.4*	*37.1*	*18.9*	*21.0*
Income	12.4	16.2	19.6	25.9	12.4	35.6	18.6	7.2
Personal income	–	–	4.8	1.4	–	18.0	–	–
Corporate income	–	–	14.7	24.5	–	17.6	18.6	7.2
Property	7.1	5.0	9.0	3.6	1.0	1.5	0.2	13.8
Others	0.0	7.8	–	0.7	0.0	0.0	0.1	–
Indirect taxes, of which:	*57.1*	*37.6*	*64.6*	*45.7*	*53.8*	*45.2*	*73.2*	*45.2*
VAT	43.3	26.3	41.7	26.1	25.7	25.0	35.9	30.3
Excise duties	8.8	7.0	9.4	11.2	10.7	12.3	9.9	12.3
Imports and export duties	1.9	2.5	10.5	6.7	16.8	5.4	22.9	2.0
Others	3.1	1.8	3.0	1.7	0.6	2.5	4.5	0.6
Total tax revenue	76.6	66.6	93.2	75.9	67.2	82.3	92.1	66.2
Social contributions	*23.4*	*33.4*	*6.8*	*24.1*	*32.7*	*17.7*	*8.0*	*33.7*
Total fiscal revenue	100	100	100	100	100	100	100	100
Administrative level								
Central government	63.7	68.9	93.2	86.5	68.6	100	100	91.3
State – local government	36.3	31.1	6.8	13.5	31.4	–	–	8.7

	1995							
	AR	BR	CL	CO	CR	MX	PY	UY
Direct taxes, of which:	*26.2*	*27.7*	*31.1*	*35.0*	*17.7*	*40.2*	*16.5*	*23.9*
Income	18.5	16.7	21.1	25.6	14.4	38.9	16.4	9.0
Personal income	–	–	6.4	–	–	15.9	–	–
Corporate income	–	–	14.7	–	–	23.0	16.4	9.0
Property	7.7	4.0	10.0	7.1	2.8	1.3	0.0	14.9
Others	0.0	7.0	–	2.3	0.5	0.0	0.1	–
Indirect taxes, of which:	*58.0*	*34.0*	*61.5*	*47.9*	*49.0*	*47.2*	*73.4*	*43.7*
VAT	41.1	24.7	41.0	28.8	26.0	28.5	38.6	30.5
Excise duties	11.6	5.2	11.7	11.2	17.0	12.9	15.0	12.2
Imports and export duties	2.5	2.4	7.0	5.9	5.4	4.9	16.6	0.7
Others	2.8	1.7	1.8	2.0	0.6	0.9	3.2	0.3
Total tax revenue	84.2	61.7	92.6	82.9	66.7	87.4	89.9	67.6
Social contributions	*15.8*	*38.4*	*7.4*	*17.0*	*33.2*	*12.6*	*10.1*	*32.3*
Total fiscal revenue	100	100	100	100	100	100	100	100
Administrative level								
Central government	61.2	70.7	92.1	84.0	65.2	100	100	90.8
State – local government	38.8	29.3	7.9	16.0	34.8	–	–	9.2

	2005p							
	AR	BR2004	CL	CO2004	CR	MXc	PYc	UYc
Direct taxes, of which:	*32.8*	*29.0*	*35.7*	*41.0*	*19.7*	*43.5*	*15.8*	*20.3*
Income	20.6	17.4	26.2	29.3	16.5	41.9	15.8	12.6

continued

Table 2.2 continued

| | 2005p | | | | | | | |
	AR	BR2004	CL	CO2004	CR	MXc	PYc	UYc
Personal income	–	–	–	–	–	–	–	–
Corporate income	–	–	–	–	–	–	15.8	12.6
Property	12.2	4.1	9.5	9.6	3.2	1.6	0.0	7.7
Others	0.0	7.5	–	2.1	0.0	0.0	0.0	–
Indirect Taxes, of which;	*55.0*	*29.8*	*57.0*	*45.2*	*49.1*	*44.5*	*75.2*	*55.5*
VAT	35.6	23.3	40.2	28.8	27.0	34.7	40.0	36.2
Excise duties	7.6	3.6	9.5	10.0	15.9	6.0	17.1	11.0
Imports and export duties	10.2	1.4	2.2	4.3	5.7	2.9	13.5	5.9
Others	1.6	1.5	5.1	2.1	0.5	0.9	4.6	2.4
Total tax revenue	87.8	58.8	92.7	86.2	68.8	88.0	91.0	75.8
Social contributions	*12.3*	*41.2*	*7.1*	*13.8*	*31.1*	*12.0*	*9.0*	*24.4*
Total fiscal revenue	100	100	100	100	100	100	100	100
Administrative level								
Central government	64.0	72.1	92.9	84.6	66.1	100	100	100
State – local government	36.0	27.9	7.1	15.4	33.9	–	–	–

Source: ILPES-CEPAL (2006).

Notes
p preliminar.
c central government.

considerably different. At one side Brazil has a tax structure based for about 41 percent on social contributions and for the remaining 59 percent on both direct and indirect taxes. In Chile and Paraguay the share of tax revenues is much higher (91–3 percent), while the share of social contributions is significantly low (7–9 percent of total revenues). The variation in the share of individual taxes between Latin American countries has continued to be considerable. For instance, in 2005 the share of direct taxes ranged from a low 15.8 percent in Paraguay and 20.3 percent in Uruguay to 41 percent in Colombia and 43.5 percent in Mexico. The share of personal income tax ranged from 12.6 in Uruguay to 41.9 in Mexico. Among indirect taxes the share of the VAT ranged from 23.3 percent in Brazil to 40 percent in Chile and Paraguay.

In the region revenues from the VAT have grown significantly over the past decade. Argentina, Brazil and Chile collect a large share of their total tax revenues from VAT. In these countries value-added taxes generate revenues levels comparable to those of the European countries. On the other hand, Mexico collects relatively little from the VAT (3.8 percent on GDP), mainly because of a significant erosion of the tax base.

Selected Latin American countries also differ in the way they provide arrangements between the central and the sub-central levels of government. Historically, Latin American governments have been highly centralized, but in the last two decades several countries have devolved and begun to share important responsibilities with sub-national governments. For most of the region, however, the assignment of tax bases still reflects the former centralized governance pattern. Tax policy, administration and revenue collection are, for the most part, concentrated at the central government level. As a result, Latin American sub-national governments widely depend on intergovernmental transfers for their financing, and have little capacity to mobilize their own resources (Lledo *et al.* 2004). Table 2.2 shows for some of these countries the attribution of tax revenues to the central and sub-central layers of general government. The degree of (tax) decentralization is still very different between selected countries. The share of central government receipts ranges from 64 percent in Argentina to 84.6 percent in Colombia and 92.9 percent in Chile where almost all taxes are legislated, collected and assessed by the central government. During the last decade the tax structure is not changed on average, with some countries (Chile, Colombia and Costa Rica) increasing their degree of decentralization and other countries (Argentina and above all Brazil) moving in the opposite direction.

Institutional features of current tax systems

Personal income tax

The degree of experience and practice in the field of personal income tax (PIT) varies a great deal across Latin American countries. Income taxes range from relative well-established ones, as in Brazil, to the most recently implemented PIT in Paraguay (2006). The present personal income taxes are the result of tax reforms implemented from the late 1990s with different patterns across countries. On the one hand, in order to reduce the distortion elements of the tax systems and following a general international trend, the number of tax brackets has been reduced and marginal tax rates have been decreased in some countries, such as Argentina, Chile and Mexico (Bès 1996; Boylan 1996; Gil Dìaz 2002). On the other hand, other countries have experienced initial forms of scheduler PIT (Paraguay and Uruguay) and most of them have increased the lowest marginal rates, even if just at a marginal level, as part of broader tax reforms (Martner and Tromben 2004; Shome 1999). As a consequence of the still-ongoing reforms, the PIT schedule is piecewise-linear in most of the countries (see Table 2.3) due to the structure of the tax brackets and rates and quite high thresholds of exemption. However, such a structure does not imply that the general effect is necessarily redistributive. Latin American countries collect little from taxes on income due to the structure itself of the PIT, large personal allowances and deductions, limited number of taxpayers and weak tax administration (Shome 1999; Tanzi 2000). Recent evidences show that the PIT in most Latin American countries does not have any significant redistributive effect (Engel *et al.* 1999; Goni *et al.* 2006). Such a failure of the taxation system in reducing inequality is an important shortcoming in an area that shows one of the highest income inequalities in the world. Any further reform of the fiscal systems should consider both an increase of the volume of the direct tax revenue

Table 2.3 Structure of personal income tax

Country	Tax unit	Number of brackets	Minimum tax rate	Maximum tax rate	Highest rate applies from	Tax base	Main exemptions	Main reliefs
AR	Individuals and undivided estates. Spouses file a separate tax return	7	9	35	$39,215	Worldwide income from real estate, capital business income and personal	Gifts, inheritances and legacies. Domestic-source dividends from registered shares. Public and private bonds and other financial sources	Family (spouse, dependent, life insurance and private pension contributions) and personal (basic, employment and self-employment) allowances decreasing with income. Deduction of maintenance payment services and social security payments.
BR	Individuals. Spouses file a joint tax return if they are not married under a separate property regime	3	0	27.5	$12,000	Worldwide income from salaries, capital, raffles and personal services	Domestic-source dividends. Interest on savings accounts	Family (dependent) and personal (basic; medical and education expenditures) allowances. Deduction of Social security payments
CL	Individuals. Spouses must file a joint tax return in some cases	8	0	40	$110,500 (tax brackets defined in taxation units)	Worldwide income from any source	Domestic-source dividends as tax credit	Deduction of instalments paid for mortgages and gifts
CO	Individuals. Spouses taxed separately	4	0	33	$34,750	Worldwide income from salaries, pensions, capital gains, gift, inheritances and business income	Domestic-source dividends	Deduction of interests paid on loan for the taxpayer home
CR	Individuals	5	0	25	$17,890	Domestic-source income only	Dividends subject to a 15% final withholding tax	Family (spouse, dependent) allowances

Table 2.3 continued

Country	Tax unit	Number of brackets	Minimum tax rate	Maximum tax rate	Highest rate applies from	Tax base	Main exemptions	Main reliefs
MX	Individuals. Spouses taxed separately	5	3	29	$9,245	Worldwide income from any source	Domestic-source dividends. Financial interest income, gifts and bequest	Personal (medical) allowances and deduction of charitable contribution, real mortgage interests and contribution to retirement and health accounts. Tax subsidy (i.e. tax credit up to 50% of tax, decreasing with income)
PY	Individuals and individual enterprises (individual farmers are subject to a tax on farming income at the rate of 25%)	2	8	10	Income over 120 monthly minimum wages ($23,000)	Domestic-source income only: employment income, 50% of dividends and the profit distributions from companies subject to CIT, capital gains derived from the transfer of property and interest income	Pensions in general and social security benefits	Personal and family allowances.
UY	Individuals on their units of monthly national minimum salary (NMS)	5	10	25		Domestic-source income only: wages, salaries and pensions	Capital income taxed separately (10%)	In addition a rate of 2% (and a surcharge of 0.25%) is payable by employers

Source: IBFD (2006).

(Colombia and Mexico) and a change in the structure of the tax and transfer system (Brazil) to get a more progressive overall fiscal system.

The number of brackets varies from two in Paraguay to eight in Chile. In most of the countries (Brazil, Chile, Colombia, Costa Rica and Uruguay) a zero tax rate has applied to the first tax bracket and it reduces substantially the coverage of the PIT. The exemption thresholds are quite high if compared to the relevant income distribution: in Brazil 90 percent of income reported in a recent national survey is below such a threshold and in Colombia the average per capita employment income is about half of the upper limit of the first bracket. The highest marginal tax rate (40 percent) is applied in Chile: the other top marginal tax rates range from 6 percent in Uruguay to 35 percent in Argentina. Paraguay and Uruguay still apply separate schedules to different sources of income but they seem to represent an exception in the area. Paraguay distinguishes between taxation of farmers' income, traders' income and a personal income subject to a new PIT from the year 2006. In Uruguay the PIT is an incomplete schedular system with different rates and exemptions applied to wages, pensions and non-professional services.

In all countries the tax unit is the individual; however in Brazil, Chile and Colombia spouses may file a joint tax return in order to get the full benefit of personal and family allowances. Standard personal relief is implemented in most of the countries through tax allowances in the form of fixed deductions from the PIT base. Family allowances can be found for instance in Argentina, Brazil, Costa Rica and Paraguay associated with the presence of a spouse and dependent children and the expenses related to the mortgage paid for the taxpayer house (Chile, Colombia and Mexico). Moreover, some personal allowances, in particular related to employment status as civil servants and employee, have been recently introduced in order to deal with the high degree of informality in the economy in Argentina, Brazil and Mexico. Nevertheless the exclusion of fringe benefit from the PIT tax base in Mexico is one of the main causes of horizontal inequity since these benefits represent about one-third of total earnings for some categories of employees.

Following the most recent reforms, tax bases are quite comprehensive, including worldwide income and, in most countries, capital incomes. The main structural link with the corporate income tax is through the exemption of the domestic-source dividends from the PIT in Argentina, Brazil, Colombia and Mexico; in other countries they are offset against taxes to be paid (Chile) or subject to a 15 percent final withholding tax (Costa Rica). Confirming the peculiarity of Paraguay and Uruguay, in both these countries, only domestic-source income is subject to taxation, a practice not consistent with the ongoing globalization process (Baunsgaard and Keen 2005). In Brazil, Chile, Colombia and Costa Rica the PIT is withheld and employment incomes and other regular sources of income are taxed at source. As a consequence, tax returns have only an adjustment purpose. In countries traditionally subject to high inflation rates, the indexation of tax brackets should play an important role as part of stabilization and equity issues. On the one hand, in order to cope with the fiscal drag, in

Chile, Colombia, Paraguay and Uruguay tax brackets are defined in taxation units. It means that the tax structure is expressed in real terms rather than in monetary amounts. On the other hand, in Brazil the monetary readjustment is sporadic and always below the price indices. Finally, there is a high level of centralization of the income tax, in particular in Argentina, Mexico and Paraguay.

The corporate income tax

As explained in more detail in the chapters on specific countries, a number of approaches to taking company profits may be observed in Latin American countries, especially in the determination of taxable income, in the integration of the corporate and personal income taxes, in the treatment of small firms and finally in the taxation of business gross assets. In general terms, two main trends have characterized the last decade: the reduction in statutory corporate tax rates and the tendency towards unification in the CIT tax rates. The process of reduction in CIT rates started during the 1980s and continued in the following decade. According to Shome (1992 and 1999) during the 1980s the unweighted average of CIT rates in the Latin American area had diminished from 44 percent to 36 percent. In our sample of eight Latin American countries the simple average of CIT rates has diminished from 31.25 percent to 25 percent in the last 15 years (1990–2005). In four countries (Brazil, Chile, Mexico and Paraguay) the reduction has been quite significant, while two countries (Argentina and Colombia) have moved in the opposite direction. The result of this process has been to move the CIT tax rates on average considerably under the top personal income tax rate (Shome 1999). During the 1980s most of the selected countries had progressive CIT rates and also different rates depending on the economic sector. The progressivity of the corporate tax was intended to pursue redistributive goals, while the use of a differentiated tax structure for the economic sector was intended by governments as a way to influence the resource allocation in the economy. During the last decade the situation has been reverted, with the reduction in the number of rates applied in each country and a tendency towards unification in CIT rates (Martner and Tromben 2004). At present among the selected countries only Costa Rica continues to keep a differentiated structure of CIT rates (10 and 30 percent). In the Latin American area the dispersion between the highest and lowest rate continues to be high; for example, Paraguay applies the rate of 10 percent, while the CIT rate is 35 percent in Argentina and 34 percent in Colombia. Present corporate taxes in Latin American countries are mainly linear and centrally collected. As illustrated in Table 2.4, currently statutory CIT rates are moderate; the statutory average tax rate of the Latin American area is 28.25 percent, compared with 25.04 percent in the EU and 29.99 percent in the Asia and Pacific area (KPMG 2006). Similarly to EU countries, the reduction of corporate tax rates has been particularly relevant during the second half of the 1990s (Shome 1999).

The selected countries apply different systems of integration with the personal income tax. Many countries apply a system of dividend exemption (Brazil, Colombia, Paraguay and Uruguay). Chile and Mexico apply the tax credit method in taxing dividend income. Shareholders may credit a percentage of dividends against their PIT liability. The credit is calculated by applying the rate at which dividends were taxed at the corporate level to dividends paid out of income already subject to the corporate income tax. Taxpayers entitled to the credit must include the credit in their taxable income and in the amount eligible for the credit. In Costa Rica dividends paid to individuals are subject to a 15 percent final withholding tax. The final withholding tax is levied at a reduced rate of 5 percent in the case of dividends distributed by stock corporations whose shares are registered on an officially recognized stock exchange, provided the acquisition and subsequent sale of the shares are effected through a stock exchange. In Argentina a different approach is followed. Dividends paid to resident individuals are taxable or not taxable, depending on the amount of distributions by the paying entity. Dividends are normally not taxable in the recipient's hands, provided they are paid out of income that has been reported by the distributing entity.

Corporate tax bases appear lower than their potential because of extensive exemptions and tax incentives (IBFD 2006). Historically, special tax treatments and incentives were given to the agricultural sector and to some specific industries (Shome 1999). The degree of tax erosion caused by preferred tax treatments is still considerable, even if decreasing in recent years (CEPAL 1998). In Argentina a number of tax incentive schemes aimed at industrial promotion have been removed during the 1990s. These schemes have been replaced by more efficient ones, targeted for instance to promote R&D projects or investments in new capital assets. R&D projects benefit from a tax credit of up to 50 percent, while investments in real capital may benefit from an anticipated refund of the input VAT or of an accelerated depreciation system. Brazil, Chile, Colombia, Mexico, Paraguay and Uruguay still make an extensive use of tax incentives targeted to promote export-oriented firms or R&D investments or regional development (IBFD 2006). For instance in Brazil several tax incentives are granted to encourage technological qualification of domestic industrial and farming enterprises; these incentives include a tax credit equal to 15 percent of R&D-related expenses and a special depreciation (at twice the normal rate) for new equipment used in the R&D activities. The government has also used incentive programs to stimulate development of the economically less developed areas of the country, namely the northeast and Amazon regions. These programs include a number of tax incentives in both the direct and indirect taxes fields. Regional incentives have proven to be the most elaborate and successful group. Also in Colombia regional development is promoted through tax incentives (in terms of reduction in the income tax rate) for companies located in certain free zones. Similar schemes are still present in Mexico, Paraguay and Uruguay. Almost all the selected countries make large use of incentives for export promotion. However, a gradual elimination of these schemes is expected in all countries in order to comply with WTO rules.

As reported in Table 2.4, in taxing corporate profits a number of approaches can be observed, especially in the determination of taxable income. In the calculation of the tax base buildings may be depreciated in all selected countries. The straight-line system is the compulsory method used in almost all countries. In

Table 2.4 Structure of corporate income tax

Country	Statutory tax rate (%)	Treatment of dividends	Depreciation of assets	Valuation of inventories	Carry forward of losses (no of years)	Tax incentives
AR	35	Generally exempt. However they are taxed (35%) when exceeding taxable profits (equalization tax)	Straight-line (different %)	Market cost at the end of the year	5	R&D Tax credit
BR	15 (+ surtax of 10% above $110,000) and 9% of social contributions	Exempt	Straight-line (10%)	Weighted average, FIFO	Unlimited (up to 30% of taxable profits)	R&D Tax credit; export tax credits; regional development tax incentives
CL	17	Taxed with full tax credit	Straight-line (different %)	Earlier direct cost or weighted average	Unlimited	Investment tax credit; export tax incentives; regional development incentives
CO	34	Generally exempt. However they are taxed when exceeding taxable profits	Fixed yearly % (different %)	Average and specific identification methods	Unlimited	Export tax incentives; regional development
CR	10–30	15 final withholding tax (reduced to 5% for dividends from quoted companies)	Straight-line (different %)	FIFO or LIFO	3–5	Export promotion
MX	29	Taxed with full tax credit	Straight-line (different %)	FIFO, LIFO or weighted average	10	Export promotion; job creation tax credit; R&D tax credit
PY	10	Exempt	Straight-line (different %)	FIFO or LIFO	3	Export promotion; industrial investment; free zone
UY	30	Exempt	Straight-line (different %)	FIFO, LIFO or weighted average	3	Export promotion; free zone

Source: IBFD (2006).

the evaluation of inventories two main methods are applied. Costa Rica, Mexico, Paraguay and Uruguay permit the last-in, first-out (LIFO) method, while Brazil allows the option for the weighted-average cost method. None of the selected countries allows a carry-back of losses; the carry-forward is allowed in all countries, subjected to restrictions. Losses can be carried forward only for three years in Paraguay and Uruguay, for five years in Argentina and Costa Rica, and for ten years in Mexico. The carry-forward is unrestricted in Chile and Colombia. A number of Latin American countries have, for many years, had presumptive taxes for small business taxpayers that:

1   are levied on gross corporate revenues;
2   substitute either for VAT or income tax.

Other Latin American countries such as Argentina and Brazil went further by creating a unique tax levied on small enterprises that replaces more than one of the major taxes, such as VAT, income and social security taxes (Tanzi 2000). Finally, it should be noted that Latin American countries have a long and sometime successful experience of business taxes on gross assets (Shome 1999). Such a tax has proved to operate well in inflationary environments (Tanzi 2000). It was first adopted in Mexico in 1988 and subsequently introduced in other countries, such as Argentina, Costa Rica, Paraguay and Uruguay (Shome 1999). In Mexico the business tax on gross assets is still in force. It was introduced with the aim of improving the fairness and efficiency of the tax system; it is levied at the rate of 1.8 percent and operates as a minimum income tax for those enterprises reporting no income tax liability in their annual tax return (IBFD 2006).

Consumption-based taxes

Indirect taxes, in the form of taxes on domestic and internationally traded goods and services, represent the bulk of Latin American tax revenues. The contribution of domestic taxes on consumption has increased in the last two decades. As shown in Table 2.2, Latin American countries rely heavily on indirect taxes which account for about 50 percent of total tax revenue (in 2005) with the exceptions of Brazil (30 percent) and Paraguay (75 percent). Value added taxes have been introduced during the 1960s in Brazil and Uruguay followed by the other countries in the 1980s and the 1990s. They have become an important component of consumption taxes, replacing cascading turnover taxes (Martinez-Vazquez and McNab 2000; Shome 1999) and compensating for poor income tax collections and decreasing taxes on foreign trade. VAT revenue covers the main share, ranging from 23 percent on total taxes in Brazil to 40 percent in Paraguay. Over the last decades, the standard rate has increased with few exceptions (Chile and Paraguay) and has had a remarkable effect on the total revenue in Mexico and Uruguay. However, the increase in the VAT revenue compensates only partially the revenue reduction due to the trade liberalization (Martner

Table 2.5 Tax rates for selected consumption-based taxes

Country	VAT			Import	Export	Excises		
	Standard rate (%)	Increased rate (%)	Reduced rate (%)			Cigarettes (%)	Unleaded gasoline (%)	Diesel fuel (%)
AR	21	27	10.5	Included	0	60	62–70	19
BR	Inter-state: 12 Intra-state: 17	Intra-state: 25–35	Inter-state: 7 Intra-state: 7	Included	0	Federal excise tax (IPI) from 0% to 365%		
CL	19	36		Included	0	60.4	6 tax units per cubic metre	1.5 tax units per cubic metre
CO	16	25–45	2–10	Included	0	55	$0.15 per gallon	
CR	13		5	Included	0	100		Different %
MX	15		0–10	Included	0	110	Different %	Different %
PY	10		5	Included	0	8	34	34
UY	23		14	Included	0	$0.5 per unit	$0.64 per liter	$0.06 per liter

Source: IBFD (2006).

and Tromben 2004): trade tariffs and import and export duties decreased by 50 percent in the last ten years, in particular in Argentina, Chile, Colombia, Costa Rica, Mexico and Paraguay (Tanzi 2000). The VAT structure is predominantly dual- or (more frequently) multiple-rates (see Table 2.5). The standard VAT rate ranges from 10 percent in Paraguay to 23 percent in Uruguay. Most countries apply one or two reduced rates, ranging between 1.6 (Colombia) and 14 percent (Uruguay), and most countries applies a zero-rate on particular goods (or leave they exempt at all). Finally, many countries apply also an increased rate on some goods and services. The reason of multiple-rate structures in the selected countries can be found in the heritage of the past multiple-rate turnover taxes and in the attempt to mitigate the regressive burden distribution of the VAT. The rate differentiation is decreasing over time as a consequence of a simplification process. However, it still appears to be an ineffective and ill-targeted instrument. It causes high administrative costs and promotes tax evasion and elusion phenomena (Martner and Tromben 2004).

The range of activities exempted from VAT or subject to reduced tax rates still appears to be wide and differentiated across countries. However, the observed trend is aimed at getting a wider tax base. In Latin American countries, VAT is generally a national tax with the main exception represented by Brazil whose three government tiers (federal, state and municipal) are granted the right to administer distinctive VATs. As known, independent and simultaneous VATs applied by overlapping jurisdictions have widely been considered to be either undesirable or infeasible (Bird and Gendron 1998). Nevertheless, it has been argued that a dual VAT – with sub-national VATs integrated with a national VAT and a high control over inter-jurisdictional trade – or even two levels of VAT in a single country can be a solution also to the issue of cross-border trade (Bird and Gendron 2001).

In Brazil, the federal and the state taxes are ruled by different legal norms among states (Afonso 2001). At the federal level, only manufactured products are subject to the value-added tax (i.e. IPI). At state level, a value-added tax on goods and selected services (i.e. ICMS) is collected on an origin basis and managed with the invoice-credit mechanism (de Mello 2007). Rules and rates differ from state to state. A number of proposals to reform the VAT system have been discussed in the last years in particular to share the ICMS between federal and state governments, to unify the legislation and standardize the rates and to define the treatment for inter-state transaction (Varsano 1999).

On average, the VAT compliance, given by the ratio between collected and potential VAT where it is the VAT average rate multiplied by final private consumption, was about 53 percent in 2002 and it has not increased significantly over the last decade (Shome 1999; Martner and Tromben 2004) with very low values in Mexico (34 percent) and Colombia (40 percent).

Focusing on excise taxation, Latin American countries show wide differences in the way they levy excises on alcoholic beverages, on tobacco products and on fuels. Most of the excises rely on *ad valorem* rates with great variability across countries, while in Chile, Colombia and Uruguay fuel and cigarettes

(Uruguay) are subject to specific rates. On the other hand, the gradual equalization of rates applied to domestic and imported products is common across countries.

Notes

1 The authors would like to thank Alberto Barreix and Luigi Bernardi for helpful comments and suggestions. All remaining errors are the responsibility of the authors.
2 Mexico and Paraguay show even lower levels (11 and 13 percent respectively), but available figures refer only to taxes collected by the central government.

References

Afonso, J. R. (2001) *Brazil: Fiscal Federalism, Tax Modernization and Consumption and Production Taxes*, AFE/BNDES.

Baunsgaard, T. and Keen, M. (2005) "Tax Revenue and (or?) Trade Liberalization," Working Paper 05/112, Washington, DC: IMF.

Bernardi, L. (2004) "Rationale and Open Issues of more Radical Reforms," in Bernardi, L. and Profeta, P. (eds) *Tax Systems and Tax Reforms in Europe*, London: Routledge.

Bernardi, L., Fumagalli, L. and Gandullia, L. (2006) "Overview of the Tax Systems and Main Tax Policy Issues," in Bernardi L., Fraschini A. and Shome, P. (eds) *Tax Systems and Tax Reforms in South and East Asia*, London: Routledge.

Bès, M. (1996) "Tax Reform, in The Economic and Social Progress report of Latin America and Caribbean," Washington, DC: Inter-American Development Bank.

Bird, R. M. and Oldman, O. (eds) (1990) *Taxation in Developing Countries*, 4th edition, Baltimore and London: Johns Hopkins University Press.

Bird, R. M. and Gendron, P. P. (1998) "Dual VATs and Cross-border Trade: Two Problems, One Solution?," *International Tax and Public Finance*, 5: 429–42.

—— (2001) "VATs in Federal States: International Experience and Emerging Possibilities," International Centre for Tax Studies, University of Toronto.

Boylan, D. (1996) "Taxation and Transition: the Politics of the 1990 Chilean Tax Reform," *Latin American Research Review*, 31(1): 7–31.

CEPAL (1998) *The Fiscal Covenant: Strengths, Weaknesses and Challenges*, Santiago de Chile: CEPAL.

Clements, B., Faircloth, C. and Verhoeven, M. (2007) "Public Expenditure in Latin America: Trends and Key Policy Issues," IMF Working Paper WP/07/21, Washington, DC: IMF.

de Mello, L. (2007) "The Brazilian 'Tax War': The Case of Value-Added Tax Competition Among the States," OECD Economics Department Working Papers, n. 544, Paris: OECD.

Engel E., Galetovic A. and Raddatz, C. E. (1999) "Taxes and Income Distribution in Chile: Some Unpleasant Redistributive Arithmetic," *Journal of Development Economics*, 59: 155–92.

Gandullia, L. (2004) "A Comparative View of Selected European Countries," in Bernardi, L. and Profeta, P. (eds) *Tax Systems and Tax Reforms in Europe*, London: Routledge.

Gil Diaz, F. (2002) "La prolugada reforma fiscal de Mexico," *Gaceta de Economia del ITAM*, 5(9): 7–62.

Goni E., Lopez J. H. and Servén L. (2006) "Fiscal Reform for Social Equity in Latin America," paper presented at the conference *Politicas Econòmicas para un Nuevo Pacto Social en Amèrica Latina*, Barcelona, October.

IBFD (2006) *Latin America – Taxation & Investment*, Amsterdam: IBDF CD ROM 1/2006.

IDB (1996, 1997, 1998, 2006) *Economic and Social Progress in Latin America*, Inter-American Development Bank, Washington, DC: Johns Hopkins University Press.

Jenkins, G. P. (1995) "Perspectives for Tax Policy Reform in Latin America in the 1990s," *Taxation Research Series* 22, Cambridge: Harvard Institute for International Development.

KPMG (2006) *Corporate Income Tax Rate: a Trend Analysis*, KPMG International.

Lledo, V., Schneider A. and Moore, M. (2004) "Governance, Taxes and Tax Reform in Latin America," IDS Working Paper 221, Brighton: Institute of Development Studies.

Martinez-Vazquez, J. and McNab, R. (2000) "The Tax Reform Experiment in Transitional Countries," *National Tax Journal*, 53(2): 273–98.

Martner, R. and Tromben, V. (2004) "Tax Reforms and Fiscal Stabilisation in Latin American Countries," Serie Gestión Pública n. 45, Santiago de Chile: CEPAL.

OECD (2006a) *Challenges to Fiscal Adjustment in Latin America: The Cases of Argentina, Brazil, Chile and Mexico*, Paris: OECD.

—— (2006b) *Revenue Statistics 1965–2005*, Paris: OECD.

Perry, G. and Herrera, A. M. (1994) *Public Finances, Stabilisation and Structural Reform in Latin America*, Washington, DC: Inter-American Development Bank.

Shome, P. (1992) "Trends and Future Directions in Tax Policy Reforms: A Latin American Perspective," IMF Working Paper WP/92/43, Washington, DC: IMF.

—— (1995) "Recent Tax Policy Trends and Issues in Latin America," in *Policies for Growth: The Latin America Experience*, Washington, DC: IMF.

—— (1999) "Taxation in Latin America: Structural Trends and Impact of Administration," IMF Working Paper WP/99/19, Washington, DC: IMF.

Tanzi, V. (ed.) (1993) *Transition to Market. Studies in Fiscal Reform*, Washington, DC: IMF.

—— (2000) "Taxation in Latin America in the Last Decade," paper presented at the conference on *Fiscal and Financial Reforms in Latin America*, Stanford University, November.

Varsano, R. (1999) "Subnational Taxation and Treatment of Interstate Trade in Brazil: Problems and a Proposed Solution," IPEA.

Websites

www.eclac.cl/Ilpes/ – ILPES-CEPAL (2006). United Nations Economic Commission for Latin America – Latin American and Caribbean Institute of Economic and Social Planning.

3 Political economy issues of taxation

Paola Profeta and Simona Scabrosetti

Introduction

Most Latin American countries have only recently experienced a transition towards democracy. With the exception of "old" democracies such as Costa Rica or Colombia, while in the 1950s only a minority of Latin American countries could be considered democracies, in the 1990s a large majority of them accomplished the transition to a democratic political organization, although with several specific features.

The democratic transition has relevant implications for economics. The recent political economy literature has analyzed the double link between democracy and economic development. On one side, countries should become more democratic as they become richer (Lipset 1959). As pointed out by the "modernization" theory (see Boix 2003; Barro 1996; Giavazzi and Tabellini 2005; Acemoglu *et al.* 2004, 2005; Acemoglu and Robinson 2006) markets can prosper only in a political framework characterized by constitutional liberties and democratic practices.[1] On the other side, democracy affects the economic outcomes and, in particular, it may affect public policies: Boix (2003) suggests that in democratic regimes taxes and public spending should be higher than in autocratic regimes, since in the latter a substantial part of the electorate is excluded from the decision-making process. Boix (2003) also shows that under the same level of per capita income, when modernization starts, the government is larger in a democracy than in an autocracy, because redistributive welfare expenditures, such as pensions, healthcare and unemployment benefits, rise after the introduction of a democratic regime. This is particularly true in countries characterized by high *ex ante* income inequality: in a democracy, the larger the group of low-income individuals, the higher the votes in favor of redistributive public policies (in the spirit of the Meltzer and Richard's seminal paper (1981)), and thus the higher the taxes, especially on labor income, and public expenditures.

Recently, Persson and Tabellini (2006) have deeply analyzed the double link between democracy and economic development, identifying a new crucial variable, "democratic capital," which is a measure of the persistence of democracy in a society: democratic capital stimulates growth, which in turn contributes to consolidate democracy creating a virtuous circle of democracy and development.

The predictions of this literature are, however, at odds with facts in the Latin American context. In general, the economic performances of Latin American countries have been rather poor and disappointing, in particular in the years right after democratization: on average the lowest growth rates are in the 1980s, that is during the transition period. This poor economic performance is difficult to be explained according to the "modernization" theories. Focusing in particular on taxation, contrary to the predictions of Boix (2003), the democratic transition in Latin America has not been associated with a growing fiscal pressure, nor with a rebalancing of tax composition in favor of more labor and less consumption taxes. We find that countries where fiscal pressure is increasing show this rising path even before the democratic transition. This suggests that there is no systematic relation between the democratic transition and an increase of fiscal pressure.[2] In other words, since the level of fiscal pressure depends on many factors (per capita income, macroeconomic variables, etc.) the democratic transition does not appear to have *ceteris paribus* a crucial positive impact. This result cannot be explained if we represent the functioning of a democracy through a standard median voter model, which aggregates voters' preferences: in this area, among the most unequal region in the world (see Chapter 2 and Barreix *et al.* 2006), the popular demand for redistribution is very high. Following Meltzer and Richard (1981), we would expect significant increases of taxation with the democratic transition. This is not what happened in Latin America and thus a puzzle emerges.

Rodriguez (2001) suggests that other political factors have to be included to account for Latin America's overall poor economic outcomes: political instability; inequality in the distribution of political and economic power; corruption and rent-seeking; and vested interests.

In this chapter we focus on taxation and we investigate this "puzzling" evidence: enormous changes in the political organization of these countries, mainly the democratization process, have not been associated with a raise in the fiscal pressure.

After assessing this evidence, we make an effort to provide possible explanations of this "puzzle." This is not an easy task. All possible arguments that we will mention have perhaps a role in this complex evidence and the best explanation has to be thought of as a combination of them. We argue that specific elements which characterize Latin America may have played a role in keeping the fiscal pressure low despite the democratic transition:

1   the quality of democracy, with a low level of representation and a relevant weight of lobby, elites, interest groups;
2   the development of financial institutions;
3   the heritage of populist economic policies.

We should also remember that international organizations, such as the IMF and the World Bank, have played a crucial role in the design of fiscal systems and fiscal reforms in many Latin American countries. The tax systems in place thus strongly reflect the plans of these external organizations, not necessarily in line with the preferences of their democratic societies.

The chapter is organized as follows: the next section focuses on democracy and summarizes the main facts of the democratic transition for each Latin American country analyzed in this book. The following section shows the existence of a puzzle comparing fiscal and political data. We then provide alternative explanations of this puzzle, before presenting the conclusions.

Democracy in Latin America

In the 1980s and 1990s, with the exception of Costa Rica and Colombia, all Latin American countries of the sample analyzed in this book experienced a democratic transition. This happened in 1983 in Argentina, in 1985 in Brazil and Uruguay, in 1989 in Chile, in 1991 in Paraguay and in 1994 in Mexico. In each country the democratic transition, which has represented the defeat of the armed forces' political power, has been characterized by specific features.

In Argentina (see Chapter 6), serious economic problems, mounting charges of corruption, public denunciation of human rights abuses and, finally, the 1982 defeat by the UK in the Falklands War, all these facts contribute to discredit the military regime that was in power since the coup against Isabel Perón in 1976. On October 1983, Argentines went to the polls in elections found by international observers to be fair and honest and the large turnouts for mid-term elections in 1985 and 1987 demonstrated continuous public support for the new strong and vigorous democratic system. As for Brazil (see Chapter 7), the military maintained power from 1964 until March 1985 because of political struggles within the regime and local elite. In 1984 many public demonstrations held in the main cities made clear that military rule could not continue and that Brazilians were starting to require changes in the electoral system to directly elect their president. So, after the end of the military dictatorship, Brazil went into a troubled process of re-democratization, with the New Constitution in 1988 and the first direct presidential election won by Collor de Mello. In Uruguay (see Chapter 13), the unpopularity of the de facto military government emerged in 1980 with the "no" in the referendum proposing a change in the constitution. In 1984, after massive protests against the dictatorship, national elections were held and the new administration, led by Sanguinetti, started to implement economic reforms and to consolidate democracy. The Chilean military regime instead (see Chapter 8) lasted until 1988, when in a plebiscite 55 percent of the voters denied a second term to General Pinochet, the chief of a junta established by the army in power since 1973. Paraguay (see Chapter 12) was progressively isolated from the world community during Stroessner's 34-year reign, characterized by severe limitations of political freedoms and persecution of opponents. In 1989, Stroessner was overthrown in a military coup headed by General Rodríguez that easily won the presidency in elections, instituted political, legal, and economic reforms and initiated a rapprochement with the international community. A democratic system of government was then established by the 1992 Constitution. As for Mexico (see Chapter 11), since 1929 the Institutional Revolutionary Party (PRI) monopolized all the political branches. It was only through the electoral reforms started by President Salinas de Gortari and consolidated by President Zedillo, by the mid-1990s, that the PRI lost its majority in Congress and the democratic transition started.

Despite these specific features that gave birth to the democratization process in each country, a common element of the successive development and, to a certain extent, of the current maturity of democracy in Latin America relies in its economic foundations. Latin American citizens seem to support democratic regimes mainly because they are convinced that these are beneficial for their economies. 72 percent of Latin Americans believe that democracy is the only political system which can contribute to economic development (Latinobarometro polls 2004, in Santiso 2006). Interestingly, this value increases up to 84 percent in Uruguay and 79 percent in Argentina, the countries which have experienced the most dramatic shocks and financial crisis in the area. In other words, as noticed by Santiso (2006), it seems that Latin American citizens are becoming "politically mature." They can distinguish between democracy as a political system, which they consider the best environment for growth (on average, according to the poll on Human Values 1995–2000, again in Santiso 2006, more than 80 percent of Latin Americans approve of democratic ideals), and the economic outcomes reached by the functioning of their democratic governments and political leaders, which may fail to satisfy their expectations. In fact the average rate of satisfaction about the accomplishments of democracy does not exceed 62 percent.

A crucial implication of this trend is that Latin American citizens are particularly sensitive to the economic performances (especially in terms of growth and inflation) accomplished by their leaders, and they are ready to punish those leaders who do not achieve the expected economic goals. At the same time, this implies that economic reforms are a main platform proposed by political parties to gain votes. This is especially true in the context of taxation, where reforms may represent a politically feasible and optimal strategy to gain support, since there still exists potential space for both increasing the fiscal pressure and rebalancing the composition of the tax revenue, currently mainly dominated by indirect taxes (see Chapter 2). However, fiscal policies do not really follow this suggested path.

Taxation and democracy: a puzzle?

Contrary to the predictions of the literature, and also contrary to what we would expect in a democratic context with essential economic foundations, after the democratic transition Latin American economic policy has not given a priority role to taxation and redistributive policies. In the period 1980–2004, while the democratization process develops, the tax burden in percentage of GDP remains quite low (in 2004 the average value for Latin America countries is 16.6 percent (ILPES CEPAL 2007)) compared with an EU(25)-average of 39.3 percent (EUROSTAT 2006)) and quite stable. The tax structure remains dominated by indirect taxes, with a low weight of income and capital taxes.

Figure 3.1 shows for each country the evolution of a democratic index and of the tax revenue in the period 1980–2004. Data on tax revenue as percentage of GDP come from ILPES CEPAL statistics and the democratic index is POLITY2 from Polity IV dataset (2005). This dataset contains many information on political regimes characteristics and transitions of a variety of countries from 1800 to 2004 and it is largely used in the most important political economy studies. According to some specific political features, such as political competition, political freedoms, constraints on the exercise of power by the executive and guarantee of civil liberties, each country is related to a one-year democracy

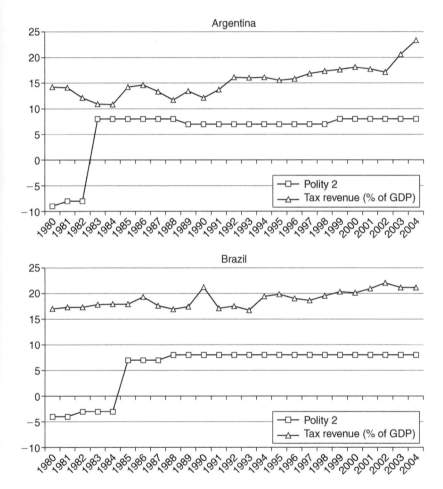

Figure 3.1 The evolution of POLITY2 and tax revenue in Latin American countries (source: POLITY2 from Polity IV dataset and tax revenue from ILPES CEPAL).

Note
Tax revenue for Argentina and Brazil refers to general government.

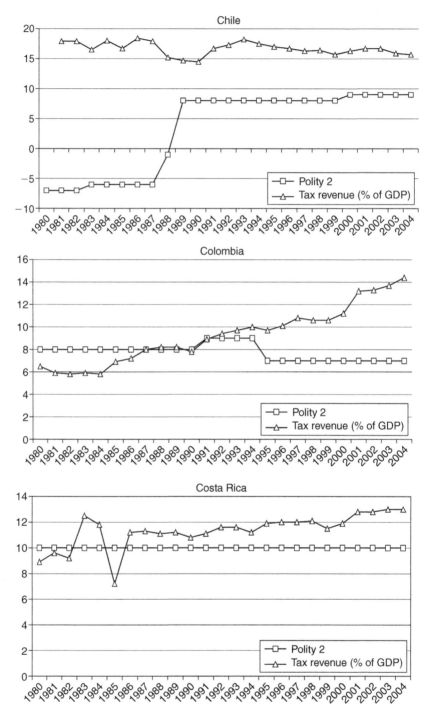

Figure 3.1 continued.

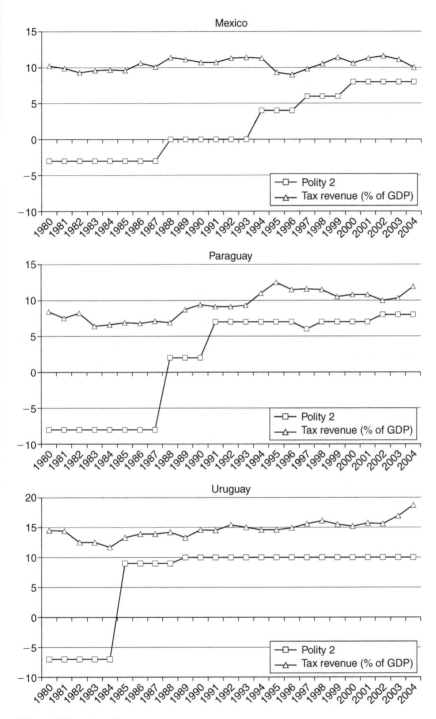

Figure 3.1 continued.

(DEMOC) and autocracy (AUTOC) index, both ranging from 0 to 10 (strong democracy or strong autocracy). POLITY2 is a combined polity score, computed by subtracting the AUTOC score from the DEMOC score and so ranging from –10 (strong autocracy) to +10 (strong democracy).[3]

According to Figure 3.1, there is no systematic relation between the evolution of democracy and the evolution of taxation. Apart from Colombia, which experienced a significant increase in tax revenue/GDP in the period 1980–2004 (the democratic transition here happened much earlier, in 1957), this ratio slightly rises over time in some countries (Argentina, Paraguay, Uruguay, Brazil, Costa Rica) and is almost unchanged in others (Mexico, Chile). Notice that for the first group of countries this slight increasing path of tax revenue in percentage of GDP seems to start even before the democratic transition, and it should thus be explained by other factors (for instance per capita income, macroeconomic performances). The timing of the transition seems to have no relation to changes in the tax burden. In other words, it is very difficult to argue that tax revenue increases after the democratic transition, as we would expect from the theories.

Concerning the tax structure, notice that indirect taxes (consumption) are more important than direct ones (income and capital). As described in the country chapters, VAT is in general a major revenue source preferred to income taxes. According to ILPES CEPAL statistics from 1990 to 2004, in Mexico in 2004 direct taxes amount to 4.6 percent of GDP while indirect taxes reach 5.3 percent of GDP. The difference in the relative weight of direct and indirect taxes is much more evident if one considers the tax structure of Paraguay and Uruguay. In Paraguay, during the analyzed period, the ratio between indirect taxes and GDP is generally more than four times that of direct taxes. In Uruguay, the importance of consumption taxes is confirmed by the fact that their revenue in 2004 are 14.3 percent of GDP against 4.3 percent of GDP of income and capital tax revenue. In Costa Rica, direct taxes increase from 2.2 in 1990 to 3.8 percent of GDP in 2004, but indirect taxes are much more important, reaching in the same years 8.6 and 9.2 percent of GDP respectively. In Chile, direct taxes/GDP and indirect taxes/GDP stay around 5 and 11 percent respectively during the 2000s. Argentina's tax structure is becoming more balanced: in 1990 the difference between the revenue of consumption and income taxes was five points of GDP while in 2004 it decreases to 3.3. Even in Colombia, we observe a similar trend: in 2004 direct and indirect taxes amount each to 7.2 percent of GDP. Brazil represents the only exception. In this country taxes on income and capital are always higher than consumption taxes.

Given the high *ex ante* inequality that characterizes Latin American countries (see Barreix *et al.* 2006), this structure of taxation with a prevalent weight of indirect taxes implies a high degree of regressivity,[4] and thus an even more unequal *ex post* income distribution. This is exactly the opposite of what predicted by a standard median voter's model (*à la* Meltzer and Richard 1981), which would suggest that, in a democratic country, when *ex ante* inequality is higher, a poorer median voter votes for higher taxes and redistributive policies and thus *ex post* inequality is reduced.

How can we reconcile this puzzling evidence with political theories? We try to address this question in the next section.

Possible explanations of the puzzle

In this section we propose possible explanations of the puzzling evidence on taxation and the democratic process in Latin America. These explanations can be grouped in three types:

1 the quality of these democracy suffers from low levels of representation, while vested interests, or lobbying and interest groups play a crucial role, leading to economic outcomes rather different than median voter's choices;
2 financial institutions, which are crucial for tax enforcement, have typically provided a low value added to Latin American firms which use them, and thus a high degree of "disintermediation" characterizes these economies;
3 the economic policies suffer from the heritage of populism, which in previous political regimes was keeping taxation very low in order to maintain the support of the masses, even at a cost of increasing debt.[5]

The quality of the democracy and the role of vested interests

One of the main issues of democracy in Latin America concerns the quality of these democracies. The POLITY2 index captures some fundamental characteristics of a democracy. However, to what extent do these democracies have a substantial rather than a formal character? This would help in explaining why the economic outcomes are somewhat different from the ones that would emerge in a true democracy.

In a democracy, a small and homogenous number of elected individuals are in charge to represent the large variety of public opinion and preferences. The quality of a democracy can thus be judged, at least in part, by the level of representation. In a democratic context, representation matters for the durability and stability of the democratic regime itself. However, the relation between representation and durability is not unambiguous. On one side, Diamond (1996) argues that underrepresentation may affect citizens' support for the system and thus increase the likelihood of a reversal to non-democratic forms of government. On the other side, as noted by Huber and Stephens (1999), in countries where poverty and inequality are prevalent, such as in Latin America, a lack of political representation may be associated with democracy consolidation, because if subordinated classes are not represented, the elites can keep their interests more secure and reduce the possible threats of breakdown. However, once the economy develops, representation may increase without affecting the stability of the democracy.

The level of representation in a democracy may also play a crucial role in explaining economic policies. We expect that a democratic transition will not induce a significant increase in taxes, even in countries with high income inequality, when low-income groups are not enough represented, i.e. the representation level is low. This lack of representation in Latin American countries may help to reconcile the evidence on taxation and formal democratic systems. Luna and Zechmeister (2005) build an index of "mandate or issue representation." Using data for 1997 and 1998 and considering the correspondence between party elites and party electorates on a variety of issues grouped in five areas (economic, foreign investment, religion, regime, law and order), they find the highest scores of this index in Chile and Uruguay, followed by Argentina. Colombia and Costa Rica stay in the intermediate range and Mexico and Brazil are the less representative countries. The old democracies, Colombia and Costa Rica, seem to be characterized by only a shallow connection between elites and citizens (see in particular the experience of Colombia until 1974), but there is room for a significant improvement in the effectiveness of political representation in the young democracies too. In other words, there is room for these new democracies to acquire a more substantial character.

While in Latin American democracies political parties weakly represent voters' political preferences, they are largely influenced by the action of lobbies, elites and interest groups. In scarcely representative democracies, the government shapes policy more to the pressures of special interests than to the preferences of the general electorate. The role of lobbies in the political process has been emphasized by Grossman and Helpman (1994). They argue that once their internal free-rider problems are solved, special interest groups can provide political contributions to influence the government's policy. The lobbying process can be seen as a two-stage non-cooperative game. Each interest group gives the government a contribution schedule that maximizes the aggregate utility of its members in which all possible policies are linked to specific contributions. Then the government chooses a policy and collects from each group the related contribution. The increasing ability to contribute and to deliver blocks of votes improves the position of special interests in the eyes of the government.

Following this reasoning, taxation in Latin America may be seen as the result of the pressure of interest groups, which lobby to keep taxes low. In particular, the elites in power are generally close to the rich. They are interested in keeping down taxes not only for themselves, but also for the middle classes, in order to obtain their support in the political competition (see also Chapters 2 and 9).

Financial institutions

In a democratic system electoral terms and mandates impose a radical transformation of the temporal horizon. In a shorter time horizon, which depends on electoral terms and mandates, the appropriate time management becomes a top priority for the government. Financial institutions are developed in this direction, since they may allow governments to act as though they had infinite horizons at their disposal.

Once introduced and developed, financial institutions may also play a crucial role for tax enforcement. According to Gordon and Li (2005a), this role becomes very important to understand why rich and poor countries have different tax revenue as a percentage of GDP and different composition of the tax burden. In poorer countries firms receive a low added value (i.e. benefits) from using the financial sector than in richer ones. This affects the threat of "disintermediation." When firms rest on the financial sector, the government can obtain much information about the scale of the firm's economic activity and use them to improve tax enforcement. Thus, the modest value added coming from the financial sector reduces the poor government's ability to collect tax revenue.[6]

Following this reasoning, a possible explanation of the low tax burden in poor countries is that the underdevelopment of the financial sector, bringing about "disintermediation," may be responsible for low tax enforcement and thus low revenue collection.

Moreover, if the benefits from using the financial sector are low, the design of the tax structure will be oriented towards a more intensive use of corporate income taxes, and tax collection will be focused on capital intensive firms. This narrow tax base in fact depends more heavily on the financial sector and has very low chances of "disintermediation." In this context, countries may use an inflation tax as an instrument to raise the costs of cash transactions and create efficiency and revenue gains by improving the capital and labor allocation between taxed and untaxed sectors and shifting new firms to using banks as intermediaries.

The results of Gordon and Li (2005a) are consistent with the Latin American context, which shows a low tax burden and a still relevant inflation tax (see Chapter 2). As a consequence, a democratic transition may not induce a significant increase in tax collection, if it is not joined by a significant economic development, which would induce a further development of a well functioning financial sector and, in general, of efficient fiscal institutions.

Gordon and Li (2005b) claim that this most intense use of taxes on corporate income in poor countries can also be justified using the lobby model of Grossman and Helpman (1994). Capital intensive firms are interest groups actively lobbying to keep a low level of corporate taxation. When these firms are not numerous, such as in poor countries, they are not able to lobby effectively and, as a consequence, the level of CIT in the tax structure increases. However, contrary to the evidence, this would suggest that the overall level of taxation is also higher in poor countries, where only few firms actively lobby.

Populism

During the 1980s in Latin America landowners exercised the kind of political monopoly that does not allow the political system to start fiscal and economic reforms to create a sufficiently high tax base. After World War I and the Great Depression of the 1930s this political monopoly stopped giving way to political parties and military leaders, supported by urban labor union and import-substituting industrialists. Political scientists named this alliance between labor and capital owners against landowners "populism." It cements in a set of economic policies designed to achieve specific political goals such as mobilizing support within organized labor and lowermiddle-class groups (Kaufman and Stallings 1991). Among the different experiences of Latin American populism we can mention the Péron regime in Argentina from 1973 to 1976, the Echevarría government in Mexico from 1970 to 1976 and the five years of Sarney governance in Brazil from 1985 to 1990. Populist politics gave rise to populist policies oriented, for example, to keep taxation very low in order to maintain the support of the masses, even at a cost of repeated cycles of growing budget deficits and increasing debt.

The heritage of these populist economic policies is our third argument that may help explaining the low level of tax burden observed in the young Latin American democracies. As mentioned above, the democratization process is perceived by citizens as an improvement and a way to attain economic development. In this sense, it could be difficult for politicians elected in a sufficiently free and fair context to increase taxes with respect to the previous political regimes. In particular, the political cost of increasing income taxes in these low-income countries, in terms of loss of support from the population, may be so high that the government prefers to tax corporations (and provide a system of incentives for them; see Chapter 4).

Conclusions

Latin America suffers an "excess of inequality" (World Bank 2005). The high levels of inequality have been quite stable over time. Thus, they are not affected by the economic or political changes that characterized the last decades in this area of the world. Inequality *ex post* is not much better than inequality *ex ante*. This suggests that taxation does not have a redistributive impact. Fiscal pressure is in fact quite low and indirect taxes dominate direct ones in many countries' tax structure.

Though the high *ex ante* and *ex post* inequality may sound consistent with the non-democratic phases of the twentieth century, it is quite surprising that they remain similar after 20 years of democracies. Political economy median voter's theories would predict an increase of taxation and redistributive policies, which, instead, has never started. We have suggested that other political factors are still relevant in Latin American democratic decision-making, which may help explaining this apparent puzzle: a low level of representation of political parties; large power of lobbies and interest groups; high "disintermediation" from the financial sector which reduces tax enforcement; the heritage of populist economic policies. Reducing the role of these factors seems to be essential to a democratic increase of fiscal pressure and redistribution which, lastly, would reduce inequality. This in turn may also have an important positive impact for growth and the overall development of Latin America (see Aghion *et al.* 1999).

Notes

1 See Cacciatore *et al.* (2006) for the problematic evidence in this theoretical context of South and East Asia.
2 Notice that we focus on tax revenue. However in countries such as Chile, Colombia and Mexico, non-tax revenues, related to the exports of non-renewable resources, are also important and they have considerably increased in the last years (see Jiménez and Tromben 2006).
3 Actually, POLITY2 is a revised combined polity score that differentiates from POLITY (see Polity IV Project Dataset User's Manual (2005) for more details).
4 Notice that the recent introduction of multi-rate VAT may alleviate this regressivity result (see Chapter 2).
5 Notice the opposite experience of new EU members, in which the transition from an autocratic regime to a democracy is associated with an increase of taxes and public expenditures, in line with the heritage of the former socialist regimes.
6 Cash transactions are used here as a synonym of informal economy, difficult to control and to tax. Firms that are not strongly dependent on the financial sector can rely on cash transactions, which do not leave a paper trail, in order to avoid (high) taxes (i.e. the cost of using the financial sector). This may increase the shadow economy.

References

Acemoglu D. and Robinson, J. A. (2006) *Economic Origins of Dictatorship and Democracy*, Cambridge: Cambridge University Press.
Acemoglu, D., Johnson, S., Robinson, J. A. and Yared, P. (2004) "From Education to Democracy?," MIT, Department of Economics, Working Paper 05.
—— (2005) "Income and Democracy?," MIT, Department of Economics, Working Paper 05.
Aghion, P., Caroli, E. and García-Peñalosa, C. (1999) "Inequality and Economic Growth: The Perspective of the New Growth Theories," *Journal of Economic Literature*, vol. 37, n. 4.
Barreix, A., Roca, J. and Villela, L. (2006) "Political Fiscal y Equidad. Estimación de la Progresividad y Capacidad redistributive de los Impuestos y el Gasto Publico Social en los Países de la comunidad Andina," in *La Equidad Fiscal en Los Paises Andinos*, IADB.
Barro, R. J. (1996) "Democracy and Growth," *Journal of Economic Growth*, 1, pp. 1–27.
Boix, C. (2003) *Democracy and Redistribution*, Cambridge: Cambridge University Press.
Cacciatore, M., Profeta, P. and Scabrosetti, S. (2006) "Democracy and Welfare without Welfare State," in Bernardi, L., Fraschini, A. and Parthasarathi, S. (eds) *Tax Systems and Tax Reforms in South and East Asia*, London: Routledge.
Diamond, L. (1996) "Is the Third Wave Over?," *Journal of Democracy*, 7, pp. 20–37.
Dornbusch, R. and Edwards, S. (eds) (1991) *The Macroeconomics of Populism in Latin America*, Chicago: The University of Chicago Press.
Giavazzi, F. and Tabellini, G. (2005) "Economic and Political Liberalizations," *Journal of Monetary Economics*, vol. 52, issue 7, pp. 1297–330.
Gordon, R. and Li, W. (2005a) "Tax Structure in Developing Countries: Many Puzzles and a Possible Explanation," NBER Working Paper 11267.
—— (2005b) "Puzzling Tax Structures in Developing Countries: A Comparison of Two Alternative Explanations," NBER Working Paper 11661.
Grossman, G. M. and Helpman, E. (1994) "Protection for Sale," *American Economic Review*, vol. 84, n. 4, pp. 833–50.

Huber, E. and Stephens, J. (1999) "The Bourgeoisie and Democracy: Historical and Comparative Perspectives," *Social Research*, 66, pp. 759–88.

Jiménez, J. P. and Tromben, V. (2006) "Política Fiscal y Bonanza: impacto del aumento de los precios de los productos no renovables en América Latina y el Caribe," *Revista de la Cepal*, 90, pp. 61–86.

Kaufman, R. R. and Stallings, B. (1991) "The Political Economy of Latin American Populism," in Dornbusch, R. and Edwards, S. (eds) *The Macroeconomics of Populism in Latin America*, Chicago: The University of Chicago Press.

Lipset, S. M. (1959) "Some Social Requisites of Democracy: Economic Development and Political Legitimacy," *American Political Science Review*, vol. 53, issue 1, pp. 69–105.

Luna, J. P. and Zechmeister, E. J. (2005) "Political Representation in Latin America," *Comparative Political Studies*, vol. 38, n. 4, pp. 388–416.

Meltzer, A. H. and Richard, S. F. (1981) "A Rational Theory of the Size of Government," *Journal of Political Economy*, 89, pp. 914–27.

Persson, T. and Tabellini, G. (2006) "Democratic Capital: The Nexus of Political and Economic Change," CEPR Discussion Paper n. 5654.

Rodriguez, F. (2001) "The Political Economy of Latin American Economic Growth," Global Development Network Research Paper.

Santiso, J. (2006) *Latin America's Political Economy of the Possible*, Cambridge: The MIT Press.

Websites

www.cidcm.umd.edu/inscr/polity/ – Polity IV dataset.

www.eclac.cl/ilpes/ – ILPES CEPAL Statistics.

epp.eurostat.ec.europa.eu/ – EUROSTAT.

web.worldbank.org/wbsite/external/datastatistics/ – World Bank (2005) World development Indicators, WDI online.

4 Corporate tax systems and policies for attracting FDI

Giorgia Maffini and Anna Marenzi

Introduction, contents and main conclusions

Reporting the experience of Latin American countries, this chapter focuses on the effects of the corporation income tax (CIT) and fiscal incentives on foreign direct investment (FDI). The CIT affects both the marginal and inframarginal return to investment through the effective marginal and the effective average tax rate (Devereux and Griffith 1998 and 2003). Hence, together with tax incentives, it is an important factor in determining the cross-country distribution of FDI (Hines 1999; De Mooij and Ederveen 2003). After the restrictive policies of the 1970s and the debt crisis of the 1980s, FDI in Latin America became a key factor for fostering growth and development. The liberalization of the economy and the deregulation and privatization of services have largely contributed to the FDI inflows in the region since the 1990s (Rios-Morales and O'Donovan 2006). Also, before that, Latin American governments have widely used tax incentives to attract foreign capital. The use of many different fiscal incentives created a complex and opaque system imposing high compliance costs on taxpayers and a serious burden on the administration (see, among others, Zee *et al.* 2002).

Today, globalization in the form of increased trade and foreign investment has put fiscal systems under even more pressure. Developing countries all around the world have to attract investment in a more competitive environment and, therefore, they still have to make use of fiscal incentives. At the same time, it is important to maintain an adequate stream of revenues for financing projects (e.g. education of the labor force, infrastructure) aimed at making the environment more attractive for FDIs. Since the mid-1990s, many countries in the region tried to reorganize their fiscal system more efficiently, mainly following the "low-rate broad-based" (LRBB) approach (Martner and Tromben 2004; Tanzi 2000). As a result, nowadays Latin America has relatively low statutory corporate tax rates although there are still differentials in the tax rates and in the maturity of the CIT system. Nonetheless, the benefits from tax competition are not equally distributed among the countries of our selected sample. For example, Chile has a modern corporate tax system which has assimilated most of the international standard rules, such as the taxation of worldwide income and the adoption of safeguards against tax arbitrage (e.g. transfer pricing rules, thin capitalization). On the contrary, Colombia and Paraguay still have a pre-global corporate tax system.

An efficient fiscal system should not support unproductive rent-seeking behaviors while trying to promote investment. Hence, it is important for fiscal incentives to be part of a coherent, broad fiscal policy generating a transparent, efficient fiscal system. Generally, this doesn't happen in the countries of our sample as they still offer generous and broad-based tax incentives mainly to foreign and domestic firms located in free-tax free-trade zones. Companies located in those areas are granted full or partial exemption from income and capital taxes (Agosin *et al.* 2005). These forms of generalized incentives did not guarantee inflows of high value-added investment in the region. Latin American countries have attracted mainly natural resources, market-seeking and efficiency-seeking FDIs. There is no substantial *technological assets-seeking* investment. The latter is more likely to induce positive spillovers into the domestic economy through technology and knowledge transfers.

It is nowadays increasingly important for Latin America to attract high value-added FDI. The latter are more likely to create positive externalities for the local economy and they are therefore crucial for growth and development. This type of investment is attracted not only by fiscal incentives but also by specific characteristics of the host country such as the education of the labor force and the availability of proper infrastructure. For building up a stock of non-fiscal capabilities able to attract foreign capital, countries in the region need to generate tax revenues as well. Latin American fiscal administrations started adopting measures to protect their tax base internationally. They endorsed transfer-pricing and thin capitalization rules and they developed a network of tax treaties against double taxation. This is a further step in the direction of a more efficient and more modern fiscal system. The reforms were not implemented by all countries of the region, though. Furthermore, complex rules such as those regulating transfer-pricing are sometimes not enforced as the administrations still lack the expertise to apply them.

The chapter is organized as follows. The first section depicts the evolution and the type of foreign direct investment in the region since the 1980s. The second section describes the policies used to promote capital inflows. The third section illustrates the corporation income tax systems and the fourth section adds a description of the main rules adopted in the selected countries to tackle issues in international taxation.

Foreign direct investments in Latina America: evolution and patterns

The increasing integration of the global economy has led to the amplified importance of FDI around the world. Since the 1980s, global net flows of FDI increased by about 100 percent from about US$57 billion in 1980 to US$665 billions in 2004 (see Figure 4.1). The sizeable growth in FDIs has been quite volatile: phases of stagnation (such as the first half of the 1980s and 1990s) were

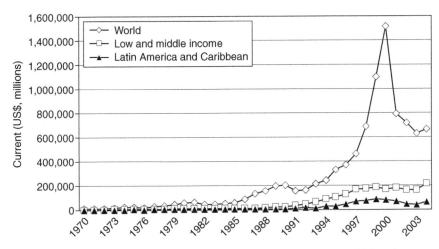

Figure 4.1 World FDI net inflows (current US$, millions) (source: World Development Indicators, World Bank, September 2006).

followed by periods of significant growth (second half of the 1980s and 1990s). FDI flows to Latin America followed a similar trend even though the region did not take advantage of the first FDI boom of the late 1980s: in the 1970s and 1980s, the countries of the region applied import-substitution industrialization policies hence building an environment of trade protection. Inflows of FDI into the region remained fairly stable from 1980 until 1993, increasing at an annual rate of less than 2 percent and lingering at around 1 percent of GDP. The FDI boom in Latin America began in 1993.

The view of Latin American governments changed radically in the 1990s: after the restrictive policies of the 1970s and the debt crisis of the 1980s FDI became a key element for fostering growth and development. FDI inflows prospered uninterruptedly until 1999. In terms of levels of net total FDI attracted, the leading countries are Brazil, Mexico, Argentina and Chile (see Figure 4.2). In terms of net total FDI as a percentage of GDP, the leading countries are Chile, Brazil, Costa Rica and Mexico (see Table 4.1). In this period, FDIs were attracted by deregulation and privatization of services and by policies opening up and liberalizing the economy (among others, Rios-Morales and O'Donovan 2006). Between 1990 and 1998, the countries in the region privatized assets for about US$154.2 billion and their high tariffs on imports and exports were reduced very quickly at about 10–14 percent (Hosono and Nishijima 2001).

New regional integration schemes were also launched and/or revitalized through trade agreements signed by Latin American countries with both their neighbors and outside players (e.g. the Southern Common Market (MERCO-SUR), the Group of Three, the North America Free Trade Agreement (NAFTA) and the Free Trade Agreement of the Americas (FTAA)).

More recently, after four years of deteriorating FDI inflows (from 2000 to 2003) as a consequence of the financial crisis, Latin America and the Caribbean

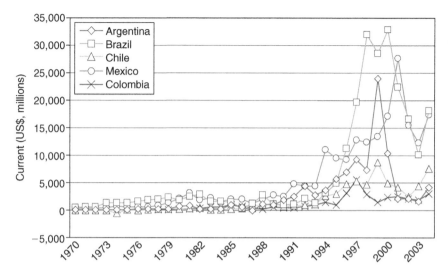

Figure 4.2 FDI net inflows in Argentina, Brazil, Chile, Mexico, Colombia (current US$, millions) (source: World Development Indicators, World Bank, September 2006).

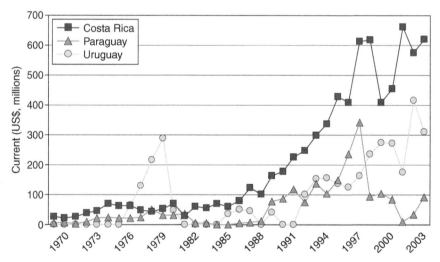

Figure 4.3 FDI net inflows in Costa Rica, Paraguay, Uruguay (current US$, millions) (source: World Development Indicators, World Bank, September 2006).

underwent first a rebound and then an increase in FDI in 2004. In 2005, FDI inflows to the whole region increased by 12 percent and amounted to $67 billion ($104 billion including offshore financial centers) of which 40 percent came from the United States[1] (UNCTAD 2006). The reasons are to be found in the global and local strong economic growth and in the high commodity prices. However, Argentina was the worst hit by the debt crisis in 2001 and it has not yet got back

Table 4.1 FDI net inflows (% of GDP – average values per period)

	1970–9	1980–9	1990–9	2000–4
Chile	–0.19	2.03	4.99	6.06
Brazil	1.13	0.66	1.58	3.70
Costa Rica	2.26	1.78	3.13	3.18
Mexico	0.80	1.16	2.24	2.85
Colombia	0.36	1.30	2.14	2.79
Argentina	0.26	0.65	2.59	2.10
Uruguay	0.73	0.52	0.61	2.06
Paraguay	1.09	0.28	1.79	0.91
Latin America and Caribbean	0.73	0.80	2.21	3.20
Low and middle income countries	0.48	0.54	1.98	2.63
World	0.47	0.63	1.42	2.62

Source: World Development Indicators, World Bank, September 2006.

to its previous levels of FDI (UNCTAD 2004). FDI flows to the region have increased substantially but other types of capital flows have remained sluggish. FDI is certainly still the central source of private external finance to Latin America in recent years. Using Dunning's well-known scheme (Dunning 1993), foreign direct investment can be classified according to the economic rationale driving them: natural resource-seeking investments; market access-seeking; efficiency seeking and strategic/technological asset-seeking (see Table 4.2).

In the last century, FDI in the region has been of the *natural-resource seeking* kind as it was primarily aimed at securing oil, gas and minerals. This type of investment rarely induces positive spillovers in the host economy, in particular when resources are exported as raw materials. The liberalization and privatization waves encouraged this type of investment also in the 1990s: transnational corporations (TNCs) could acquire state assets in the form of either privatized companies or gas, petroleum (Venezuela, Colombia and Argentina) and mineral rights (Chile, Peru and Argentina). But the reforms occurred in the last decade of the twentieth century also fostered *market-seeking* FDI,[2] especially in the services sector where newly privatized telecommunication and energy companies became good investment opportunities, together with the sale of private sector activities such as banks and other financial institutions (Mortimore 2000). A major example is Brazil: it is the biggest recipient of FDI in Latin America and in particular, between 1991 and 1998, 28 percent of FDI entered the country through the privatization program (Mortimore 2000) mainly in the telecommunications (e.g. Telebras and cellular phone concessions) and electricity sector. In general, between 1996 and 2002, 59 percent of the FDI inflows in Latin America targeted the services, while 28 percent targeted manufacturing and only 13 percent the primary sector (Rios-Morales and O'Donovan 2006). More specifically, the south cone received more *market-seeking* investments in services (financial services, telecommunications, electricity and gas distribution) and manufacturing (agro-industry, chemicals and automotive) while Mexico and

Table 4.2 Type of FDI in Latin America

Sector	Natural resource seeking	Market-seeking	Efficiency-seeking
Goods	*Petroleum and gas* Bolivia, Colombia, Ecuador, Peru, Venezuela, Argentina, Trinidad and Tobago *Mining* Chile, Argentina, Bolivia, Colombia, Ecuador, Peru, Venezuela	*Automotive* Argentina, Brazil, Paraguay, Uruguay *Chemicals* Brazil *Food* Argentina, Brazil, Mexico *Beverages* Argentina, Brazil, Mexico *Tobacco* Argentina, Brazil, Mexico	*Automotive* Mexico *Electronics* Mexico Caribbean Basin *Apparel* Mexico Caribbean Basin
Services	*Tourism* Mexico Caribbean Basin	*Finance* Mexico, Chile, Argentina, Venezuela, Colombia, Peru, Brazil *Telecommunications* Brazil, Argentina, Chile, Peru, Venezuela *Retail trade* Brazil, Argentina, Mexico *Electricity* Colombia, Brazil, Chile, Argentina, Central America. *Gas distribution* Argentina, Chile, Colombia, Bolivia	*Administrative services* Costa Rica

Source: ECLAC (2005, Table 1.6).

the Caribbean Basin traditionally collected mainly *efficiency-seeking* flows aimed at securing lower production costs and establishing export platforms (ECLAC 2006). FDI from the automobile industry exemplifies this pattern[3] but it is important to remember that *efficiency-seeking* investments in the Caribbean also entered the electronics, apparel, and services sectors (e.g. electronics and the administrative services in Costa Rica). In Brazil and Argentina investments from foreign (mainly European) automobile companies aimed at either consolidating their position or at gaining access to local automotive markets. On the contrary, investment in Mexico, largely from US companies, was in search of lower production costs to better compete in the home country market.[4] The difference between the two sub-regions lies in institutional and geographical factors. First, the MERCOSUR countries lacked the geographic closeness with a major market and, at the same time, their large market attracted *market-seeking* investments almost by definition.[5] But their institutional environment was also very different from the Mexican one. The Mexican authorities implemented the *maquila*[6] program which allowed foreign export-oriented firms to operate tax-free. They also allowed the assembling of vehicles with a high percentage of imported parts, vehicles which were exported once assembled. The NAFTA was also a key element in boosting automotive FDI from the US: the agreement grants special provisions for the automobile sector. Its regional norms of origin establish that a good is considered to be produced within the NAFTA countries if 62.5 percent of its production costs are incurred in that area. This has favored investment of the US corporations in Mexico as goods (and their value-added) produced in the NAFTA region attract lower indirect taxes when exported back to the US. MERCOSUR countries have free-trade zones as well. Nonetheless, Mortimore (2000) highlights that they are not as advantageous as the Mexican export-processing zone for assemblers. Countries in the south cone also kept barriers to the import of motor vehicles and high levels of mandatory regional content.

Table 4.2 shows there are no substantial *technological assets-seeking* investments aimed at securing technology-intensive production assets. This type of FDI is more likely to induce positive spillovers into the domestic economy through technology and knowledge transfers. The literature argues that this is the main weakness of the Latin American FDI attraction model (Rios-Morales and O'Donovan 2006). Not only this is likely to be the reason why the literature does not find evidence of positive spillovers from foreign investment to the regional domestic economy (among others, Aitken *et al.* 1996) but it also makes the region vulnerable to the competition of Asian countries. Actually, Latin America continues to lose headway to destinations such as China and other Asian nations, even though FDI remains the biggest source of external private funding for the region. In the 1980s, the area received about 12 percent of global FDI. The percentage shrank to 10 percent in the following decade and to 8 percent since 2000 (ECLAC 2006).[7] According to ECLAC (2006), while countries such as Singapore, Korea, China, Malaysia and Thailand implement more active and focused policies for attracting FDI, in Latin America strategies are still passive and not targeted at specific high-quality investments. Furthermore, whilst the more competitive European and Asian countries target their incentives to efficiency-seeking and strategic or technological-asset seeking FDIs, incentives in South America and the Caribbean are principally fiscal in nature and very general. Moreover, many countries of the region score quite low in various indexes measuring the quality of the business environment. Except for Costa Rica and Chile, the other countries appear in the bottom two quintiles of the Index for Economic Freedom (Heritage Foundation),[8] Doing Business (International Finance Corporation),[9] the Corruption Perception Index (Transparency International)[10] and the A.T. Kearney Globalization Index.[11] This places the area far behind the developed nations and the Asia-Pacific region.

Investment promotion policies in Latin America

Before the FDI boom, most of the countries of our selected sample (e.g. Argentina, Mexico and Brazil) implemented batteries of diverse tax incentives aimed mainly at their less developed regions and at specific industries (Bird and Chen 2000). The incentives were not part of a broadly consistent industrialization and/or development policy. Therefore, they did not have much effect in terms of promoting growth and development even if they might have had some positive effects on specific sectors (e.g. manufacturing and tourism in Mexico and Costa Rica). Being fragmented across sectors and regions and being implemented through particular laws, incentives were very likely to be abused, especially in federal systems such as Brazil and Argentina where local authorities are more exposed to lobbies' pressure (UNCTAD 2000).

The political economy literature attempts to pin down the mechanisms leading to some specific investment promotion policies (Jensen 2003) such as those mentioned above. Among others, Li and Resnick (2003) explain the level and type of investment incentives with the nature of the host country political institutions. The hypothesis is then tested in Li (2006). Using a cross-section of 52 developing countries, including the countries studied in this book, the author finds evidence that the institutional characteristics of the host political system (i.e. democracy versus autocracy) affect the level of tax incentives granted to foreign investors. Generally, more democratic regimes offer effective property rights protection. Hence, strong tax incentives are not needed to compensate FDIs for the high risk of expropriation, seizure of assets, contract repudiation, and government corruption. Nonetheless, not all autocracies adopt the same incentives policy. Since tax incentives imply a transfer of benefits from domestic to foreign capital, the choice of which type of investment to promote is strictly bond to the economic elite's interests and their lobbying power. In Argentina, during the last military government, the incentives were implemented mainly for domestic political reasons either in response to domestic lobbies or to "compensate" some regions (e.g. Tierra del Fuego) for being far from the economic centre of the country (Byrne 2002). Border security reasons also encouraged governments to promote a program of fiscal incentives for industries in some poor and underpopulated provinces such as the Manaus Free Zone in the Brazilian Amazon.

Since the 1990s, countries in the region tried to rationalize the investment incentives systems (see Chapter 2) as the different and fragmented rules in place displayed many shortcomings. First, they were highly distorsive with respect to agents' economic decisions as they also encouraged corruption and unproductive rent-seeking activities. They made the fiscal systems more complicated and less transparent, imposing high compliance costs on taxpayers and a serious burden on the administration. Another major drawback consisted in great revenue losses. This could potentially prevent the authorities from developing infrastructure, education and health programs. The latter features can make the countries attractive for FDI. While rationalizing the fiscal system, in a world where an increasing number of countries compete to attract limited investment capital, tax authorities have to encourage capital inflows by offering investment tax incentives (see, among others, Morisset and Pirnia 2001; Holland and Vann 1998; Rios-Morales and O'Donovan 2006). This practice can lead to a race to the bottom where all countries end up with a comparable amount of total investment and with serious revenue losses (Thomas 2000). In this respect, all the countries[12] in our sample relied upon free-trade zones which granted exemptions mainly from import duties and indirect taxes (e.g. VAT). Many of the free-trade areas also exempt profits and their repatriation for a limited amount of years.[13] The aforementioned tax benefits were also extended to domestic firms (Agosin *et al.* 2005). Most of the fiscal advantages accruing in those areas have been phased out (e.g. Mexico) or will be eliminated as they are not compatible with many of the trade agreements signed by the countries in our sample (e.g. MERCOSUR and WTO).

As mentioned above, Latin America has attracted mainly natural resources, market-seeking and efficiency-seeking FDI with a "the-more-the-better" approach (Rios-Morales and O'Donovan 2006). In this environment, according to the UNCTAD FDI Indices,[14] between 2002 and 2004, Chile and Costa Rica have attracted a good amount of FDI with respect to their capability (see Table 4.3).

Chile has performed well in attracting foreign capital as it is politically and economically stable. In addition, it has a low corporate tax rate (17 percent) coupled with the a full integration system in which the CIT paid is creditable against income taxes imposed on resident (Global Complementary Tax) and foreigner individuals (Additional Tax). Moreover, in order to boost financial markets, the government allowed full/partial exemption of capital gains on the disposal of certain assets. In 2002, a new and favorable tax regime for platform companies[15] was launched with the aim of encouraging multinational corporations to set up their regional headquarters in Chile. For tax purposes, platform companies are considered as non-resident or domiciled taxpayers so that only income generated in the country is taxed and dividends and profits that they may receive from subsidiaries abroad would be exempted. Chile has also signed a great number of tax treaties with other Latin American countries (e.g. Argentina, Brazil, Mexico, Paraguay), developed (e.g. Canada, France, Spain, Sweden and the UK) and developing countries (e.g. Malaysia) allowing a reduction in withholding taxes.

Costa Rica profits from a stable economic and political climate and from a well-educated labor force. The country has greatly used incentives to attract

Table 4.3 Matrix of inward FDI performance and potential, 1988–90 and 2002–4

1988–90	*High FDI performance*	*Low FDI performance*
High FDI potential	Chile, Colombia, Costa Rica, Mexico	Brazil, Uruguay
Low FDI potential	Argentina, Paraguay	
2002–4	*High FDI performance*	*Low FDI performance*
High FDI potential	Chile	Argentina, Brazil, Mexico
Low FDI potential	Costa Rica	Colombia, Paraguay, Uruguay

Source: UNCTAD, FDI Indices.

capital flows, in particular in the manufacturing sector (e.g. electronics with the Intel semiconductor assembly and testing plant) which has prospered under the tax-free zone system.

Finally, both Chile and Costa Rica have specific institutions assisting and guiding foreign companies to set up their operations in the two countries.

In the actual highly competitive setting where many developing countries can offer generous treatment to attract low value-added FDI (D'Amuri and Marenzi 2006), it is important for the development of Latin America to attract the "right" type of FDI. In other words, governments should stimulate foreign direct investment likely to generate spillover benefits in the host economy (e.g. transfer of knowledge). Positive externalities of FDI are normally ignored by private investors and they are not incorporated in their decision-making process so that the level of investment could be sub-optimal. In this direction, Brazil and Mexico granted incentives for qualified investments to encourage technological qualification of enterprises: a tax credit (15 and 30 percent, respectively) is available for R&D expenses incurred in the tax years and different forms of accelerated depreciation incentive are allowed for investment on new fixed assets and for new equipment used in R&D activities (see Chapter 2).

Corporate taxation and investment in Latin American countries

The CIT affects both the marginal and inframarginal return to investment through the effective marginal and the effective average tax rate (Devereux and Griffith 1998, 2003). Hence, together with tax incentives, it is an important factor in determining the cross-country distribution of FDI (Hines 1999; De Mooij and Ederveen 2003). Specifically, tax burden on FDI depends on three elements: domestic corporate taxation of home country and host country; international taxation of cross border income flows (dividend, interest, etc.); and interaction of tax systems between home and host countries.

The systems of corporate taxation

The current corporate tax systems of the selected countries are the result of several fiscal reforms mainly started in the beginning of the 1990s and, for certain countries, still underway. Generally, most countries have realized a consistent reduction in the statutory tax rate in the last decades. At the same time, they have adopted base-broadening measures, such as, taxation of worldwide income, adoption of safeguards against tax arbitrage and reduction of tax exemptions and incentives (see, among others, Tanzi 2000; Martner and Tromben 2004; Agosin et al. 2005). Wibbels and Arce (2003) suggest that, as trade and financial liberalization consolidate, CIT revenues get less relevant for Latin American countries. In fact, the share of corporate income tax as a percentage of GDP declined from an average of 5 percent in 1975–8 to 3.9 percent in 1997–2002.

Each country has developed its own tax system in a different social, economic and political framework; this has conditioned the evolution of the national tax systems. As a result, the countries show different level of maturity in their corporate tax systems. In this respect, it is possible to identify three groups of countries.[16] Chile and Mexico display a corporate tax structure that assimilates most of the international standard rules, such as transfer pricing guidelines. A second group of countries (Argentina, Brazil and Colombia) exhibit a system where the current CIT reflects a protracted process of gradual changes, principally responding to macroeconomic fluctuations and shocks rather than to a well defined tax design project. Among these countries, Colombia has a pre-global system, primarily focusing on collecting revenues from internal transactions and local trade rather than favoring capital flows and foreign investments. The transition towards a modern tax system is the main aim of the new wave of tax reforms undertaken by the countries of the third group in the mid-2000s (Costa Rica, Uruguay and Paraguay). For different reasons, their full implementation has been delayed but these reforms could potentially modernize the tax systems. In particular, the proposed tax reforms in Costa Rica and Uruguay include several elements of international taxation: a transition towards the worldwide income taxation model and the introduction of a set of traditional instruments, such as transfer pricing rule, definition of permanent establishment and tax haven regulations. Finally, the reform underway in Paraguay broadens the CIT tax base and reduces the tax rate. It should reposition the Paraguay system from a primitive to a one that is more appealing for capital and trade.

The main features of the corporate tax system of the countries analyzed in this book are summarized in Table 4.4.

A domestic company is liable to be taxed on its worldwide income in Argentina, Brazil, Chile, Colombia and Mexico and it is granted tax credits for taxes paid abroad. A foreign company is normally taxed only on its host-source income. Costa Rica, Uruguay and Paraguay adopt the territorial system,[17] although the proposal of moving to a worldwide system is actually under discussion for the first two countries.[18] Hence, in Costa Rica, Uruguay and Paraguay income arising from foreign sources and received by resident companies is not taxed at all, and foreign taxes are not deductible or creditable. Both Costa Rican and Uruguayan tax systems provide relief to non-residents with respect to source income. Under certain circumstances, Costa Rica may exempt or reduce income tax when there is evidence that the residence country does not grant any credit or deduction for the Costa Rican income tax. In Uruguay dividends and technical assistance are exempted from corporate taxation. Generally, subsidiaries of multinationals are taxed using the same basis of local entities. A different tax rate is applied in certain countries (Chile, Colombia, Costa Rica and Paraguay) to branches of foreign enterprises.

As noted by Martner and Tromben (2004) and Tanzi (2000), in the 1990s most countries began to reduce and unify their national corporate tax rate in order to be more in line with international standards. As a result, today Latin American countries have relatively low statutory corporate tax rates although the tax rate

Table 4.4 The main features of the corporate income tax systems

	Argentina	Brazil	Chile	Colombia	Costa Rica	Mexico	Paraguay	Uruguay[d]
Territorial scope	Worldwide	Worldwide	Worldwide	Worldwide	Source	Worldwide	Source	Source
Standard CIT rate (%)	35[a]	15 + 9 (SC)	17	35	30	28	10	25
• Surtax rate		10		10 (2002–6)				
• Branch profit tax			35	7	15		15	
Inter-company dividends	Fully/partially excluded	Fully excluded	Fully excluded	Fully excluded	Fully excluded	Fully excluded	Fully/partially excluded	Fully excluded
Capital gains	CIT rate	CIT rate	CIT rate	CIT rate	generally not taxed	CIT rate	CIT rate	CIT rate
Rule against thin capitalization	Yes	Yes	Yes	None	Yes	Yes	None	None[e]
Net worth or Assets tax (%)	1 on assets	None	None	0.4 on net worth	None	1.25 on assets	1 on assets	1.5–3.5 on net worth
Tax treaties	18	+25	13	4		+30	5	2
Revenue protection	TP/TC/CFC	TP/CFC	TP	TP	None	TP/CFC	None	TP/CFC
Withholding taxes (%):								
• dividends	0[b]	0	0–40[c]	7	15	0	15	7
• interest	15.05–35	15	35	39,55	15	4.9–10–28	15 (i.e. 50% of 30%)	12
• royalties	17.05–28–31.5	15	30	39,55	25	28	15 (i.e. 50% of 30%)	12

Source: UNCTAD (2000); Byrne (2002); KPMG (2003) and others.

Notes

a A regional turnover taxes averaging 1–3.5% is in force.

b Distributions that exceed taxable profits are subject to the 35% equalization tax.

c Dividends distributed to individuals resident or domiciled are subject to Global Complementary Tax (GCT) of 0–40%. CIT is creditable against GCT.

d The information reported in the table refer to the tax reform approved by the Uruguayan Parliament in 2006.

e The new measures will be effective July 1 2007.

f The social contribution on net profits; TP = transfer pricing; TC = thin capitalization; CFC = controlled foreign company legislation.

Legend: SC = rate of social contribution on net profits; TP = transfer pricing; TC = thin capitalization; CFC = controlled foreign company legislation.

differentials across countries can still be significant. The Latin American average CIT rate was 28.3 percent in 2006: the highest values are those of Argentina and Colombia (35 percent), the lowest one is that of Paraguay (10 percent). All countries apply a standard flat corporate tax rate (see Table 4.4). However, most of the countries in the region display multiple regimes together with the standard corporate tax rate, there also exist presumptive, preferential and simplified treatments (see also Chapter 2).

Preferential and special regimes

The use of a presumptive taxation system is a common feature of several Latin American countries (Tanzi 2000; Gonzalez 2006), such as Argentina, Brazil and Colombia. Generally, these systems estimate taxpayer's income using some specific base such as assets, gross receipts/turnover, or external indicators of income or wealth. For example, the Argentinean presumptive minimum income tax works as an assets tax. In Brazil annual turnover is the tax base for the regime of presumed profit. In Colombia, the minimum presumptive income is equal to 6 percent of the corporation's net worth, minus a fixed abatement.

Moreover, in most countries the current CIT regimes allow preferential treatments for enterprises operating in specific sectors. Mining companies in Chile are taxed under a progressive scheme with tax rates ranging from 0 to 5 percent. Small enterprises in Uruguay are exempt from CIT and pay a monthly lump-sum tax. In Brazil micro-companies and small enterprises have the option to be taxed under a simplified regime[19] with a progressive rates ranging from 3 to 5 percent for micro-companies and from 5.4 to 8.8 percent for the small enterprises.[20] Medium and large-sized Mexican companies engaged in transport and agriculture activities pay little or no CIT under the simplified regime. In Costa Rica the simplified regime replaces either the CIT or the VAT for qualified taxpayers[21] that adopt it. Simplifying regimes are normally introduced for reducing compliance costs for certain "weaker" entities. Nonetheless, it is widely recognized that some so-called simplified regimes may be actually very complicated (Chen and Martinez-Vazquez 2003).

Dividends, capital gains taxation and other taxes

In all countries of the sample, excluding Paraguay, inter-company dividends are partially or fully exempt from corporate income tax for resident companies. In Argentina an equalization tax applies where distributions are in excess of taxable profits. Capital gains accruing to corporations are usually treated as ordinary income for tax purposes. Latin American countries tend to impose high rates of withholding taxes (see Table 4.4). Net worth taxes are levied in Argentina, Colombia, Mexico and Uruguay with different characteristics across countries (Tanzi 2000; Sadka and Tanzi 1993). As already mentioned, a presumptive minimum income tax is levied on firms incorporated in Argentina: the tax is levied at a rate of 1 percent on the value of all assets held at the end of

Table 4.5 Effective corporate tax rate on foreign capital investment

	Argentina	Brazil	Chile	Mexico[a]
Services	44.2	41.6	31.0	24.0
Manufacturing	31.6	34.5	22.3	19.3

Source: Chen and Martinez-Vezquez (2003).

Notes
The simulation of METRs is based on 2001 tax legislation. Statutory CIT rate were: 35% in Argentina and Mexico, 34% in Brazil and 15% in Chile.
a The METRs incorporate the 2002 post-reform tax system.

each fiscal year. In Mexico the net worth tax operates as a minimum tax (1.8 percent) for enterprises reporting no income tax liability in their annual tax return. Finally, in Colombia and Uruguay the tax is imposed on the net worth (which depends on the relevant taxpayer and on the type of assets involved) of resident and non-resident companies. The tax rate is fixed at 1.2 percent in Colombia and at 1.5 percent in Uruguay.

Finally, depending on the interaction across the different features of the corporate tax system, effective tax rates may differ substantially from statutory rates. Generous deductions and exemptions or large multifaceted incentives contribute to lowering effective tax rates. At the same time, taxes other than the corporation income tax, such as turnover taxes, gross or net taxes, and property taxes, may significantly increase the effective tax burden on capital investment. A recent comparative measure of total real tax burden affecting foreign capital in some countries of our sample has been produced by Chen and Martinez-Vazquez (2003). The authors calculate the marginal effective tax rates (METRs) on FDI of US multinationals in manufacturing and services sectors for Argentina, Brazil, Chile, Mexico and Peru. The all-inclusive effective corporate tax rates are reported in Table 4.5.

The results indicate that Mexico and Chile provide the most tax-advantageous environment to US investors. Mexico has a relatively generous CIT regime in term of depreciation allowance (5 percent for buildings, 25 percent for vehicles, 30 percent for computers, and from 5 to 2 percent for machinery[22]) and the lowest property tax among the four countries. Chile has the lowest legal tax rate.

Aspects of international taxation in Latin America

The competition for attracting FDI imposes two main constraints on tax administrations. First, they should avoid any double taxation on non-residents' income. Second, they should preserve the tax base so to finance projects (e.g. infrastructure building, education programs) to appeal more to high value-added FDI. Countries have established a series of treaties to avoid double taxation (DTTs) and the erosion of the tax base, specifying when the source country is allowed to levy a tax, whereas the country of residence is required to concede the right to credit. Tax treaties contribute to create a stable and transparent environment for trade development and FDI promotion through clear and steady rules. Furthermore, tax treaties contain specific limitations on the withholding tax rates on dividends, interest, and royalties imposed by the source country, as prescribed in the OECD Model Convention. Alternatively, the withholding tax rate levels are left to bilateral negotiations, as in the UN Model Convention for developing countries. DTTs should also include rules for the exchange of information between countries to facilitate the protection of the tax base. Unfortunately, this is rarely the case for developing countries and, hence, withholding taxes are levied at higher rates.

In general, when compared with the tax treaty network of more developed countries, Latin America's one is rather limited (see Table 4.4). Nonetheless, it is rapidly expanding, especially for countries such as Argentina, Brazil, Chile and Mexico. Chile is very active in terms of DTTs negotiation: it signed 21[23] treaties since the end of the 1990s. In general, Chilean treaties are based on the OECD model,[24] which contains reduced withholding tax rates for different kinds of income and grants tax credits for taxes paid in the host countries.[25] Argentina signed 18 tax treaties with, among others, Austria, Belgium, Denmark, Finland, France, Germany, Italy, Norway, Spain, Sweden, Switzerland, the Netherlands and the UK. Most of the treaties are based on the OECD model. Brazil also has an extensive network including treaties with Belgium, Canada, France, Italy, Japan, Luxembourg, the Netherlands, Portugal, Spain, Argentina, Chile and Ecuador. It has recently concluded negotiations with Mexico, Israel, Belgium and South Africa starting a trend of reducing withholding taxes on royalty payments (from 10 percent to 15 percent) within the framework of the OECD Model Convention. By contrast, Colombia's tax treaty network is underdeveloped. Until now, Colombia has one bilateral tax treaty signed with a traditional capital exporting country (i.e. Spain, ratified on 1 July 2006). Another major treaty signed with the Andean Community created significant tax restrictions for the movement of services.[26] Since Costa Rica, Uruguay and Paraguay enforce the territorial model, there is no need to grant double taxation relief for their residents with respect to foreign-source income. All countries, in different ways, provide relief to non-residents with respect to source income. The transition towards a worldwide taxation system recently proposed in Costa Rica and Uruguay will require a revision of the current rules, however.

A number of anti-avoidance and anti-deferral measures such as transfer pricing regulations, thin capitalization rules and controlled foreign company (CFC) legislation have been adopted in the last ten years for protecting the national tax base (Table 4.4). With the exception of Paraguay and Costa Rica, all countries in our sample have implemented transfer pricing rules incorporating at least generally the arm's length principle contained in the 1995 OECD Transfer Pricing Guidelines. The process started in 1995[27] in Mexico, the only OECD member in the region.[28] Other countries followed suit: Argentina[29] (1998 and 1999), Chile (1997), Colombia (2004), Peru (2001), Venezuela (1999 and 2001) and Uruguay (2007) enacted transfer-pricing rules based on the OECD principles even if the individual legislation has differentiated aspects in each country. Brazil does not follow the international arm's length principle established by the OECD. Actually, the Brazilian legislation ratified in 1997 departs from international norms. It settled on a maximum amount for both deductible expenses on inter-company import transactions and for taxable revenues on inter-company export transactions. It also imposes some specific methods and fixed margins for determining the correct transfer pricing for Brazilian tax purposes. The introduction of transfer-pricing rules is an important step towards a modern fiscal system able to protect the national tax base. Enforcement activities are becoming more and more frequent in Argentina, Brazil, Chile and Mexico. Nonetheless, the tax administration's lack of experience in dealing with complex rules has created a situation of arbitrariness chiefly in Brazil and Argentina (Villela and Barreix 2002). OECD arm's length principles have been nominally adopted in many countries of the region. The administrations which have applied transfer pricing rules in practice (e.g. Mexico and Argentina) departed from the OECD model, though. In fact, many Latin American tax administrations have employed more protective principles for calculating the tax base (Velayos *et al.* 2007).

Transfer-pricing rules become ineffective if companies in tax havens receive a great part of the profits generated in another developing country. Legislation defensive against low-tax jurisdictions is already in place in Argentina, Brazil and Mexico and will be effective in Uruguay as from 1 July 2007. CFC legislation prescribes that income from a controlled foreign entity situated in an offshore location will be attributed to the domestic taxpayer and subject to tax in her/his country of residence. There can be very different ways to apply this rule. In Latin America, the existing and more widely used model is to adopt a blacklist of low tax jurisdictions. Mexico adopted this approach in 1996,[30] Brazil (1996) and Argentina (1999) followed suit.[31]

The international aspects of taxation and tax incentives are crucial elements for Latin American countries willing to compete in today's world. The aforementioned implementation of anti-avoidance and anti-deferral measures is not enough: regional integration has to be encouraged even further through the free flow of information between governments and between governments and investors (Bird 2007).

Notes

1 The second biggest investor was the Netherlands (but caution should be used as many multinational groups locate their holding companies in the Netherlands because of fiscal privileges). Spain followed with 6 percent of total investment. Additional key players were other countries in the region as a result of the activity of some "Trans-Latin" corporations such as the Argentinean Technit, the Mexican America Movil and the Brazilian Camargo Correa.
2 This type of investment was typically targeted at gaining access to local markets.
3 Foreign direct investment in the automotive industry was a very important component of FDI in Latin America and the Caribbean during the 1990s. According to Mortimore (2000), in 1998 seven of the ten biggest companies in the region by consolidated

sales belonged to that industry. They were General Motors, Volkswagen, Ford, and Chrysler in Mexico and Volkswagen, General Motors and Fiat in Brazil.

4 Mortimore (2000) highlights that during the 1980s, European and particularly American corporations faced stiff competition from their Asian (in particular Japanese) counterparts in the automotive, apparel and electronics industries. By relocating part of the production (mainly the assembly process) in the Caribbean, American companies were able to fight back. They could assembly their final products at lower costs in the region and, thus, export them back in their home market at lower prices.

5 It is worth noting that as a consequence of the MERCOSUR, the market in the south cone is even bigger.

6 A *maquiladora* is a Mexican corporation, wholly or predominantly owned by foreigners, that assembles products to export in other countries.

7 In 2005 South, East and Southeast Asia attracted about $165 billion, with China alone accounting for about $72 billion. China was the third largest recipient of FDIs in 2005 totaling about 22 percent of total investment going to developing countries and about 7 percent of global investment (UNCTAD 2006).

8 The index measures ten broad economic factors: trade policy, tax burden, government intervention, monetary policy, foreign investment, banking, wages and prices, regulation, rights of ownership and degree of market informality.

9 This index measures how easy it is to do business for a start-up company. It records the simplicity of company registration procedures, licensing agreement, and so on.

10 This index measures the perceived and not the objective corruption in a country.

11 This index measures four different aspects of globalization: economic integration (through trade and FDI inflows and outflows), technological connectivity (through number of internet users), and political engagement (number of country's memberships in international organizations and UN peacekeeping missions) and personal contact (through monitoring tourism and international travel).

12 Argentina is the only exception.

13 For an analysis of the costs and benefits of tax holidays, see OECD (2001).

14 See www.unctad.org.

15 Law 19,840 enacted in November 2002 enables foreign investors to set up a platform company in Chile for channeling and managing investments in third countries. Companies set up as a Business Platform must be incorporated in accordance with Chilean law and can either be open stock corporations or closed stock corporations, subject to the same regulations and governmental supervision as listed stock corporations.

16 In considering the proposed classification, it should be noted that the income tax systems of Brazil, Colombia, Costa Rica and Uruguay have a general income tax levied on both individual and business enterprises. The lack of a separate corporate tax law is a relevant element in evaluating the degree of maturity of a tax system.

17 In the past, Latin American countries, as most of the developing countries, used to rely on territorial taxation system for two reasons. First, having a net external liability position, countries in the region had to gain more from taxing income of foreign investors than exempt residents' foreign income. Second, it was difficult for the tax administration to find out how much foreign income accrued to residents (see Zee *et al.* 2002).

18 In particular, according to the Base Report presented in August 2005 by the Tax Reform Commission, the Uruguayan tax system should move from residential approach to the territorial one, after a transitory period (see Chapter 13).

19 Among other legal entities, subsidiaries, branches and permanent establishments of foreign companies do not qualify for the simplified tax regime.

20 The tax rate covers, mainly, corporate taxation, social contributions on profit, and federal social security tax and excise tax.

21 The simplified regime is targeted to corporate and individual taxpayers with annual purchases not greater than a certain amount and with no more than three employees,

provided their business activity is one of the 11 included in this regime (china and porcelain production, furniture production, handmade shoes manufacturing, etc.).

22 Among the four countries, the less generous regime of depreciation allowance is that in Argentina with the following percentages: 2 percent for buildings, 20 percent for vehicles, 33 percent for computers, and 10 percent for machinery.

23 Countries which have in force a Double Tax Treaty with Chile are Argentina, Poland, Spain, Peru, Ecuador, Korea, Brazil, Mexico, Canada, Norway, the UK, Denmark, Croatia, Sweden and New Zealand, Malaysia, France, Ireland, Paraguay, Russia, Portugal. The following countries are negotiating a treaty with Chile: Finland, Cuba, Hungary, the Netherlands, Colombia, Switzerland, the US, Venezuela, Italy, Czech Republic, China, Thailand, South Africa, Australia, Belgium, Kuwait, India.

24 Chile is not a member of the OECD but only an observer.

25 Following the United Nations model, the treaty signed with Argentina in 1986 represents an exception as it grants the right to taxation almost entirely to the country of source.

26 In order to avoid double taxation with regard to air and maritime transportation Colombia has signed some international tax agreements with Chile, Germany, the US, Venezuela, France and Brazil.

27 In 1995 the transfer-pricing legislation was enacted for *maquiladoras* and in 1997 for all taxpayers.

28 Mexico joined the OECD in 1994.

29 Argentina is an observer at the OECD.

30 In 2006, Mexico has changed its system form the "blacklist approach" to a more complex system in which the tax administration assesses whether a specific structure is in fact a low-tax structure.

31 Colombia has also adopted CFC rules but it has not defined its "blacklist" yet.

References

Agosin, M. R., Barreix, A., Gómez Sabaini, J. C. and Machado, R. (2005) "Tax Reform for Human Development in Central America," *Rivista de la CEPAL*, Santiago, Chile: CEPAL.

Aitken, B., Harrison, A. and Lipsey, R. E. (1996) "Wages and Foreign Ownership: A Comparative Study of Mexico, Venezuela, and the United States," Journal of International Economics, vol. 40, n. 3–4, pp. 345–71.

Bird, R. M. (2007) "Tax Incentives for Foreign Investment in Latin America and the Caribbean: Do They Need to be Harmonized?," in Barreix, A., Villela, L. and Velayos, F. *Taxation and Integration*, Banco Interamericano Desarrollo.

Bird, R. M. and Chen, D. (2000) "Tax Incentives for Foreign Investment in Latin America," XII Seminario de Polica Fiscal, *Compendio de Documentos 2000*, Santiago, Chile, pp. 169–216.

Byrne, G. (2002) "Tax Incentives for FDI in Seven Latin American Countries," *Banco Interamericano Desarrollo*, June 2002.

Chen, D. and Martinez-Vazquez, J. (2003), "Efficiency Effects of Mexico's Tax Reform on Corporate Capital Investment," Andrew Young School of Policy Studies, Working Paper 03–08, Georgia State University.

D'Amuri, F. and Marenzi, A. (2006) "Features and Effects of Corporate Taxation on FDI," in Bernardi, L., Fraschini, A. and Shome, P. (eds) *Tax Systems and Tax Reforms in South and East Asia*, London: Routledge.

Devereux, M. P. and Griffith, R. (1998) "Taxes and Local Production: Evidence from a Panel of US Multinationals," *Journal of Public Economics*, vol. 68, pp. 335–67.

—— (2003) "Evaluating Tax Policy for Location Decisions," *International Tax and Public Finance*, vol. 10, pp. 107–26.
De Mooij, R. A. and Ederveen, S. (2003) "Taxation and Foreign Direct Investment: A Synthesis of Empirical Research," *International Tax and Public Finance*, vol. 10, pp. 673–93.
Dunning, J. H. (1993) *Multinational Enterprises and the Global Economy*, Reading, MA: Addison-Wesley.
ECLAC (2005) "Foreign Investment in Latin America and the Caribbean 2004," United Nations Publication.
—— (2006), "Foreign Investment in Latin America and the Caribbean 2005," United Nations Publication.
Gonzalez, D. (2006) "Regimenes especiales de tributacion para pequenos contribuyentes en America Latina," *Banco Interamericano Desarrollo*, June 2006.
Hines, J. R., Jr. (1999) "Lesson from Behavioral Responses to International Taxation," *National Tax Journal*, vol. 52, pp. 305–22.
Holland, D. and Vann, R. J. (1998) "Income Tax Incentives for Investment," in Thuronyi, V. (ed.) *Tax Law Design and Drafting*, vol. 2, ch. 23, International Monetary Fund, pp. 1–33.
Hosono, A. and Nishijima, S. (2001) "Prospects for Closer Economic Relations between Latin America and Asia," RIEB Discussion Paper n. 121.
Jensen, N. (2003) "Democracy Governance and Multinational Corporations: The Political Economy of Foreign Direct Investment," *International Organization*, vol. 57, n. 3, pp. 587–616.
Li, Q. (2006) "Democracy, Autocracy, and Tax Incentives to Foreign Direct Investors: A Cross-National Analysis," *The Journal of Politics*, vol. 68, n. 1, pp. 62–74.
Li, Q. and Resnick, A. (2003) "Reversal of Fortunes: Democracy, Property Rights and Foreign Investment Inflows in Developing Countries," *International Organization*, vol. 57, n. 1, pp. 175–214.
Martner, R. and Tromben, V. (2004) "Tax Reforms and Fiscal Stabilsation in Latin American Countries," CEPAL Series – Gestion Publica, n. 45, Santiago, Chile.
Morisset, J. and Pirnia, N. (2001) "How Tax Policy and Incentives Affect Foreign Direct Investment," in Wells, L.T.Jr. *Using Tax Incentives to Compete for Foreign Direct Investment: Are they Worth their Costs?*, FIAS Occasional Paper n. 15, World Bank.
Mortimore, M. (2000) "Corporate Strategies for FDI in the Context of Latin America's New Economic Model," *World Development*, vol. 28, n. 9, pp. 1611–26.
OECD (2001) "Corporate Tax Incentives for Foreign Direct Investment," OECD Tax Policy Studies n. 4.
Rios-Morales, R. and O'Donovan, D. (2006) "Can the Latin American and Caribbean Countries Emulate the Irish Model of FDI Attraction?," *CEPAL Review*, vol. 88, pp. 49–66.
Sadka, E. and Tanzi, V. (1993) "A Tax on Gross Assets of Enterprises as a Form of Pre-sumptive Taxation," *Bulletin for International Fiscal Documentation*, vol. 47, n. 2, pp. 66–73.
Tanzi, V. (2000) "Taxation in Latin America in the Last Decade," paper presented at the conference on *Fiscal and Financial Reforms in Latin America*, Stanford University, November 2000.
Thomas, K. P. (2000) *Competing for Capital: Europe and North America in a Global Era*, Washington: Georgetown University Press.

UNCTAD (2000) "Tax Incentives and Foreign Direct Investment. A Global Survey," UNCTAD, Geneva.

—— (2004) "World Investment Report 2004: the Shift towards Services," UNCTAD, Geneva.

—— (2006) "FDI from Developing and Transition Economies: Implications for Development," UNCTAD, Geneva.

Velayos, F., Barreix, A. and Villela, L. (2007) "Regional Integration and Tax Harmonization Issues and Recent Experiences," in Barreix A., Villela, L. and Velayos, F. *Taxation and Integration*, Banco Interamericano Desarrollo.

Villela, L. and Barreix, A. (2002) "Taxation and Investment Promotion," *Banco Interamericano Desarrollo*, August 2002.

Wibbels, E. and Arce, M. (2003) "Globalization, Taxation, and Burden-Shifting in Latin America," *International Organization*, vol. 57, pp. 111–36.

Zee, H. H., Stotsky, J. G. and Ley, E. (2002) "Tax Incentives for Business Investment: A Primer for Policy Makers in Developing Countries," *World Development*, vol. 30, n. 9, pp. 1497–516.

5 Fiscal havens in Latin America and the Caribbean

Jeffrey Owens and Alessandra Sanelli

Introduction[1]

Tax havens play an increasingly important role in world financial markets, particularly in the Caribbean and Latin American regions. Tax havens thrive in a climate characterized by excessively strict bank secrecy, a lack of transparency and where countries are not prepared to cooperate to counter abuse. Over the last 30 years, we have seen many Caribbean islands move into offshore financial activities. This has had profound implications for the structure of their economies. It has also had profound implications for both developed and developing countries. This chapter examines the role of Caribbean tax havens, the response of the international community and sets out what is the current position of these jurisdictions in the light of the international initiatives aimed at curbing harmful tax practices.

The chapter is organized as follows. The next section identifies the growing concerns about tax havens, particularly those of national tax administrations, and reviews the theoretical and empirical literature on tax havens and information exchange. The third section tracks the origins of the Caribbean tax havens, while the fourth section examines their present weight in the international financial and economic landscape. The fifth section reviews the international initiative undertaken at the OECD level to counter fiscal abuse through tax havens and the response of Caribbean jurisdictions. Finally, the last section examines the possible future prospects for these economies.

Tax havens: a growing concern for the international community

In recent years, improved communications and liberalization of financial markets have fostered an impressive growth of both cross-border financial transactions and foreign direct investment (FDI). The rising volume of international transactions has brought new risks, among which the wider potential adverse effects of financial crises and financial instability and the larger possibilities to hide abroad the proceeds of illicit activities.

A fundamental concern of national governments, both in developed and developing and transitional economies, relates to the possible erosion of national tax bases arising from the transfer of their residents' capital to offshore financial centers. In fact, while there may be legitimate reasons to use offshore financial centers, including tax reasons, they are often used for tax evasion and avoidance purposes. This is due to the fact that offshore financial centers are often referred to as "*tax havens*," because these are often countries or territories which attract foreign capital by promoting themselves through a combination of low or no taxation, advanced communication facilities, reliable legal systems and a high degree of confidentiality for financial data, such as those on beneficial ownership, companies, trusts and bank accounts.[2] Tax havens are used both by individuals and companies. In the new era of "banking without borders" wealthy individuals can easily evade capital income taxes in their country of residence by transferring capital abroad and channeling passive investments through tax havens. This type of tax evasion is facilitated by the existence of jurisdictions with strict bank secrecy rules which prevent information exchange with the residence country, and by the increased recourse to foreign institutional investors and shell companies with opaque structures based in offshore financial centers, which can make it very difficult for domestic tax authorities to track the capital income. With the growth of cross-border capital flows, the potential for abuse created by the lack of access to bank information for tax purposes and the resulting adverse consequences have increased exponentially. At the same time, tax authorities find it more and more difficult to monitor foreign portfolio investments of their residents because of the removal of traditional sources of information on these transactions (e.g. exchange controls). The decision by one country to prevent or restrict access to bank information for tax purposes now is therefore much more likely than ever before to adversely affect tax administrations of other countries. Furthermore, the progressive elimination of withholding taxes at source on non-residents' portfolio investment income allows more and more taxpayers to escape all form of capital income taxes. Quite often, even when investing in their own countries, resident investors use foreign financial intermediaries and corporate or trust vehicles based in bank secrecy jurisdictions or offshore financial centers to disguise themselves as non-residents and evade domestic taxes. Thus, for example, a significant part of the investment into China via Hong Kong is made by Chinese residents; Cyprus plays a similar role for Russia. An increasing proportion of investment into Asia is channeled through structures established in the British Virgin Islands. Even more significant is the possible use of bank secrecy jurisdictions to escape domestic taxes on income and wealth of a different origin (business income, inherited wealth, etc.) that represent the "*principal*" of the foreign investment.

Companies make use of tax havens mostly for tax minimization purposes. They shift income to tax havens through their foreign affiliates in order to reduce or defer residence-country taxes. In this respect, the most attractive features of tax havens are the low level of taxation and the availability of flexible and tax-advantaged vehicles to channel international business, such as shell or holding companies. Investments in high-tax countries, for example, may be financed with loans from affiliates in tax havens; the resulting interest payments reduce taxable incomes in high-tax locations while producing taxable income in the havens. Another method is the use of transfer pricing. Even if most high-tax countries require firms to use transfer prices that would be paid by unrelated parties, following the OECD's 1995 Transfer Pricing Guidelines, difficulties in enforcement makes it possible for firms to reduce the overall tax burden. Tax havens can be also used to avoid repatriating foreign income in the firm's home country and thereby producing a home country tax obligation. The resulting tax savings can be substantial, contributing to the value of tax haven operations (Dharmapala and Hines 2006). Bank and financial confidentiality may nonetheless play a role, both for closely held or passive investment companies and, more generally, because it makes it more difficult for home-country tax administration to track tax haven activity aimed at tax avoidance and evasion.

The effects of tax havens have recently been the object of a theoretical and empirical literature (see boxed text below).

Tax havens: theoretical analysis and empirical findings

The nature of tax havens and the effects of tax haven activity on the economies of high-tax countries have been examined in the context of the tax competition literature.

A first question addressed by the theoretical studies concerns the factors that influence the desirability of becoming a tax haven (see Dharmapala and Hines 2006, and Slemrod and Wilson 2006, for a review). A common result is that small open economies have an incentive to undercut large countries in order to attract mobile capital: whilst they are not able to influence the interest rates prevailing on international markets through their mainstream economic policies, they can quite easily attract international capital flows by reducing their tax rates, either directly and/or by offering a "favorable" tax climate for non-resident investors. The budgetary cost of these tax reductions need not be very high, since the tax reduction is accompanied by a larger tax base due both to greater investment by non-residents and to greater taxable income of residents.[3]

This result seems confirmed by the patterns observed in tax havens' economies. Tax havens tend to be small countries with extremely open economies and substantially smaller natural resource endowments that non-havens. Also the experience of tax haven economies over the last two decades is consistent with the predictions of the theory. The period of globalization has been very favorable for tax havens, which grew at an average annual real per capita rate of 3.3 percent between 1982 and 1999, compared to the 1.4 percent growth rate of the world as a whole (Hines 2004). This result is consistent with the growth of FDI in the same period[4] and with the empirical evidence showing that both the volume and location of FDI are sensitive to tax differentials.[5]

The effect of tax haven activity on the economies of non-haven countries is a highly controversial point. A common fear of non-haven countries is that tax havens may help diverting economic activity away from them, eroding tax bases that might otherwise be used to raise government revenue. This fear is more acute in the case of nearby tax havens, which might divert activity from other countries within the same region or economic federation. In this respect, the empirical evidence seem to suggest a complementary rather than substitute relationship between investment in tax havens and investment in nearby countries: the availability of tax havens seem to stimulate, rather than divert, economic activity in nearby non-haven countries (Hines 2004; Desai *et al.* 2004). However, as suggested by Sullivan (2006), it is possible that the complementary relationship holds for certain types of foreign investments in low-tax countries (for instance, those aimed at establishing "export platforms" that provide market access for goods and services from the home country), while a substitute link holds for other types of FDI (those aimed at establishing production facilities for goods and services). Thus, the overall impact of tax havens on the welfare of high-tax countries is still ambiguous. Tax haven operations may stimulate activity in nearby countries by facilitating the avoidance of taxes in that country, the avoidance of taxes elsewhere, or by reducing the cost of goods and services that are inputs to production or sales in high-tax countries. At the same time, tax haven activity could provide governments of high-tax countries with a device to move toward a less-distorting tax regime, that could not otherwise be implemented, mainly for political constraints. The use of tax havens could in fact allow high-tax countries to apply a lower effective tax rate on mobile firms compared to the one applied on immobile firms. On the other hand, tax avoidance and evasion will erode the tax base and therefore tax revenues of high-tax countries. In a recent study, Slemrod and Wilson (2006) demonstrate that the full or partial elimination of tax havens would improve welfare in non-haven countries, reduce compliance costs and lead to a more balanced tax structure.

Even if the conclusions of the theoretical and empirical analysis are somewhat still controversial, policymakers in non-haven countries are increasingly concerned about the potential adverse effects of tax haven activity on their national tax systems and, more generally, on their economies. These concerns have prompted many governments to consider international cooperative efforts designed to preserve their economies from the negative externalities due to tax havens. Following an endorsement by the G-7 at the Lyon Summit in June 1996, the OECD launched in 1998 the *Harmful Tax Practices* initiative[6] to discourage

OECD member countries and certain tax havens outside the OECD from pursuing policies that were thought to harm other countries by unfairly eroding tax bases.

The OECD initiative has evolved considerably since its launch in 1998, offering a forum for constructive dialogue between on and offshore financial centres. Over time, an increasing emphasis has been put on access to bank and financial information and on exchange of taxpayer-specific information between national tax authorities, which are increasingly viewed as necessary pre-conditions for the effective functioning of national tax systems in a context where the ever-increasing levels of foreign direct investment and of portfolio cross-border capital flows implies the risk of a growing demand for tax haven operations. In the OECD's view, an effective information exchange should allow all countries to protect the integrity of their tax system from the effects of international tax evasion, while preserving the right to tailor their tax systems to their own needs.[7] Put another way, effective cooperation to counter abuse is an essential requirement to get the full benefits of a more competitive environment.

Conversely, the existence of obstacles hampering the access to financial information by domestic and foreign tax authorities leads to adverse consequences. First, it distorts international capital flows, since funds can be attracted by or routed through countries whose strict secrecy provisions offer a favorable environment to tax evaders. Second, it has adverse consequences on the structure of national tax systems, since the tax burden is shifted from capital to less mobile factors (such as labor) or consumption, in an attempt to limit the erosion of the tax base. Preventing the full taxation of income arising from portfolio investments, the lack of access to bank information jeopardizes the overall equity of the tax system, both between compliant and non-compliant taxpayers and among different income sources. Strict bank secrecy rules may represent a significant constraint for governments wishing to raise a given amount of tax revenues in order to be able to deliver the desired amount of public goods. This latter effect is particularly serious for developing countries where capital flight towards bank secrecy jurisdictions may give rise to an erosion of their already potentially weak tax base, which can seriously undermine the ability of governments to make the vital investments in social services and economic infrastructure upon which sustainable economic development depends. Finally, strict bank secrecy regimes may have adverse effects in domains other than taxation, attracting money laundering and other types of criminal activities, ranging from terrorism to financial fraud.

The issues of bank secrecy and information exchange and, in more general terms, the need for an increased level of transparency, have become a priority also on the political agenda of other international organizations, particularly those dealing with the different forms of financial abuse or taking care of the stability of the international financial system: both the Financial Stability Forum (FSF) and the Financial Action Task Force on Money Laundering (FATF) have undertaken efforts to convince offshore financial centers to comply with international standards by requiring, among other things, enhanced transparency.[8]

The lifting of bank secrecy and the need for information exchange have received considerable attention in the economic literature (see boxed text below), which has also tried to answer the question of whether information exchange agreements can arise spontaneously.

The theoretical and empirical analysis on information exchange: a survey

In the theoretical literature, the lifting of bank secrecy and the need for information exchange between national tax authorities have received consideration within the analysis of the impact of tax policy on mobile financial capital in a context of open economies (Giovannini 1990; Bacchetta and Espinosa 1995; Huizinga and Nielsen 2000; Makris 2003; Sørensen 2001; Keen and Ligthart 2003). Information exchange between tax authorities and the prerequisite of access to relevant information have been recognized as essential for the taxation of capital income according to the residence principle. The residence principle is recommended by several authors as a second-best measure to the full coordination of tax policies (interpreted as a system of uniform tax rates and uniform tax bases: see, for instance, Giovannini 1990, and Sørensen 2001), since it allows national governments to choose their own preferred tax rates without violating international production efficiency, i.e. without distorting the location of international investment (the Diamond and Mirrlees theorem (1971)).[9] Other reasons in favor of the residence principle are interpersonal equity, as it allows for the progressive taxation of worldwide capital income, and a fair distribution of tax revenues among countries (since each country is able to tax its own residents).

An effective implementation of the residence principle is only possible when national tax authorities have full information on foreign source income earned by domestic taxpayers. This condition is met when information exchange covers all types of foreign source income and when foreign tax authorities have access to all relevant information. In practice, however, information exchange is far from perfect, mainly for two reasons: transaction costs and differences in country incentives. The last factor is probably the most important: the level of information sharing with foreign governments is considered a strategic variable and is taken into account by national governments when designing the optimal international tax system in the same way as the tax rate on domestic and foreign source income (Bacchetta and Espinoza 1995). Since countries face a diverse set of incentives to exchange taxpayers' information, it is far from clear that information exchange agreements can be self-enforcing.[10] This question has been addressed by several studies. Assuming perfect capital market integration, Eggert and Kolmar (2002) show that there exist equilibriums where information exchange arises spontaneously. However, this happens in a paradoxical context, where the high elasticity of capital makes governments unable to apply any tax that could potentially benefit from the exchange of information (typically, taxes on capital income). In other words, if capital is perfectly mobile, information exchange arises spontaneously but is useless, since all the taxes that are potential candidates for information-induced tax-base effects simply disappear. In the authors' opinion, this model can help explain why in recent years the growing integration of capital markets is being accompanied by some progress in measures of tax information exchange.

Apart from the paradoxical case of perfect capital mobility described by Eggert and Kolmar, three sets of circumstances have been identified in which countries may find in their interest to provide information (Keen and Ligthart 2003). The first can be modeled as a two-stage game where countries first decide the level of information exchange and then set the tax rates. Assuming that the institutional features of the tax system are given from the outset to tax authorities, Bacchetta and Espinosa (1995) find that a country may choose to provide at least some information to foreign tax authorities if this enables the information-receiving country to increase its own income tax rate. These conclusions are confirmed by Sørensen (2001). On the other hand, using the same two-stage game framework, but with the different assumption that all the institutional features of the tax system (i.e. the degree of information exchange and the level of tax rates) are chosen by the tax authorities instead of being given from the outset,[11] Makris (2003) finds not only that the non-cooperative equilibrium is characterized by zero information transmission, but also that there is no scope for cooperation in information sharing policies, irrespective of the transactions cost function and of the double taxation schemes. In fact, he shows that a coordinated increase in information exchange not only will make no difference, but in the case where information exchange is an equilibrium outcome, it will even leave countries worse off.

The second possibility, explored in a later paper by Bacchetta and Espinoza (2000) and by Huizinga and Nielsen (2002), is one where countries view the choice of tax rates and information provision as an infinitely repeated game and continuously adapt their decisions to those of other countries. In this setting, information exchange arises spontaneously if the possible advantages that each country can have by defecting from (or not entering) the agreement are balanced by some form of punishment.[12] The result of this balance – and hence the long-term sustainability of cooperative information exchange agreements – depends on several variables. The attractions of defection will be greater the higher are policymakers' discount rates (information exchange is more likely to be chosen if governments have little discounting of the future, i.e. if they are long-term oriented), the more imbalanced are capital flows and the more sensitive are capital flows to their effective tax treatment. One clear implication of this approach is that small capital-importing countries are likely to have least to gain from information exchange: for these countries, the advantages arising from the choice of lower tax rates in order to attract inward investment – an increase in the size of the banking and financial industry, a resulting increase of the wage tax base and of welfare in general – largely compensate the losses of any revenue from the small domestic capital tax base.

The third possibility consists in introducing some kind of compensation rather than punishment in order to induce countries to exchange information, as proposed by Keen and Ligthart (2003, 2004). Countries may redistribute to the information providing jurisdictions a certain proportion of the additional revenue they are able to collect thanks to the exchange of information, in order to compensate them for the adverse economic effects of voluntarily engaging to exchange information. Keen and Ligthart (2004) show that while large countries always prefer information exchange with any level of revenue sharing (since they always gain more from taxing their residents thanks to the information they receive compared to what they lose from the transfer of a certain amount of revenues to the information providing countries) small countries only have attractions to information exchange if the difference in size with the information receiving country is not very pronounced and if the share of revenue they receive from the residence country is sufficiently large.[13]

An issue connected with the implementation of information exchange is the "third country problem," i.e. whether a group of countries (i.e., the OECD or the EU) as a whole can gain from reaching an agreement on information exchange if the rest of the world does not join into the agreement. Unless all countries take part in the information exchange, the gains to any subset from agreeing to exchange information are likely to be reduced to the extent that third countries continue to provide an opportunity to invest without declaring the proceeds. These latter countries could even become more aggressive in tax competition because of their enhanced monopoly power in the provision of strictly confidential saving schemes and in consideration of their potentially higher gains. Since small countries have probably more to gain from remaining outside information exchange agreements, and since the number of small jurisdictions is quite high, the difficulties of implementing a truly comprehensive information exchange agreement are obvious. However, it is also possible that the small dimension of these countries represents a factor of vulnerability on which bigger countries can rely to persuade the small ones to agree to exchange information.

To sum up, it turns out from the theoretical literature that it is unlikely that full information exchange will spontaneously emerge, particularly because offshore financial centers have little interest to agree to any inter-national agreement that will curb their ability to attract capital, unless some form of positive incentive is given. This solution requires a coordinated effort on a multilateral basis and needs to be extended to as many tax havens and bank secrecy jurisdictions as possible in order to reduce the risk of defections.

The empirical literature on the implications of bank secrecy is more limited. A few studies (Grilli 1989; Alworth and Andresen 1992; Huizinga and Nicodème 2004) have found a certain degree of sensitivity of inter-national bank deposits to bank secrecy and other tax variables, from which it could be argued that cross-border financial flows are, at least to a certain extent, "tax-driven," i.e. affected by tax cheating purposes.

Origins and evolution of the Caribbean tax havens

Most tax havens are small, very open economies, and this is particularly true in the Caribbean region where the majority of islands have, over the last 30 years, moved into the offshore financial business. At least three reasons can explain this development.

1 *The agricultural sector* in the Caribbean area was increasingly unviable as preferential trading schemes were removed and more efficient producers entered their traditional markets.
2 *Few of the islands* have any natural resource endowments.
3 *Tourism*, which was highly successful in certain of the islands, was volatile and, in some cases, it could not be further exploited.

Financial services have been seen as an area in which, for a modest initial investment, Caribbean islands could upgrade the skills of the population, gener-ate employment and revenues for their governments and, more generally, boost their GDP by taking advantage of the high growth rate of the industry.

For some of these dependencies the move towards the offshore financial center and tax haven status was quite successful and led to significant rates of economic growth. Their colonial heritage gave them important competitive advantages, among which a modern-style legal system (usually based on the Anglo-Saxon model), English language (for most of them), a currency tied to that of the mother country, and in many cases the benefit of tax treaties which had been extended to them. These advantages were strengthened through the introduction of attractive rules for the incorporation of international busi-ness companies (IBCs) and for the establishment of trusts, the adoption of zero or very low taxes on incomes, profits and wealth tax (particularly for foreign-source and non-resident income), the absence of exchange controls and the introduction of strict bank secrecy and confidentiality of information rules.[14] Further advantages were the political stability, a pleasant physical environment and, more importantly, the proximity to or links with major on-shore financial centers (such as the US and the UK).[15]

In the Caribbean region these factors allowed first the Bahamas and then the Cayman Islands to become leading offshore financial centres, moving from poor subsidized economies in the beginning of the 1960s to net providers of resources to the Commonwealth since the 1980s. The Bahamas is nowadays ranked among the top five locations in the world for offshore mutual funds and trust funds and has also developed a significant inter-bank market. The Cayman Islands are nowadays the world's fifth largest banking centre, and the first among offshore jurisdictions, with a prominent position both in the inter-bank business and in private banking. The Caymans also host half of the world's hedge funds, hundreds of major non-financial subsidiaries of US corporations and the world's second-largest captive insurance market. The British Virgin Islands have developed into one of the most successful centers for IBCs and trust arrangements.

The Netherlands Antilles developed as a typical "treaty tax haven," being used in the 1960s through the mid-1980s to allow non-resident investors to receive portfolio income from the United States tax free.[16] Once the US abolished its withholding tax, there was no longer any motive for taking this route. Nowadays, the country is not anymore among the most prominent offshore jurisdictions, and is trying to develop other sectors of the offshore industry, namely incentives aimed at international business companies.

In more recent years, the demand for tax haven facilities has considerably expanded, owing to the high growth rates of cross-border investment and to the increased number of potential customers arising from the new possibilities offered by the new technological and communication infrastructures and the growing use of multiple layers of transactions to structure offshore operations through vehicles located in different countries. The gradual relaxation of reserve requirements, interest rate controls and capital controls in the main "onshore" markets and the creation of offshore banking facilities in some of the main industrial countries (the US and Japan) have reduced the regulatory advantages of offshore financial centers, making them less attractive for conventional banking. On the other hand, the tax avoidance facilities of OFCs have become more and more important, particularly for FDI and asset management.[17] The limited initial investments needed to enter the offshore industry have induced new countries, especially the smaller ones, to implement the "offshore package" of financial services and asset protection products in order to join in the competition for attracting internationally mobile capital:[18] hence, the number of tax havens has grown remarkably. This process have involved also some new entrants in the Caribbean area: Antigua and Barbuda, St. Kitts and Nevis, Grenada, Dominica, St. Lucia.

In this more competitive environment, the choice of a tax haven is increasingly determined by their "specialization" and by their proximity to target investment markets, although in some cases the geographical proximity to tax-payers still acts as a driver.[19] Some Caribbean tax havens have been able to succeed or to retain their market share thanks to product diversification and specialization in specific market niches. For instance, Bermuda is nowadays one of the world's biggest insurance and reinsurance markets; the British Virgin Islands have become one of the world's favorite locations for international business corporations (which are used exclusively as offshore vehicles); the Bahamas have developed a significant inter-bank market. Furthermore, in order to enhance their reputation, some of the most significant Caribbean offshore centers have taken the political decision to commit to tax information exchange by entering into Tax Information Exchange Agreeements (TIEAs).[20]

Some of the late arrivals in the Caribbean region and elsewhere, however, have had little success, because they have not been able to offer any advantage over the more established centers.[21] Overall, it is fair to say that with the exception of the Bahamas, Bermuda, the British Virgin Islands, the Cayman Islands and Panama, the other Caribbean offshore financial centres are struggling to make their financial activities a sustainable part of their economies.

The position of the Caribbean tax havens in the global financial markets

The relative importance of Caribbean tax havens can be measured through several indexes. However, a difficulty often encountered when trying this kind of estimate is the limited availability of reliable and internationally comparable data for many sectors of the OFC industry.

Suss *et al.* (2002) collect some relevant indicators with reference to 2001 or previous years. Overall, these indicators show that the size of the Caribbean tax havens and offshore financial centers varies significantly from one country or territory to another, and that there is a wide range of specialization across the region. So, for instance, while the British Virgin Islands is the largest register of international business companies (estimated to account for 48 percent of global IBC incorporations), the Cayman Islands, estimated to be the fifth largest off-shore financial center in the world, has fewer registered IBCs, but significantly more banks, insurance companies and trusts. Among recent entrants into the OFC sector, St. Kitts and Nevis has the largest number of registered IBCs, while Antigua and Barbuda has the most diversified OFC industry, including not only IBCs, but also banks and trusts.

The study also examines the contribution of the OFC sector to specific economic indicators. So, for example, it emerges that in many Caribbean jurisdictions employment opportunities arising from the OFC industry are significant. In 2000 the estimated employment in the OFC sector represented 15 percent of the labor force in the British Virgin Islands, 8 percent in Antigua and Barbuda, 1 percent in the Bahamas and 0.5 percent in Dominica. The wide range of variation depends both on the relative size of the economy and on the type of OFC business prevailing in each jurisdiction (for instance, offshore banks and shell companies do not require physical presence and, as such, do not require a significant number of people).

Another significant indicator used in the study is the amount of the fees collected by the central government from OFCs service providers. As of end-2000, Antigua and Barbuda derived over 7 percent of central government revenues from offshore sector fees, followed by Grenada at 4.5 percent and Anguilla at 3.6 percent. Among the more established OFCs, the British Virgin Islands, which is the world market leader in incorporation of international business companies, collected fees representing 55 percent of government revenues, equal to 13 percent of GDP. The Cayman Islands also rely heavily on fees collected from offshore banks, which accounted for 14.5 percent of government revenues by end-2000. In contrast, the governments of Bahamas and Barbados were less dependent on offshore sector fees (respectively: about 1 percent of government revenues and between 0.2 percent and 0.4 percent of GDP).

Further information on the weight of the financial industry and offshore business for tax havens can be obtained looking at the contribution of these sectors to GDP. According to the limited information publicly available, it can be estimated that at the end of 2001 the contribution of all offshore services to GDP ranged from around 25 percent in the Cayman Islands to 30 percent in the Bahamas and 45 percent in the British Virgin Islands. For other tax havens, the only available information was the GDP share of the whole area of services; quite often, the financial sector and tourism represent the main components of this share. According to available information, at the end of 2001 the GDP share of all services was 89 percent for Bermuda, 84 percent for the Netherlands Antilles, 81 percent for Montserrat, 77 percent for Antigua and Barbuda.

With reference to the offshore banking sector, a more detailed set of comparable statistical data can be taken from the Bank for International Settlements *Locational Statistics* as complemented, in some cases, by national sources.

Table 5.1 reports (in the first column) the size of foreign bank liabilities as a multiple of GDP[22] for a set of offshore financial centers that have historically relied heavily on bank secrecy and for other representative offshore and mainstream financial centers; the second column of the table reports each country's share of global foreign bank liabilities. Countries in each group are ranked according to the amount of their foreign liabilities vis-à-vis all sectors, banks and non-banks.

The Caribbean tax havens amount to just under 8.5 percent of the world foreign bank liabilities. As can be expected, the foreign liability/GDP ratio is much higher in small havens compared to other financial centers, however, even within small countries, the ratio shows a wide diversity, ranging from the highest value of 617.87 in the Cayman Islands to less than 0.11 for Aruba. Apart from the Cayman Islands and, to a lesser extent, the Bahamas, the Netherlands Antilles and Bermuda, for the remaining tax havens the banking business with non-residents seems to be far less important, confirming the specialization of the different Caribbean jurisdictions.

Table 5.1 Weight of foreign banking activity in selected OFCs (2001)

	Bank liabilities vis-à-vis non-residents as multiple of GDP	Country share of total bank liabilities vis-à-vis non-residents (%)
Caribbean OFCs Identified as tax havens by the OECD		
The Cayman Islands	617.87	6.97
The Bahamas	20.86	0.94
Netherlands Antilles	13.33	0.28
Bermuda	3.91	0.13
Panama	0.73	0.11
Aruba	0.11	0.0020
Antigua and Barbuda	0.20	0.0013
St. Kitts and Nevis	0.26	0.0012
The Commonwealth of Dominica	0.31	0.0011
St Lucia	0.13	0.0010
Grenada	0.24	0.0009
St. Vincent and the Grenadines	0.12	0.0006
Anguilla	0.65	0.0006
Other non-OECD OFCs		
Singapore	4.36	3.63
Hong Kong SAR	1.58	2.35
OECD OFCs		
Switzerland	3.16	5.70
Luxembourg	16.93	3.57
Belgium	1.16	2.71
Austria	0.46	0.90
Other selected financial centers		
United Kingdom	1.65	20.77
United States	0.13	11.42
Germany	0.47	8.77
France	0.49	6.76
Japan	0.15	4.64

Sources: data on foreign liabilities are taken from BIS Locational Statistics and from national sources; data on GDP are from World Bank (World Development Indicators database), from national sources or from other international organizations estimates.

Notes
Data on foreign liabilities and GDP are for 2001 when available, otherwise latest available.

Table 5.2 reports similar indicators with reference to the amount of bank deposits of non-bank non-residents for a subset of countries for which relevant data are available. These indicators can be useful to assess more specifically the value of private banking in each tax haven. Once again, the Cayman Islands show a very high ratio (bank deposits vis-à-vis non-bank non-residents being equal to 230.87 times the country GDP), followed at a distance by the Bahamas (21.52). Also the share of total bank deposits of non-resident non-banks which is held by the most prominent offshore financial centers appears to be significant: as can be seen from the last column in the table, the Cayman Islands hold more

Table 5.2 Weight of foreign private banking in selected OFCs (2001)

	Bank deposits of non-resident non-banks as multiple of GDP	Country share of total bank deposits of non-resident non-banks (%)*
OFCs		
The Cayman Islands	230.87	10.83
The Bahamas	21.52	4.04
Bahrain	2.02	0.89
Netherlands Antilles	3.21	0.28
Singapore	1.31	4.52
Hong Kong SAR	0.44	2.71
Switzerland	1.43	10.72
Luxembourg	5.37	4.70
Belgium	0.36	3.44
Austria	0.04	0.35
Other selected financial centers		
United Kingdom	0.33	17.46
United States	0.02	7.01
Germany	0.15	11.33
France	0.04	2.34
Japan	0.01	1.13

Sources: Data on non-residents bank deposits are from BIS Locational Statistics; data on GDP are from World Bank (World Development Indicators database), from national sources or from other international organizations estimates.

Notes
Data at end 2001 when available, otherwise latest available.
* Total stock for BIS reporting countries.

than 10 percent of the global stock of these deposits, a share comparable to that of Switzerland and higher than the United States.

The OECD initiative on harmful tax practices and the position of Caribbean jurisdictions

The OECD harmful tax practices initiative

In 1998, the OECD Ministerial Council established a forum which identified the following four key criteria for identifying harmful tax practices:

1   no or nominal taxes, in the case of tax havens, and no or low taxation, in the case of member country preferential tax regimes;
2   lack of transparency;
3   lack of effective exchange of information;
4   no substantial activities, in the case of tax havens, and ring-fencing, in the case of member country preferential regimes.

The no/nominal/low taxes criterion was intended merely as a gateway to determine those situations in which an analysis of the other criteria is necessary. The adoption of low or zero tax rates is *never* by itself sufficient to identify a jurisdiction as a tax haven. The OECD does not prescribe appropriate levels of taxation or dictate the design of any country's tax system. This work has received considerable political support.[23]

In 2000, the OECD identified 35 jurisdictions that were found to meet the tax haven criteria.[24] A process was also established whereby the identified tax havens could commit to improve transparency and establish effective exchange of information for tax purposes. Those jurisdictions that were not willing to make such commitments would be included in a list of uncooperative tax havens. Thus, the key distinction for OECD countries became whether a tax haven was cooperative or uncooperative. The *2001 Progress Report* made certain modifications to the tax haven work. There were two principal modifications. First, a tax haven that committed to eliminating lack of transparency and lack of effective exchange of information would be considered cooperative and therefore would not be included on the OECD's list of uncooperative tax havens. A second modification was that a potential framework of coordinated defensive measures would not apply to uncooperative tax havens any earlier than it would apply to OECD countries with harmful preferential tax regimes. In April 2002, the OECD published the list of uncooperative tax havens, containing seven jurisdictions that still were at that time unwilling to commit to transparency and exchange of information for tax purposes; two jurisdictions – Nauru and Vanuatu – made commitments in 2003 and the list now contains only five jurisdictions: Andorra, Liberia, Liechtenstein, the Marshall Islands and Monaco.

The 33 jurisdictions that made commitments to transparency and effective exchange of information are referred to as Participating Partners. The OECD and non-OECD Participating Partners have worked together in the Global Forum on Taxation to develop the international standards for transparency and effective exchange of information in tax matters. The Caribbean offshore financial centers have played a particularly active role in the forum. They took part in the specially created working group which developed the 2002 Model Agreement on Exchange of Information on Tax Matters.[25]

In order to determine exactly where countries stand in relation to transparency and information exchange, the Global Forum decided at its June 2004 meeting in Berlin that it was important to carry out a review of countries' legal and administrative frameworks in these areas so as to assess progress towards a level playing field. In addition to Global Forum Participating Partners (Table 5.3), other significant financial centers (Table 5.3) were invited to participate in the review.[26] Overall, the factual assessment covered 82 countries.

The report *Tax Co-operation: Towards a Level Playing Field – 2006 Assessment by the Global Forum on Taxation* issued in May 2006 reflects the outcome of the factual review carried out by the Global Forum. All the

Table 5.3 Countries covered by factual assessment

Global forum participating partners

Anguilla	Dominica	Korea	San Marino
Antigua and Barbuda	Finland	Malta	Seychelles
Aruba	France	Mauritius	Slovak Republic
Australia	Germany	Mexico	Spain
The Bahamas	Gibraltar	Montserrat	Saint Kitts and Nevis
Bahrain, Kingdom of	Greece	Nauru	Saint Lucia
Belize	Grenada	Netherlands	Saint Vincent and the Grenadines
Bermuda	Guernsey	Netherlands Antilles	Sweden
British Virgin Islands	Hungary	New Zealand	Turkey
Canada	Iceland	Niue	Turks and Caicos Islands
Cayman Islands	Ireland	Norway	United Kingdom
Cook Islands	Isle of Man	Panama	United States
Cyprus	Italy	Poland	US Virgin Islands
Czech Republic	Japan	Portugal	Vanuatu
Denmark	Jersey	Samoa	

Invitees

Andorra	Guatemala	Monaco
Argentina	Hong Kong, China	Philippines
Austria	Liberia	Russian Federation
Barbados	Liechtenstein	Singapore
Belgium	Luxembourg	South Africa
Brunei	Macao, China	Switzerland
China	Malaysia (Labuan)	United Arab Emirates
Costa Rica	Marshall Islands	Uruguay

OECD and non-OECD Participating Partners in the Global Forum on taxation have endorsed the principles of transparency and exchange of information for tax purposes that are reflected in the report. They have also agreed to their legal and administrative frameworks being reviewed in the light of these principles. For the first time, other significant non-OECD economies such as Hong Kong, China and Singapore have participated in the work of the Global Forum in these areas. Six of these non-OECD economies have also endorsed the principles of transparency and exchange of information and agreed to work with the Global Forum towards a level playing field: Argentina; China; Hong Kong, China; Macao, China; the Russian Federation and South Africa.

How do the Caribbean and other financial centers measure up to these criteria?

The results of the Global Forum assessment of legal and administrative practices concerning transparency and information exchange is a valuable means to examine the current standpoint of the Caribbean tax havens towards the OECD harmful tax practices initiative. Their position regarding the different aspects of the assessment is as follows:

A Exchanging Information

Many of the Caribbean jurisdictions have (or are in the process of negotiating) exchange of information arrangements that permit them to exchange information for both civil and criminal tax purposes in the form of double tax conventions or TIEAs (some exceptions are Anguilla, Panama and Turks and Caicos). In addition, as a practical matter, Panama is rarely, if ever, able to exchange information in criminal tax matters. None of the Caribbean jurisdictions reported having a *domestic tax interest*, i.e. being unable to respond to a request for information where they have no interest in obtaining the information for their own tax purposes. Also, none of the Caribbean jurisdictions reported applying the principle of dual incrimination to all their information exchange relationships concerning the administration or enforcement of domestic tax law. However, Saint Lucia and Saint Vincent and the Grenadines apply this principle in connection with exchange of bank information (see section B).

B Access to bank information

While in 77 countries covered by the factual assessment governmental authorities have access to bank information and/or information from other financial institutions for at least some tax information exchange purposes, among the Caribbean jurisdictions Panama have indicated an inability to access bank information for any exchange of information purposes. In 17 countries, access to bank information is granted only for the purpose of responding to a request for exchange of information in criminal tax matters. Of these the Caribbean jurisdictions of Saint Lucia, Saint Vincent and the Grenadines (in addition to Andorra, Austria, Cook Islands, Luxembourg, Samoa, San Marino, and Switzerland) apply the principle of dual criminality in connection with access to bank information for exchange of information purposes.

C Access to ownership, identity and accounting information

Of the 82 countries reviewed, 78 – including all the OECD countries – generally have powers to obtain information that is kept by a person subject to record-keeping obligations which may be invoked to respond to a request for exchange of information in tax matters. In addition, 71 countries reported that they also generally have powers to obtain information from persons not required to keep such information which may be invoked to respond to a request for information. Anguilla, Montserrat, Panama and Turks and Caicos Islands have very limited powers to obtain this kind of information for criminal tax matters.

D   Availability of ownership, identity and accounting information

COMPANIES

Of the 82 countries reviewed, 77 require companies to report legal ownership information to governmental authorities or to hold such information at the company level. Three countries (Montserrat, Saint Kitts and Nevis and the US Virgin Islands) each have one form of company where this is not the case.[27] More stringent ownership reporting requirements exist in the financial sector in certain countries. All but five countries (Aruba; Guatemala; Hong Kong, China; Macao, China; and Singapore) indicated that applicable anti-money laundering legislation would normally require corporate service providers or other service providers to identify the beneficial owners of their client companies.

In 75 countries, all domestic companies are required to keep accounting records. No such requirements exist for international business companies in Belize, Brunei and Samoa or for limited liability companies in Anguilla, Montserrat and St. Kitts and Nevis.[28] In the Bahamas, only public companies and regulated companies in the banking, securities and insurance sectors are required to keep accounting records. Mandatory accounting records retention periods of five years or more exist in 63 countries.

Bearer shares may be issued in 48 countries. Of these, 39 have adopted mechanisms to identify the legal owners of bearer shares in some or all cases. Furthermore, ten of these 39 countries (Antigua and Barbuda, Belize, British Virgin Islands, Cayman Islands, the Cook Islands, Dominica, Grenada, Montserrat, St. Kitts and Nevis and St. Vincent and the Grenadines) also require bearer shares to be immobilized or held by an approved custodian. The remaining 29 rely mainly on anti-money-laundering rules, investigative mechanisms or a requirement for the holders of shares to notify the company of their interest in the shares. Anguilla is one of the nine countries that reported not having any mechanism to identify the owners of bearer shares, although it indicated to plan to adopt such mechanisms in the near future.

Bearer debt instruments may be issued in 52 countries and 40 of these have adopted mechanisms to identify the owners of such instruments. In general, these mechanisms rely on anti-money laundering rules, on investigative powers or, in the case of EU member states and their associated or dependent territories, on procedures set out in the EU Savings Tax Directive and savings tax agreements.

TRUSTS

Of the 82 countries reviewed, 54 have trust law. Of these, Macao, China and the Seychelles have no trust law applicable to residents, but have trust law applicable to non-residents. Information on the settlers and beneficiaries of domestic trusts is required to be held under the laws of 47 countries. In 36 of the countries with trust law, a domestic trustee of a foreign trust would also be required to have information on the identity of settlers and beneficiaries, in some or all cases. Of the 28 countries that do not have trust law, 18 indicated that their residents may act as trustees of a foreign trust. In all of these, except for Luxembourg, there is a requirement on resident trustees to identify settlers and beneficiaries of foreign trusts. Of the 54 countries which have trust law, 45 countries reported requiring all trusts formed under their law to keep accounting records. Dominica, St. Lucia and Turks and Caicos are among the seven countries that have not reported a requirement to keep records under their trust law.

The way forward for Caribbean offshore financial centers

The future for Caribbean offshore financial centers depends, to a large extent, on their willingness to meet the new international standards that have been developed by such bodies as the FATF, the FSF and the OECD. Meeting these standards will enhance their reputation and make them more attractive as financial centers in which to carry out legitimate transactions.

For the more established centers, such as the Bahamas, the Cayman Islands and the British Virgin Islands, which have already developed relatively strong and extensive legislative and regulatory frameworks, the cost of introducing the additional measures necessary to comply with international standards need not be substantial. At the same time, the international community is committed to helping these countries and territories to implement effectively these standards. The main mechanism for this implementation in the tax area is Tax Information Exchange Agreements (TIEAs). These agreements provide an effective mechanism that minimizes the risk that these centers are misused by residents of other countries to evade their tax responsibilities. Over the last few years, all the major Caribbean offshore financial centers, other than Panama, have entered into one or more TIEAs. We can expect that this trend will accelerate and that these OFCs will extend their network of TIEAs, not just with OECD countries, but also with major non-OECD countries (China, India, Brazil and South Africa have already begun negotiations).

In the case of some of the smaller Caribbean OFCs, they may decide that the burden of meeting these new standards means that the cost of having an offshore sector outweighs the benefits. In these cases, the international community needs to stand ready to provide assistance so that other economic activities are open up for these islands.

Notes

1 The views expressed in this article are those of the authors and do not in any way commit the OECD and its member countries nor the Banca d'Italia.
2 These different factors may have a different weight for each tax haven. This also means that there may be different groupings of tax havens, depending on the combination of relevant factors chosen to identify them.
3 The explanation lies in the classic argument of Diamond and Mirrlees (1971) that governments unnecessarily distort production when they tax intermediate production, from which it follows that in small open economies governments with a sufficient

number of available tax instruments can make all domestic residents better off by not taxing internationally mobile capital. In fact, since small open economies are price-takers in world markets, they are unable to shift any of their tax burdens on foreign investors: any attempt to do so would simply distort their economies by putting additional costs on domestic factors in the form of lower wages and land prices. It follows that domestic residents would be made better off by removing any taxes on foreign investors and instead directly taxing the returns to local factors of production. In addition to the price-taker position of small economies and to the availability of a sufficient set of tax instruments for the governments of the same economies, another basic assumption on which the Diamond and Mirrlees argument relies is that foreign investors do not earn economic rents from their investments in the small economies.

4 Between 1982 and 1999 total world foreign direct investment grew from around 0.5 percent to around 3.5 percent of world GDP. See Hines (2004) that reports data from the World Bank database *World Development Indicators.*

5 Empirical studies have shown other relevant features of tax havens. For instance, better-governed countries seem more likely to become tax havens (Dharmapala and Hines 2006). A possible interpretation of this is that only better-governed countries can credibly commit not to expropriate foreign investors. It is not clear, however, whether it is the decision to become a tax haven that affects the quality of local governance or the quality of governance itself is influenced by economic and political conditions that also determine whether or not a country becomes a tax haven. Another relevant finding (from studies referring to American multinational firms) is that the highest share of tax haven operations seem to come from large firms with high volumes of international activity, high R&D intensity and significant volumes of intrafirm trade (Desai *et al.* 2006). For these firms tax haven affiliates appear to facilitate the relocation of taxable income from high to low tax locations and to reduce the cost of deferring home country taxation of income earned in low tax foreign locations. Of course, the issue at stake here is not the tax haven characteristics of the jurisdiction, but the existence of a low rate of tax.

6 OECD (1998), hereafter "the 1998 Report." Luxembourg and Switzerland abstained on the approval of the report.

7 OECD (2004a).

8 In April 2000 the Financial Stability Forum (FSF) launched an assessment of the compliance of supervisory and regulatory systems of the OFCs' financial sector with international standards with the prospect of enhancing financial stability and fighting financial fraud and the financing of terrorism. The assessment led to the identification of several OFCs, especially in the smaller and poorer jurisdictions, having critical deficiencies. In the same year the Financial Action Task Force on Money Laundering (FATF) undertook an initiative to identify non-cooperative countries and territories in the fight against money laundering. Between 2000 and 2001 the FATF identified a list of 21 non-cooperative countries and territories, among which were several Caribbean OFCs. Thanks to the significant and rapid progress in addressing deficiencies, all countries have been gradually removed from the list.

9 The residence principle is consistent with the Capital Export Neutrality (CEN) condition, since it implies that the taxpayer faces the same tax burden on domestic and foreign source income. In the presence of different marginal tax rates across countries, the CEN condition implies that the international allocation of investments is neutral because the cost of capital (the required pre-tax rate of return) is equated across countries. For this reason the residence principle is considered superior to the source principle of taxation, which implies taxation of capital income at different rates depending on the country of the investment. The source principle allows for neutrality in the international allocation of savings and is thus consistent with the condition of Capital Import Neutrality (CIN), since it assures that capital income is taxed in the source country (usually through withholding taxes) at the same rate for

residents and non residents and that foreign source capital income is exempted from tax in the investors' home countries. However, it distorts the investment decisions because it allows the pre-tax rates of return to differ among countries.

10 Some countries may choose to not release bank information to foreign jurisdictions in the attempt to enhance their attractiveness for foreign investors, thereby increasing the size of their financial industry, employment and national welfare. Other countries, particularly those which have substantial capital outflows, may be interested in obtaining information on portfolio investments made abroad by their residents, in order to limit the erosion of their tax base due to underreporting of foreign source income. In general, the discrepancy in the values placed by any two countries on each other's taxpayer information depends on a number of factors (Tanzi and Zee 2001). The most relevant are: asymmetries in the economies' size (as GDP level, taxpayers' number, capital flows, etc.); differences in the capital account balances (taxpayer information provided by the tax authorities of a capital-importing country to a capital-exporting country is more valuable to the latter than similar information to the former provided to it by the latter); differences in the completeness and reliability of information gathered by national tax administrations.

11 Unlike Bacchetta and Espinoza, Makris assumes that all distortionary tax rates can be different and endogenously determined.

12 Since in this context it is likely that uncooperative behavior by any country would lead to other countries also behaving non-cooperatively, each country must balance the long-term gains from continued cooperation with the temporary gain from failing to provide information and with the permanent cost of non-cooperative behavior by the other countries.

13 When the difference in size with the information receiving country is very pronounced, small countries may resist moving to exchange information, whatever the share of revenue sharing. If, however, the size of the two countries is sufficiently close, the small country will prefer information exchange even if all the additional revenue it generates is retained by the information receiving country (the residence country).

14 For instance, the rules for the legal protection of bank secrecy were introduced in 1966 in the Cayman Islands and in 1980 in the Bahamas.

15 Sullivan (2004) reports that, according to the Cayman Islands Monetary Authority 2002 Annual Report, about 70 percent of the international assets and liabilities booked through the Cayman Islands originate from the US.

16 Until 1984, interest income received by non-residents from US sources was subject to withholding tax, either at 30 percent or at a lower rate as provided in a tax treaty. Since the treaty between the US and the Netherlands Antilles reduced the withholding tax rate to zero, and the Netherlands Antilles did not charge any withholding tax, the country was used to route interest payments from the US to third-country recipients free of taxes at source.

17 With reference to this latter market, it is possible to reduce inheritance and other capital taxes for individual investors that acts as a prime incentive and has led to a large expansion in offshore fund management activity, in particular by the use of investment vehicles such as trusts and private companies.

18 For example, Malta launched its international financial center facilities in 1994.

19 Thus in the last few years, we have witnessed the growth of some new OFC and tax haven practices in the East Asia region, where some jurisdictions (Labuan in Malaysia, and Samoa) are emerging thanks to their ability to intermediate in a "tax-efficient" way the growing capital flows which circulate in the area. Given the significant economic growth rates currently reached by some of the biggest countries in the region, such as China and India, the global weight of Asian OFCs – both of well established ones, such as Singapore and Hong Kong, and of those which seem to be emerging more recently – is likely to increase.

20 The Cayman Islands, for example, have a TIEA with the United States and Bermuda; Antigua has one with Australia; the Netherlands Antilles have signed a TIEA with Australia and New Zealand.
21 This was the case, for instance, of Dominica, Grenada, St. Lucia and, to a lesser extent, St. Kitts and Nevis.
22 Data on GDP are from the *World Development Indicator* of the World Bank.
23 The G-7–8 finance ministers have consistently provided political support for the project and the G-8 heads of government confirmed their support at the Gleneagles Summit in July 2005. Also, at the November 2004 meeting of the G-20 finance ministers a strong statement in support of this work was issued and further endorsement of this work was provided in the most recent G-20 Communiqué issued in November 2006 and in a Communiqué from the Caribbean-UK Forum on 28 April 2006.
24 Andorra; Anguilla; Antigua and Barbuda; Aruba; The Bahamas; Bahrain; Barbados; Belize; British Virgin Islands; Cook Islands; Dominica; Gibraltar; Grenada; Guernsey; Isle of Man; Jersey; Liberia; Liechtenstein; the Maldives; Marshall Islands; Monaco; Montserrat; Nauru; Netherlands Antilles; Niue; Panama; Samoa; Seychelles; St. Lucia; St. Kitts and Nevis; St. Vincent and the Grenadines; Tonga; Turks and Caicos; US Virgin Islands; Vanuatu. Six other jurisdictions – Bermuda, Cayman Islands, Cyprus, Malta, Mauritius and San Marino – were not included in the 2000 report because they committed to eliminate their harmful tax practices prior to the release of that report.
25 Available on the OECD website at http://www.oecd.org/ctp. The Model Agreement, released in March 2002, was developed by the Global Forum Working Group on Effective Exchange of Information which consisted of representatives from OECD countries and delegates from Aruba, Bermuda, Bahrain, the Cayman Islands, Cyprus, Isle of Man, Malta, Mauritius, the Netherlands Antilles, the Seychelles and San Marino. The work of that group has been complemented by the work of the Global Forum's Joint Ad Hoc Group on Accounts which has developed guidance on accounting and recordkeeping requirements for corporations, partnerships, trusts and other entities or arrangements.
26 All Global Forum participating partners except Antigua and Barbuda and Grenada responded to the questionnaire which forms the basis of the factual assessment. The information of the factual assessment about Antigua and Barbuda and Grenada is based on publicly available information or information previously provided by Antigua and Barbuda and Grenada. Among the invitees, all but two – Brunei and Liberia – responded to the questionnaire used as the basis for the factual assessment. Liberia was unable to do so due to its current political situation.
27 With respect to Grenada there was not sufficient information to reach a conclusion.
28 In these cases only records that the directors of such consider necessary or desirable need to be kept.

References

Alworth, J. and Andresen, S. (1992) "The Determinants of Cross-border Non-bank Deposits and the Competitiveness of Financial Market Centers," *Money Affairs*, 5, pp. 105–33.
Bacchetta P. and Espinosa, M. P. (1995) "Information Sharing and Tax Competition among Governments," *Journal of International Economic*, n. 39, pp. 102–21.
—— (2000) "Exchange-of-information Clauses in International Tax Treaties," *International Tax and Public Finance*, vol. 7, pp. 275–93.
Desai, M. A., Fritz Foley, C. and Hines, J. Jr. (2004) "Economic Effects of Regional Tax Havens," NBER Working Paper n. 10806.

—— (2006) "The Demand for Tax Haven Operations," *Journal of Public Economics*, 90, pp. 513–31.

Dharmapala, D. and Hines J. Jr. (2006) "Which countries become Tax Havens," paper submitted to the conference organized by the International Tax Policy Forum, Washington, DC, December 2006.

Diamond, P. and Mirrlees, J. A. (1971) "Optimal Taxation and Public Production II: Tax Rules," *American Economic Review*, vol. 61, pp. 261–78.

Eggert, W. and Kolmar, M. (2002) "Residence-based Capital Taxation: Why Information is Voluntarily Exchanged and why it is not," *International Tax and Public Finance*, vol. 9, pp. 465–82.

Giovannini, A. (1990) "International Capital Mobility and Capital Income Taxation," *European Economic Review*, n. 34, pp. 480–8.

Grilli, V. (1989) "Europe 1992: Issues and Prospects for the Financial Markets," *Economic Policy*, vol. 4, pp. 387–421.

Hines, J. Jr. (2004) "Do Tax Havens Flourish?," NBER Working Paper n. 10936.

Huizinga, H. and Nicodème, G. (2004) "Are International Deposits Tax-driven?," *Journal of Public Economics*, vol. 88, n. 6, pp. 1093–118.

Huizinga, H. and Nielsen, S. B. (2000) "The Taxation of Interest in Europe: A Minimum Withholding Tax?," in Cnossen, S. (ed.) *Taxing Capital Income in the European Union*, Oxford University Press.

—— (2002) "Withholding Taxes or Information Exchange: The Taxation of International Interest Flows," *Journal of Public Economics*, n. 87, pp. 39–72.

Keen, M. and Ligthart, J. E. (2003) "Information Sharing and International Taxation: A Primer," mimeo, Washington, DC: IMF – Fiscal Affairs Department.

—— (2004) "Incentives and Information Exchange in International Taxation," CentER Discussion Paper 2004–54.

Makris, M. (2003) "International Tax Competition: There is no Need for Cooperation in Information Sharing," *Review of International Economics*, vol. 11 (3), pp. 555–67.

OECD (1998) *Harmful Tax Competition – An Emerging Global Issue*, Paris.

—— (2000) *Improving Access to Bank Information for Tax Purposes*, Paris.

—— (2004a) *The OECD's Project on Harmful Tax Practices: the 2004 Progress Report*, Paris.

—— (2004b) "A Process for Achieving a Level Playing Field," outcome of the OECD Global Forum on Taxation in Berlin, 3–4 June 2004.

—— (2006) *Tax Co-operation, Towards a Level Playing Field*, Paris.

Slemrod, J. and Wilson, J. D. (2006) "Tax Competition with Parasitic Tax Havens," NBER Working Paper n. 12225.

Sørensen, P. B. (2001) "Tax Coordination in the European Union: What are the Issues?," *Swedish Economic Policy Review*, vol. 8, pp. 143–95.

Sullivan, M. A. (2004) "US Citizens Hide Hundreds of Billions in Cayman Accounts," *Tax Notes International*, vol. 103, n. 8, pp. 956–64.

—— (2006) "A Challenge to Conventional International Tax Wisdom," *Tax Notes International*, December 11.

Suss, E. C., Williams O. H. and Mendis C. (2002) "Caribbean Offshore Financial Centers: Past, Present, and Possibilities for the Future," IMF Working Paper, WP/02/88.

Tanzi, V. and Zee, H. H. (2001) "Can Information Exchange be Effective in Taxing Cross-border Income Flows?," in Andersson, C., Melz, P. and Silfverberg, C. (eds) *Modern Issues in the Law of International Taxation*, Dordrecht: Kluwer Law International.

Part II

Country studies of tax systems and tax reforms in Latin America

6 Argentina

Martin Bès

Introduction and contents[1]

Upon taking office in July 1989, President Menem embraced a reform agenda aimed at reverting the previous decade of economic stagnation. The reform program faced serious implementation issues, as exemplified by the initial privatizations that did not adequately address regulatory issues while attempts at stabilizing the economy after the hyperinflation bouts of 1989 and 1990 were short-lived. In January 1991 Domingo Cavallo was appointed Economy Minister, and his first concern was re-establishing credibility in the Administration's economic policies. At the heart of this lack of credibility were the fiscal imbalances that had stubbornly resisted policymakers over the previous decade and which ended up being monetized and reflected in very high inflation.

Cavallo introduced a currency board, which came to be known as *convertibilidad*. This monetary regime required that the monetary base be backed by foreign currency at an exchange rate of one peso per one US$. This rule prevented the government from balancing its accounts by printing money, reduced the ability of the Central Bank of acting as a lender of last resort to the financial sector and eliminated the possibility of indexation, all of which were perceived as the ultimate causes of inflation.[2] A law was passed in support of the monetary regime in order to enhance its credibility, demonstrating the political system's commitment to it. *Convertibilidad* was in place for over a decade, until its collapse amid Argentina's political and economic meltdown in December 2001.[3] An improvement in fiscal performance was a requirement of *convertibilidad*. On the expenditure side, there was a widely held view that while the level of spending was more or less rigid its composition was not. Financial support of state enterprises would be eliminated as a result of the privatization program, but these resources would be required to increase health and education spending as well as the transitional costs of economic reforms. The conclusion was that the thrust of improvements in fiscal accounts would need to come from the revenue side. The reform of the tax system implemented in the early 1990s was designed to support fundamental economic reforms required by the new development paradigm adopted by the country.

A brief reference to the time period will enhance the readers' understanding of the reforms. While 16 years may not seem an extensive period in a country's

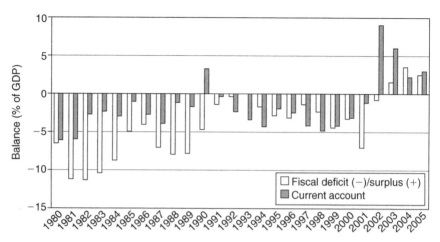

Figure 6.1 Argentina's external and fiscal balance (% of GDP).

history, it would be a mistake to assume that the economic policies implemented since 1990 were unchanged throughout this period. As a result several sub-periods are specified in order to facilitate the understanding of this chapter. In the field of tax policy, changes were introduced in response to the government's reform agenda, to variations in policymakers' preferences as well as to changes in the economic constraints, mainly from the international arena. A timeline summarizes the domestic and the international events that took place during this period and provides context for the policy reforms in tax policy described in the chapter.

The first period runs from mid-1989 to 1995, during Menem's first term. Its highlights are an initial four years of economic reform, which taper out as the constitution is modified in order to allow the president's reelection while the first major emerging market crisis of the decade takes place (Tequila). During the second period, which runs from 1996 to 1999, the reform agenda was reduced to fine-tuning first generation reforms as no political consensus emerged regarding the direction of additional measures. This was mainly due to Menem's ambitions of a third presidential term, which distracted political capital from economic reform. Even though the country's expansive fiscal policy was inconsistent with *convertibilidad*, access to international financial markets allowed policymakers to procrastinate in adopting policies that would reduce fiscal imbalances. This was a period of intense volatility in emerging markets, triggered by Thailand and South Korea's external collapse in 1997 and followed by comparable events in Russia (1998), Long Term Capital Management (1998) and Brazil (1999).

The third period extends from December 1999 to December 2001. The main focus of the new government that took office in December 1999 was to restore fiscal solvency, an increasingly challenging task as the economy reacted negatively to fiscal adjustment and international financial markets signaled Argentina as the next major emerging economy that would face a currency crisis. While

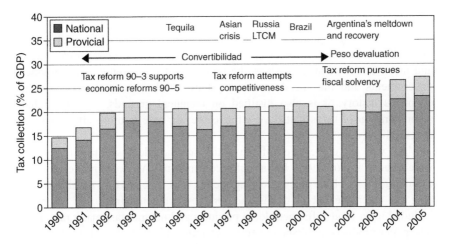

Figure 6.2 Argentina's timeline 1990–2005; background: tax collection (% of GDP).

different changes in economic policies were attempted, they hardly qualify as economic reforms, but rather as desperate, and in the end futile, attempts to ward off devaluation and default. The fourth and last period began in 2002 and continues until today. It started when the authorities formally abandoned the currency board regime in the midst of a political meltdown and an unprecedented economic collapse. The new monetary and exchange rate framework that emerged in 2002 was followed by policies devoted to produce a fiscal surplus in response to the goal of reducing economic vulnerabilities and to the limited access to private financial markets and foreign resources.[4]

An overview of the development of the tax system since the early 1990s will be the subject of the second section. The economic goals pursued by policymakers, their choice of tax policy instruments and the main results presented within a macroeconomic framework will be explored in this section. A description of the main taxes currently collected in Argentina will be presented in the third section. At the national level this involves the income tax, the VAT, excises on a group of selected products, export taxes, import tariffs and social security taxes. The two main tax assignments of the provinces, the turnover tax and property taxes are also presented.[5] A final section will explore some ideas for a reform agenda for Argentina's tax system.

The evolution of the tax system since the early 1990s

This section explores the main changes introduced in Argentina's tax system since 1990. These reforms are conceptually linked and, revenue-sharing arrangements aside, these taxes ultimately all feed into the government's revenue pool. However for presentation purposes they are organized around three categories: domestic, trade and social security taxes. A brief description of tax administration strengthening is included at the end of the section.

Reforms in domestic taxation

Argentina's tax assignments are heavily biased in favor of the central government. The central government is responsible for VAT, excises, trade, payroll and income taxes, but must share the proceeds of tax revenue with provincial governments and the social security system. While this is the result of the country's history, it is also justified on technical grounds, as a centralized administration of taxes that have a moveable tax base is more efficient than a decentralized one.[6]

VAT was the centerpiece of the initial steps of domestic taxation reform, which began in late 1989. Initial enhancements in VAT were implemented by extending the tax base and increasing the tax rate. The starting point was reducing the extensive list of goods and services exempted from this tax, which included most foodstuffs, petroleum products and natural gas, many raw materials, paper products, published material, certain capital goods and most services. This list was greatly reduced between 1989 and 1990 and coverage was extended to public services whose provision was being transferred to the private sector through an ambitious if not always well-planned privatization process. The tax rate was increased from 15 percent to 16 percent, after an initial short-lived reduction to 13 percent. Although the tax base was expanded somewhat during the following years, increases in the tax rate became the instrument of choice when changes were introduced in VAT. The rate was raised to 18 percent in 1992 and a temporary surcharge of three percentage points was introduced in 1995 in response to fiscal constraints faced during the Tequila Crisis. This surcharge was made permanent in 1996. As a result of these measures as well as improvements in tax administration the share of VAT in total tax collection almost trebled between 1990 and 1995 reaching 6.8 percent of GDP. While these measures aimed at increasing government revenue, they also improved the design of the tax system by eliminating a large amount of excise taxes and optimizing those that remained. These were maintained as they taxed a small group of relatively expensive goods (e.g. automobiles and car parts), had an inelastic demand (e.g. oil products) and/or also had negative externalities (e.g. alcoholic beverages, tobacco products).

Measures to reform direct taxation were introduced in 1990. The initial changes were centered on reducing tax rates of the corporate and personal income taxes. This reform followed the precepts of the US income tax reform of 1986, which reduced the tax burden on corporations and individuals and simplified the tax system. The different tax rates in place for domestically owned firms and foreign owned firms were reduced in 1990 from 33 percent to 20 percent and from 45 percent to 36 percent respectively. They were eventually unified at 30 percent in 1992 and subsequently raised to 33 percent in 1996. The maximum rate of the personal income tax was reduced from 35 percent to 30 percent, while six income brackets replaced the previous eight. Initial changes in the tax base of the corporate income tax involved provisions designed to increase allowances for loss carryovers as well as temporary measures authorizing expensing of incremental investment. Changes in rates on withholding tax on dividends and other payments were introduced with the dual aim of reducing dispersion and the level of rates. The concept of world income in the definition of the tax base was also introduced. Changes in the tax base of personal income tax were centered on limiting medical expense deductions.

The taxation of personal and business assets was also modified. On the one hand the capital gains tax as well as taxes on corporate and personal net worth were eliminated while a tax on the gross assets of businesses was introduced in 1989, with a tax rate set at 1 percent. It was designed to address non-compliance of the corporate income tax as payments made on the gross asset tax could be credited against income tax liabilities but payments exceeding these liabilities did not create a tax credit for the corporations. Finally, the tax rate on checking accounts was reduced from 0.007 percent to 0.003 percent and payments could no longer be credited towards other tax liabilities. Aside from isolated measures such as the increase in the VAT tax rate and some additional adjustments in the income tax designed to reduce existing loopholes, the fundamental reforms of the domestic tax system were in place by the end of 1992. Increasingly however, between 1992 and 1995, tax policy was selectively employed to improve the competitiveness of economic sectors facing difficulties arising from the fixed exchange rate regime. An example of these measures was the elimination of the federal stamp tax as well as the exemption of the gross asset tax for sectors that faced declining prices in international markets for their products. The latter comprised the bulk of agricultural and industrial commodities produced in the economy.

Some additional modifications to the domestic tax system were made in 1998. The first significant change was the introduction of a simplified tax regime, aimed at improving compliance of small entrepreneurs and the self-employed. Income tax, VAT and social security taxes were met through a single presumptive tax, appropriately called the *monotributo*. Payments were made monthly on the basis of four basic parameters: gross annual sales, unit prices charged for services, physical size of businesses and their energy use. While the *montributo* was a pragmatic approach to improving compliance of the informal sector of the economy, it introduced a bias against declaring economic activities above the thresholds defined for these parameters.[7] Persisting unemployment drove the need for additional tax legislation seeking to address the existing factor bias against labor and in favor of capital and was finally approved in December 1998. These measures attempted to reduce the cost of labor by reducing payroll taxes, compensating the loss of revenue by increasing the collection of VAT and corporate income taxes as well as other taxes on capital. A constraint of the reform was that it had to be revenue neutral as the fiscal imbalance and mounting debt obligations did not allow further deterioration of the government accounts. This required a political negotiation of the revenue sharing agreement as social security contributions are not shared between the central and provincial governments while VAT and income taxes are. While employer contributions to the social security system varied by geographical region and economic sector, the average rate was estimated at 10.5 percent. The goal of the policy was to reduce this in several steps to 4.5 percent starting in 1999.

Changes in VAT consisted of increases of the tax rate of some services to the full rate (21 percent) and extending the base for cable TV at a rate of 10.5 percent. A reduction of the tax rate to 10.5 percent for a basket of goods was also approved in the legislation.

Several elements of the corporate income tax were also modified. In the first place, a surcharge of two percentage points, from 33 percent to 35 percent, was applied on annual profits that exceeded US$200,000 while the tax base was extended by including cooperatives. Additional measures to deal with cross-border tax avoidance schemes of domestic and foreign corporations were also introduced. A modified version of the gross asset tax, named the presumptive minimum profits tax was introduced. The tax base and rate were similar to that of the gross assets tax but payments of the corporate income tax were now credited towards the new tax. From a conceptual point of view, the most significant change in this set of tax legislation was the introduction of a tax on paid interest. The tax base were the interest payments made on the debt owed by non-financial enterprises and the tax rate was set at 15 percent if the lender was a corporation and 35 percent if it was an individual. The tax aimed at reducing thin capitalization, the bias in favor of debt financing in a firm's capital structure that arises from the possibility of deducting interest payments in income tax assessments. Thin capitalization was believed to be a widespread vehicle for tax avoidance adopted by locally owned firms and by affiliates of foreign owned firms. While the former may act through shell companies in tax havens or through back-to-back operations with a bank, the latter typically is implemented through a loan from the parent company to the affiliate.[8]

As was mentioned earlier in this chapter, a key element of the reform of domestic taxation implemented at the beginning of the decade was the introduction of a greater degree of neutrality in the tax system, supporting the fundamental reforms that reflected the new development paradigm adopted by the country. However, the policy changes introduced in December 1998 were an attempt to offset significant distortions in relative prices that resulted from the rigid exchange rate system that was in place since 1991 and that discouraged the employment of the non-tradable factor (labor) and encouraged that of the tradable factor (capital). Ultimately, changes in tax policy were no match when Brazil devalued its currency in 1999 while Argentina held on to its currency board: economic activity declined and fiscal accounts worsened. The morale of the story is that while tax policy can improve allocation decisions, it cannot compensate for significant inconsistencies in other policies.

A new government was sworn into office in December 1999. The incoming economic authorities faced an unsustainable fiscal deficit, which had worsened as a result of the recession triggered by the said Brazil's devaluation.[9] Given the commitment of the newly elected government to maintaining the currency board, the need to jumpstart the economy was constrained by the limited access of resources to finance expansive fiscal policy. Revenue measures were introduced under an IMF supported program with the aim to raise revenue in order to reduce the imbalance of government accounts by 1.8 percent of GDP. The rationale behind fiscal tightening in this recessive scenario was that markets would reward these measures by reducing the risk premium, stimulating economic activity through the consumption and investment channels. Among the adopted tax policy measures were adjustments in the personal income tax which reduced deductions, raised tax rates and introduced an emergency surcharge. An increase in the personal wealth tax was also put in place. Changes in indirect taxation involved the introduction on new excise taxes as well as the equalization of tax rates on gasoline and some extension of the VAT base. These measures were eventually complemented by cuts in public expenditure that included reductions of salaries of government employees and of pensions in nominal terms. A new economic team took office in March 2001 and announced further expenditure cuts, resigning shortly after due to the lack of political support.

Cavallo was appointed Minister of Economy again in March 2001 as a desperate attempt to address the looming economic crisis within the framework of *convertibilidad*. A financial transactions tax was introduced in April 2001, initially at a rate of 0.25 percent while the base was the gross value of debit and credit transactions. The rate was increased to 0.4 percent a month later with the increase credited towards VAT and income tax liabilities. A third rate increase was introduced in August 2001, raising it to 0.6 percent. Exemptions and reductions in gasoline taxes and the income tax were also eliminated in August 2001, but by then the economy was in a tail-spin. In early December 2001, a run on bank deposits forced a de facto suspension of *convertibilidad*. The currency board was formally abandoned a month later as the country sank deeper into its political and economic crisis.

Although fiscal solvency remained a key challenge in early 2002 and in some areas policy reversal was contemplated and/or implemented during this period, reforms in domestic taxes, social security and trade liberalization were largely unaffected, though export taxes were introduced once again as will be seen in the section on reforms in trade taxes. Nominal collection of domestic taxes was stagnant in 2002, the result of a collapse of 10.9 percent of GDP and an inflation rate of 41 percent. The economic team that took over in May 2002 resisted attempts to introduce additional shocks to the economy, including tax policy. Income tax brackets were not adjusted for inflation and corporations were not allowed to index their depreciation allowances, although these gains in terms of tax collection were partially offset by the carryover of losses that took place during 2001 and 2002. The result was a significant increase in tax revenue, which responded to strong economic recovery summarized by an average annual growth rate of 9 percent in real GDP and 7.4 percent in inflation between 2003 and 2005.

Reforms in trade taxes

By the end of the 1980s, the main elements of Argentina's trade policy were:

1 widespread use of quantitative and administrative restrictions on imports;
2 high import tariffs;

3   a large dispersion of import tariffs;
4   export taxes on primary products;
5   drawback payments on some manufactured goods;
6   an overvalued exchange rate;
7   restrictions on purchasing currency for imports and of disposing foreign currency earnings of exports.

The poor performance of the economy during the 1980s, characterized by sluggish growth, high inflation and frequent fiscal and current account crises can undoubtedly be traced to the economy's anti-trade bias as well as to its debt overhang. Initial measures towards trade reform were taken in 1987, consisting mainly of reducing quantitative restrictions on imported goods. By July 1990, administrative restrictions on trade were lifted for the majority of goods, although some administrative and quantitative restrictions still applied to a small group of manufactured products, including steel and automobiles. Currency restrictions were increasingly relaxed.

Reform of tariff rates was introduced in 1989, when they were grouped around six tiers and dispersion between them was reduced. The maximum *ad valorem* tariff was reduced from 50 percent to 24 percent while the minimum tariff rate was increased from 0 to 10 percent. The result was a reduction of the weighted average tariff from 28 percent to 18 percent by June 1989 (IMF, RED 1990). The government maintained taxes on exports of primary products and initially extended them to manufactured goods after the massive devaluations that took place during 1989. It did this with a twofold goal: raising government revenue and mitigating regressive income distribution by moderating price increases of agricultural products, which are an important component of the consumption basket of low-income groups. Export taxes on manufactured products were eliminated in 1990 when currency markets stabilized, while those affecting primary products were reduced to 11 percent by December 1990, from a high of 27 percent a year earlier. A further simplification of the tariff structure was introduced in April 1991. A new three-tier tariff structure was introduced: raw materials and capital goods were not taxed, intermediate products were taxed at an *ad valorem* rate of 11 percent while final products were subject to a rate of 22 percent.[10] The lower rates and reduced dispersion resulted in a weighted average tariff rate of 9 percent. All remaining export taxes were eliminated with the exception of those on soybeans and sunflower seeds. Quantitative and administrative restrictions were eliminated, while quotas on automobile imports were auctioned. Furthermore, exchange rate restrictions were lifted, as they were not consistent with the country's currency board. This meant not only that exporters no longer had to surrender foreign exchange earnings to the Central Bank but that this institution gave up its role a provider of export financing and pre-financing, an activity which would be handled by private markets. The prevailing rebate arrangements were changed, reducing the rates and making all payments in cash instead of bonds.

The analysis of trade reform in Argentina would not be complete without examining MERCOSUR. On March 1991, Argentina, Brazil, Paraguay and

Uruguay signed the Treaty of Asunción, creating MERCOSUR (*Mercado Común del Sur*). The four countries signed the Ouro Preto Protocol in December 1994 creating a customs union and adopting a common external tariff AEC (*Arancel Externo Común*). Some exemptions persisted, e.g. for the automobile industry. The AEC is an eleven-tier tariff structure starting at 2 percent. Each tier increases by two percentage points and higher tariffs are associated with higher value-added products. A uniform tariff increase of three percentage points was put in effect in 1998, although countries retained flexibility in applying it. Temporary tariff increases were adopted in 2001, 2002 and 2003 in response to the economic crisis affecting the region, but by 2004 they were eliminated.

The implications of trade liberalization should not be minimized. From a resource allocation perspective, they reversed a decades old policy that has often been associated with the country's disappointing economic performance in the postwar era. The new trade regime dramatically improved governance, as quantitative restrictions and administrative controls were replaced by automatic price mechanisms that reduced the opportunity for discretion in the system. The fact that a government of a recently re-established democratic regime accomplished this should not be lost to the reader.[11] The elimination of export taxes and quantitative and administrative restrictions on imports, the reduction of the level of import tariffs and their dispersion as well as the creation of MERCOSUR resulted in a significant increase in trade during this period. Imports and exports grew at an annual rate of 7.5 percent between the early 1990s and 2005. The fiscal implications were no less important. The customs union reduced the tax base as the share of imports from MERCOSUR doubled by 2005 while the tariff rates applied to the remaining set of goods was greatly reduced, although the net effect in terms of revenue was ultimately positive due to a greater volume. Additionally, by eliminating export taxes in 1991, the government surrendered a major source of resources, equivalent to 8.4 percent of its tax revenue in 1990.

Foreign exchange restrictions and export taxes were re-established as a result of the collapse of the currency board regime in December 2001. The former was associated with the need to preserve international reserves while economic agents fled local currency as a result of a massive shift in portfolio preferences and the meltdown of the country's banking system. The latter was aimed at propping government revenue and simultaneously moderating domestic price increases. The exchange rate was floated after being pegged briefly. The float coexisted with currency restrictions affecting transactions in the current and the financial accounts of the balance of payments. These restrictions sought to accelerate the surrendering of foreign currency by exporters and extend payment periods of importers and private debt obligations and they were gradually relaxed as economic conditions improved.[12] While import tariffs were not changed, quantitative restrictions were introduced in a few sectors such as textiles and home equipment. Export taxes were set at 10 percent for primary products (agriculture and energy commodities) and 5 percent for industrial goods during March 2002. Export taxes on primary products were raised to a range of

20 percent to 23 percent and most energy products were later taxed at a shifting scale as the price of oil increased in the international market. Trade reform has proved resilient to severe changes in the economic scenario. This is the result of the structural changes of the economy, which has become more open to international competition over the past decade through MERCOSUR and exposure to other markets. The use of export taxes does not qualify this conclusion even if an export tax could be seen as a second best solution from a revenue point of view. Indeed, export taxes should be seen as a pragmatic response to the practical limitations and weaknesses of administrating income taxes in the agriculture and energy sectors as well as the dual goal of moderating the domestic price level in the context of weaker real exchange rate.

Social security reform

By the early 1990s, the main problems faced by the social security system were the inconsistency between the expected retirement benefits and the resources provided to fund them, the incentive structure embedded in the social security system, judicial rulings requiring increased benefits as well as the country's demographic trends. Legislation to reform Argentina's social security system was passed by Congress in 1993 and the new system, known as "*Sistema Integrado de Jubilaciones y Pensiones*" (SIJP) came into effect in July 1994. The new legislation reformed the pension schemes of employees of the central government, the private sector and of individuals who were self-employed.[13] Employers' contributions remained at 16 percent of wages, while employee contributions were increased by one percentage point, reaching 11 percent of wages.[14] The minimum retirement age was raised by five years to 60 years in the case of women and 65 years for men while the number of years required to contribute into the system was raised by ten years and was set at 30 years. Finally, a mixed component was introduced and workers were allowed to choose between a defined benefit government-managed pay-as-you-go (PAYG) pension scheme and a defined contribution (capitalization) scheme operated by private pension funds. The 1994 pension reform introduced a greater degree of discipline to the social security system. It clearly defined the conditions and contributions required for individuals in order to access pension benefits, reducing administrative discretion in defining the level of benefits which led to fraud, abuse and excessive litigation.[15] A complementing piece of legislation, the Pension Solidarity Law, was approved in 1995. Its aim was to limit pension expenditures and particularly those at the upper end of the scale by:

1   requiring that any future increase of pension benefits be linked to the budget instead of wage increases;
2   restricting payments of arrears based on court decisions to the amount defined in that year's budget; and
3   fixing the maximum monthly pension paid by SIJP at US$3,100.

Policymakers' initial attempts to improve the economy's competitiveness and reduce the anti-labor bias of the tax system by reducing employer contributions to the social security system began in 1994. These initiatives were fine-tuned in the following years with the aim of ensuring horizontal equity across economic sectors, although geographical disparities remained. A more comprehensive attempt, aimed at improving neutrality between labor and capital, was mentioned in the above section on reforms in domestic taxation. By 2001, policymakers reduced employee contributions from 11 percent to 5 percent in an attempt to jumpstart the economy. This was later partially reversed, raising the rate to 7 percent as economic conditions improved but increasing the rate back to 11 percent is still pending.

While it has overcome attempts of policy reversal, the social security reform faces major challenges if it is to fulfill the goals set out when it was approved 13 years ago. Any summary of these challenges should include:

1 the system's relatively low coverage, in which only 55 percent/60 percent of the workforce contributes on a regular basis;
2 future benefits of the privately managed accounts which will result from the reduced employee contributions of privately managed accounts;
3 the high cost associated with the capitalization scheme, representing around 2.5 percentage points of employee contributions;
4 the high fiscal cost of the reform;
5 the impact of the country's debt default on portfolio of private pension funds, since they were forced to acquire government debt during the period preceding the crisis;
6 improving the allocation of privately managed employee contributions, helping the development of the domestic capital market and financing the economy's investment needs.

Tax administration reform

The three entities assigned the administration of the domestic tax system, customs, and social security at the federal level are *Dirección General Impositiva* (DGI), *Dirección General de Aduanas* (DGA) and ANSES respectively. These institutions had not been immune to the fiscal constraints of the 1980s and were in need of major investment in information technology, process re-engineering and human capital formation, including managerial skills. Their performance was also hampered by the lack of data sharing among the three institutions as well as the distortion of taxpayer information caused by a decade of triple-digit inflation and the hyperinflation bouts of 1989 and 1990, which made most assessments by these entities almost meaningless. Furthermore, dealing with taxpayer non-compliance was made more difficult by the low share of transactions done through the banking system.

Taxpayer segmentation was the centerpiece of the institutional reform strategy at the DGI. This was initially focused on upgrading the collection function and by the mid-1990s information on about 350,000 taxpayers, representing close to 80 percent of domestic tax collection, was available on a daily basis. Another key element of the improvement in tax administration was the widespread use of withholding. DGI identified chains of economic activity and required the more formal elements of each chain to withhold tax liabilities from suppliers (back withholding) and clients (forward withholding). This proved to be extremely effective in terms of collection and was applied in other tax administrations in the region. Finally, the simplification of tax policy and modern information technology were the basis of improvements in the audit function, which was clearly observed in the case of VAT: non-compliance dropped from 65 percent in 1990 to under 25 percent a decade later.[16] Unfortunately these improvements were not always reflected in increased revenue as a lengthy and at times corrupt judiciary thwarted the tax administration's attempts of enforcing compliance. The increased volume and diversification of imports that resulted from trade reform guided the institutional reform process of the customs administration. Legislation was updated and processes were re-engineered in order to allow a greater selectivity of inspections. Investment in information technology became crucial as the greater volume of trade had increasing impact on domestic taxation (mainly VAT and excises), if not for tariffs and export taxes.

DGI was assigned the collection of payroll taxes in 1994, while ANSES retained the administration of benefits and claims. DGA and DGI were consolidated under a new entity called *Administración Federal de Ingresos Públicos* (AFIP) in 1996. The concentration of the collection, auditing and enforcement functions improved tax administration and were a key element in later increases of tax revenue. Challenges remain however, associated with the degree of informality in the economy, the complexity of the tax system and the shortcomings of the judiciary.

Features of Argentina's main taxes

This section describes the salient features of the main taxes collected in Argentina until December 2005. At the national level this involves the income tax, taxation of assets, the financial transactions tax, VAT, excises on a group of selected products, social security taxes, the simplified tax regime (*monotributo*) and trade taxes.[17] The two main tax assignments of the provinces, the turnover tax and property taxes (real estate and automobiles) are also included in this section.

Income tax

The income tax is a federal government tax assignment. It is paid by individuals, undivided estates, firms incorporated in Argentina and foreign beneficiaries of locally generated income. Argentina residents have to pay income tax on their world income while non-residents are only taxed domestically from their income from Argentina sources. Religious institutions, public charities and foundations

Table 6.1 Tax burden in Argentina (% of GDP)

	1990	1991	1992	1993	1994	1995	1996	1997	1998	1999	2000	2001	2002	2003	2004	2005
Income, assets, etc.	1.6	2.3	2.0	2.2	2.6	2.7	2.9	3.1	3.5	3.9	4.4	5.4	4.8	6.3	7.4	7.6
Income tax	0.5	0.6	1.1	1.8	2.3	2.5	2.5	2.9	3.2	3.3	3.8	3.5	2.5	3.6	4.7	5.3
Personal	0.0	0.0	0.3	0.6	0.7	0.8	1.0	0.9	1.0	1.1	1.4	1.4	1.1	1.3	1.4	1.5
Corporate	0.0	0.6	0.8	1.3	1.5	1.7	1.6	2.0	2.2	2.2	2.4	2.1	1.4	2.3	3.4	3.8
Personal assets tax	0.0	0.0	0.0	0.1	0.1	0.1	0.2	0.2	0.3	0.2	0.4	0.3	0.2	0.4	0.4	0.3
Presumptive min income tax	0.3	0.5	0.3	0.2	0.1	0.1	0.0	0.0	0.0	0.0	0.0	0.2	0.2	0.4	0.3	0.2
Financial transactions tax	0.3	0.9	0.3	0.0	0.0	0.0	0.0	0.0	0.0	0.0	0.0	1.1	1.6	1.6	1.7	1.8
Others	0.5	0.3	0.3	0.2	0.1	0.2	0.3	0.2	0.3	0.6	0.7	0.6	0.6	0.8	0.7	0.3
Consumption taxes	5.3	6.1	8.2	8.9	8.7	8.5	8.7	9.2	9.1	9.0	9.2	8.1	7.1	7.7	9.0	9.0
VAT	2.3	3.4	5.9	6.9	6.7	6.8	6.9	7.0	7.0	6.6	6.7	5.7	4.9	5.6	6.9	6.9
Excises int unificados	0.8	1.3	1.2	1.1	1.1	1.0	0.9	0.8	0.8	1.1	1.2	1.0	0.7	0.8	0.9	1.0
Energy	1.7	1.4	1.2	0.9	0.9	0.8	0.9	1.4	1.3	1.3	1.3	1.4	1.5	1.4	1.3	1.1
Trade taxes	1.5	0.9	1.0	1.1	1.1	0.8	0.9	1.0	1.0	0.8	0.7	0.6	2.0	3.0	3.0	3.0
Import (inc. statistics)	0.3	0.5	0.9	1.0	1.1	0.8	0.8	1.0	0.9	0.8	0.7	0.6	0.4	0.6	0.7	0.7
Export (inc. statistics)	1.1	0.3	0.0	0.0	0.0	0.0	0.0	0.0	0.0	0.0	0.0	0.0	1.6	2.5	2.3	2.3
Social security	3.7	4.3	5.0	5.6	5.4	4.7	4.0	3.8	3.7	3.5	3.4	3.2	2.8	2.8	3.0	3.1
Other	0.3	0.7	0.4	0.5	0.4	0.4	0.0	0.0	0.0	0.1	0.1	0.1	0.1	0.1	0.2	0.7
Gross collection national	12.5	14.4	16.6	18.3	18.1	17.2	16.4	17.1	17.3	17.5	17.9	17.5	16.9	20.0	22.7	23.4
Net collection national	12.5	14.3	16.5	17.9	17.7	16.7	16.1	16.9	17.1	17.3	17.7	17.3	16.5	19.6	22.3	22.4
Provincial taxes	2.3	2.6	3.3	3.7	3.8	3.6	3.6	3.7	3.9	3.9	3.8	3.6	3.4	3.8	4.0	4.1
Gross collection total	14.8	16.9	19.8	22.0	21.9	20.7	20.0	20.8	21.2	21.4	21.7	21.1	20.3	23.8	26.7	27.5
Net collection total	14.8	16.9	19.7	21.6	21.5	20.3	19.7	20.6	21.0	21.2	21.5	20.9	19.9	23.4	26.4	26.5

Source: Based on data from Ministerio de Economia y Produccion – Secretaria de Hacienda.

are the main private agents exempted from this tax. Income from public and private bonds and some other financial sources are also exempted from it.

Personal income tax

The personal income tax applies to individuals and undivided estates. Four income categories are defined: income from real estate, from capital, business income and from personal services. This allows taxpayers that do not keep accounting records to submit detailed tax returns with different types of income. The tax base is the net income of each category, after deduction of allowed expenditures. The main deductible expenditures are maintenance payments, social security payments, personal and family allowances and minimum thresholds. Current annual values for family and personal allowances are presented in Table 6.2.[18] Special deductions included in this table have been introduced in order to compensate for the degree of informality in the economy. The relatively higher tax compliance of employees and public officials vis-à-vis the self-employed explains the difference in the level of allowances.

A salient feature of the personal income tax is that these allowances are subject to a decreasing scale in response to higher net income, which is presented in Table 6.3.

Finally, specific tax rates are applied at different levels of income (Table 6.4).

The personal income tax is self-assessed. Statements are filed and payments are made through the banking system. The banking system consolidates payments and information and submits it to the tax administration. Five advance payments,

Table 6.2 Argentina's PIT: annual family and personal allowances

	US$
Threshold	1.960
Spouse	1.570
Child	785
Other exemptions	785
Special deductions for self employed	1.960
Special deduction for retirees, employees, and public officials	7.450

Table 6.3 Argentina's PIT: reduction of allowances

Taxable income		% of reduction
0	12.745	0
12.745	21.240	10
21.240	29.740	30
29.740	42.480	50
42.480	63.725	70
63.725	72.220	90
72.220	–	100

Table 6.4 Argentina's PIT: tax brackets

Taxable income			Amount due		
			Fixed amount	Plus %	Over the excess
0	–	3,270	–	9	–
3,270	–	6,535	295	14	3,270
6,535	–	9,805	750	19	6,535
9,805	–	19,610	1,370	23	9,805
19,610	–	29,410	3,630	27	19,610
29,410	–	39,215	6,275	31	29,410
39,215	–	–	9,315	35	39,215

estimated on the previous year's net income are made every two months. Tax-payers file the previous year's income tax return in April and any balances are paid in May.

Corporate income tax

The corporate income tax applies to firms registered in Argentina. The income tax law authorizes deductions of expenses associated with income generation as well as those associated with ensuring the permanence of the corporation. The law also provides a comprehensive set of rules for the treatment of expenses and specifies the items that may be deducted when estimating the tax liability. Expenses can only be deducted if invoices support them, while those made abroad are presumed to be associated with foreign income and are not deductible unless the taxpayer can prove otherwise. The usual expense categories apply and the main ones are the following:

1 *Compensation paid to employees, including social security payments.* The law caps the amount of directors' fees that may be deducted for tax purposes.
2 *Interest payments.* The law requires that: total liabilities may not exceed 250 percent of total equity and total interests must not exceed 50 percent of taxable net income computed before the deduction of interest. These limitations aim at preventing tax avoidance through thin capitalization.
3 *Depreciation.* The only depreciation rate set in legislation is that of buildings (2 percent per annum) while the deduction of automobile depreciation is limited to US$6,540 (net of VAT). The generally accepted rates are 10 percent for equipment and 20 percent for vehicles. The cost of research and development may be expensed in the same period it is incurred.
4 *Charitable contributions.* They are limited to 5 percent of taxable profits. Any excess of this amount may not be carried forward.

Losses faced by taxpayers may be offset against future income for a period of five years. Corporations are required to combine the operating profits and losses of all branches in the country. However, the Argentine branch of a non-resident corporation is treated as a separate business, requiring that the income from the national source be identified. Losses generated from transactions in corporate stock can only be offset against the same source within the next five years. The same applies to foreign source losses. The corporate income tax is self-assessed and payments and filing of statements is done through the banking system. The banking system consolidates payments and information and submits it to the tax administration. Ten monthly advance payments are made, estimated on the basis of the previous year's net income. The first payment is equivalent to 25 percent of this amount while the following nine payments are equal to 8.33 percent. The corporate tax rate is 35 percent. Shares or any other instrument supporting property rights in a corporation are nominative.

Taxation of assets

There are three main taxes on assets: the personal assets tax, the tax on presumptive minimum income and the tax on property (real estate and vehicles). The first two are central government tax assignments while the latter is assigned to the provinces.

Personal assets tax

This tax is levied on assets held by individuals or undivided estates at the end of each year. Argentina residents must pay this tax on their assets, regardless of their location while non-residents are only taxed on their assets located in Argentina. The principal assets included in the tax base are real estate, vehicles and financial assets. Argentina residents are exempted with a threshold of US$33,431. The tax rate for assets above this threshold and up to US$65,360 is 0.5 percent while a rate of 0.75 percent is applied to assets above this amount. A higher rate of 1.5 percent is applied when tax avoidance by domestic residents is presumed. Examples of these are real estate (residence, vacation home) held by a foreign corporation or financial assets held by a foreign corporation where the country of origin does not register such assets. These apply to corporations whose main line of activity is to invest funds outside their country of origin. The personal assets tax is self-assessed and payments and filing of statements is done through the banking system. The banking system consolidates payments and information and submits it to the tax administration. Five advance payments are made every other month, amounting to 20 percent of the estimation of the previous year's net income.

Presumptive minimum income tax

Firms incorporated in Argentina, trusts, investments funds, single-individual firms and civil associations and foundations not specifically exempt from it, pay this tax. Individuals and undivided estates also pay this tax on their holdings of farm property. The main assets exempted are those located in Tierra del Fuego, used in mining activities as well as those belonging to taxpayers registered under the simplified tax regime for small taxpayers. The tax base is the value of all assets held at the end of each fiscal year. There is a tax holiday for assets that may be amortized during the first two years they were acquired, with the exemption of automobiles. Banks and insurance companies will assess as their tax base 20 percent of their assets liable for this tax. The equivalent percentage for traders of agricultural primary products will be 40 percent. There is an exemption for the first US$65,360 in assets held by a taxpayer. Taxpayers may credit payment made to foreign tax authorities on similar taxes of assets located abroad. The tax rate is 1 percent. The presumptive minimum income tax is self-assessed and payments and filing of statements is done through the banking system. The banking system consolidates payments and information and submits it to the tax administration. Eleven monthly advance payments are made, amounting to 9 percent of the estimation of the previous year's net income. Payments made on this tax are credited to income tax liabilities. Payments made on the income tax and on the financial transactions tax may be credited towards payments made to the presumptive minimum income tax.

Tax on property

Taxation of real estate and motor vehicles are an assignment of provincial governments. Each of the 23 provinces, and the city of Buenos Aires, has the autonomy to assess property values and tax rates, which explains the dispersion of the contribution of this tax to government revenue. Given the large number of jurisdictions, this analysis of real estate taxes in Argentina is based on the province of Buenos Aires. Property is classified as urban and rural. As in most places, this tax is predetermined by the tax administration (i.e. it is not self-assessed). The assessment of urban property disaggregates between the price of land and any construction built on it. Public and private entities participate in the assessment of the land prices, which is updated periodically. An estimation of the construction cost of a building is made on the basis on its records (i.e. construction permit, physical inspections, etc.), adjusted by an amortization allowance. The resulting tax-base will fall in one of the 13 tax brackets that were defined for the current year. The tax is the sum of a fixed amount of any bracket and a variable item that is estimated as a percentage of the difference between the assessed value and the lower range of any bracket. The tax rate only exceeds 1 percent in the higher brackets, but the effective rate is usually lower as property assessments do not keep up to market values.

Financial transactions tax

The basis of this tax is the gross value of debit and credit bank transactions. While some transactions are exempt, the basis of the tax is fairly comprehensive. The main exemptions are credits on salaries and pension payments as well as debits up to a similar amount to the same beneficiaries, clearing mechanisms by the financial system, accounts of promoted economic activities (mining, forestry, alternative energy), accounts of religious groups. The tax rate is 0.6 percent per transaction. Reduced rates are charged for traders of agricultural primary products, operators of payment systems (credit cards, food coupons, etc.). Payments made on this tax are credited to income and presumptive minimum income tax liabilities.

Value added tax (VAT)

Argentina's VAT follows the destination principle, in which the tax is imposed on the value added of domestically consumed goods and services. The tax base of domestic transactions is the net price, including associated services provided jointly with it. A tax credit is originated by each purchase made. The VAT is self-assessed on a monthly basis, with payments made through the banking system within the month following the filing of the tax liabilities. The tax basis of imports is the price declared in the customs invoice, which must include any import tariff levied in the good or service. VAT on imports is paid jointly with import taxes before the goods or services leave customs. The tax covers the sale of most goods and services, as some exemptions exist. The main exempt goods are, at the consumption stage, books and other published material, bread, milk and mineral water. Medicines are taxed at the production or import stage, whichever the case may be. Airplanes are also exempted. The main VAT exemptions on the service side are educational services, health services supplied by non-profits, international transport services of goods and individuals and monthly rents below US$490.

A general tax rate of 21 percent is defined for the majority of goods and services. However, the main public utilities (electricity, natural gas, water and sanitation, telecommunications) are taxed at a rate of 27 percent. Similarly, a lower rate of 10.5 percent is applied on primary agriculture production, agrochemical products, domestic transport services of individuals, home repair, newspaper, magazines and other published material, services provided by registered worker cooperatives. The tax rate of exports is 0 percent, giving rise to a refund of accumulated tax credits. Tourists receive a rebate for purchases above US$23.

Table 6.5 Summary of VAT rates in Argentina (%)

	Rate
General rate	21
Higher rate: public utilities: electricity, natural gas, water and sanitation, telecommunications	27
Reduced rate: primary agriculture production, agrochemical products, domestic transport services of individuals, home repair services, newspapers and other published goods, services provided by registered workers cooperatives	10.5
Zero rate: exports	0

While the VAT is structured as a tax on consumption, a special feature of VAT in Argentina is the rebate introduced in favor of consumers when purchases have been made by debit and credit cards. This feature was introduced in order to mitigate the regressive impact of consumption taxes on low-income individuals while at the same time improving tax-compliance by requiring electronic transactions. Eligible expenditures are capped at US$330 per month and the refund is 2.12 percent on the purchase of fuel and 4.13 percent on the purchase of other goods and services when the transaction is made using a debit card. The equivalent rates for credit cards are 1.27 percent and 2.48 percent. The amounts credited to cardholders are netted of the VAT, income tax, and presumptive minimum income tax liabilities of card issuers.

Excise taxes

This tax is levied in a single stage for a limited number of goods and services. As the destination principle is followed, it is applied at the level of the manufacturer or importer. The taxable products are tobacco, alcoholic beverages, soft drinks, motor vehicles and parts, recreation watercraft and aircraft, certain electronic appliances and fuel. Certain insurance activity and cellular telephone services are also taxed.

Excises on goods

The tax base of most excises is the sale price, net of discounts, VAT and other financial costs. The cigarette tax base is the price paid by the consumer. In the case of imports, the tax base will be 130 percent of the amount resulting from the addition of the price of the good, import tariff and any other tax with the

Table 6.6 Excise rates in Argentina (%)

Product	Rate
Tobacco	
Cigarettes	60
Cigars	16
Tobacco consumed as leaves	20
Alcoholic beverages	
Whiskey, cognac, brandy, pisco, gin, rum, etc.	20
Beer	8
Soft drinks and mineral waters	4 to 8
Luxury articles	20
Automobiles, motorcycles, recreational boats and airplanes	
Sales price higher than $4,900 and up to $7,190	4
Sales price higher than $7,190	8
Electronic devices	17

exception of VAT. This generates a tax credit for the importer that is netted against other taxes when the good is sold in the domestic market.

Excises on services

Excises are levied on insurance activity and cellular telephone services. The insurance premiums are the tax base of insurance services, net of VAT payments. Agricultural, life, personal accidents and surgery and maternity insurance are exempt. The tax rates applied are 2.5 percent for work-related injury insurance, 8.5 percent for general risk insurance and 23 percent for a general risk insurance policy that is issued by a company that is not authorized to operate in Argentina. In the latter case, the individual contracting the insurance is responsible for paying the tax at the time the premiums are payable. Excises on cellular telephones services are levied on final users at a rate of 4 percent. Exemptions include international roaming fees, connection fees to other networks as well as other value-added services.

Excises on fuels

The sale of fuel is taxed in Argentina. The tax base is the sale price, net of discounts, VAT, other excises and financial costs. Tariffs are added for imported fuel. In the case of compressed natural gas, the tax base is the price faced by consumers. Although fuels are taxed at an individual *ad valorem* rate, law specifies a minimum amount to be paid per unit of fuel.

There are additional taxes levied on fuel consumption. The most important ones are:

1   A surcharge of 20.2 percent on gas-oil and liquefied gas for car use. This surcharge is implemented at a single phase and exports of these products are exempt (Law 26.028).

Table 6.7 Excise rates on fuels in Argentina

Product	Rate (%)	Minimum amount – dollars per litre
Gasoline		
Unleaded – up to 92 octane rating	70	0.18
Unleaded – more than 92 octane rating	62	0.18
Leaded – up to 92 octane rating	70	0.18
Leaded – more than 92 octane rating	62	0.18
Virgin	62	0.18
Turpentine/solvent	62	0.18
Gas-oil/diesel-oil/kerosene	19	0.05
Compressed natural gas	16	–

2   A surcharge of US$0.02 per liter of gasoline and per liter of natural gas used for cars. These resources are earmarked for investment projects in the transportation and water sector as well as recovery of land affected by floods (Decree 1381/01).
3   A surcharge of 7.5 percent of the price of natural gas at the point of entry of the transportation system. These resources are earmarked to consumers of gas and liquefied petroleum gas in the provinces that are producers of these products (Law 25.565).
4   A surcharge of US$0.001 per kWh. This tax is structured as a single phase, imposed at the wholesale level (Law 15.536 and its modifications).

Gross turnover tax

The gross turnover tax is a provincial tax assignment, generating approximately two-thirds of the tax revenue collected by the provinces. The cascading effect that results from its multi-phase design imposes a bias against exports and in favor of imports as the latter are taxed only when the goods arrive at customs while the former are taxed during each phase. Another undesirable effect of this tax is that it introduces an incentive towards vertical integration in order to avoid the tax. Each province sets the tax rate, which differs by economic activity. The rate on primary production and manufacturing has been set at zero if these activities take place in the province that is setting the rate. This percentage rises to 1 percent/1.5 percent if the goods are sold in a different province. There is a wide dispersion of tax rates between sectors and between provinces within a sector. The average tax rate for construction activity is set at 2.3 percent, with a low of 0 percent and a high of 3.7 percent. Something similar occurs in the financial sector, where most rates are set within a range of 4.1 percent/5 percent but some provinces charge up to 8.5 percent.[19]

Social security taxes

Although the national social security system covers employees, self-employed individuals and domestic help, due to brevity concerns only the first one of these will be covered in this section.

MOPRE (*Módulo Previsional* or retirement module) is the unit employed to define the payment adjustments of the PAYG regime, the amount of the presumed income of the self-employed and the maximum income level subject to social security taxes. The value of MOPRE when this chapter was written was set at US$26. The minimum income on which social security taxes must be paid is set at a multiple of three of the value of MOPRE, or US$78. At the other end of the income scale, incomes are capped at 60 times the value of MOPRE, or US$1,570. Employees and employers must make five different contributions to the social security system: the integrated retirees and pensioners system; the healthcare system of retirees and pensioners; the family subsidy regime; the national employment fund; and contributions to health services. The employer

Table 6.8 Social security system tax rates in Argentina

Concept	Employee PAYG (%)	Employee capitalization (%)	Employer (%)
1 Retirement	11	7[1]	
2 Retirees health services (INSSJP)	3	3	
3 Family subsidy regime	–	–	
4 National employment fund	–	–	
Subtotal (1 + 2 + 3 + 4)	*14*	*10*	*17 or 21[2]*
5 Health benefits	3	3	6
Total	*17*	*13*	*23 or 27*

Notes
1 Employee contributions were set at 11 percent when the social security reform was implemented in 1994. This rate was reduced to 5 percent in 2001 in an attempt to jumpstart the economy by increasing disposable income. The rate was set at 7 percent as economic conditions improved in 2003, and a timeline has been adopted for raising the rate to 9 percent in October 2006 and to 11 percent in 2007.
2 A rate of 17 percent has been set for small and medium enterprises, government entities as well as some other non-profit organizations. The remaining employers are taxed at a rate of 21 percent.

withholds the employee's tax liabilities and makes payments on a monthly basis. Payments are made to AFIP, which then distributes the proceeds to the different public institutions as well as to the privately managed pension funds in the case of employees that have opted for this system. The cumulative rates, once employee and employer contributions to all components of the system are taken into account, are in the range of 36 percent to 44 percent.

Two additional features of employer contributions must be highlighted. In the first place, employers have to contract insurance for employment-related activities. Insurance premiums are set by private parties and they depend on the employers' line of economic activity as well as their safety measures. The second feature is that, subject to geographical considerations that favor less developed regions of the country, employers may credit part of their share of social security contributions towards their VAT liabilities.

Simplified tax regime – monotributo

The simplified tax regime covers VAT, income and social security taxes for small taxpayers. Small taxpayers are defined as individuals that sell goods, works and services, members of registered workers cooperatives, undivided estates and partnerships of up to three members as long as their economic activities do not exceed certain financial and physical parameters. Physical parameters are used as a proxy for taxpayer income. Importers of goods and services are excluded from this regime. The main financial parameters to qualify under the simplified tax regime are the following:

1   gross sales of services and or rentals shall not exceed US$23,530 per fiscal year;

2 gross sales of any remaining economic activity shall not exceed US$47,060 per fiscal year;

3 the maximum unit sale price shall not exceed US$285.

The tax liability is determined by taking gross revenue and the physical parameters into account, with a scale ranging from US$11 to US$70 per month for rentals and providers of services and US$11 to US$165 for the remaining economic activities. The main contribution of the *monotributo* is that it allows AFIP to focus on taxpayers of greater revenue generating potential while providing the rest of them with an opportunity for formalizing their economic activities.

Trade taxes

Argentina applies taxes on imports and on exports. Import tariffs for most goods are applied on an *ad valorem* basis, which range from 0 to 20 percent. An exception is the automobile sector, which faces a maximum rate of 35 percent, as well as some sectors (e.g. textiles) where specific tariffs are applied. Export taxes were introduced in 2002. Exports of goods are taxed at rates that vary in a range of 5 percent to 25 percent, with an inverse relationship between the export tax and the value added of the good.

1 Oil is taxed at 25 percent. An additional surcharge was introduced in August 2004, which triggers when the price of the barrel of West Texas Intermediate (WTI) exceeds US$32. The surcharge follows the schedule in Table 6.9.

2 Gasoline is taxed at a rate of 5 percent, propane and butane at a rate of 20 percent.

3 Grains, edible oil and pellets are taxed at percent. Soybeans and sunflower seeds at 23.5 percent.

4 Meats are taxed at a rate of 15 percent.

5 Products classified as regional production (fruits, vegetables, rice, honey, etc.) are taxed at a rate of 10 percent.

6 Cheese is taxed at 10 percent and the rest of dairy products at a rate of 15 percent

Table 6.9 Surcharges in oil taxation in Argentina

Price range of WTI – US$ per barrel	Surcharge (%)
32.01 to 34.99	3
35.00 to 36.99	6
37.00 to 38.99	9
39.00 to 40.99	12
41.00 to 42.99	15
43.00 to 44.99	18
45.00 and higher	20

7   The remaining products (i.e. manufactured goods) are taxed at a rate of 5 percent.

Some ideas for a reform agenda of Argentina's tax system

This section explores ideas for a reform agenda of Argentina's tax system. Several elements of this reform agenda should be highlighted. In the first place, fiscal solvency should not be undermined by any "improvement" in the tax system. The reason is all too evident since until recently policymakers' neglect of fiscal solvency has led to macroeconomic instability and unsustainable debt accumulation that ended in economic collapse and debt default. A second element is that policymakers should not be dazzled by taxes that may be analytically superior but that ultimately can't be collected by the tax administration. Tax policy should internalize the degree of informality under which different sectors of the economy operate and adopt pragmatic responses to this environment. A third element of a possible reform agenda is that tax policy should include automatic and transparent incentives to promote growth. Devolution of tax assignments to lower levels of governments is a fourth element of this agenda. However, devolution must acknowledge the relatively weak institutional capacity of provincial tax administrations vis-à-vis AFIP as well as the difficulties of decentralizing the administration of taxes that have a movable tax base. Finally, even though a goal of a more equal income distribution is probably better served through targeted expenditure policy, there is a scope for improving the design of the tax system while at the same time contributing to greater equity.[20]

Devolution

The goal of increasing provincial tax assignments faces several constraints. In the first place, the federal government's fiscal balance must not deteriorate.[21] A second concern is that provincial governments must exploit their tax assignments, avoiding the politically less costly alternative of not taxing their constituencies and demanding federal funds through tax-sharing mechanisms instead. Additional elements are the relative institutional weaknesses of provincial tax administrations vis-à-vis AFIP as well as the relative ease of centrally administrating taxes with a movable tax base. Some tax reform ideas that would support the goal of devolution are the following.

Personal income tax

A surcharge on the federal government's tax rate could be introduced. Congress would authorize a range for this surcharge, between 0 and 5 percent, and each provincial government would set the tax-rate it would apply within the authorized range, simply *piggy-backing* on the federal government's schedule as is done in the US. The tax would continue to be administered by

AFIP, overcoming the issues of institutional weaknesses and movable tax base previously mentioned.

Personal assets tax

AFIP's role in administrating this tax derives from the bfact that individuals frequently have assets in more than one province, and occasionally in more than one country, as well as to the need to check the consistency of asset and income tax data. However, due to the relatively low level of the country's financial depth, a large share of an individual's wealth is held in real estate. Increasing the accuracy of real estate assessments would greatly improve the revenue collected by this tax and that is a task of provincial governments. A similar rationale applies to other real property (e.g. vehicles, boats, etc.). A possible incentive to improve the productivity of this tax would be to replace the revenue sharing formula currently employed by devolving taxation of real property held by individuals to the provinces and preserving the taxation of financial assets and assets held abroad at the national level.

Export taxes on agricultural production

Under the current tax assignments, the federal government levies export taxes while the each province collects the rural property tax and neither tax is shared. The export tax on agricultural products could partially be replaced by an increase in the rural property tax, although a revenue neutral outcome would require reducing the amount of tax revenue shared between the federal and provincial governments from other sources. Under this alternative, the federal government would compensate the loss in revenue by reducing the amount of tax revenue it transfers to the provinces that concentrate agriculture production (e.g. Buenos Aires, Córdoba, Entre Ríos, La Pampa and Santa Fe). This group of provinces would offset the loss of shared tax revenue by increasing rural property taxes. This arrangement has the potential of significantly increasing tax revenue for these provinces, as the collection of the rural property tax is poorly implemented in Argentina.[22] In addition to the benefits deriving from devolution and the possible increase in revenue, replacing export taxes with rural property taxes would have the advantage of reducing the welfare losses at the production and consumption level associated with the export tax. This should increase agricultural production and the volume of exports in response to the higher output and reduced consumption. Additionally, replacing a portion of the export tax with the rural property tax would help isolate government revenue from the cyclical behavior of commodity prices, reducing volatility in fiscal accounts. There are two main costs to be paid if this proposal would be implemented. In the first place, export taxes are not expensive or technically challenging to administer vis-à-vis property taxes. The second consideration refers to the regressive impact on low salaries of a higher price level in food products, as it would reduce the wedge between domestic and international prices of food commodities.

Incentives to promote investment and growth

Several investment incentives have been in place in Argentina's tax system for some time, implemented around the corporate income tax and the VAT.[23] More recently, legislation was passed in 2004 creating limited investment incentives, consisting of accelerated depreciation allowances to be deducted in the corporate income tax as well as immediate devolution of VAT credits in new projects. While care should be taken in order to avoid an undesirable erosion of tax-bases, the tax system could benefit from explicit rules in terms of a stable regime of saving and investment incentives. A set of possible ideas would be the following.

Personal income tax.

An amount of an individual's yearly income could be deferred from the personal income tax if it were invested for a minimum amount of time in the purchase of financial assets through the formal financial sector. These funds would be channeled through individual saving accounts that would be managed by the financial sector. The latter would withhold tax liabilities when assets were sold.

Corporate income tax.

Two sets of incentives could be introduced. The first one consists of rules allowing accelerated depreciation to be deducted from income tax liability as well as immediate devolution of VAT credits in new projects. The second one consists of reducing the tax rate on retained income to 25 percent and taxing distributed income at 10 percent. This creates an incentive to build equity in firms, especially benefiting small and medium enterprises that usually finance their expansion through retained earnings as they have less access to credit. Establishing an implementation period during which this rule would be phased in could mitigate short-term concerns regarding the fiscal impact of the erosion of the tax base.

Increasing VAT productivity and equity measures

A direct consequence of Argentina's very disappointing economic performance over the past three decades has been increased poverty and worsened income distribution. While the country's tax system cannot be blamed for this outcome, it has not contributed to reverting it either. Some measures could be introduced in the tax system to alleviate poverty and target inequality in income distribution, even though the main results in this field will come from better jobs and targeted expenditure policy promoting human capital formation, water and sanitation, housing and security.

Value Added Tax

A brief description of goods and services exempted from VAT were presented in the above section on VAT. The overriding argument that is used when exempting goods and services is the need to avoid the negative distributional impact of including them in the tax basis. The problem with this rationale is that exemptions benefit all consumers and not only low-income groups. An alternative would be to follow a targeted approach that would extend the tax base in order to include the greatest possible universe of goods and services and at the same time introduce refunds to low-income groups. Extending the tax-base would improve tax administration, which would be reflected in the improvement of VAT's productivity, currently around 0.37 in Argentina. Individuals receiving the two lowest deciles of income would receive refunds for their increased VAT payments, which would be credited electronically to a debit or credit card. The amount of refunds would be capped at 10 percent of the income of the two lowest deciles. This program would build on the existing system of tax rebates implemented by AFIP described in the above section on VAT as well as on the government's program of conditional cash transfers to low-income individuals. A reduction of the VAT general rate could be analyzed if net tax revenue (i.e. after transfers to low income individuals) increases above certain levels.

Personal income tax

As proposed by Barreix and Roca (2006), the income from financial assets should be included in the tax base of the personal income tax. The tax rate should be in the range of 10 percent, although a lower rate of 5 percent could be applied in peso denominated assets in order to discourage dollarization.

Social security system

The social security system faces challenges on several fronts. Although over the past four years only the lowest pensions have been increased, Supreme Court rulings require extending these increases to the rest of the beneficiaries, which will erode the fiscal surplus. A second concern is in regard to the benefits of future retirees affiliated with the privately administered pension funds, as they are contributing at a lower rate than the one required by the system. The high cost associated with the management of individual accounts is also an issue of concern and will require a review of insurance premiums paid as well as the commercial activities employed by the industry in capturing clients. Additionally, pension reform has contributed very little towards capital market development, a claim made by early supporters of the reform. Finally, initiatives are required to address the issue that less then half of employed workers are making retirement contributions. Some ideas that would contribute to solving the problems that were identified previously are as follows.

Employee contributions

The current contribution rate of 7 percent should be increased over time to 11 percent as originally envisioned to ensure funding of future pensions.

Employer contributions

Rates paid by employers could be reduced from the current 17 percent/21 percent by three to five percentage points. A minimum threshold could be introduced, partially financed by raising the current ceiling that caps contributions on salaries at US$1,570 per month. The rationale is to encourage the formalization of low-income individuals, as they accumulate fewer assets towards their retirement.

Coverage

Measures mentioned regarding employer contributions should be complemented by administration efforts to ensure formalization of employment relations. Non-contributory pensions should target individuals that have not been employed in the formal sector at their retirement age.

Cost of the privately managed system

Pooling disability and life risks will reduce the dispersion in insurance costs for individuals contributing to the privately managed system. Additionally, competition would be enhanced with the introduction of standardized retirement accounts, investing in bank deposits, government bonds and AAA private securities that would serve as an alternative vehicle to privately managed pension funds.

Role of pension funds

Pension funds should play a more pro-active role in channeling pension saving towards meeting the economy's investment needs, avoiding the excessive concentration of government securities in their portfolios. This requires building the institutional capacity as well as the legal framework that would enable investments in, e.g. trust funds financing infrastructure, industry or mortgage based securities.

Transactions with "tax havens"

To a large degree, the success of a tax administration in enforcing tax legislation depends on the possibility of analyzing the consistency of information provided by taxpayers with other sources of data. While domestic data is usually not a major issue, some countries do not share information, encouraging individuals or corporations to set up tax avoidance schemes in them. An example of this is provided by agribusiness exports: according to AFIP (2006), 83 percent of the US$3 billion dollars exported by Argentina in 2005 of edible oil and grease is done through countries that will not provide tax information. The presumptive elements of the tax system should be re-enforced, penalizing transactions with those tax jurisdictions that refuse to share taxpayer information. Penalties would range from imposing steep surcharges on existing rates on these transactions to deny authorization of operating in Argentina. While Argentina's tax legislation already applies surcharges (e.g. section on personal assets tax), a greater rate is required to effectively discourage these transactions.

Notes

1 I want to acknowledge the discussions on fiscal issues maintained over the years with A. Barreix as well as his insightful comments to this chapter. I have also benefited with discussions with and/or comments from R. Carciofi, J. Roca, R. Ruiz del Castillo, E. Díaz Bonilla, M. Brusa and A. Marenzi. M. V. Cabo was invaluable in collecting information and assisting with the formatting of this document. Of course any mistakes in it are my own. Finally, all opinions expressed in this document are of my sole responsibility.
2 Additionally, the widespread use of indexation mechanisms made changes in relative prices costlier in terms of inflation and/or economic activity, reducing the effectiveness of exchange rate adjustments in order to increase the relative price of tradables vis-à-vis non-tradables.
3 The Convertibility Law was abandoned on January 2002. This only formalized the end of currency board, which had effectively collapsed by early December, 2001, when the "Corralito" was introduced. Measures were implemented between March and December of 2001 with the aim of introducing flexibility in the monetary regime to jumpstart the economy, which was by that time in a period of severe depression, and avoid default in Argentina's sovereign debt. For a description of Argentina's collapse see Mussa (2002) and Blustein (2005).
4 Consensus emerged in Argentina after default regarding the need to avoid the debt orgy of the 1990s, when debt grew from $55.1 billion to $144.3 billion between 1990 and 2001. After economic collapse in early 2002, Argentina's government initially requested significant net resources from an IMF led support program. However, by mid-2002, a new economic team indicated that it would not attempt to access net resources but rather requested a program designed to roll-over multilateral debt as it matured. The principal reason for this change was the profound discrepancy between Argentina's policymakers and the IMF regarding policies to be adopted by the country. This was consistent with the shifting paradigm regarding multilateral support programs that the new US Administration had been promoting since 2001. The result was that Argentina was the only major economy at the time that faced an economic crisis without multilateral assistance, making net payments to the IMF, World Bank and Inter-American Development Bank of $26.5 billion between January 2002 and April 2006.
5 Some provincial governments also receive royalties from mining and oil and gas operations. The main source of municipal revenue is a user fee that is very similar to a real estate tax. Neither royalties nor municipal revenue will be analyzed in this chapter.
6 This arrangement originated in the Constitution adopted by Argentina in the nineteenth century, which assigned taxes on trade to the federal government while consumption taxes were to be shared by the federal and provincial governments. A revenue sharing scheme was adopted between the national and provincial governments, as expenditure decisions were increasingly decentralized. Basically four taxes were assigned at the provincial level in 1990: on real estate, on vehicles, a gross sales tax and a stamp tax. The first two are predetermined by the tax administration while the latter two are self-assessed by the taxpayer.

7 This problem is referred to as *enanismo fiscal* (fiscal pigmies) in Argentina.

8 Greater tax neutrality regarding the capital structure of firms benefit smaller sized companies as they have less access to credit than larger corporations. See FIEL (2006).

9 The federal government's fiscal deficit was $7.1 billion dollars in 1999. This amount rises to around $11 billion dollars if one-time proceeds from privatization are added, representing 3.9 percent of GDP.

10 Resolution 1239/92 modified the tariff structure without affecting the essence of the policy reform. Imports of automobiles were subjected to a special regime.

11 See Rodrik (2002).

12 The government introduced restrictions on the *inflow* of capital as domestic economic conditions improved and liquidity increased in international markets. The aim was to reduce volatility in the exchange rate, which in the short run would impact through currency appreciation.

13 Other pension systems, e.g. provincial government employees, security forces, and professional groups were not part of the reform. Provincial governments were allowed to transfer their social security systems to the SIJP.

14 Additional payroll taxes amounting to 22 percent of wages were not affected by the reform. They were earmarked for retiree health insurance (5 percent), employee health insurance (9 percent), family allowances (7.5 percent) and a National Employment Fund (1.5 percent).

15 The non-contributory component of the pension system PNC (*pensiones no contributivas*) was not part of the SIJP. PNC is made up of seven programs that target specific groups:

1   old age individuals who have not contributed to the system;
2   handicapped individuals;
3   mothers of seven or more children;
4   relatives of individuals who were victims of state terrorism (*desaparecidos*);
5   veterans of the Malvinas War;
6   assigned by specific laws;
7   assigned by Congress (*graciables*).

16 Non-compliance in 2005 was estimated at 23.3 percent by the tax administration. See AFIP (2006) for an explanation of the methodology employed.

17 The main source of this section is *Ministerio de Economía y Producción* (2005), available at www.mecon.gov.ar. A feature that will not be presented in this text is the earmarking of tax revenue for specific destinations. The interested reader should consult *Ministerio de Economía y Producción* (2006).

18 All values in this section will be expressed in US dollars and will be rounded. The exchange rate used throughout this section is 3.06 argentine pesos per one US dollar.

19 For a table of tax rates see FIEL (2006).

20 An additional element of the reform agenda is the introduction of environmental taxes, which should be increasingly employed in a post-Kyoto framework to curb carbon emissions.

21 After decades of deficits, the federal and provincial government showed significant surpluses between 2003 and 2005. While still high the fiscal surplus is threatened by demands for increases in public employee wages and pensions in the PAYG segment as well as by public investment requirements.

22 Using 2005 data, we can estimate that a reduction of a percentage point in the export tax rate of cereals, grains and edible oils requires an increase of US$1.63 per hectare per year in the rural property tax of the five provinces mentioned above in order to obtain a revenue neutral yield. This estimation is on the high side as it ignores second order effects: the positive supply response of higher prices of these products as well

as a reduced consumption, both of which will result in increases of exported volumes and hence increases in export tax revenue.

23 For an analysis of these incentives see González Cano (2005).

References

AFIP (2006) "Recaudación de Recursos Tributarios," Buenos Aires: Administración Federal de Ingresos Públicos.

Barreix, A. and Roca, J. (2006) "Arquitectura de la Reforma Tributaria 2005," Montevideo: Universidad Catolica del Uruguay.

Blustein, P. (2005) "And the Money Kept Rolling In (and Out): Wall Street, the IMF and the Bankrupting of Argentina," *Public Affairs*, New York.

FIEL (2006) *Presion tributaria sobre el sector formal de la economía*, Buenos Aires.

González Cano, H. (2005) "Análisis de la armonización tributaria en el MERCOSUR desde la situación y perspectiva de Argentina," in Tanzi, V., Barreix, A. and Vilela, L. (eds) *Tributación para la integración del MERCOSUR*, Washington, DC: Departamento de Integración y Programas Regionales, Banco Inter-Americano de Desarrollo.

International Monetary Fund (IMF) Several Publications dated between 1989 and 2004 (Recent Economic Developments – RED, Article IV Consultation, Program Reviews), Washington, DC: IMF.

Ministerio de Economía y Producción (2005) "Tributos vigentes en la Republica Argentina a Nivel Nacional – Actualizado al 31 de diciembre de 2005," Buenos Aires: Dirección Nacional de Investigaciones y Análisis Fiscal, Subsecretaria de Ingresos Públicos, Secretaria de Hacienda.

—— (2006) "Destino de la Recaudación de los Impuestos al 31 de marzo de 2006," Buenos Aires: Dirección Nacional de Investigaciones y Análisis Fiscal, Subsecretaria de Ingresos Públicos, Secretaria de Hacienda.

Mussa, M. (2002) "Argentina and the Fund: From Triumph to Tragedy," Washington, DC: Institute for International Economics.

Rodrik, D. (2002) "The Rush to Free Trade in the Developing World: Why so Late? Why Now? Will it Last?," Cambridge, MA: NBER Working Paper n. 3947.

Sturzzeneger, F. (2006) "Justificando una estructura impositiva 'distorsiva'," *Indicadores de Coyuntura* n. 464, Buenos Aires: Fundación de Investigaciones Económicas Latinoamericanas (FIEL).

7   Brazil

José Roberto Afonso and Rafael Barroso

Introduction[1]

Brazil is Latin America's largest nation in demographic, economic and geographical terms, and boasts the world's tenth largest gross domestic product – GDP (US$796 billion), the fifth largest population (184.2 million) and the fifth largest land area. The Brazilian economy experienced profound structural changes throughout the last century and the nation became urbanized at a very rapid rate. Following a long period of stagnation during much of the nineteenth century, the Brazilian economy registered the fastest pace of growth of any country in the world in the period between the 1870s and the 1970s. In the last 25 years however, this rate of economic growth, which had been especially robust following World War II, has suffered a strong downturn. Between 1951 and 1980, a period encompassing the so-called Brazilian Miracle, the average annual rate of growth was of 7.3 percent, whilst in the period that followed (1981–2005) this pace dropped back to just 2.5 percent. As a result, the country's per capita income is ranked 86 (US$7,450)[2] and 22.8 percent of the population still lives below the poverty line.[3] An even more worrying aspect of this situation is the high degree of income concentration: the Gini Index for Brazil was at 0.568 in 2005, placing the country amongst the world's most unequal under this gauge. The present federative structure is composed of three tiers: the central tier, referred to as the Union, is better known as the federal government; the intermediate tier is made up of 26 states plus the Federal District; and the local tier is made up of 5,564 municipalities. The institutional framework existing today was imposed by the Federal Constitution of 1988, which resulted in a sharp decentralization, that was not only political but also administrative and fiscal.

The tax system is made up of taxes, fees and contributions. The latter have specific characteristics in Brazil as they are not exclusively levied on payrolls. The 1988 Constitution diversified their sources, which resulted in social contributions also being levied on the revenues and profits of employers as well as on lotteries, government revenues and licensing, among others. The two most relevant social contributions are called PIS/PASEP and COFINS and are levied on any type of revenue earned by the firms. These two contributions are discussed in more detail below. Today, these different contributions already account for half the total Brazilian tax burden (19.5 percent of GDP in 2005, or over one percentage point more than was raised through traditional taxes), thanks to strong expansion since the last reform. This has basically been due to the fact that central government has taken on exclusivity in levying contributions, that is, it does not have to share them with sub-national governments, as in the case of taxes on similar bases.

The tax burden went through an expansionist phase in the postwar period, which accelerated towards the end of the last decade (see Table 7.1). The bases of the present tax system were defined in the mid-1960s. From that time until 1993, the total tax burden averaged around the equivalent of 25 percent of GDP, which was already a high level compared with many other emerging economies, and especially those in Asia. The stabilization of the economy in 1994 resulted in two expansionist cycles. First, the Real (R$) took the tax burden to 29 percent of GDP levels,[4] which in reality was already the prevailing rate but which had been somewhat hidden until then by the so-called Tanzi effect.[5] Either way, had the burden stayed at that level then Brazil would be on a par with other emerging market economies today. The second cycle came in the wake of the serious external crisis of 1998, when the country began an impressive and steady process of expansion of the total tax burden that continued, even after the change of government in 2003 and the resulting crisis of confidence had dissipated.

As a consequence, by far the most striking characteristic of the Brazilian tax system today is the size of its total burden: 39 percent of GDP. This percentage exceeds, and considerably, the average of emerging market economies[6] and is a serious hindrance to the competitiveness of Brazilian goods. Worse than the burden's size, is its structure that is concentrated on indirect taxes: more than half of the total tax revenue comes from different forms of taxing the domestic market of goods and services, with many of these taxes being of a cumulative nature. This places a burden directly on capital goods (and helps increase the cost of fixed investment, whose participation in national accounts is very low), and indirectly on exports (even in the case of value added type taxes, it is not easy to recover accumulated tax credit balances). The most perverse side of this system can be seen in the distribution of the tax burden amongst households, where the poorest families pay proportionally more tax relative to their household income than the richest families – and this in a country that is already marked by a high level of poverty and social inequality.

Despite these distortions, all the initiatives undertaken to try to reform the tax system have failed and indeed there has been no lack of such projects in recent years. Some have argued for a radical change (such as the popular creation of a single tax), whilst others have suggested specific changes to be implemented on a gradual basis, with some of these changes proposed by federal government bills (in principle, with greater parliamentary backing), but the majority put forward by individual congressmen (more sensitive to the demands of sub-national governments and taxpayers). As the definition of tax responsibilities is

Table 7.1 Total tax burden composition evolution in Brazil: 1980–2005 (% of GDP)

Tax/year	1980	1985	1990	1995	2000	2001	2002	2003	2004	2005
Total	24.52	24.06	28.78	29.41	33.36	35.12	36.63	35.85	37.03	38.94
International trade	0.70	0.40	0.39	0.76	0.77	0.76	0.59	0.52	0.52	0.46
Goods and services	9.98	10.06	14.06	13.73	15.63	16.37	16.16	15.81	16.85	17.25
General Tax ICMS	*4.87*	*5.44*	*7.24*	*7.30*	*7.41*	*7.65*	*7.65*	*7.53*	*7.73*	*7.92*
Industrial products	*2.19*	*1.84*	*2.40*	*2.01*	*1.59*	*1.51*	*1.31*	*1.15*	*1.19*	*1.24*
Revenues (social security)	*1.02*	*1.43*	*2.66*	*3.34*	*4.31*	*4.74*	*4.70*	*4.76*	*5.41*	*5.51*
Financial transaction	*0.00*	*0.00*	*0.00*	*0.50*	*1.59*	*1.73*	*1.80*	*1.78*	*1.79*	*1.80*
Property	0.27	0.17	0.27	0.80	1.01	1.02	1.04	1.02	1.04	1.07
Income and gains	3.01	5.13	5.67	5.65	5.15	5.62	6.53	6.30	6.21	7.10
General income tax	*3.01*	*5.13*	*5.13*	*4.76*	*4.36*	*4.86*	*5.61*	*5.30*	*5.12*	*5.81*
Profits (social security)	*0.00*	*0.00*	*0.54*	*0.91*	*0.79*	*0.75*	*0.92*	*1.01*	*1.09*	*1.29*
Payroll	5.98	5.84	6.56	5.41	6.95	7.43	7.59	7.56	7.81	8.10
Social security	*4.68*	*4.73*	*5.11*	*4.85*	*5.25*	*5.61*	*5.92*	*5.95*	*6.21*	*6.43*
Other taxes	4.60	2.46	1.82	2.03	3.86	3.91	4.72	4.64	4.60	4.96

Source: Afonso and Meirelles (2006), Araújo (2005). Global Tax Burden defined according to the National Account System.

Notes

Other taxes = fees, economic contributions (such as royalties), other taxation bases, small amount revenues from above mentioned tax bases.

set down in writing in the National Constitution, which also details the norms set down for many taxes (especially the state tax on the circulation of goods, whose interstate taxation system is fully regulated by the text), any attempt at reform, however limited its scope, would inevitably require an amendment to the Constitution (which depends on the approval of two-thirds of the members of the two Houses of Congress, in two rounds of voting). The few tax reform proposals that have been discussed have always avoided issues sensitive to the federative debate. The few measures that have managed to be approved have involved merely topical changes that have almost always been aimed at increasing the tax burden.

The debate on tax reform has returned to the national political agenda since the announcement that economic growth had fallen short of estimates, once again. There is absolute consensus over the need for such reform, but when the debate shifts to the details of proposals, so dissention increases. This lack of agreement in relation to the ideas and measures put forward comes from the broad gulf that separates different interests, not only between taxman and taxpayer (which is natural in any system around the world), but also between the governments of different regions and at different levels (see the federative question) and between sectorial interest groups (many benefited by constitutional earmarkings).

This chapter aims to describe the present tax system in Brazil and to reflect on its recent evolution and attempts at its reform. It has been organized into five sections, including this introduction. The next section sets out a general view of public finances. The third section details the characteristics of the main taxes. The fourth discusses topics that are relevant to the present day, such as the issue of regressive taxation and the federative question and the final section looks at the recent debate over tax reform initiatives, both those that have failed and those that are necessary.

A general view and the recent development of taxation

Brazil has had a long history in which the state has played a leading role in the economy and, at the same time, seen a strong decentralization of public administration (Afonso and Rezende 2006). The option for a federal regime (imposed "from the top downwards" to ensure national integrity) explains the tendency towards lengthier constitutions. This is especially the case of the tax system: the distribution between different levels of government of the responsibilities for taxation has helped shape the division of power in the federation.

Sub-national governments have always benefited from a broad level of autonomy, both in terms of legislating on their taxes, levying them directly, and also deciding on how to allocate resources, and generate and provide accounts. In view of the profound regional inequalities that have always existed, a vertical division of revenues has always been adopted, from upper to lower levels of government, and with a horizontal distribution in favor of less developed regions and localities. The historical relevance that state governments have always had within the federative division of tax powers, explains the predominance of indirect taxation at the different levels of government. These governments applied a tax on sales in general, which was then substituted by the reform program imposed by the military in 1965 with an innovative tax on the circulation of goods of the value added type. Not only was this the first time in the world that such a tax was created on a national scale, but it was also the only time that such a tax was delegated to an intermediate tier of government. From a political standpoint, ending the state government power to levy tax on goods is seen as an impossible task, largely because this has become the largest single source of own income for this tier of government, and the more developed the state, the more income it receives. The last tax reform was carried out by the National Constituent Assembly 1987–8. This reform was neither innovative nor did it alter the tax structure significantly, largely because efforts were rather concentrated on fiscal decentralization. Five federal taxes on strategic inputs were eliminated (fuels, electric energy, minerals and transport and communication services).

These had previously been levied using a single rate with resulting cumulative effects, and their bases were now integrated into the old state tax on the circulation of goods (ICMS), which was theoretically non-cumulative. Its management was entirely delegated to these state governments, who furthermore had the power to freely fix tax rates on the internal circulation of goods (rates on interstate flows remained in the hands of the Senate). Central government continued to levy tax on value added, but limited this to other industrialized products (IPI) and the local governments maintained their tax (cumulative) on services in general (ISS). Most of the attention in the 1988 reform was focused on continuing to raise the sharing out of federal tax revenues in favor of subnational governments: the percentage of the two main federal taxes, on income (IR) and on industrial products (IPI), transferred to the state (FPE) and municipal (FPM) participation funds increased from 18 to 44 percent between 1980 and 1993; in the case of the IPI, a further 10 percent was set aside for exporter states. The implementation of this system remodeling resulted, first in a strong decentralization of tax revenues and, second, in a steady and vigorous increase in the tax burden (see Table 7.2). The redistribution of resources had clear directional results: in vertical terms, all the relative gains favored the municipal tier, when adopting the concept of available revenue (own exclusive tax revenues plus or minus the constitutional sharing out of tax revenues), meaning that both the federal tier and the state tier lost out in terms of their proportion of the total tax revenue; in horizontal terms, the additional resources of sub-national governments were transferred in greater proportion to less developed regions – rather than reverting the high economic concentration in wealthier regions through the sharing out of available tax revenues as well as expenditure. Central government effectively reacted to the decentralization of taxes by creating and successively expanding the incidence of contributions (non-shared), which resulted in a rise in the tax burden and the cumulativeness of indirect taxes. It especially placed a heavy burden through the levying of contributions on strategic inputs and

Table 7.2 Historical evolution of the total tax burden and tax revenue federative division in Brazil

Concept	Central	State	Local	Total	Central	State	Local	Total
	Tax burden in % of GDP				Composition in % of GDP			
Own taxation								
1960	11.14	5.45	0.82	17.41	64.00	31.30	4.70	100.00
1980	18.31	5.31	0.90	24.52	74.70	21.60	3.70	100.00
1988	16.08	5.74	0.61	22.43	71.70	25.60	2.70	100.00
2005	26.72	10.01	2.26	38.99	68.50	25.70	5.80	100.00
Available revenue								
1960	10.37	5.94	1.11	17.41	59.50	34.10	6.40	100.00
1980	16.71	5.70	2.10	24.52	68.20	23.30	8.60	100.00
1988	13.48	5.97	2.98	22.43	60.10	26.60	13.30	100.00
2005	22.53	9.70	6.76	38.99	57.80	24.90	17.30	100.00

Source: Afonso and Meirelles (2006) – based on data from STN, SRF, IBGE, Social Security Ministry, CEF, Confaz e Local Gov Balances.

Notes
National Accounts System methodology includes taxes, fees and contributions, including financial transactions tax and other taxes levied on the payroll, as well as the revenue obtained from the stock of overdue taxes.
Direct taxation: tax revenue collected by every government level with its own means. Available revenue: direct taxation plus/minus intergovernmental transfers.

services, which had escaped from the scope of the IPI, and, more recently, also on imports.[7] Recent changes to the composition of the national tax burden suggest disregard for the process of gradual change combined with reasonable flexibility in federative relations (Serra and Afonso 2006). Public policies, from macroeconomic to social point forcefully to a fiscal re-centralization, not least to satisfy the growing pressure from enormous federal government spending on the transfer of income. This ranges from pension and assistance benefits to interest on public sector debt in treasury note form.

International comparisons of tax burdens show that Brazil is significantly above the prevailing standard among emerging market economies (Figure 7.1).[8] The Brazilian tax burden is on a par with the average burden of developed nations (39 percent of GDP), and a full 12 points above the developing nation average. It is important to look deeper into our analysis and divide up the burden according to bases of incidence: although the Brazilian tax burden is equal to that of many rich nations in percentage of GDP terms, the situation is quite different when we look at types of incidence. In the case of taxes on income and profit, the average of the rich nations is 84 percent greater than that of Brazil: 14.4 percent against 7.9 percent of GDP. An expressive difference can also be seen in taxes on assets: the average of rich nations is 70 percent greater than that of Brazil: 2.1 percent against 1.2 percent of GDP. The highest burden falls considerably in the case of contributions incident on payrolls: the rich nations levy 24 percent more than Brazil: 10.8 percent against 8.6 percent

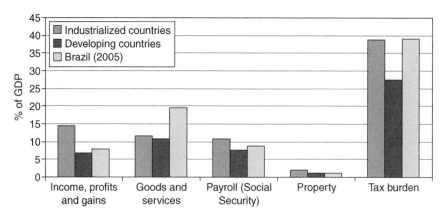

Figure 7.1 Tax burden per incidence in Brazil and in a group of nations (2004) (source: IMF 2006).

of GDP. This picture changes radically when we look at taxes incident on the domestic market for goods and services in Brazil, which exceeds the average of the world's most industrialized nations by 70 percent: 19.5 percent against 11.5 percent of GDP.

In other words, it is the stark difference of the indirect tax burden that creates the unusual situation of the country being on the same level in terms of total taxation as the world's richest nations, and which ends up harming the country's competitiveness and fiscal fairness. A pioneering move to adopt a tax of the value added type on a national scale through reform in the mid-1960s, did not lessen the distortions because Brazil's indirect tax did not keep up with the evolution of the tax in other countries – the non-cumulative tax is limited to large taxpayers (by right or in fact) and even then continues to be tied to the old taxman regime, conceding capital gains tax credits with considerable delay and obstructing or even denying rebates of accumulated credit balances, especially by exporters; the greatest symptom of a cumulative system is the taxing of financial transactions.

Institutional characteristics of the principle taxes levied

This section details the main characteristics of the Brazilian taxes resorting to the International Monetary Fund's typology for its explanation. Before analyzing the characteristics of the principle taxes levied in Brazil, one should stress the relative importance of each block or even each tax. This can be done by looking at the details of a recent composition of tax revenues: which totaled 38.9 percent of GDP in 2005 (Afonso and Meirelles 2006). In principle, the methodology usually adopted in international statistics, interpreted in the strictest sense, divides up revenue between: taxes, in the broadest sense (78 percent of the total), and social contributions, in the strictest sense, incident only on payrolls

(22 percent of the total). A broader analysis by type of incidence can also be adopted, using the classification recently adopted by the IMF (see Table 7.3).

Indirect taxation generates a little over half of natural tax revenue if we include it in addition to taxes on the domestic market (16.4 percent of GDP), those which are incident on financial transactions – and is, alone, the size of the total tax burden of many Latin American and even emerging market economies.[9] The most relevant tax category is that which is levied on production and sales in general form: 42 percent of national tax revenue, ranging from the state tax on the circulation of goods to federal contributions on turnover and revenue.

The very small size of the burden of taxes considered as selective or specific (less than four points of national tax revenues) can be explained by the unusual form in which the above-mentioned category of generic indirect taxes is levied. They do not follow general rules and do not always apply single tax rates and, in fact, in the case of the exclusive bases of specific taxes (such as fuels, cars, tobacco and beverages) it is common practice to adopt different tax bands, rising from zero to higher rates levied by each tax (without mentioning the generalized use of tax substitution and other forms of presumption).

The taxation of salaries constitutes the second large block, despite the loss of relative importance of salaries within income, a world phenomenon that in Brazil has taken on dramatic forms that have reduced the income of salaried workers to a level that constitutes merely one-quarter of national income (excluding taxes). By computing the many different forms by which salaries, the

Table 7.3 Tax revenues composition in Brazil (2005)

Global revenue and by categories	R$ billions	R$ per inhabitant	% of total revenue	Tax burden % GDP
Global	754.4	4,160	100.0	38.94
Goods and services	355.1	1,958	47.1	18.33
General goods and services	*317.7*	*1,752*	*42.1*	*16.40*
Excises taxes	*27.7*	*153*	*3.7*	*1.43*
Public services	*9.8*	*54*	*1.3*	*0.50*
Payroll	178.7	985	23.7	9.22
Employees. Public Servants. Self-employed	*37.8*	*208*	*5.0*	*1.95*
Employers	*128.5*	*709*	*17.0*	*6.63*
Others	*12.4*	*68*	*1.6*	*0.64*
Income and gains	152.7	842	20.2	7.88
Families	*46.5*	*256*	*6.2*	*2.40*
Companies and shareholders	*75.8*	*418*	*10.0*	*3.91*
Others	*30.5*	*168*	*4.0*	*1.57*
Financial transactions	35.1	194	4.7	1.81
Property and wealth	23.7	131	3.1	1.22
International trade	9.0	50	1.2	0.47

Source: Afonso and Meirelles (2006), in accordance to the IMF Government Finance Yearbook classification.

payroll or manual labor wages are taxed, one comes to a burden equivalent to 9.2 percent of GDP (in 2005), of which 6.6 percent of GDP is retained at source by employers, reflecting the fact that Brazil is one of the countries that adopts among the highest aggregate employer tax rates in the world (close to the highest European examples). Contrary to the situation that exists in richer economies, taxation of income and profits and gains in Brazil accounts for one-fifth of the total tax burden (8 percent of GDP). The difference (on the downside) is even more evident in the case of income tax levied on individuals: 6 percent of the national tax burden. On the other hand, taxation on the profits of companies and shareholders brings 10 percent of the total. One can consider as low, on the one hand, taxation levied on assets (1.2 percent of GDP) when comparing with the average in the richest countries, and on the other that levied on foreign trade (0.5 percent of GDP) relative to less developed economies, which reflects regional treaties and agreements, such as the MERCOSUR trade block, but covers up the fact that, implicitly, taxes and contributions on sales in general end up taxing exports via inputs. Finally, it is worth noting the decentralization (that has in the past been greater) in the direct generation of the tax burden of 38.9 percent of GDP in 2005: 68.4 percent was raised by central government (of which only 20 percent in the form of taxes); 26 percent by the state govern-ments (of which 20 percent related to tax on goods); and 5.6 percent by munici-pal governments (who collect more tax on services than they do through traditional taxes on urban property – 0.7 percent against 0.5 percent of GDP).

Taxation of income, profits and gains

Individuals

Brazil has had a long history of taxation – the first form of tax on the income of individuals (IRPF) was implemented in 1923. The taxation of individual incomes brought into state coffers 2.4 percent of GDP in 2005, of which only 0.4 percent was stated in, and paid under the annual income tax return. In other words, the bulk of this was paid at source.

Salaried workers are discounted tax direct at source in their pay packets and the employer pays the income tax retained at Source (IRRF) on their behalf. Liberal professionals (self-employed) are obliged to issue receipts and pay tax due, direct and on a monthly basis. Lottery winnings are also taxed as income at source. The federal tax authorities raised 1.5 percent of GDP in 2005 through retentions related to income from work.[10] Retention of tax at source is also applied to other forms of income that are not considered salaries: income from capital, raffles, earnings abroad and services received by companies. In the spe-cific case of financial investments (including gains in variable income invest-ments) and withdrawals by shareholders of their companies' results, these are taxed exclusively at source (the normal tax rate is 15 percent but it rises to as much as 22.5 percent in the case of shorter-term investments) and are not levied according to the annual table (raised 1 percent of GDP in 2005).

The annual tax declaration or return is only for adjustment purposes – in other words, used to check on any additional tax due from those who have more than one source of income; or to establish whether any tax already paid needs to be refunded (rebate), due to the standard deduction (20 percent) or to deductible expenditures (dependents, allowances, schooling, health plans, private pension plans, or even donations to cultural or social entities such as charities, always subject to limits and ability to provide evidence of payment). Taxation on income of individuals (at source and in the annual tax declaration or return) applies only two tax rates (15 percent and 27.5 percent) in accordance with brackets of income.[11] With the implementation of the economic stabilization plan in 1994, the automatic indexation of this table to past inflation was extinguished; readjustment of the tax brackets was made sporadically and always below the cost of living. As a result, the number of taxpayers who declared income tax rose from 7.64 million in 1996 to 22 million in 2006, of which 21 million made their declarations or returns by means of the Internet. The coverage of income tax in Brazil is relatively low (the economically active population totaled 91 million), the direct result of a decreasing formalization of the labor market (only 44 percent of workers are formally registered with signed labor documents) and low salaries or wages paid (almost 90 percent of income declared by families in a household survey was within the exemption bracket, below US$7,000 earned in the tax year). Tax income from annual declarations is even more limited: of the total 16 million tax declarations or returns filed in 2003, only 31 percent concluded with tax due – according to (SRF 2006b).[12]

Companies

Companies pay corporate income tax (IRPJ) as well as a social contribution on net profit (CSLL), which is linked to financing social security and was created by the 1988 Constitution. Firms also pay a general revenue contribution, which is discussed thoroughly below. Although they are two distinct taxes, the bases for incidence and the rules for levying are the same (the contribution is settled before the tax and offers fewer options of incentives). The tax rates within the normal accounting regime (real profit) are 15 percent in the case of the tax, and 9 percent in the case of the contribution. An additional 10 percent tax is payable on annual profits exceeding about US$110,000 p.a. In 2004, slightly fewer than three million annual company tax declarations were filed, which between them declared a total corporate income equivalent to 189 percent of GDP (SRF 2006a). The regime of real profit (2003) included a mere 6 percent of all taxpayers (176,030 companies and 2,693 financial institutions), but generated 81 percent of total tax revenues (156 percent of GDP in 2003). As it offers the opportunity for deductions and incentives, at the end of the declaration period, corporate income tax (IRPJ) was found owing in 69,623 companies (in a total amount equivalent to 1.6 percent of GDP) and social contribution on net profits (CSLL) found owing in 62,439 companies (0.6 percent of GDP). In other words, out of the total number of companies, only 3.3 percent of the net revenue from their declared activities was found to be due in tax. The case of financial institutions was no different. They collected 0.5 percent of GDP, in both IRPJ and CSLL, but this was equivalent to a mere 1.4 percent of the total of their revenues from financial activities.

Companies with an annual turnover that is less than around US$22 million, may opt for the regime of presumed profit under which they only need to declare their turnover and apply a tax rate to that, which is differentiated by economic activity and reflects a profit margin that is set by legislation (varying from 1.6 to 32 percent on gross revenue).[13] A similar system is also applied to micro and small companies, who can opt for a simplified tax regime (SIMPLES), also applicable to other federal taxes (including substituting the employer's contribution to social security due on the payroll), in such a way as to levy a percentage on earnings that is differentiated by sector (the collecting entity is responsible for separating the proportion of each tax originally due within the official accounts).[14] Profits and dividends distributed by companies and interest on own capital, are not taxed. Finally, one should mention that some transactions are taxed at source. Typical examples include remittances abroad (at a rate of 15 percent, which rises to 25 percent if these remittances are earnings from business activities) and, of less importance, benefits from private pension plans and prizes or awards won in intellectual and artistic competitions, among others. These taxes raised 0.5 percent of GDP in 2005.

Taxation of payrolls and the workforce

This IMF adopted category is not taxed in Brazil but it is levied through various contributions other than those linked to social security, although many are even levied on the same tax collection payment slip. Compared to the classic social contribution, the aggregate revenue from this group is relatively small: 0.6 percent of GDP in 2005. The most important in this category is the salary-education contribution (0.3 percent of GDP in 2005), set down within the constitutional text itself in the chapter on education, and meant to provide an additional source of financing for public elementary education. Another two types of contribution that can also be levied on salaries have in common the fact that they are compulsory (once again, based on rulings set down in the Federal Constitution of 1988), and that the proceeds from both are passed on to private entities such as union, employer and worker representations (associations, trade unions etc.), which means that the management and application of these contributions does not form part of public budgets.

Property taxation

This category deals with taxes which are levied in the case of the ownership of an asset or right, or the transfer thereof. In this sense, a restricted interpretation here also classifies the taxation of the transmission of financial assets, such as checks and other forms of bank debit. In other words, this category also includes the CPMF as levied in Brazil (and in few other emerging market economies). Thus, the tax burden on property and its transmission reached 2.7 percent of GDP in 2005, which was a very high percentage even when compared with the richest nations; but, excluding the exceptional contribution (CPMF), this percentage dropped to 1.2 percent of GDP (largely the result of sub-national taxation on urban property and vehicles).

There is no general form of taxation on property, nor on corporate assets (such as in some countries).[15]

The taxation of real estate in Brazil has always been separated into two distinct taxes – the tax on urban properties (IPTU), which has always been levied by municipalities and presently raises 0.5 percent of GDP; whilst the tax on rural property (ITR), at times in the past levied by other tiers of government, is now the domain of central government.[16] However, the ITR has always generated derisory revenues, which were equivalent to just 0.014 percent of GDP in 2005. The IPTU (tax on urban properties), meanwhile, has been given increasing attention by municipal governments, with revenues going from 0.14 percent to 0.5 percent of GDP between 1988 and 2005.

State governments are responsible for the tax on the ownership of automotive vehicles (IPVA), which accounted for 0.5 percent of GDP in 2005. The IPVA is levied each year on owners of cars, boats, trucks, motorbikes and aircraft, on the purchasable value, a definition that is based on market prices with rates fixed by each state's legislation of, and differentiated by, type and usage.

The taxation of debits and other bank transactions, as mentioned previously, is the most profitable and singular form of taxing the transfer of assets, in this case of financial assets. Initially, a federal tax was created (the IPMF), which was only levied in 1994, at a rate of 0.25 percent and produced revenue equivalent to 1 percent of GDP. In 1996, it was recreated, but this time in the form of a provisional contribution (the CPMF – contribution on financial transactions) to be used to finance the public health system, with a rate set at 0.2 percent. The term of validity of the CPMF was later successively extended (there have already been six constitutional amendments since the first tax) and is presently valid until 2007, with a single rate of 0.38 percent (since 1999) now applicable generating annual revenue that has been stable at around 1.5 percent of GDP since 2002. Its base of incidence includes financial transactions and its system of levying is very simple: it is levied on any operation that is settled or any issue that is carried out, which represent the contractual or physical circulation of money, which result, or not, in the transfer of ownership of such monies, credits or rights. Thus, the CPMF is applied to withdrawals, deposits and bank loans, as well as payment orders and transactions in the futures or stock markets. Exemption is given to transfers by a title holder to himself (e.g. an individual or company transferring money from one account in their name to another account in their name), government and charitable transactions, simplified accounts of low-income individuals and public share offerings.

Taxes on goods and services

The taxation of goods and services in the domestic market constitutes by far the most important tax block within the national tax burden: it was equivalent to 18 percent of GDP in 2005, of which 15.8 percent was in the form of general type taxes. Of these, the equivalent of 9.2 percent of GDP came from value added taxes (thus defined constitutionally, although they leave a lot to be desired in practice), and 5.8 percent came from contributions on sales in general (part levied in the form of a non-cumulative regime since 2003).

The three tiers of government all exercise tax powers within this block, contrary to the principles initially drawn up in the reform of 1988. These had attempted to divide up the bases in such a way that goods in general and communications would only be levied the state tax (the ICMS), services would be levied the municipal tax (the ISS) and industrialized goods (almost in the form of a selective tax) would be levied the federal tax (the IPI). Social and economic contributions, however, had their bases and, later, their rates successively expanded and increased by central government and this allowed for an excessive increase in the federal and the total tax burden on all bases. In fact, today, contributions on revenues (such as the COFINS and the PIS) have a broader base and a more sector diversified collection than the traditional state ICMS tax.

Value added taxation

Brazil made a pioneering move in 1965, when it replaced a state cumulative sales tax with a tax on the circulation of goods – the ICM (excluding fuels, electricity and minerals; items that were taken under the federal umbrella as a single levy tax), in which the charge was based on the value added, using however a system of physical credit[17] (maintained to this day) and a mixed system for apportioning the revenue from inter-state transactions. Under the same reform process, the central government was assigned a tax on industrialized products – the IPI (once again failing to cover the bases mentioned earlier), which was also levied on the value added but, in practice and over time, effectively became a selective federal tax, since the charges were concentrated on a limited tax base. An old municipal tax on professions was also replaced by a tax on services in general (the ISS), but it was charged cumulatively. The 1988 constitutional reform did not change the apportionment of the three taxation tiers, despite the already ample international experience of charging VAT on a national scale and familiarity with the problems, limitations and criticism of charging this tax in Brazil at the state level. The only step taken in 1988 was to do away with the selective federal taxes, including them instead within the state taxation base (as ICMS – value-added tax on the circulation of goods and services). This was done in such a way as to explicitly preclude the levying of federal IPI on such strategic inputs.

The ICMS is easily the greatest revenue earner among the nation's taxes, yielding the equivalent of 8 percent of GDP, and has dominated attention during all the various attempts to institute tax reforms. In theory, state governments ought to observe the principles established in the Constitution (which addresses the issue in considerable detail) and the general regulations set down in complementary laws. However, this does not always occur. Local governments resorted to a variety of creative expedients to get around the requirements, including fake loans and other credits, setting off an unprecedented fiscal war that has endured for more than a decade. The ICMS became, in practice, 27 different taxes, each with its own rules and rates, which vary considerably from state to state.

With regard to the rates, the first Brazilian anomaly is that the ICMS calculation base includes the tax itself. For inter-state transactions, it is set by the Federal Senate, which in 1989 created a dual system: the normal rate is 12 percent, but this drops to 7 percent on goods moving from the richer states to the poorer states (with the exception of fuels and electricity, where the distribution is constitutionally guaranteed). State law sets the nominal rates for internal transactions, the normal rate is 17 percent (in practice, the charge is 20.5 percent of the base value); two reduced rates are commonly used (set at 7 percent on goods that form part of the basket of staple goods and for low charge energy consumers, and at 12 percent on goods whose production is to be encouraged, such as automobiles and alcohol or diesel fuel), as well as two higher rates (set at 25 percent on fuels, electricity and communications and, occasionally, 35 percent for certain items considered superfluous, or weapons – equivalent to 33 and 53 percent, respectively, of the base value).

The Constitution assures that ICMS is to be non-cumulative and, since 1996, that it is not levied on exports; however, serious problems persist, for there is no safeguarding of the use of eventual accumulated credit balances; credits relating to the acquisition of capital goods can only be used over a period of four years; and those relating to consumer and durable goods are even today frequently undeclared. Even after the change, the states continued to tax exports, fully or in part, until they were stripped of this power by national law in 1996 (in exchange for compensatory transfers from the federal government); but up to this day, they resist and place barriers in the way of rebates of accumulated tax credit balances.[18] Once fiscal competition ceased to be a means of attracting productive investment to the smaller and poorer states and became a nationwide practice, together with the fact that dynamic activities such as services escaped this tax (and even municipal ISS, since the federal government took advantage of the lower taxation of the sector to increase its burden of contributions), the state administrations focused their efforts on raising the rates on strategic inputs and the output of oligopolies: 42 percent of the national ICMS revenue comes from oil and fuels, communications and electricity (19, 12 and 11 percent, respectively). The proportion is even higher, the less developed the state, where the rest of the ICMS revenue comes more and more from tax substitution and the advanced charging of inter-state revenues. At any rate, what was created as the most generalized domestic market tax has been whittled down over the past ten years, taking on more and more the appearance of a selective or specific tax.[19]

The traditional federal value-added tax is the IPI, but the revenue generated is limited: just 1.2 percent of GDP and barely 3 percent of the overall tax burden, because the federal authorities largely ignored this tax after the 1988 reform raised the allocation of other tiers of government and regional funds to 57 percent (suffice it to say that the revenue was 3.5 times greater in 1968). In practice, it became a selective tax, and in this way met a principle established in the Constitution itself, which determines that its rates should take into account the essential degree of the product: hence, they were defined on a case by case basis, using a table divided into 21 sections and 97 sub-sections, and ranged from 0 (for staple essential consumer goods) up to 42 percent on perfumes and 45 percent on snow or golf vehicles. On top of the sheer complexity of the tariff structure, the IPI is frequently used as a means for granting sectorial incentives (as in the recent case of the construction industry), since it does not involve much sacrifice, most of which is borne by the state and local government tiers. Never has the revenue from the IPI been so low, since its inception, and it is largely concentrated on just three superfluous items – automobiles, beverages and tobacco (one-third of the total) and imports (accounting for a further 22 percent).

General sales – revenues taxation

The taxing of revenues in general (not just on commercial, but on other types as well, such as financial income and even income from government work) is carried out by means of two social contributions charged by the central government: one is known as COFINS (contribution for the financing of social security); the other embraces two contributions (the social integration program and the public service employee savings program – PIS/Pasep), created in 1970 and, following the most recent constitutional reform, tied to the funding of unemployment benefit.

The COFINS raised the equivalent of 4.5 percent of GDP in 2005, making it the country's fourth largest source of tax revenue, behind the ICMS, income tax and payroll contributions to social welfare. It was raised to 3 percent of total revenue,[20] but special regimes were established, under which financial institutions pay 4 percent of their net income from financial intermediation; large companies (which pay corporate income tax on their realized profit) pay 7.6 percent of the difference between what they sell and what they buy (known as the non-cumulative regime) and importers pay the same 7.6 percent at the moment of customs clearance (created following a constitutional amendment, in mid-2004, to give equal treatment to domestic and imported products).[21] Exports are not taxed and are granted specific exemptions and specific and varied treatment, according to specific cases (allowing large companies in certain sectors, for example, to avoid the non-cumulative regime).

There was evident harm caused by the cumulative effect of the earlier COFINS system, aggravated by the excessively high rate of 3 percent, (see Varsano *et al.* 2001) and the recent changes have been mindful of the need to improve the quality of the taxation. However, they have brought fresh problems, such as a huge increase in the burden, resulting from the willfully excessive level of the rate for the non-cumulative regime (the same change, effected a year before on the charging of PIS/PASEP, had clearly demonstrated the consequences of increasing the burden) and its retention even after the broadening of the calculation base by including imports, as well as the growing complexity. It should also be noted that contributions were not converted into authentic non-cumulative taxes, because the companies within the non-cumulative regime buy from and sell to companies outside it – not to mention the special regimes; in effect, the COFINS and PIS have become a kind of distinctive bundle of indirect taxes. On the other hand, compared to the state ICMS, the COFINS at least has the advantage of being more productive, and applies national regulations and raises revenue in a more diversified fashion (for example, fuels, power and communications account for 22 percent of the total, 20 points less than in the case of the ICMS; moreover, services provided to companies and financial institutions, two bases not covered by ICMS, generate 12 percent of the total COFINS). Looking at it in another way, the COFINS will tend, in the future, to follow the country's indirect taxation reform agenda, taking over the former role of the ICMS, which has become less productive, more complex and heavily concentrated. As already mentioned, the second contribution levied on sales in general is the PIS/PASEP, which yields the equivalent of 1.1 percent of GDP and, for companies and financial institutions, adopts exactly the same levying arrangements as the COFINS, for the same contributors, but at much lower rates: 0.65 percent for companies under the cumulative regime and 1.65 percent under the non-cumulative regime. This contribution has one advantage over the COFINS: the contributor population is broader still, covering all legal entities, so that not-for-profit organizations also contribute, paying 1 percent of their payroll, while public administrations pay 1 percent of their current budget revenue. Another difference is with regard to the allocation: while the COFINS is of a general nature (financing social security as a whole), the PIS/PASEP is of a specific nature (for the workers' support fund, which covers unemployment benefit, an annual bonus and professional training, with a 40 percent reserve directed towards investment programs); in addition to a provisional constitutional ruling that set aside 20 percent for allocation by the central government (also applied to the other contributions).

Specific taxation

The most important specific tax is that levied on services (the ISS) and has been exacted by the municipalities ever since the reform back in 1960s. They have the autonomy to legislate, charge and inspect, but they can only levy against those services provided internally, that do not come within the sphere of the ICMS (inter-state communications and transport) and are specifically identified in a complementary national law (the last update occurred in 2003). To avoid the fiscal war that had been burgeoning, as the leading municipalities learned how to best exploit this tax, a constitutional amendment introduced a minimum rate (set at 2 percent) and prohibited the granting of tax incentives at a lower rate. Since each municipality can set its own rates, there is a broad and varied spectrum – the most common being 5 percent.

A federal tax (the IOF) is levied on credit, foreign exchange and insurance transactions and also those involving bonds or securities, the purpose of which is strictly regulatory (that is to say, its use is determined more by the guidelines of monetary, foreign exchange or credit policy than as simply a revenue source). It is true that, in 1990, it was utilized to effect the confiscation of 20 percent of national savings – under what was known as the Collor Plan.[22] Other specific duties (which are not taxes, as such) have also been introduced by the federal government since the late 1990s, to be levied on strategic inputs, such as fuels and communications, on the pretext of financing infrastructure investments in the respective areas. In practice, there was a reversal of all the original endeavors by the members of the Constitutional Assembly to do away with the old single levy taxes on such inputs (which were initially included in the base of the general contributions, COFINS and PIS, and were also later to have other taxes, contributions and even disguised charges levied on them, often as a result of constitutional amendments) and reserve such bases for state ICMS or municipal ISS (which had been left behind during the building up of the overall tax burden, despite their rates having been raised substantially every time it was felt that the federal government was about to encroach upon these tax bases). The most significant example is the contribution on intervention within the economic domain (CIDE), charged by the federal government since 2001 on imports and the commercialization of oil and oil products, natural gas and fuel alcohol, at specific rates, yielding the equivalent of 0.4 percent of GDP.[23]

One source that is always surrounded by controversy, as to whether it should or should not be classified as a tax, is that of royalties and other forms of stake holding in the revenues and results from the production of oil, gas and electricity and the extraction of minerals. The aggregate revenue is sizeable: equivalent to 0.8 percent of GDP in 2005 (but it could even exceed 1 percent, given the relative growth of the GDP and oil prices, which accounts for the greater part of the revenue).

There is a wide range of other small forms of specific taxation of goods and services, or their use, or the permission to perform certain activities, which are always linked to actions or services of collective or individual interest.

Taxes on foreign trade

The federal import tax (II) currently yields the equivalent of 0.5 percent of GDP, which does not constitute a significant revenue inflow, despite the commercial opening up of the economy promoted since 1990; this is largely a reflection of the structure and regional trade accords. Thus, rates are defined within the sphere of the MERCOSUR trade bloc, comprising the TEC (common external tariff), with a minimum rate of zero and a maximum rate of 35 percent – that is to say, full members tax the same products at a unified rate and these products circulate freely within the trading bloc. Until 2008, each country may retain a list of exceptions, of up to 100 products, taxed at different rates to the TEC, and half yearly reviews may be conducted (allowing the changing of up to 20 percent of the items on the list). By definition, the tariff structure should have a low spread and a small number of different rates.

The federal tax on exports, meanwhile, has a basic rate of 30 percent, and the government has the authority to reduce it or increase it by up to 150 percent, for foreign exchange or foreign trade policy purposes or to regulate supply. However, it is rarely charged and the revenue is negligible.

Payroll social contributions

The manuals and international experience define social contributions as those levied upon the payroll, generally being due from both the employer and the employees, and used to finance benefits and other forms of social support. In Brazil, the category social contribution, in legal terms, includes other calculation bases. However, in accordance with the methodology of the IMF, we will deal here with just the traditional contribution format: in line with the pattern of the wealthier countries, in 2005 they represented an important portion of the overall tax burden (22 percent), yielding the equivalent of 8.6 percent of GDP, of which 5.6 points was channeled into the general welfare regime and three percentage points went to the specific regimes of the public employees and the establishment of a worker's compulsory savings scheme. The size of these revenues would appear to reflect the imposing of an extremely heavy aggregate burden on the payroll, in excess of the norm for the majority of emerging economies and close to the total burden imposed in the European countries that give the greatest priority to the welfare state.

General welfare contributions

Of the total amount paid into social security, 44 percent comes from employers' contributions (companies pay a 20 percent rate and financial institutions 22.5 percent of the payroll, with no ceiling for the amount of the contribution) and 18 percent from wage earners (rates vary from 7.65 percent up to 11 percent of monthly earnings, on a progressive scale, but with a ceiling of one contribution salary (which is also the ceiling for normal retirement benefit) – currently set at US$1,300 a month).

This system means that the charges on higher incomes are proportionally much higher for the employer than for the employee, thus discouraging the formal hiring of higher-income employees and frequently stimulating the dismissal of such employees, for subsequent re-engagement as service providers, either as private enterprises or as self-employed professionals (nevertheless, this last segment represents less than 4 percent of the total revenue collected).

Attention is drawn to the fact that around one-third of the social security revenue comes from sources other than the above-mentioned standard contributions – among which are the contributions of the owners of micro and small businesses under the "simples" regime, whereby a rate is paid on the company's turnover; amounts retained at source by the hirers of services provided by third parties (20 percent of the amount paid to individual workers and 15 percent in the case of cooperatives); and amounts retained at source against transfers of federal taxes to the majority of state and municipal governments that had not paid in their social security contributions in the past.

It should be pointed out that this general welfare regime applies to workers with signed work papers, the vast majority being in the private sector plus a few public employees (in the rare cases of local governments that have not organized a specific regime for them). Rural workers and self-employed professionals get differentiated treatment: with the former, the employer contributes at the rate of 2 percent of the gross income from the sale of his/her rural products, and workers can retire on a pension of one minimum wage (if they wish to receive more, they can contribute at a rate of 20 percent of the desired amount, up to a ceiling); in the case of the self-employed, they must pay a higher rate (20 percent) than wage earners, and this encourages a large proportion of this segment to remain outside the state system.

Other social contributions

Another social contribution levied on the payroll and due only from the employer (at a rate of 8 percent) is the FGTS (length of service indemnity fund), which brings in the equivalent of 1.8 percent of GDP, but is of a quasi-fiscal nature: although it is set down in law, its revenue is not included in the public budgets, because it is credited on a monthly basis to the individual accounts of the workers, held at an official lending institution.[24] The majority of the governments have organized their own social security regimes for their public employees (known as the RPPS), but an adequate actuarial assessment has never been performed and the charging of contributions from those covered was only normalized following the constitutional reform approved towards the end of 2003. It is estimated that the contributions, including the employer's portion, yield the equivalent of 1.2 percent of GDP. In the case of the federal government, active public employees contribute at a rate of 11 percent – inactive employees also contribute, under special conditions. The lower tiers of government have the freedom to introduce different rates for their own regimes, just as long as these are not inferior to those adopted for the federal regime.

Other issues

It might also be worthwhile to address two further issues in order to develop a broader awareness of all the aspects of the Brazilian pattern of taxation: the most recent issues that affect fiscal federalism, fundamental to a full understanding of tax reform; and the taxation system's regressive nature, whose effects are as harmful as they are unknown in domestic literature.

Dilemmas of federalism

It is a mistake, commonly made by analysts, to think that the federation is a great hindrance to reform, as if the federative allocation of tax revenues had remained constant since the implementation of the system determined by the 1988 Constitution. In recent years, the Federation has ceased to be a thorn in the side of the so-called economic order, to the point that it has become a factor contributing to the success of short-term macroeconomic policy (at least in terms of managing the debt and surplus targets). However, there is still a long list of issues that need to be faced by the Brazilian Federation over the coming years, including a gradual re-centralization of tax control.

In the last few years, important changes have been made in the pattern of financing and public spending, with increasing influence of the central government. Recent taxation measures have taken to the extreme the option of raising unshared contributions, while focusing the granting of benefits on those taxes that are shared with the states and municipalities, thereby throwing the federative structure into disorder (Table 7.2).[25] Seen from a longer perspective, after four decades, the municipalities have assumed the position of the states as the dynamic force of Brazilian federalism, judging by the changes in the federative allocation of the available taxation revenues. The state governments have had ten percentage points cut from their share – which fell from 35 percent of total revenues in 1965, prior to the reform carried out by the military government, to around 25 percent 40 years later. The municipal governments, meanwhile, have seen their share grow from 10 percent to 17 percent of the overall revenues. An area in which little or no progress has been made is that of the so-called fiscal war between the states, conducted by manipulating their respective ICMS rates and the granting of benefits (especially the refunding of that portion of the tax that was due to other states) disguised as subsidized loans and even shareholdings. The principal effect has been to reduce the overall effectively available state revenue, and to increase the fiscal pressure of these government tiers on the central government, as well as diluting the historical tendency towards regional economic decentralization. The recent case of the automobile assembly plants is a typical example: given the generalized concession of incentives, the most developed states ended up making the most of their obvious advantages – market location and better economic and social infrastructure, in comparison with the less developed ones. The implications of the ICMS war extend beyond the fiscal sphere, as it has a lot to do with the direction of the industrial and foreign trade policies, essential to a stable upturn in economic growth. In a more open economy, there is less solidarity and more variation in interests and outlooks between the more and less developed regions, especially in terms of trade and industrial policy.

Table 7.4 Impact of taxation on total household income in Brazil: 1996 and 2004

Monthly household income	% of the household income						Tax Burden Addition (in %)
	Direct taxes		Indirect taxes		Global tax burden		
	1996	2004	1996	2004	1996	2004	
up to 2 MW	1.7	3.1	26.5	45.8	28.2	48.9	20.6
2 to 3	2.6	3.5	20.0	34.5	22.6	38.0	15.4
3 to 5	3.1	3.7	16.3	30.2	19.4	33.9	14.5
5 to 6	4.0	4.1	14.0	27.9	18.0	32.0	14.0
6 to 8	4.2	5.2	13.8	26.5	18.0	31.7	13.7
8 to 10	4.1	5.9	12.0	25.7	16.1	31.6	15.6
10 to 15	4.6	6.8	10.5	23.7	15.1	30.5	15.4
15 to 20	5.5	6.9	9.4	21.6	14.9	28.5	13.5
20 to 30	5.7	8.6	9.1	20.1	14.8	28.7	13.9
over 30	10.6	9.9	7.3	16.4	17.9	26.3	8.4

Notes
Elaboration: Fecomercio (2006). Primary sources: POF/IBGE (2004), Vianna *et al.* (2000).
MW=minimun wage.

Taxation regressiveness

One particularly weighty consideration in the analysis of taxation is the question of its distribution according to the different population strata, but in Brazil this rarely gets much attention in political and technical debate. Recent data reveals one awful aspect of the sheer size and recent increase in the taxation burden in terms of a large and growing level of regressiveness. As has already been mentioned, the taxation burden is largely based on the indirect levying of taxes. This is true even in the case of social contributions, whose effects are possibly even more harmful than those of the taxes.

However progressive may be the levying of taxes on income and assets, the impact is very small in comparison with the enormous weight of the indirect taxes. Studies (Fecomercio 2006) show a direct and continuous relationship between family or household income and the impact on it of indirect taxes: it is estimated that the average burden on a family in the lowest decile, with an average monthly income of less than two minimum wages, is three times that on those in the highest decile, with a monthly income of more than 30 minimum wages (Table 7.4). The same estimate shows that the recent increase in the burden, being more strongly backed by indirect taxes than by direct ones, means that this increase proportionally affects the lower income families more.

Tax reform

For years, tax reform has been on the agenda for national political and economic debate, so it is appropriate to provide a personal opinion as to the reasons behind the failure of so many projects and why such an overhaul is becoming ever more necessary.

Disruptive adjustment

Fiscal discipline has never been a simple consensual issue in Brazilian history, which has thrown up examples of moratoria: international, in the case of the central government, but also by the lower tiers of government. Concern over the matter, which was ignored by the 1988 reform, only came to the surface with the introduction of the Real Plan: the diagnosis was that inflation masked a structural public account deficit and that, as long as no long-term reforms were put forward and implemented, it would be necessary to effect a provisional fiscal adjustment. This adjustment would involve a temporary increase in the burden of taxation, particularly through social contributions, and the creation of a mechanism for unlinking these revenues, so that additional sums from these same contributions could be utilized for other purposes. Despite being introduced as temporary constitutional rules, their validity has been successively extended and they will continue to be in force until 2007.

At the heart of the concept of fiscal adjustment as a necessary evil are two structural issues that date back to the constitutional reform of 1988: the need to cater for the expansion of social security and, at the same time, try to reduce or even partially reverse the decentralization of taxation. To begin with, federal spending was affected by the increase in pension benefits, within the general regime and also for its own public employees (and much more recently, in welfare benefits), to which it responded by increasing the contributions. Next, the federal accounts, which had been under pressure since the creation of the Real Plan, due to the growing cost of public debt brought about by the extremely high real interest rates, began to require ever greater primary surpluses, following the eruption of the external crisis of 1998. This also led to an increase in the tax burden, although of a different nature and without depending on the unlinking of the federal revenues – now, the sources originally linked to social security were beginning to generate surpluses that were used to finance the burgeoning fiscal spending, not only on retired public employees, but on servicing the public debt. In practical terms, the consequences have been the opposite of those originally intended: a vicious circle has been created, wherein the very emergency measures themselves have led to a relaxing of the federal authorities' efforts and the delaying of the restructuring of public spending; in other words, the measures focused on the continuous increase of the tax burden have ended up provoking imbalance and got stuck in a cycle whereby the adjustment causes maladjustment.

Reform proposals and the reasons for their failure

The 1988 constitutional reform had been in effect for just a few years when projects to change the taxation system started to appear, advocated in large part by segments close to the taxpayers who were given little elbow room in the constitutional debates, which, as mentioned before, had focused attention on the federative issue. Among others, one that gained considerable attention was an unusual project with popular appeal that proposed replacing all the taxes with a single tax on financial transfers. The idea was so strongly defended that the federal government ended up proposing and approving the creation of a provisional tax of this kind, which was introduced only in 1994; later, it was to be reintroduced as a contribution to finance health spending (CPMF), also on a provisional basis.

The first important project for reforming the taxation system, proposed by the federal government in 1995, explicitly rejected the idea of promoting the re-centralization of revenues. The main objective was to consolidate the national VAT legislation, thwart a fiscal war and create a federal tax that was identical to the state one (same base, justification and legislation), as well as to unify the present social contributions and replace their base, levied on the total sales turnover, with value added, with a view to eliminating its negative impact on the economy's competitiveness. With the prospect of establishing a VAT model with collection shared between the federal government and state governments, the simultaneous application of two rates was provided for, permitting the introduction of the principle of destination in inter-state transactions. This would avoid the evasion stemming from the mere elimination of the charge on the shipping of goods to other states, as well as stopping the predatory fiscal war between Brazilian states. The core of the proposal developed in Brazil, based on what was termed Dual VAT, was to be an ICMS that would be shared between the federal and state governments: it became known as the "little boat model," due to the innovative treatment proposed for inter-state transactions – according to Varsano (1999).

However, the best opportunity in recent years to push through a sweeping revision of the country's taxes was wasted, because the federal government was afraid of jeopardizing its short-term fiscal efforts, aimed at mitigating the severe external crisis. The government had introduced a program of fiscal stabilization that, in reality, was founded on a sharp and rapid increase in the overall burden of taxation, especially through contributions on turnover, profits and financial transfers that would be altered, merged or eliminated in the reform that was before Congress.[26] The fear of assuming very short-term risks led to the abandonment of the process, on the only occasion that an agreement had been reached to introduce changes in the taxation that were authentically structural and long term (Dain 2005). A short time afterwards, alleging once again the lack of tax reform, the government sought and gained approval for the extension of the unlinking of revenues (DRU) and the provisional taxation of bank account transfers contribution (CPMF).

In 2003, the new president of the Republic of Brazil also presented a reform project to Congress which, essentially, had the same long-term objectives. This time, state governors were mobilized, amid much fanfare and it appeared that tax reform would be pushed through, but the proposed constitutional amendment to reform the state ICMS, so as to nationalize the legislation and standardize the rates, was not approved and until today is circulating within the House of Representatives. The same fear of losing control over the short-term adjustments was seen again in 2003, despite the change in government and arguments. In truth, the project only touched, and even then only partially modified, the ICMS, but even so it did not get through. Yet again, what was necessary to a more immediate fiscal adjustment was passed unanimously – the extension of the CPMF and DRU, though in enlarged form (the DRU was extended to cover economic contributions and the CPMF rate was constitutionalized) and supplemented by other measures that would lead to a further increase in the tax burden (notably, the contributions on turnover were extended to cover imports). The only consolation is that, during this post-constitution period, though there has been no change in the constitutional framework, significant changes have been made in the supplementary legislation, especially once the economy had stabilized. Following important modifications, such as doing away with monetary correction on company balance sheets and the creation of a simplified system of federal taxation on micro and small businesses (the "simples"), the federal government supported the changes in the state ICMS forwarded by the Kandir Law and the social contributions on sales (the PIS and, later, the COFINS).

From a federative viewpoint, the measure that had the most direct impact was established by the Kandir Law, a supplementary law of September 1996, which eliminated the direct imposition of ICMS on all exports, including those of primary and semi-prepared manufactured products. The states only agreed to surrender their power to tax exports in return for financial support from the federal government, agreed at the time as a transitory system (for a maximum of twelve years), in the form of a revenue guarantee (with resources passed on only to those states that suffered a reduction in their revenues, and proportional to that loss); this was subsequently converted into a federal transfer (about US$2 billion a year), with predetermined apportionment, in the nature of compensation. The Kandir Law has however ended up generating two ongoing causes of friction that impair federative relations and economic competitiveness. On the one hand, the transfers are subject to annual renegotiation, during the process of approving the federal budget, because there are no clear principles to govern the determining of the overall amount to be transferred, nor adequate criteria for the distribution of the resources among the neediest states. On the other hand, the fact that exoneration is not automatic (no transfers to third parties or cash indemnification) has meant that, depending on the state authority in question, exporters can accumulate large ICMS credit balances, in contravention of the spirit of that law and even of the Constitution itself (since a partial reform, in 2003, elevated the principle previously declared in the Kandir Law to the constitutional level). What is more, it has disseminated among state governments the idea that exporting is bad, as it generates no revenues but nevertheless generates expenses: some governors not only hold up or refuse the repayment of credits, but sometimes also resist the granting of incentives and infrastructural support to new projects aimed largely at foreign markets.

The need for more widespread reform

The Brazilian tax system has become a singular case: it is the only one in the world in which revenues from contributions exceed those from taxes, because it is the only one in which contributions are not levied exclusively on payrolls. According to the law, we have two systems of taxation. In fact, there is a single system in which the contribution is simply a legal short-cut to enable the compulsory extraction of resources from society in a manner that is much quicker and easier than the traditional form of taxation. The prolonged use of a strategy for short-term fiscal adjustment based on raising the burden of taxation has hindered economic growth. It is important to make clear that this is not a case of arguing that a high tax burden is, in itself, something that slows down the economy – indeed, if this were the case, then countries of Western Europe would not have grown, and would not still be growing. Nevertheless, it cannot be denied that the tax burden became a problem in Brazil as from the second half of 1990s, breaking with the historical postwar tradition whereby the burden of taxation would rise during the upside of the economic cycle (when the expansion of revenues tended to exceed the rate of GDP growth) and would remain stable during the downside. Despite some oscillations, the economy has grown rather slowly since the introduction of the Real (about 2.2 percent a year, on average), while at the same time, the average annual growth of national taxation revenues has been close to three times that figure. In such a peculiar scenario, it is inevitable to suppose that taxation has been an important factor in slowing down or braking economic growth, particularly when the taxing of exports has been retained and the charges on capital goods have been increased.

It is time to abandon the strategy of conducting tax reform through a process of gradual change and minimalist projects and face up to the basic issues, which point towards discussion and changes in social security (including addressing the thorny question of pensions) and in the federation itself (whose spending is also on the table for discussion). It is in the area of taxation that the most concrete and effective steps can be taken to curb the growth of public spending and, if such be the case, to initiate a reduction. Restricting the use of provisional measures (temporary laws) in dealing with taxation issues (limited, in exceptional circumstances, to handling the few regulatory taxes), giving the same treatment to contributions and other types of charges as that given to taxes, and beginning the gradual depletion of the CPMF and the DRU, are the shortest routes to, first of all, slowing down the propagation of spending and, second, if possible, starting to reduce it.[27] It is undeniable that the weight of the tax burden has been defined by the amount of spending, but it does not mean that that is the cause. Ever since it became easier, as well as seductive, to create and inflate unshared federal taxes (since the two transitory regulations mentioned earlier came into effect), public spending in Brazil started to grow – and not only pulled up by the increase in taxes and the cost of servicing the public debt.

For this reason, the unlinking of revenues has never been a solution for controlling spending, and as it has changed over the last few years, it has even induced an increase in spending. Budgetary rigidity is merely a symptom of the disease, not the cause of the infection, the origin of uncontrolled spending and finances. It is necessary therefore to reverse the trend, making it harder to increase and use tax revenues, in order to force a review of the pattern of spending.

Notes

1 The opinions expressed herein are those of the authors and not necessarily of the institutions to which they are linked. The authors would like to thank Maria Cristina Barroso, Ana Carolina Freire and Kleber Castro for their research assistance.
2 According to the 2002 World Bank classification related to *per capita* gross domestic product, measured using purchasing power parity.
3 According to FGV (2006), which considers those with per capita income of less than R$121 per month as poor. This was the same source used in the Gini Index.
4 The Real Plan was also made up of some revenue raising measures aiming at covering the fiscal gap that would emerge with the end of the inflationary revenues.
5 The Tanzi effect is the name given to the tax loss that occurs, in high inflation periods, between the moment the due tax is generated or calculated and its payment. Thus, the nominal tax burden becomes greater than the real one. Once the inflationary process ceases, the real tax burden converges to the nominal one.
6 Excluding transition economies like the East European countries.
7 The performance of the federal tax burden structure speaks for itself. On one hand, there has been a drastic reduction in the burden of the only value added type federal tax, the IPI: in 1970, this raised the equivalent of 4.4 percent of GDP; in 2005, revenue from IPI fell to just 1.2 percent, one of the lowest levels in its history. On the other hand, social contributions levied on revenues in general and on earnings (PIS and COFINS) have been vigorously expanded since the last reform: in 1980, revenue was the equivalent of only 1 percent of GDP; in 2005 it hit a record 5.6 percent of GDP; if we also include revenue equivalent to 1.5 percent of GDP obtained with contribution on financial transaction (CPMF) and 1.3 percent of GDP CSLL levied on profit, the total tax burden of these four contributions alone hit 8.4 percent of GDP in 2005. The total raised through such contributions was equivalent to more than six times that raised through federal industrial tax and already exceeded state value added tax or even federal income tax.
8 Taking as a base, data from 2004 contained in the last government finance yearbook published by the International Monetary Fund (IMF 2006). In the correlation between income per capita and level of taxation, Brazil is level with the economies of the old Communist block, such as Belorussia, the Ukraine and Bulgaria, the only countries that manage to ignore the rule and combine low income with a high tax burden.
9 Excluding some transition economies like the Eastern European countries.
10 A further 0.5 percent of GDP was collected by state and municipal administrations which, for example, do not pay the central government what they have retained at source from salary payments made to their public sector workers (this is the only form of concurrent tax responsibility existing in Brazil).
11 In 2006, the brackets were as follows: exemption, on up to approximately US$7,000 earned in the tax year; rate of 15 percent, on between US$7,000 and US$12,000; rate of 27.5 percent on anything over US$12,000 earned in the tax year. Application is gradual. Retention at source adopts the same table except with the annual amounts divided by 12.
12 The total income declared was equivalent to 33.1 percent of GDP in 2002 (the tax year in question), but the taxable amount in the declarations fell to 24.1 percent of GDP (the significant difference was basically caused by tax-exempt income, such as low value pensions and earnings from savings accounts); the total sum of net income was reduced even further after allowable deductions were made, to just

17.8 percent of GDP. In the end, tax due was equivalent to 1.7 percent of GDP and constituted an effective total average tax rate of 7.1 percent on the taxable income in the declarations. The total rebate or tax refund was 2.5 times greater than the amount of tax due. Despite the low level of coverage, those declaring income tax also declared a total of assets and rights that were equivalent to 120 percent of GDP.

13 The presumed profit regime was used by 683,000 corporate taxpayers (22 percent of the total number of taxpayers), who between them had revenues equivalent to 17 percent of GDP. They collected a total of 0.6 percent due in IRPJ and CSLL in 2003, which represented 3.7 percent of the total sales (a proportion slightly higher to that found in the case of the real profit regime).

14 The largest contingent of companies (two-thirds of the total) was made up of 1.6 million micro companies and 334,000 small companies, which opted for the special regime (SIMPLES) and declared revenue that was equivalent to 11.6 percent of GDP and tax due (not only income tax but all federal taxes) totaling 0.6 percent of GDP. This consumed 5.3 percent of the revenue pile, therefore an average proportion that goes against the popular belief that this regime should produce a significant reduction in the tax burden for this corporate segment.

15 The Constitution of 1988 innovated by attributing to central government the responsibility for taxing large fortunes. However, no such tax has even been implemented nor has there ever been any proposal put forward to regulate it.

16 The contribution on improvements is a tax that for decades, according to the Constitution, the three tiers of government have been able to levy on any gain in value of property resulting from the carrying out of public works. It has however, been rarely applied, by just a few municipal governments in wealthier regions of the country, and presently raises a derisory 0.007 percent of GDP.

17 In the physical credit system, companies can only appropriate tax credits in a "competence basis" rather than in a cash basis which is the rule in all other value added tax system in the world. That is to say that in Brazil a firm that buys a new machine for its plant will only get the tax credit in 48 months, albeit an European firm would get the whole tax credit in the cash disbursement for the machine.

18 The main legislative focus of this tax was on inter-state taxation: created originally as a purely at-source tax, it gradually transformed into a mixed tax, although it tends to be more beneficial to the state receiving the goods, above all in the less developed regions. As a result, the last constitutional reform included within its main body of text, a considerable quantity of detailing of rules.

19 A good illustration of the depleting of the ICMS over time is to compare the 1968 tax burden with that of 2005: in that first year, the state ICM, without the major bases and with a general rate of 15 percent, accounted for 7.3 percent of a total of 8 percent of GDP, but fell to around 20 percent of the national tax burden, despite becoming the ICMS with the incorporation of fuels, power and communications, the significant rise in the general rate and the creation of special higher rates.

20 COFINS is the tax that has grown the most, by far, since the 1988 reform – indeed, in that year, it yielded a mere 0.8 percent of GDP and the general rate was 0.5 percent of gross turnover.

21 Special regimes were also created in order to impose tax substitution (as in the cases of cigarettes and vehicles) or even single levy tax regimes (for fuels and pharmaceuticals, among others) levied on certain specific activities – with rates ranging from 3.2 percent to 10.8 percent.

22 The regulations are diverse and complex, with many exemptions and reduced rates: the maximum general rates are presently 1.5 percent per day, in the case of bond or security operations (but with a zero rate for 23 types of credit operation), and 25 percent on exchange operations (but falling to zero in the case of contracts stemming from the exporting of goods and services or the importing of services,

among others); in the case of gold purchases, the rate is 1 percent, based rather unusually on the text of the constitution (since revenue from this specific source pertains in its entirety to the government of the state and municipalities where the gold is produced, to compensate for the fact that no ICMS is charged on gold).

23 A similar case is that of telecoms services, which contribute at the rate of 1 percent of operating revenue to the fund for universal telecom service coverage and at the rate of 0.5 percent to other fund to finance the operations of the sector's regulatory agency. The most peculiar feature of these revenues is that the lesser part actually goes towards those investments for which they were created – the greater part is put aside as a disguised indirect means of increasing the federal government's primary budget surplus.

24 This was introduced in 1966, as a kind of reserve fund, to be drawn down in the event of the worker being dismissed without just cause: in which case the employer would have to pay an additional fine, equivalent to 40 percent of the balance of the worker's FGTS account, as a way of discouraging a high labor turnover.

25 Between 2002 and 2005, the overall taxation burden increased by the equivalent of 2.3 percentage points of GDP: state ICMS accounted for 12 percent of this rise, but the effect of the increase in the federal contributions on sales (PIS/COFINS) was three times greater. The allocation of the revenue (after constitutional transfers) shows a significant increase in the federal share, which in the last five years has grown by 1.8 percentage points, from 55.8 percent to 57.6 percent of the total taxation revenue (Table 7.2).

26 In 1999–2000, the federal authorities broke off the agreement that had been made in the House of Representatives, as well as with the state and municipal authorities, regarding what was known as the Mussa Demes amendment, despite the fact that it would bring about an undeniable and deep rooted improvement in the system of taxation and that its implementation would be gradual and the effects only felt in the long term. The federal government feared that this reform would hinder or even cancel out the endeavors it was making in the very short term.

27 Not to mention the CPMF trap, which means that, when real interest rates are finally reduced to a sensible level (the bank rate is presently six times the average level for emerging economies), the current rate of 0.38 percent on bank transfers will discourage financial intermediation, in addition to the other problems associated with this type of charge (Campodonico *et al.* 2006).

References

Afonso, J. R. R. and Araújo, É. A. (2006) "Municipal Organization and Finance: Brazil," in Shah, A. (ed.) *Local Governance in Developing Countries*, Washington, DC: The World Bank.

Afonso, J. R. R. and Barbosa Meirelles, B. (2006) "Carga Tributária Global no Brasil, 2000/2005: Cálculos Revisitados," Cadernos NEPP/Unicamp, n. 61, Unicamp, Campinas.

Afonso, J. R. R. and Rezende, F. (2006) "Brazilian Federalism: Facts, Challenges, and Perspectives," in Wallack, J. S. and Srinivasan, T. N. (eds) *Federalism and Economic Reform: International Perspectives*, New York.

Araújo, É. A. (2005) "Análise das Contribuições Sociais no Brasil," Brasília, CEPAL.

Campodonico, J. B., De Mello, L. and Kirilenko, A. (2006) "The Rates and Revenues of Bank Transaction Taxes," OECD Working Paper n. 494, Paris: OECD.

Dain, S. (2005) "A Economia Política da Reforma Tributária de 2003," *Econômica*, v. 7, n. 2, pp. 293–318, Rio de Janeiro.

Fecomercio, Federação do Comércio do Estado de São Paulo (2006), "Simplificando o

Brasil: Tributação e Gastos Públicos," Caderno Fecomercio de Economia n. 11, São Paulo.

Fundação Getúlio Vargas (FGV), Centro de Políticas Socias (2006) *Miséria, Desigualdade e Estabilidade: O Segundo Real*, Getúlio Vargas Foundation, Rio de Janeiro, September.

IBGE, Instituto Brasileiro de Geografia e Estatística (2004) "Pesquisa de orçamentos familiares 2002–2003: primeiros resultados: Brasil e grandes regiões," IBGE – ordenação de Índices de Preços, Rio de Janeiro: IBGE.

International Monetary Fund (2001) *Government Finance Statistics Manual 2001*, Washington, DC: IMF.

—— (2006) *Government Finance Statistics Yearbook, 2005*, Washington, DC: IMF.

SRF (Secretaria da Receita Federal) (2006a) "Consolidação da Declaração do Imposto de Renda da Pessoa Jurídica 2004," *Estatísticas Tributárias* 11, Internal Revenue Department, Brasília: SRF.

—— (2006b) "Carga Tributária no Brasil 2005," *Estudo Tributário* n. 15, Brasília, Ministério da Fazenda.

Serra, J. and Afonso, J. R. R. (2006) "Uma Visão Panorâmica do Federalismo Fiscal no Brasil," mimeo.

Varsano, R. (1999) "Subnational Taxation and Treatment of Interstate Trade in Brazil: Problems and a Proposed Solution," The World Bank, Conference, Valdivia, Chile.

Varsano, R., Pereira, T., Araújo, É. A., Silva, N. and Ikeda, M. (2001) "Substituindo o PIS e a COFINS – e por que não a CPMF? – por uma Contribuição Não-cumulativa," IPEA, Texto para Discussão n. 832, Rio de Janeiro: IPEA.

Vianna, S. W., Magalhães, L. C. G., Silveira, F. G. and Tornich, F. A. (2000) "Carga Tributária Direta Indireta sobre as unidades familiares no Brasil: Avaliação de sua incidência nas Grandes Regiões Urbanas em 1996," IPEA, Texto para Discussão n. 757, Brasília.

8   Chile

Matteo Cominetta

Introduction and contents

Stretching from the Antarctic region to the eighteenth parallel and covering 756,950 km^2 Chile is the seventh largest country in Latin America. It is populated by 16 million people with a high degree of ethnic homogeneity, given that 95 percent of the population is of "White or White-Amerindian" parentage. With US$4,408 of per capita GDP, it is the richest country in the region, excluding Trinidad and Tobago and other small-sized countries of the Caribbean. After the PPP adjustment, the above figure reaches US$11,200, making Chile the second richest Latin American country after Argentina. The same ranking emerges from the Human Development Index. The distribution of such income is extremely uneven: the Gini index is 0.571 while the ratio of the income accrued by the richest 20 percent of the population to that accrued by the poorest 20 percent is 18.7. Such high values are not exceptional within Latin America. However, they are exceptionally high on a global level. Only a handful of African countries present higher values. Chile is thus one of the most uneven countries on the planet. From the sectoral distribution of the GDP (primary 9 percent, secondary 34 percent, tertiary 57 percent) one can see that Chile stands in the middle between rural pre-industrial countries with dominating primary sectors and post-industrial ones where services typically account for more than 60 percent of the GDP while the primary sector is below 3 percent.

This chapter analyzes the most significant features of the Chilean taxation system. The analysis is organized as follows: the second section sketches the history of the taxation system and investigates the recent evolution of the government budget. The third section looks at the present structure of the system from an institutional point of view. The main taxes are described. The fourth section analyses the effect of taxation on Chileans' income distribution via the computation of effective tax rates. The fifth section is concerned with the last interventions and with the current debate on taxation matters. The sixth section concludes.

A general overview of the Chilean tax system and its development

An initial overview of its economic, budgetary and expenditure features

On the wave of booming copper prices, of which Chile is the world's first producer, the general[1] government's (preliminary) net lending reached 4.9 percent of the GDP in 2005. A year before this figure reached 2.1 percent. It was a return to the norm, after the 1998–2003 period of net borrowing. In the last 15 years the fiscal authorities have indeed pursued a policy of tight discipline. The primary result turned negative in 1999 only, when the economy suffered a –1.1 percent growth as a consequence of the drop in copper prices and the financial turmoil caused by the East Asian and Russian crises. In 2002, the second worst year, the government balance nearly broke even, standing at –0.1 percent of GDP. Again, low copper prices and extraordinary macroeconomic shocks (the Argentinean crisis) were the causes behind this negative result. Apart from these two years, Chile generated substantial supervises, and used those to reduce its debt from 47.3 percent to 7.5 percent of the GDP (see Table 8.1).

Disaggregating the 2004 total government revenues highlights three main sources: taxes (18.8 percent of GDP); copper (3.8 percent of GDP); and social contributions (1.4 percent of GDP). The copper industry, still partly in public hands after the nationalization by the Allende Administration, is the second biggest contributor to government revenues after taxes. A look at Table 8.1 shows that, while revenues from taxes and social contributions remained fairly stable since 1990, yields from copper were the main cause of the shifts in government borrowing. Social security contributions represent a secondary source of revenues: an unsurprising fact, considering that all but the police's and the armed forces' pensions funds are managed by the private sector. Other headings are of negligible size and have been therefore omitted in the table.

Turning to the expenditures, the bulk of those are made up by three headings: public employment (5.3 percent of GDP); subsidies and donations (4.6 percent of GDP); and social security (4.8 percent of GDP). Regarding the latter, it is worth highlighting the imbalance between social security contributions and expenditures that characterizes the entire period under investigation. This "social security deficit," roughly 3 to 4 percent of GDP a year, is generated by the costs of transition from a Pay-As-You-Go (PAYG) scheme to a Fully Funded (FF) scheme, such as the one introduced in 1981. While contributions were transferred to the new privately owned pension managers, the costs of the old PAYG system kept and keeps weighing on public finances. These costs are mainly the pensions still paid to workers who retired before or after the reform under the PAYG scheme,[2] the benefits gained by workers that contributed to the old PAYG system and then shifted to the FF one[3] and, lastly, the PAYG scheme still granted to the police and the armed forces (for a detailed analysis of the transition costs, see Arenas de Mesa 2000). To this issue a section is dedicated to it at the end of this chapter.

Table 8.1 Structure and development of operations in the general government – selected figures and years – Chile (% of GDP)

	1990	1991	1992	1993	1994	1995	1996	1997	1998	1999	2000	2001	2002	2003	2004
Revenues	25.4	25.1	25.4	25.3	24.9	25.6	23.6	23.5	23.1	22.5	23.7	23.9	23.2	23.0	24.2
Total fiscal revenues	15.7	17.9	18.6	19.5	18.8	18.4	18.0	17.7	17.9	17.3	18.0	18.1	18.2	17.6	17.3
Copper	4.9	2.5	2.1	0.9	1.5	2.6	1.3	1.3	0.4	0.4	0.9	0.5	0.5	0.9	3.1
Social contributions	1.7	1.6	1.6	1.5	1.5	1.3	1.3	1.3	1.4	1.4	1.4	1.4	1.5	1.4	1.4
Expenses	20.5	20.6	20.1	20.3	19.8	18.8	17.9	18.0	19.0	20.7	20.9	20.7	20.7	19.9	18.6
Public employment	4.7	4.7	4.8	5.2	5.3	5.2	5.0	5.2	5.6	6.0	6.0	6.0	6.0	5.8	5.4
Goods and services	2.9	2.8	2.8	2.8	2.7	2.6	2.6	2.5	2.7	2.6	2.6	2.7	2.6	2.5	2.5
Debt interests	3.3	3.1	2.6	2.4	2.1	1.8	1.4	1.2	1.2	1.3	1.2	1.2	1.2	1.2	1.0
Subsidies and donations	3.7	4.2	4.2	4.3	4.2	4.1	4.0	4.1	4.2	5.0	5.2	5.0	5.2	4.9	4.7
Social security	5.8	5.7	5.5	5.5	5.3	5.0	4.8	4.7	5.1	5.6	5.6	5.6	5.6	5.3	4.9
Others	0.1	0.1	0.1	0.2	0.2	0.1	0.2	0.2	0.2	0.2	0.2	0.2	0.2	0.2	0.2
Gross operative result	4.8	4.5	5.3	5.0	5.1	6.8	5.6	5.5	4.1	1.8	2.8	3.1	2.5	3.1	5.6
Total revenues	25.5	25.3	25.6	25.4	25.1	25.7	23.6	23.6	23.1	22.5	23.8	23.9	23.3	23.0	24.3
Total expenses	23.0	23.3	23.2	23.8	23.4	22.2	21.5	21.5	22.7	24.6	24.5	24.4	24.5	23.5	22.1
Primary surplus/deficit	5.9	5.0	4.9	4.0	3.8	5.3	3.5	3.4	1.6	-0.8	0.5	0.7	-0.1	0.8	3.1
Net lending/borrowing	2.5	2.0	2.4	1.6	1.6	3.5	2.2	2.1	0.4	-2.1	-0.7	-0.5	-1.2	-0.4	2.1
Debt financing															
Financial assets acquisition	0.2	2.2	2.3	0.1	0.8	0.7	0.2	1.1	-0.9	-2.6	-1.4	-0.8	-1.6	-0.4	1.4
Net financial liabilities	-2.3	0.2	0.0	-1.5	-0.8	-2.8	-1.9	-1.1	-1.3	-0.5	-0.7	-0.3	-0.4	0.0	-0.8
Net external borrowing	-0.7	0.6	-0.3	-1.7	-0.7	-2.7	-1.1	-0.6	-0.3	0.5	-0.3	0.6	0.8	1.0	0.2
Net internal borrowing	-2.4	-1.1	-0.4	-0.3	-0.4	-0.4	-1.0	-0.5	-1.0	-0.7	-0.1	-0.5	-0.8	-0.4	-0.4
Bonos de reconocimiento	0.8	0.8	0.7	0.5	0.4	0.2	0.2	0.1	0.0	-0.2	-0.3	-0.4	-0.4	-0.5	-0.6
Public sector gross debt	47.3	40.8	33.7	31.4	25.5	19.6	15.1	13.2	12.5	13.8	13.7	15.0	15.7	13.1	10.9

Source: Budget Directorate, Ministry of Finance.

The tax system from the 1990s onwards compared with those of the other Latin American countries

Total fiscal revenues reached a level of 17.1 percent of GDP in 2004 (last official datum available, see Table 8.2). Disaggregating the latter gives insight into the contribution of each tax to the bulk of revenues.

The last column of the Table 8.2 shows the revenue of each item as the percentage of total fiscal revenues, excluding SSC, for the year 2004. It is evident from this that indirect taxation dominates over direct taxation: the former accounted for 65.5 percent of total fiscal revenues whereas the latter for 34.5 percent. Income taxation yields 4.3 percent of GDP, equal to 24.4 percent of total fiscal revenues or approximately two-thirds of direct taxation revenues. The corporate income tax, yielding an amount almost triple that of personal income taxation, is the main source of direct taxation revenues. Second comes the tax on wealth, which contributed a 2.1 percent of GDP, or 11.93 percent of total fiscal revenues. Personal income taxation is a minor source of fiscal revenues (6.25 percent of those). Indirect taxation is based on the VAT. This is the highest yielding tax in Chile, accounting for 8.1 GDP percentage points, 46 percent of total fiscal revenues and 72.32 percent of indirect taxation revenues. The remaining 28 percent is made up mainly by excise duties on tobacco, alcohol and fuels. Import duties and local taxes are all of negligible importance.

Developments of the system from 1970

As highlighted by Bulmer-Thomas (2003), since independence the main source of finance for Latin American governments' had been the taxation of international transactions. This situation, shared by Chile as well, changed abruptly following World War I: the worldwide recession, together with the drop in prices of Chile's main exports, nitrate and copper, caused a fall in the government's revenues. This rendered a system of internal taxation necessary for the survival of the state (SII 2006a). The process of creating an internal taxation system reached its final step in 1972 when the General Directorate of Internal Revenue is established. This structure then became the Servicio de Impuestos Internos (SII), which is up to now in charge of the administration of the taxation system.

Two years later, in 1974, the laws 824 and 825 are passed. These substituted the obsolete system based on the taxation of international transactions with a modern one, based on income and consumption taxation, effectively laying the basis of the system that still exists today. The system introduced in 1974 was based on five pillars: a corporate tax on all incomes coming from businesses; a unified and progressive scheme of personal income taxation for residents; a flat rate tax on incomes accruing to the non-resident; a general tax on consumption and a set of excises, the most important of which on tobacco, alcohol and fuel. The current system reflects closely the structure it had back in 1974. Indeed, it has been left virtually untouched since. The only major intervention was the 1990 reform, implemented in concomitance with the return to democracy. In the

Table 8.2 Structure and development of fiscal revenues in Chile as a percentage of GDP, 1990–2005

	1990	1991	1992	1993	1994	1995	1996	1997	1998	1999	2000	2001	2002	2003	2004	2005p	% Tot
Total tax revenues	*15.7*	*17.9*	*18.6*	*19.5*	*18.8*	*18.4*	*18.0*	*17.7*	*17.9*	*17.3*	*17.9*	*18.3*	*18.2*	*17.5*	*17.1*	*18.8*	*100.00*
Direct taxes	*4.1*	*5.6*	*5.8*	*6.0*	*5.8*	*5.6*	*5.7*	*5.6*	*5.8*	*5.5*	*6.0*	*6.5*	*6.7*	*6.4*	*5.9*	*7.2*	*34.50*
Income tax	2.6	4.1	4.2	4.2	4.1	3.9	3.9	3.8	3.9	3.5	4.1	4.5	4.6	4.3	4.0	5.3	23.39
Personal income	0.7	0.8	0.9	1.1	1.1	1.0	1.0	1.0	1.2	1.2	1.2	1.3	1.2	1.1	1.1	n/a	6.43
Corporation income	1.8	3.2	3.2	3.2	3.0	2.9	3.0	2.7	2.8	2.4	2.8	3.2	3.4	3.2	2.9	n/a	16.96
Wealth	1.5	1.5	1.6	1.8	1.7	1.8	1.8	1.9	1.9	2.0	1.9	2.0	2.1	2.1	1.9	1.9	11.11
Indirect taxes	*11.6*	*12.3*	*12.8*	*13.5*	*13.0*	*12.7*	*12.3*	*12.1*	*12.1*	*11.7*	*11.9*	*11.8*	*11.5*	*11.1*	*11.2*	*11.5*	*65.50*
VAT	7.0	7.7	8.4	8.7	8.6	8.2	8.0	7.9	7.8	7.6	7.9	7.9	8.0	8.0	8.1	8.1	47.37
Excise duties	1.9	2.0	2.0	2.0	1.9	1.9	1.8	1.9	2.2	2.3	2.3	2.3	2.3	2.1	1.9	1.9	11.11
Taxes on international transactions	2.4	2.3	2.2	2.3	2.0	2.1	2.0	1.8	1.7	1.4	1.4	1.2	0.9	0.6	0.4	0.4	2.34
Other indirect	0.2	0.2	0.3	0.5	0.5	0.6	0.5	0.5	0.5	0.4	0.4	0.4	0.2	0.3	0.7	1.0	4.09
Social contributions	*1.7*	*1.6*	*1.6*	*1.5*	*1.5*	*1.3*	*1.3*	*1.3*	*1.4*	*1.4*	*1.4*	*1.4*	*1.5*	*1.4*	*1.4*	*1.4*	
Total fiscal revenues	*17.4*	*19.4*	*20.2*	*21.1*	*20.3*	*19.7*	*19.3*	*19.0*	*19.3*	*18.7*	*19.3*	*19.7*	*19.7*	*18.9*	*18.5*	*20.2*	
Administrative level:																	
Central government	15.6	17.3	17.8	18.4	17.6	16.8	17.9	17.6	17.8	17.1	17.8	18.2	18.1	17.4	n/a	n/a	
Local government	1.1	1.2	1.3	1.2	1.1	1.2	1.4	1.4	1.5	1.6	1.5	1.5	1.6	1.6	n/a	n/a	

Source: ILPES elaboration on data from the Ministry of Finance and Internal Revenue Service of Chile.

Notes
p Provisional.
% Tot: revenue from item as percentage of total fiscal revenues excluding SSC, year 2004.

delicate moment of the transition, it was crucial for the political class to ensure popular support to the frail Chilean democracy. For this reason, tackling the social problems left by the military rule was vital. The 1990 reform thus aimed at generating the revenues necessary to finance an ambitious program of welfare expansion. The declared target was to increase government fiscal revenues by 3 percent of the GDP between 1991 and 1993 (see Boylan 1996 for a detailed description of the reform). This was pursued with a quadripartite intervention; an increase in the lowest business tax rate from 10 percent to 15 percent; a shift from estimated to actual profits as the base of the above tax for the highest contributors; an increase in personal taxation rates for middle and high-earners (obtained via a widening towards the bottom of higher brackets); and an increase in the VAT rate from 16 percent to 18 percent. As can be seen in Table 8.2, the reform accomplished its mission, raising total fiscal revenues of 24.2 percent from 15.7 percent to 19.5 percent of GDP across the 1990–3 period. Revenues from direct taxation increased by 46 percent, mainly as a consequence of the sharp increase in business taxation. The latter's yield raised from 1.8 percent to 3.2 percent of GDP, a 77 percent increase. The effects on personal income taxation were instead small. The yield from this increased by around 57 percent, but considering its very low starting level, the change remains small in absolute terms. Personal income taxation remained exceptionally low in Chile. In the same period, indirect taxation's yield increased by 16.4 percent, rising from 11.6 percent to 13.5 percent of GDP. The first impression is that indirect taxation was subject to a much smaller increase than direct taxation. However, this is not true in terms of GDP percentage: both indirect and direct taxation revenues increased by 1.9 GDP points. Unaffected by the 1990 reform, social contributions' yields remained stable at previous levels.

In 1993 the reform reached its full implementation. The effects of the VAT and business taxation increases had unfolded and the fiscal pressure reached its peak. In the following years these were partly offset by the massive drop in revenues from import duties and other forms of international transactions taxation. In 1993 trade-related revenues equalled 2.3 percent of GDP. The same figure dropped to 0.4 percent 11 years later, representing an 82 percent decrease. Tanzi (2000) shows that the effective tax on Chilean imports, computed as the ratio between revenues from import duties and total value of imports, followed a similar path, dropping from 16.7 to 5.8 in the period 1985–2000, a 65 percent reduction. The abandonment of the import-substitution model of development and the liberalization of foreign trade determined this drop. Revenue losses from trade liberalization offset the increase generated by the VAT, bringing indirect taxation yields back to pre-reform levels. Fiscal pressure declined and stabilized itself around 18 percent of the GDP, excluding social contributions. Direct taxation remained instead at higher levels than before the reform. As a consequence, the weight of direct taxation revenues relative to indirect taxation ones increased slightly. In 1990 these generated respectively 26 percent and 74 percent of total revenues, excluding social contributions, whereas in 2004 the two figures were, respectively, 34.5 percent and 65.5 percent.

Since the mid-1980s, a remarkable similarity of interventions took place across the Latin American region. With the consolidation of the so-called Washington Consensus,[4] the efficiency of tax systems remained high in the agenda of governments in the area. In this light, Latin American countries maintained their attention on reducing the most distortionary elements of their taxation systems as well as simplifying their structure. With this goal, the top rates of personal income taxes were heavily reduced. In 1986, the Latin American average top rate was 49.5. In 2004 this figure dropped to 28.8 (see Sabaini 2005). Chile followed a similar path, reducing its top rate from 50 percent to 45 percent, 43 percent and finally 40 percent in 1997, 2002 and 2003, respectively (see Table 8.3).

A similar phenomenon took place regarding the corporate income tax (CIT): in 1986 all Latin American countries but Colombia had different CIT rates according to the sector of business activity. Since then, Argentina, Brazil, Chile and Mexico among others have introduced a flat CIT. A reduction in the rate accompanied this simplification: the flat CIT rate is often closer to the bottom than to the top rate applied in the early 1990s. In Chile, CIT rates were in the range between 10 percent and 37 percent in 1986. In 1999 this multi-rate scheme was substituted with a unified rate applied to profits from any sector of activity, currently at 17 percent. One pillar of the Washington Consensus paradigm was the liberalization of trade and the shift towards the latter as the engine of development. It is then unsurprising that the most notable effect on taxation of this new trend is the reduction of taxes on international transactions. Export taxes, widely spread in the region at the beginning of the 1990s, are negligible now. Similarly, import duties have been substantially reduced due to the signing of various free-trade agreements within Latin American countries as well as between these latter and countries external to the region (e.g. the NAFTA). The notable loss in trade-related revenues, together with the unification and reduction of income tax rates without a widening in its bases, reduced overall tax revenues. To fill this gap, all Latin American governments relied heavily on the VAT: higher rates were introduced and fewer exemptions were allowed. As noticed by Baunsgaard and Keen (2005), various developing countries did not manage to recover from other sources the revenues they lost from trade liberalization. This, however, does not seem to be Chile's case. Looking back at Table 8.2, one can see that the loss in revenues from trade was almost fully covered by the increase in VAT yields, leaving the level of indirect taxation revenues only slightly reduced from 1990.

Some quantitative and institutional features of main taxes

The Chilean Constitution imposes taxes not to have a predetermined target. Tax revenues are allocated year by year with the Ley de Presupuesto (Budget Law). It follows that social contributions, defined as those contributions intended to cover welfare costs, are non-existent[5]. The costs of education, health and welfare in general are covered with revenues from direct or indirect taxation, as is the

Table 8.3 Evolution of the income taxation rates, Chile 1992–2005

	1992		1997		1998		1999		June-01		December-02		July-03		Jul-04		July-06	
	Min	Max	Min	Max	Min	Max	Min	Max	Min	Max	Min	Max	Min	Max	Min	Max	Min	Max
Personal income	5	50	5	45	5	45	5	45	5	45	5	43	5	40	5	40	5	40
Corporate income	15	35	15	35	15	35	15	15	15	15	16	16	16.5	16.5	17	17	17	17

Source: ILPES elaboration on data from the Ministry of Finance and Internal Revenue Service of Chile.

rest of government expenditure. The Chilean taxation system is then based on direct and indirect taxation only, with a few high-yielding headings generating the bulk of the revenues. The high degree of the Chilean republic's political centralization is mirrored in its taxation structure. Local authorities have very little power to levy taxes, while regional authorities have no such power at all. In terms of revenues, the central government virtually corresponds to the general government, the discrepancy between the two revenue levels being relatively small (1.6 percent of GDP in 2003, equivalent to 9 percent of general government's revenues). The above considerations all suggest that Chile has a fairly simple taxation system, similar to those diffused in most Latin American, as well as OECD, countries. An introductory description of this structure follows.[6]

Direct taxes

Income taxation was introduced by Law 824 of 1974. Under this act, residents or persons domiciled in Chile are subject to tax on income derived from any source, either domestic or non-domestic, while non-residents are taxed only on income generated within the national borders. Similarly to that of industrialized countries, Chilean income taxation is based on a flat corporate tax and a progressive tax on personal income. The former applies to all kinds of profits, irrespective of their origin. In a similar way, personal income taxation is subject to a unique progressive tax, irrespective of the origin of that income (the global complementary tax, GCT). As we will see in detail in the next section, this personal income taxation scheme is implemented via a bipartite system: a tax on dependent work (the second category tax, SCT) withheld monthly, and a global tax on total income (GCT) levied annually. The scheme does not apply to income accrued by individuals residing abroad. These are instead subject to a flat rate tax, the additional tax, or AT. All income taxes are charged on the income of the previous financial year, beginning on 1 January and ending on 31 December.

Taxes on personal income: resident individuals

The Second Category Tax (SCT). Any person resident in Chile is subject to the Impuesto de segunda categoria (Second Category Tax, SCT). This applies to income from dependent work such as salaries, pensions and other remunerations. Rates follow a progressive scheme, ranging from 0 percent to 40 percent. Tax brackets are defined in UTM, which stands for Unidades Tributarias Mensuales (monthly taxation units). These are currency units expressed in Chilean pesos, monthly adjusted in line with the consumer price index behavior. In practice the UTM scheme defines the tax brackets in real terms. It is intended to eliminate the so-called fiscal drag. In terms of 2005 US$, the SCT rates range between 0 percent for an individual earning less than US$830 a month (or US$9,900 a year) to 40 percent for those earning more than US$9,220 a month (or US$110,500 a year).[7] As we will see, all progressive taxes in Chile are

Table 8.4 Chile: main taxes

Type of tax	Name of tax	Acronym	Rate (%)
Direct taxes – income taxes	Corporate income tax (*Impuesto de Primera Categoria*)	FCT	17
	Personal income tax (*Impuesto de Segunda Categoria*)	SCT	0–40
	Global income tax for residents (*Impuesto Global Complementario*)	GCT	0–40
	Global income tax for non-residents (*Impuesto Adicional*)	AT	
Indirect taxes	Value added tax (*Impuesto al Valor Agregado*)	IVA	19
	Excises taxes (*Impuestos selectivos al consumo*)		13–60
	Custom duties (*Impuesto al comercio exterior*)		11
	Other taxes (on inheritances and donations, stamps, etc.)		0.25–1.6

Source: adaptation from SII, Santiago de Chile, Chile.

indexed against inflation as measured by the consumer price index. Table 8.5 provides the brackets and rate for the SCT as in January 2007.

SCT is computed on total salary and remuneration for work, less social security payments to AFP. The tax is withheld and paid monthly by the employer. In order to maintain the progressivity of the tax, employees with more than one employer have their rate computed on the gross total of their remunerations.

The Global Complementary Tax (GCT). Any person resident in Chile is subject to the Impuesto Global Complementario (Global Complementary Tax, GCT). As suggested by its name, the GCT is a tax on the global income of the resident, irrespective of its source. The GCT applies to the total of all gross (pre-tax) incomes of the person. It is intended to give a unified treatment to any source of income of the Chilean citizen. Rates and brackets are the same as the SCT ones, translated in annual terms. Annual taxation units (UTA) therefore substitute monthly taxation units (UTM). The former are indexed against inflation in a way analogous to UTM. Rates are again between 0 percent and 40 percent. Substituting UTA for UTM in Table 8.5, we thus have the brackets and rate structure for the GCT. The changes introduced in recent years on the SCT rates (namely, the reductions of maximum rates) applied equally on GCT's ones.

All the amounts paid for the First and Second Category Taxes constitute a tax credit usable against the GCT. In other words, taxes already paid as FCT or SCT are subtracted from the amount due as GCT. Therefore, this tax can be viewed as a mechanism of ensuring that, whatever their origin, the same levels of income pay the same amount of taxes.

Taxes on personal income: non-resident individuals

Persons neither resident nor domiciled in Chile are not subject to personal income taxation in the form of SCT and GCT. Instead, they are subject to a unique tax called the Impuesto Adicional (Additional Tax, AT). AT is levied on all incomes derived from Chilean sources (generally, when the income is made available from Chile to a person resident in a foreign country). The general AT rate is 35 percent, although there are several exceptions for various types of

Table 8.5 Second category tax in Chile: brackets and rates

Bracket	Monthly income in UTM	Tax rate (%)
1	0,0 to 13,5	Exempt
2	13,5 to 30	5
3	30 to 50	10
4	50 to 70	15
5	70 to 90	25
6	90 to 120	32
7	120 to 150	37
8	more than 150	40

Source: Servicio Interno de Impuestos (SII).

income (for a detailed description of such exceptions see SII 2006b). As for the GCT, the tax base is the sum of all pre-tax income. The AT might be seen as the equivalent of the GCT for foreigners. It ensures that any type of income is subject to the same fiscal burden. As for the GCT, the amounts paid for other taxes are indeed reclaimable as a tax credit. Of course, the major difference between the GCT and the AT is that the latter is not progressive.

Corporate income tax

Profits deriving from industrial, commercial or any other kind of activity carried out by an enterprise are subject to the Impuesto de Primera Categoria (First Category Tax, FCT). The rate is flat, its level being 17 percent. All enterprises but those involved in mining activities are subject to this regime. The latter are instead taxed under a progressive scheme. Rates ranges from 0 percent for mining exploiters whose annual sales are inferior to 12,000 metric tons to 5 percent for those whose annual sales exceed 50,000 metric tons. Moreover, it is worth noting that the value of a metric ton (and therefore the boundaries of the tax brackets) is computed according to the average value of that metal in the London Metal Exchange. Apart from being exceptionally low, the tax is then partly protecting the mining sector from fluctuations in metal prices. On top of this, it has been documented that private copper mining companies, representing almost 50 percent of Chilean production, underreported their profits via transfer pricing (exporting profits disguised as interest payments for debt with subsidiaries, for less tax is usually paid on interest payments than on profits) and paid virtually no taxes between 1992 and 2002 (see Riesgo 2005 and the response paper by Lagos and Lima 2005). This preferential regime is explainable by the central role, both in terms of income generation and employment, played by the mining industry in the Chilean economy.

An important feature of the FCT is that it applies only to profits that are withdrawn from the enterprise or, equivalently, on capital assets that are disposed of. In other words, retained profits are exempt form the FCT and therefore a *de facto* split system is in place, introducing incentives to re-invest profits in the company. Various other incentives similar to the split system just described are also present. A brief list of these follows:

1   14 bilateral Double Taxation Agreements (DTA) are in force and seven more have been signed and are waiting their implementation. Under these schemes, any tax paid in one country represents a tax credit in the other.
2   The Business Platform Law offers favorable fiscal treatments to foreign investors setting up a platform company in Chile for managing investments in third countries. When a company is set up as a "Business Platform," it is not considered to be resident or domiciled in the country. Therefore, it is liable to Chilean taxes only on the income generated in the country. This income is treated as that of a standard non-resident taxpayer, and therefore subject to FCT and AT.

3   Instead of standard treatment of the FCT 17 percent rate and personal income taxation in the form of CGT or AT, capital gains originating from public companies limited by shares are subject to a flat 17 percent rate. In practice, capital gains pay in this case the FCT only. Furthermore, capital gains from the sale or transfer of shares in SA are tax-free if these are acquired in the stock market, in a public tender share offer or in an initial public offering by foreign institutional investors. In various cases, capital gains on the sale or transfer of real estate are again tax-free (for a detailed description visit *www.sii.cl*).

4   The most northern and southern regions of the country, denominated Zonas Extremas (Extreme Zones), enjoy an extremely favorable fiscal regime offered to businesses locating in the regions (see World Bank 2005). Its main features are duty-free areas, employment subsidies, and tax credit for investment and sales subsidies.

Indirect taxes

Impuesto sobre el valor agregado (IVA)

IVA is a general consumption tax equivalent to the VAT. It was introduced with the 1974 reform and is levied on sales of all goods and services. The tax base is the difference between the tax debit (the total sales of goods and total supply of services) and the tax credit (the sum of all purchases of goods and use of services) owned by the taxpayer. A flat rate of 18 percent is currently applied on this base and must be paid on a monthly basis. Since its introduction, the VAT allowed for various exemptions that cannot be listed in full here (if interested, see Diario Oficial 1976). The two most important are the total exemption of the exporting sector and the VAT reimbursement in the case of acquisitions of fixed assets. Some products are subject to a surtax whose base is the same as the VAT, while the rates vary from case to case. Together, these surtaxes generate almost 11 percent of total fiscal revenues and 2 percent of the GDP. Products subject to the surtaxes are: alcoholic beverages (13 percent to 17 percent surtax); non-alcoholic beverages with sweeteners, colorants or flavorings (13 percent surtax, but retail sellers are exempt); luxury vehicles whose value exceeds US$18,873 (13.75 percent surtax on the excess value, going to 0 percent in January 2007. If the vehicle is imported, the relevant value is the custom one).

Excises

Sales of tobacco products, fuels and luxury goods are targeted with excises. For tobacco products, the tax base is computed on the value of the sale to the final consumer. The rates range from 51 percent to 60.4 percent depending on the type of product. For fuels, the base is the value of import or of first sale if produced in Chile. These rates are not expressed in percentage, but instead in UTM.

In 2007, they stood at 1.5 UTM per cubic meter for diesel, 6 UTM per cubic meter for gasoline. Finally, luxury goods such as gold, jewels, furs pay a 15 percent excise.

Local taxes

Local taxes are of negligible importance in Chile. Regional taxes are non-existent (as noticed above, there are however a number of tax incentives for individual and businesses locating in the extreme regions of the country), while municipal taxation is of minor entity. The collection of taxes is thus highly centralized. Nonetheless, local authorities have notable autonomy in expenditure management. Spending for infrastructures and education is indeed allocated by the central government but managed by local authorities, and in the future health expenditure management might be decentralized as well. Moreover, the Impuesto Territorial and the Patente Commercial are both levied and managed at a local level. The former is a tax on real estates and is to be paid quarterly by the owner to the council in which the estate is located. Forty percent of its revenues are directed to the council and constitute one of its main sources of income. The other 60 percent flows into a national "inter-council" fund that is intended to redistribute resources from rich to poor councils. The tax has a progressive feature, as the rates range between 1.2 percent and 2 percent according to the cadastre value of the estate. The latter is an annual duty payable to the municipality in which professional, commercial or industrial activities are carried out (see Godoy Ibanez for details).

Other taxes

A stamp duty on documents containing money credit agreements, checks and protests is levied as a percentage of the amount specified in the agreement or as a fixed amount (for checks and protests). Transfers of property in the form of inheritances and donations are subject to a progressive tax. Finally, an 11 percent tax on the custom value is levied on all imported goods. In the contest of regional integration Chile has signed bilateral agreements with Canada, Mexico and the United States that will eliminate all custom duties in ten years time. Similar agreements have been signed with Colombia, Venezuela, Peru and Ecuador and the MERCOSUR members and in the contest of the ALADI (Asociaciòn Latinoamericana De Integraciòn, Latin American Integration Association) agreement.

Social contributions

When the Fully Funded (FF), privately-managed pension scheme substituted the previous Pay-As-You-Go (PAYG) one in 1981, the armed and security forces called out of the reform, preferring to keep the old scheme for themselves only. This dichotomy is still in place, and the only social contributions present in Chile are therefore the ones paid by the armed and security forces. These account for roughly 1.4 GDP points.

The fiscal burden

The distribution of taxation charge

In a region such as Latin America, plagued by extreme income inequality, the issue of redistribution is a debated one. With regard to taxation systems, equity is generally defined in two senses: horizontal and vertical. The former requires that individuals with the same income pay the same amount of taxes, the latter requires that individuals with higher income pay a higher proportion of their income in taxes (i.e. progressivity of the taxation system). The vertical equity of the Chilean system has been investigated by Engel *et al.* (1998a). Using data from the CASEN survey[8] of 1996 and computing the before- and after-tax Gini coefficients of income distribution, their paper concluded that the redistributive ability of the system is substantially null. If anything, the system appears to be regressive, the after-tax figure (0.496) being slightly higher than the before-tax one (0.488). Moreover, the authors found that the fiscal pressure is equal between income deciles, standing around 15 percent of income. The Engel *et al.* study thus proves that the Chilean taxation system is vertically unequal. The study had a big effect on the debate, fostering the demand for an increase in direct taxation (see ARCIS 2001 and Martner 2005). Others, such as the authors themselves, highlighted the importance of considering the distributional effect of public expenditure together with revenues when judging the progressivity of a taxation system. Thus, they suggest to focus on increasing the expenditure directed to the poor instead of increasing direct taxation, which, they argue, is more distortionary than a flat VAT and it is hardly feasible due to the administrative limits still present in Chile. On the other side, conservative think tanks such as Libertad Y Desarrollo (LyD 2005) and the Centro de Estudios Publicos (Fontaine and Vergara 1997; Johnson (2002) oppose the increase in income taxation on the ground that this latter is distortionary and obstructs economic growth. They propose to drastically reduce the tax rates on the PIT, either lowering the top rate to 20 percent or introducing a 20 percent flat rate or even eliminating the personal income taxation and relying exclusively on VAT with a system of consumption subsidies for the poorest strata of the population.

As well as vertical, horizontal equity is debated. The issue here is the split system. Jorratt (2000) underlines the discrimination introduced by the split system against workers, who cannot defer the payment on their incomes. According to SII estimation, an employee with an average income faces a 35 percent rate of PIT while an entrepreneur with the same income pays 17 percent (quoted in Serra 1998, p. 24). This fact clearly represents a horizontal inequity and for this reason Jorratt argues for the elimination of the split system. On the other side, Hsieh and Parker (2006) argue in favor of the split system, citing that this is among the principal causes behind the investment boom enjoyed by Chile since then and helps explain Chile's outstanding levels of corporate savings for Latin American standards.

Another tool for investigating the distributional effect of the taxation system are the implicit tax rates. By comparing the fiscal revenues generated by capital, labor and consumption with their tax bases, the effective rates give an estimate of the actual fiscal burden placed upon the three factors, which can be very different from the one implied by the statutory rates as a consequence of exemptions, deductions, tax credits and evasion. The effective tax rate on consumption (C) compares revenues from VAT and excises with total consumption; the effective rate on labor (L) shows the relationship between revenues from employed work including SSC and the wages and salaries of the employees. Finally, the effective rate on capital (K) compares revenues from taxes on corporate income, capital gains and property with the operating surplus of the overall economy. A detailed description of the implicit tax rates' formulae and the related issues is beyond the scope of this work. If interested, see Mendoza *et al.* (1994), Carey and Tchilinguirian (2000), or Martner and Tromben (2004) for an application to Latin America.

Figure 8.1 shows the implicit rates (henceforth IR) on consumption, labor and capital for the period 1993–2002. Unfortunately, data on the reform period 1990–3 is not available, so that an analysis of the distributional effect of the 1990 reform cannot be carried out. Focusing on the following decade, some stylized facts emerge. First, the burden of taxation lies disproportionately on consumption. The effective rate on the latter, C, floated around 18 percent for the whole period considered. This should come as no surprise, given the predominance of indirect taxation in Chile. Although the phenomenon is common in Latin America, it's worth underlining that Chile's IR on consumption is exceptionally high for Latin American standards as well: Martner and Tromben (2004) find the Latin American average effective rate on consumption to be around 12 percent in 2000, five percentage points lower than in Chile. It is also worth noting how the trade liberalization-related loss of revenues was offset by the increase of VAT, leaving C fairly stable across the period.

Second, K floated around 7 percent for the 1993–9 period, remaining slightly above the Latin American average (estimated at 6 percent, see Martner and Tromben 2004). This might seem puzzling, given that Chile has the lowest statutory rate on corporate income in the region. However, this might be explained by a higher degree of tax compliance. In general, Chile shows degrees of tax compliance higher than those of its neighbors (see Jorratt 2000 and Bergman 2002). The introduction of a unique 15 percent rate and the elimination of various exemptions took place in 1999. This intervention's effects can be seen in Figure 8.1, were the K increased by two percentage points in three years. One would expect K to decrease after the reduction of all FCT rates to the lowest one. It is then surprising to see that it actually increased after 1999. This is explained by the widening of the taxable incomes due to the elimination of various exemptions and, more importantly, by the fact that the revenues from capital taxation are the sum of FCT and AT revenues.[9] These latter rose sharply in the 1999–2002 period, driving up K. In the following two years the unified

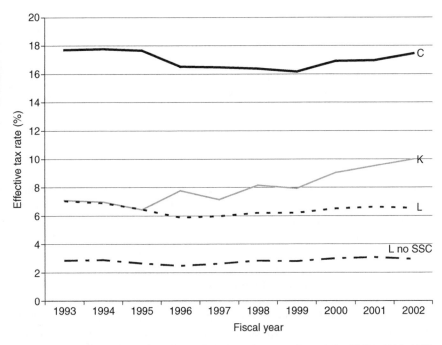

Figure 8.1 Implicit tax rates on consumption, labor and capital, Chile 1993–2002 (source: personal calculations on data from SII, Banco Central de Chile).

Notes
C: effective rate on consumption.
K: effective rate on capital.
L: effective rate on labor including social security contributions.
L no SSC: effective rate on labor excluding social security contributions.

rate was increased up to 17 percent. The effects of this increase on K are unfortunately not computable due to the lack of data.

Finally, employed labor bears an exceptionally low part of the taxation burden. When excluding SSC, the IR on labor is roughly 3 percent. Not that this phenomenon is peculiar to Chile: the Latin American average IR on employed labor is even lower, staying around 2 percent (see Martner and Tromben 2004). It would not be an exaggeration to say that income from employed labor is almost untaxed in Chile and in Latin America. Altogether, this analysis confirms the findings of Engel *et al.* (1998b) that the Chilean taxation system is regressive. The effective rates analysis identifies the source of its regressive nature, which is the dominance of consumption taxation and the almost-exemption of personal income.

Recent tax reforms and future prospects

After the successful transition to democracy, the stabilization of the macroeconomic environment, the strong reduction of public debt and the covering of revenues loss due to trade liberalization, Chile entered the new millennium in a position to focus on medium-term goals such as enhancing the efficiency of its taxation system, as commonly defined (see Slemrod and Yitkzaki 1996). In 1998–2000 the SII carried out various inquiries on the state of the system (Serra 1998; Barra and Jorratt 1998; and Jorratt 2000). The documents' aim was to identify its shortcomings and to propose the most appropriate interventions to tackle them. Four areas of intervention were proposed: the simplification of the system; the reduction of its distortionary elements; the reduction of the costs of compliance; and the fight against evasion. The main proposals to achieve these goals were the elimination of various exemptions and franchises to the general CIT and VAT treatment; the unification of the CIT rate; the substitution of the complex saving incentive scheme with a split system excluding all withheld profits from the CIT base, the reduction of the PIT top rate and a comprehensive plan to fight against tax evasion.

Judging from recent interventions, the inquiries turned out to be very influential. As we have seen above, in 1999 the split system replaced the previous incentive scheme and the unique CIT rate substituted the multi-rate system while the top PIT rate that was reduced in 2002 and 2003. On the other side, most exemptions and franchises (e.g. to the building sector and to exporters) are still applied to both CIT and to VAT. Remarkable attention has been given to the minimization of compliance costs, defined as the costs in terms of time and money undergone by the taxpayer in order to fulfill her duties. The simplification of the system was indeed accompanied by a noteworthy development in the computerization of the taxation process, which reached in Chile a higher degree than in OECD countries (see Barraza Luengo (2000) for early developments and the SII website for the latest ones). For example, since 2001 the personal income tax is wholly payable on the Internet. The main rationale behind the minimization of compliance costs was to foster the fight against evasion. This issue had attracted the attention of the Chilean authorities since the mid-1990s (see Jorratt 1996; Engel *et al.* 1998b; Trujillo Puentes 1998). According to the Silvani and Brondolo (1993) study, Chile had the highest estimated rate of VAT compliance in all Latin America. Their findings are confirmed by the SII internal study of Barra and Jorratt (1999). Moreover, Chilean citizens appear to have a higher "tax morale" as well as higher respect for the tax authorities than citizens of neighbor states (Bergman 2002). However, with an estimated 20 percent and 24 percent of VAT and total evasion (Jorratt 2000) respectively, the phenomenon still represented a significant damage to public finances. In June 2001, Law 19,738 launched the Plan de Lucha Contra la Evasion Tributaria (plan against tax evasion, PATE). Its declared goal was to reduce tax non-compliance from the estimated 24 percent figure to 20 percent in 2005. In order to achieve this goal, between 2001 and 2004 a number of laws (especially the Tax Procedure Code and the VAT Law) have been modified so as to enhance the enforcement power of the SII, while its auditor staff has been expanded. Penalties for non-compliance have been sharply increased and efforts to better coordinate the tax administration system (the SII, the Treasury and National Customs Service) have been carried out (for a summary of the PATE law see SII 2001). The results of the PATE have been investigated in SII (2005) and they depict a clear success. Estimated tax evasion has dropped to 19.8 percent or 15.6 percent of the GDP, depending on the estimation method used. In both cases, the 20 percent threshold has been passed. Simultaneously, VAT evasion dropped from 19.4 percent in 2001 to 14.3 percent in 2005.

The current debate

As outlined above the privatization of the pension system implemented in 1981 generated a sizeable "social security deficit." Furthermore, the system proved to guarantee adequate pensions only to workers able to contribute constantly over their lifetime. Temporary and "off-the-books" workers (mainly women and low-skilled workers) therefore face serious risks of poverty at retirement age. If they contributed for less than 20 years, they do not have the right to claim the minimum pension guaranteed by the government. Meanwhile, as a consequence of market concentration (the three biggest AFP market shares reaches 75 percent), low demand elasticity (employees are obliged to contribute to AFP) and huge marketing costs, the administrative costs of the system are extremely high (2.4 percent of workers' monthly wages) and AFP secure themselves out-standing profits (25 percent on average in 2005). In March 2006, the Chilean president Bachelet appointed a commission of experts to investigate possible interventions to tackle these problems. The commission's report (available at www.consejoreformaprevisional.cl) proposed a vast number of interventions, the most important of which are: eliminating the 20-year requisite for minimum pension eligibility; equalizing women and men to a retirement age of 65 (cur-rently 60 and 65, respectively); opening the AFP market to banks (currently forced to set up an ad hoc company to enter); allowing the separation of pension fund and account management services companies; and, finally, allocating new workers (220,000 a year) to the cheapest AFP via yearly auctions conducted by the social security governmental watchdog. The report, published in June 2006, is currently under scrutiny of the government and the social parties. Discussions for an encompassing reform law should start in 2007.

Conclusions

In the last decade the Chilean tax authorities invested relevant energies and resources in reducing the distortionary elements, the compliance costs and the administrative costs of the taxation system. This investment paid off: Chile has now a simple system that generates the highest yields in the Latin American context with relatively low costs of compliance and little distortionary elements. Moreover, thanks to these elements and a firm stand against evasion, it is the Latin American country with the lowest estimated evasion. On the other side, the predominance of indirect taxation and the almost-exemption of personal income make the Chilean system regressive. In a country with such income disparities, this issue cannot be ignored. The other matter of concern is the relevant imbalance that the social security system will produce in the next decades. However, with sound fiscal and macroeconomic fundamentals, strong growth and an efficient tax authority, Chile has the opportunity to tackle these problems. Whether this will happen is a political more than an economic issue.

Notes

1 Figures for the central government are almost identical (2.2 percent), which is not surprising since local taxes are negligible in Chile. The fiscal system is highly centralized.
2 Workers contributing at the moment of the reform were guaranteed the right to choose between the PAYG and FF scheme.
3 These benefits are paid to the worker via the "Bono de Reconocimiento" (last row in Table 8.1) at the moment of transferral to the FF scheme.
4 A term that should to be handled with care, see Naim (1999).
5 Since 1981, 10 percent of workers' monthly wages are withheld by the employer and paid to the private pension funds (Administradoras de Fondos de Pensiones, AFP). Strictly speaking, there are therefore social contributions, but they may not be considered "taxes" as their revenue is not accrued by the government.
6 The following description is based on information available on January 2007. Tax brackets and rates are therefore those applied to the fiscal year ending on 31 December 2006.
7 The conversion to US dollars is computed using the yearly average value of the UTM and the yearly average Peso/dollar exchange rate.
8 The CASEN survey is an household survey with social, economical and demographical information carried out by the ministry of planification (MIDEPLAN) every four years. It constitutes the principal source of micro-level data regarding the socio-economical state of the country.
9 The AT is levied on non-resident individuals. These cannot be employees in Chile. Therefore, I have assumed the AT base to be all profits and therefore I have included AT revenues in the numerator of K. This means I have ruled out by assumption the existence of self-employed workers carrying out their activity in Chile but residing abroad. Although possible it does not appear to be a numerically relevant situation.

References

ARCIS (2001) *El Sistema Tributario Chileno*, Universidad ARCIS, Santiago de Chile.
Arenas de Mesa, A. (2000) *El Sistema de Pensiones en Chile: Principales Resultados y Desafios Pendientes*, CEPAL, Santiago de Chile.
Barra, P. and Jorratt, M. (1998) "Un Analisis del Sistema Tributario Chileno," SII, mimeo.
—— (1999) "Estimacion de la evasion tributaria en Chile," Departamento de Estudios del SII, Santiago de Chile, mimeo.
Barraza Luengo, F. (2000) "Desarrollo de los Sistemas Informaticos y sus Aplicaciones," CIAT, mimeo.
Baunsgaard, T. and Keen, M. (2005) "Tax Revenue and (or?) Trade Liberalization," IMF Working Paper 05/112, Washington, DC: IMF.
Bergman, M. (2002) "Who Pays for Social Policy? A Study on Taxes and Trust," *Journal of Social Policy*, vol. 31, n. 2, pp. 289–305.

Boylan, D. (1996) "Taxation and Transition: The Politics of the 1990 Chilean Tax Reform," *Latin American Research Review*, vol. 31, n. 1, pp. 7–31.

Bulmer-Thomas, V. (2003) *The Economic History of Latin America since Independence*, 2nd edition, Cambridge: Cambridge University Press.

Carey, D. and Tchilinguirian, H. (2000) "Average Effective Tax Rates on Capital, Labor and Consumption," OECD Economics Department Working Papers n. 258.

Diario Oficial (1976) "Decreto Ley n. 1606," *Diario Oficial* 03–12–1976.

Engel, E., Galetovic, A. and Raddatz, C. (1998a) "Taxes and Income Distribution in Chile: Some Unpleasant Redistributive Arithmetic," NBER Working Paper n. 6828.

—— (1998b) "Efectos de la Accion del Servicio Internos de Impuestos sobre la Recaudacion de Iva y Renta," Departamento de Estudios del SII, Santiago de Chile, mimeo.

Fontaine, B. and Vergara, R. (1997) "Una reforma Tributaria para el Crecimiento," *Estudios Publicos*, n.67.

Godoy Ibanez, M. "Contribuciones de Bienes Raices o Impuesto Territorial," Departamento de Estudios del SII, Santiago de Chile, mimeo.

Hsieh, C. and Parker, J. A. (2006) "Taxes and Growth in a Financially Underdeveloped Country: Evidence from the Chilean Investment Boom," NBER Working Paper n. 12104.

Johnson, C. (2002) "Una Propuesta de Reforma Tributaria Eficiente," *Estudios Publicos* n. 87.

Jorratt, M. (1996) "Evaluacion de la Capacided Recaudatoria del Sistema Tributario y de la Evasion Tributaria," Departamento de Estudios del SII, Santiago de Chile, mimeo.

—— (2000) *Diagnostico del Sistema Tributario Chileno*, Departamento de Estudios del SII, Santiago de Chile.

Lagos, G. and Lima, M. (2005) "Pay your Taxes! Faulty Calculations or Ideological Prejudice?," in *The Pay Your Taxes Debate: Perspectives on Corporate Taxation and Social Responsibility in the Chilean Mining Industry*, Program on Technology, Business and Society Paper n. 15, UNRISD, Geneva.

LyD (2005) "Impuestos: Chile contra la Corriente," *Temas Publicos* n. 719.

Martner, G. (2005) "¿Existe un costo en eficiencia de la redistribución del ingreso?," Universidad de Santiago, Santiago de Chile, mimeo.

Martner, R. and Tromben, V. (2004) "Tax Reforms and Fiscal Stabilisation in Latin American Countries," ILPES research centre, CEPAL, Santiago de Chile.

Mendoza, E. Razin, A. and Tesar, L. (1994) "Effective Tax Rates in Macroeconomics: Cross-Country Estimates of Tax Rates on Factor Incomes and Consumption," NBER Working Paper n. 4864.

Naim (1999) "Fads and Fashion in Economic Reform: Washington Consensus or Washington Confusion?," Working Draft of a Paper Prepared for the IMF Conference on Second Generation Reforms, Washington, DC, 26 October 1999.

Riesgo, M. (2005) "Pay Your Taxes! Corporate Social Responsibility and the Mining Industry in Chile," in *The Pay Your Taxes Debate: Perspectives on Corporate Taxation and Social Responsibility in the Chilean Mining Industry*, Program on Technology, Business and Society Paper n. 15, UNRISD, Geneva.

Sabaini, J. (2005) "Evolucion y situacion tributaria actual en America Latina: Una Serie de Temas para la Discusion," CEPAL, Santiago de Chile, mimeo.

Silvani, C. and Brondolo, J. (1993) "Medición del Cumplimiento en el IVA y Análisis de sus Determinantes," Conferencia Técnica del Centro Interamericano de Administraciones Tributarias (CIAT), Venice, Italy.

Serra, P. (1998) "Analisis de la Eficiencia del Sistema Tributario Chileno," Departamento de Estudios del SII, Santiago de Chile, mimeo.

SII (Servicio de Impuestos Internos) (2001) "Resumen del Contenido de la Ley sobre Evasion y Elusion Tributaria," Departamento de Estudios del SII, Santiago de Chile, mimeo.

—— (2005) "Ley contra Evasion Tributaria: Compromisos y Cumplimentos en el ambito de la Administracion Tributaria Interna," Departamento de Estudios del SII, Santiago de Chile, mimeo.

—— (2006a) "Mision, Objectivos e Hystoria del SII," Departamento de Estudios del SII, Santiago de Chile, webpage.

—— (2006b) "Aspectos Generales del Sistema Tributario Chileno," Departamento de Estudios del SII, Santiago de Chile, mimeo.

Slemrod, J. and Yitzhaki, S. (1996) "The Costs of Taxation and the Marginal Efficiency Cost of Funds," IMF Staff Papers, vol. 43, n.1, pp. 172–98.

Tanzi, V. (2000) "Taxation in Latin America in the Last Decade," prepared for the conference *Fiscal and Financial Reforms in Latin America*, Stanford University, US.

Trujillo Puentes, J. (1998) "La experiencia Chilena en el Combate a la Evasion," Departamento de Estudios del SII, Santiago de Chile, mimeo.

World Bank (2005) "Chile: Políticas de Excepción en Zonas Extremas," Informe n. 27357-CH, Departamento de Reducción de Pobreza y Gestión Económica Región de Latinoamérica y el Caribe, Washington, DC.

9 Colombia

Luigi Bernardi, Laura Fumagalli
and Elena Fumagalli

Colombia's environment, economy and public budget[1]

Colombia is a historically important country, covering about 1 million km² and inhabited by about 43 million people. It won independence from Spain in 1810, and since then power has been in the hands of two parties, both of whom represent the interests of the country's large landowners and other wealthy citizens. At the outset of the 2000s, Colombia was governed by a conservative, demagogic government led by A. Uribe and backed by the US government. Uribe was subsequently re-elected in 2006. Since the 1960s onwards, the country has been plagued by the spread of guerrilla warfare involving different groups, and by the Colombian mafia's influence on the trade in agricultural goods, emeralds and, of course, cocaine. This environment was, and remains, unfavorable to the building and working of the tax system and to the taxpayer's relationships to this system. This sensitive activity is performed within a context of civil war, crimes, illegal activities, corruption and social deprivation.[2] Further, the substantial size of an informal or illegal economy, together with wide tax evasion, means that high caution should be taken when using economic data.

In 2005 GDP stood at US\$98 billion (Cia-Factbook), while per capita income was US\$2,240, US\$7,900 if adjusted for PPP. Income distribution is very uneven: the Gini coefficient for household income stood at 0.54 in 2005. The share of Colombians living in poverty is nearly 50 percent. The unemployment rate is also quite high, standing nearly 15 percent. Colombia's GDP grew at a yearly rate of about 5 percent in 2005 and 2006. Inflation fell to 4.5 percent in 2006. Both macro and public budget indicators are forecast to go well in both the short and medium run (IMF 2006; CONFIS 2006). In 2007, real GDP is forecast to grow by 4 percent, while inflation should fall to 4 percent, values that ought to be maintained in the medium run (to 2010).[3]

Focusing now on the public budget, we first need to distinguish between the non-financial public sector (NFPS), general government and central government.[4] We shall refer to the NFPS when evaluating the overall financial position of the public sector, whereas we shall consider the general government level when analyzing tax revenue.

Table 9.1 Structure and development of operations in the non-financial public sector – selected figures and years – Colombia (% of GDP)

	1990	1995	1996	1997	1998	1999	2000	2001	2002	2003	2004	2005
Total revenue, of which:	*20.0*	*27.8*	*31.0*	*31.3*	*30.5*	*33.9*	*33.7*	*35.1*	*34.7*	*35.4*	*37.5*	*34.9*
Total taxes	12.6	16.5	17.3	17.8	18.0	16.2	16.0	17.4	17.3	17.6	18.6	18.0
Non-tax current revenue	7.3	9.4	11.4	10.9	10.3	16.7	17.2	17.6	17.2	17.6	18.7	16.9
Total expenditure, of which:	*20.6*	*28.1*	*32.7*	*34.1*	*34.2*	*38.0*	*37.5*	*39.1*	*38.1*	*38.0*	*38.6*	*35.5*
Current primary expenditure	10.9	15.7	17.6	18.9	20.2	25.8	25.0	25.8	25.5	25.3	26.3	25.3
Interest on public debt	3.2	3.3	3.9	3.7	4.6	3.7	4.3	4.8	4.5	4.7	4.5	4.0
Capital expenditure	6.5	9.2	11.2	11.5	9.4	8.3	8.2	8.5	8.1	8.0	7.7	5.9
Primary surplus	*2.6*	*3.0*	*2.2*	*0.9*	*0.9*	*-0.3*	*0.4*	*0.7*	*1.0*	*2.1*	*3.6*	*3.7*
Budget balance	*-0.6*	*-0.3*	*-1.7*	*-2.8*	*-3.7*	*-4.1*	*-4.0*	*-4.1*	*-3.5*	*-2.6*	*-0.9*	*-0.3*
Total public debt of NFPS	*–*	*–*	*29.7*	*34.6*	*39.1*	*50.1*	*57.8*	*62.9*	*71.5*	*67.7*	*62.6*	*60.2*
Total public debt of central government	*14.8*	*13.9*	*14.4*	*17.8*	*24.5*	*34.6*	*42.7*	*48.4*	*55.9*	*54.9*	*52.0*	*51.0*

Source: ILPES-CEPAL on Colombian data of Ministerio de Hacienda and CONFIS.

Note
The figures for 2005 are provisional.

Both the total revenue and the total expenditure of the NFPS increased by 75 percent between the early 1990s and the early 2000s.[5] Taxes constitute just half of the NFPS' current revenue, with the remaining share mainly accounted for by profits from public utilities and the state-owned oil company. This allows Colombia to finance a sizeable welfare expenditure (on education, health and old-age pensions) without excessive fiscal pressure.[6] This clearly raises some questions about the future sustainability of Colombia's public finances, since:

1   the contribution made by non-renewable resources will inevitably decrease;
2   more than one utility will be privatized.

In both cases, non-tax revenue will have to be replaced by permanent structural taxes, and this will not be an easy task.[7] At the beginning of the 1990s, the budget was balanced, but this situation subsequently deteriorated during the years 1996–9, at which point an adjustment plan was adopted and the financial position of the NFPS improved as a consequence. The overall NFPS balance stood at –1.9 percent in 2006, and it is forecast to stabilize at –0.4 percent by 2010. At that time, the public debt/GDP ratio should decrease by about ten points (down to about 50 percent). Half of the funding of Colombia's public debt is forecast to come from internal sources, while the other half is due to be provided by foreign capital.

The rest of the chapter is organized as follows. The next section discusses a general overview of the Colombian tax system from the early 1990s onwards. The third section describes the main features of the major national and local taxes, updated to include the tax reform introduced in December 2006. The fourth section discusses a couple of significant tax policy issues: the personal distribution of the tax burden; and the financing of lower government tiers. The fifth section provides a brief overview of the broad reform submitted by the government in July 2006 but subsequently withdrawn in November 2006, and also outlines our suggestion for a more radical reform of taxation designed to reduce social deprivation in Colombia, but which would probably be met by strong political opposition.

A general outline of the Colombian tax system and its development since the early 1990s

The Colombian tax system from the early 1990s onwards

In the 1960s and 1970s, Colombia's tax system was a relatively simple one. However, from the 1980s onwards the system was subject to repeated reforms of a non-radical nature (Shome 1995).[8] Seven major reforms were introduced between 1990 and 2003 (Government of Colombia 2006),[9] mainly designed to increase revenue (Lozano 2000).[10] These reforms focused principally on VAT: the standard rate was increased from 10 to 16 percent, while its tax base was also enlarged. On the other hand, trade liberalization led to a reduction in revenue from customs duties. As far as direct taxes were concerned, the generous allowances of the early 1990s were only slightly reduced, while tax rates as such were not substantially modified either for individuals and for corporations. During the early 1990s, taxation on financial capital was eased to stimulate savings and investment; however, at the end of the decade the Colombian government introduced a wealth tax.[11]

Subsequent to the adjustment plan introduced towards the end of the 1990s, two small tax reforms were made in 2002 and 2003; these were partly designed to finance the battle against guerrilla warfare, which was a central issue in the Uribe government's program. The main tax measure introduced in 2002 consisted of a 10 percent surcharge on both income and corporate tax, while the 2003 reform increased the rate of the financial transaction tax (introduced in 1998 as a part of the adjustment plan) from 0.2 to 0.4 percent.[12] Taken together, these two measures yielded approximately 0.7 percent GDP. However, there was a real problem with the said reforms, they were all introduced as temporary measures, but were subsequently extended (in general to 2006–7), as about 1.2–2 GDP percentage points of revenue (wealth tax included) was due to evaporate, and this lost revenue had to be replaced in some way.[13] In 2005–6 the increased openness of the economy encouraged a number of new specific tax measures (International Law Office 2006), including new legislation designed to avoid double taxation among Andean countries (thus replacing the one in place dating back to 1971[14]), and new tax regimes for Free-Trade Zones and for Low-Tax Jurisdictions. With reference to the latter, a higher withholding tax rate is currently due to be applied to cross-border payments made to beneficiaries located in a list of foreign tax havens. However, the government has yet to publish the list of those countries acting as such tax havens.

An overview of the current fiscal structure, and a comparison with that of other Latin American countries

As a consequence of the above-mentioned reforms and of the buoyancy of the tax bases, general government's total fiscal pressure almost doubled between the early 1990s and the early 2000s, increasing from 10.5 percent of GDP in 1990 to 20.4 in 2004 (Table 9.2).[15]

This substantial increase was generated by direct taxation, and in particular by corporation, property and wealth taxes. Indirect taxation rose by more than three points, and this was entirely accounted for by the increase in VAT. Social security contributions more than tripled, partly as a consequence of the 1993 pension reform (Clavijo 1998), although their point of departure in 1990 was only GDP 0.8 percent. Thus total fiscal revenue in 2004 consisted mainly of taxes (17.5 percent of GDP), rather than of social security contributions (2.8 percent of GDP). The respective weights of direct and indirect taxes were evenly balanced. More than one of the above-mentioned features is characteristic of Colombia, to be found in very few other Latin American countries, and is not to be found in the continental average (see Chapter 2).

In the case of direct taxes, up until the late 1990s the most important ones were those levied on large companies and multinationals, whereas the personal

Table 9.2 Structure and development of consolidated general government revenue in Colombia 1990–2004 (% of GDP)

	1990	1991	1992	1993	1994	1995	1996	1997	1998	1999	2000	2001	2002	2003	2004
Total tax revenue	*9.6*	*10.7*	*11.2*	*11.5*	*12.1*	*11.8*	*12.5*	*13.2*	*13.1*	*13.4*	*13.9*	*15.8*	*16.0*	*16.6*	*17.6*
Direct taxes, of which:	3.6	4.6	4.9	5.0	4.8	4.7	4.6	5.2	5.2	5.7	5.9	7.0	7.6	7.7	8.4
Income and profits	3.2	4.2	4.4	4.5	4.2	4.0	3.8	4.4	4.3	4.2	4.3	5.3	5.2	5.1	6.0
Households	–	–	–	–	0.2	0.2	0.2	0.2	0.2	0.2	–	–	–	–	–
Corporations and businesses	–	–	–	–	3.9	3.8	3.6	4.2.	4.1	4.0	–	–	–	–	–
Property	0.4	0.4	0.4	0.4	0.5	0.6	0.7	1.4	1.2	1.4	1.2	1.4	2.0	2.1	2.0
Other direct taxes	0.1	0.1	0.1	0.1	0.1	0.2	0.1	0.1	0.1	0.4	0.4	0.4	0.4	0.4	0.4
Indirect taxes, of which:	6.0	6.1	6.4	6.5	7.3	7.1	7.8	8.1	7.9	7.7	8.0	8.8	8.6	9.1	9.2
General taxes on goods and services	2.4	2.8	3.2	3.3	4.1	4.1	4.7	4.8	4.6	4.4	4.8	5.3	5.2	5.7	5.9
Specific taxes on goods and services	1.8	1.8	1.8	1.7	1.9	1.8	1.8	1.8	1.8	1.8	1.9	1.9	1.9	2.0	2.0
International trade	1.3	1.0	0.9	1.0	1.1	1.0	0.9	1.0	1.2	0.9	1.0	1.1	1.0	0.9	0.9
Other indirect taxes	0.5	0.5	0.4	0.5	0.3	0.3	0.3	0.4	0.3	0.5	0.3	0.4	0.4	0.4	0.4
Social security contributions	*0.8*	*1.8*	*1.9*	*2.1*	*2.8*	*3.7*	*4.1*	*4.4*	*3.8*	*3.6*	*2.9*	*2.9*	*2.6*	*2.4*	*2.8*
Total fiscal revenue	*10.5*	*12.4*	*13.1*	*13.6*	*14.9*	*15.5*	*16.6*	*17.6*	*16.9*	*16.9*	*16.8*	*18.6*	*18.8*	*19.21*	*20.4*

Source: ILPES-CEPAL on Colombian data of Ministerio de Hacienda and CONFIS.

income tax burden has been virtually non-existent (0.2 percent of GDP up until 1999).[16] This remarkable figure may be explained in political-economy terms (see also Chapter 3). Very few Colombians actually pay income tax,[17] as tax exemptions and deductions are substantial. We believe that the country's landlords and its other wealthier citizens deliberately chose to avoid directly taxing the middle classes (and themselves) to obtain political consensus. The most important indirect tax is VAT, while other forms of indirect taxation play a secondary role. Taxation by the various levels of government is highly centralized.[18] Central government only grants departments and municipalities the power to raise a limited amount of money from property and from specific goods and services.

Total fiscal pressure and tax structure differs substantially from one Latin American country to another (see Chapter 2). A quick comparison of taxation in Colombia with that of other Latin American countries must necessarily be deemed to be purely indicative.

Nevertheless, the few figures shown in Table 9.3 may provide some insight into the comparative position of Colombia. In the first few years of the 2000s, fiscal pressure in Colombia has been close to the Latin American average; the increase in Colombia's taxes during the 1990s, on the other hand, was a multiple of the Latin American average. Moreover, the data show that Colombia has a relatively high share of direct taxes. If we compare these figures with those in Table 9.2, the picture becomes more complex. It is immediately clear that up until 2000, the structure of Colombian taxation was not that far removed from the one revealed by the average figures for Latin America as a whole. The reforms implemented in the late 1990s and during the first few years of the 2000s were mostly temporary measures, and their impact should not be overestimated. Hence the rise in the share of direct (corporate) taxation can only be seen as a temporary phenomenon.

Table 9.3 Central and general government revenue in Colombia compared with the Latin America average

	Central government – 2005		General government – 2004*	
	Colombia	LA average	Colombia	LA average
Total fiscal pressure	17.6	15.2	20.4	21.1
Percent increase from 1990	98.0	31.0	94.2	27.1
Percent share direct taxes	42.2	27.6	41.1	28.9
Percent share indirect taxes	43.2	59.9	45.1	48.0
Percent share social contributions	15.6	12.5	13.8	23.1

Source: ILPES-CEPAL.

Notes
* Only Argentina, Bolivia, Brazil, Chile, Colombia, Costa Rica, Ecuador, Uruguay. The 2005 figures are provisional.

The institutional features of Colombia's principal taxes

The following section illustrates the Colombian fiscal system (IBFD 2006) and includes the changes recently made by the tax reform passed by parliament on 27 December 2006, and which came into force on 1 January 2007 (Congreso de Colombia 2006; Colombian Tax Flash 2007; Parra, Escobar & Cia 2006). At the end of the chapter we shall see that a broader, more ambitious reform had been submitted by the government to parliament in July 2006; but after a heated debate outside of parliament, the government withdrew the reform proposal.

National taxes

Direct taxes

The income tax system consists of a general tax levied on both individuals and business enterprises. For practical purposes, we distinguish between the tax applicable to individuals (personal income tax – PIT) and that applicable to businesses (corporate tax – CT).

Personal income tax – PIT

Colombian PIT is a global income tax. It is levied at the same rate on the total income of an individual. Special taxation plays a very marginal role and is levied on a few items. The deemed minimum annual net income of individual taxpayers is 3 percent of their net wealth. Married couples are taxed separately: each spouse is taxed on his/her income, but spouses cannot divide their joint income for taxation purposes. There are separate tax regimes for two specific groups of taxpayers: Colombian national and foreign residents pay individual income taxation (IIT), while non-resident income tax (NIT) is levied on non-residents in the form of a withholding tax.[19] Resident Colombian citizens are taxed on their worldwide income, while resident foreigners who have been living in the country for less than five years are subject to tax on their income earned in Colombia. As of their fifth year of residence, foreigners resident are also taxed on their worldwide income.

Individual income taxation – IIT

IIT is based on a broad concept of income that places considerable emphasis on the personality of taxation. The main kinds of income comprised within the tax basis are as follows:

1   wages, and all other incomes from employment, together with retirement, old age, disability and company pensions received after 1998 or, regardless of when received, that amount over and above a certain threshold;

2   capital gains, gifts and inheritances, including any such sums from deceased foreign residents;
3   business and investment income.

On the basis of certain personalized targets, a considerable amount of tax exclusions and exemptions are granted: for example, the following are exempt from income tax:

1   those incomes which do not exceed some thresholds (not automatically adjusted for inflation);
2   the following incomes (up to a certain threshold established by law):
    a)   25 percent of employees' earnings when they are not over (2006) COP7,033,000[20] per month;
    b)   pension-fund related payments and life insurance payments and proceeds;
    c)   accident, sickness, maternity benefits, and sums received as severance or job's end payments.

The IIT is progressive with four brackets and marginal rates, shown in Table 9.4. Note the high thresholds in a country where the PCI of those not living in poverty and/or the employed is estimated to be about US$4,500. Income tax is directly *withheld* monthly by employers from their employees' wages. The 10 percent surcharge, in force up until 2006, has recently been abolished.

Non-residents income tax – NIT

NIT is levied on non-residents on the part of their income pertaining to activities located in Colombia, which in principle is subject to taxation at 33 percent. However, the income paid abroad is de facto subject to a final *withholding tax*, which may be levied at a rate of well below the said rate, either at 10 or even at 0 percent, according to the various incomes in question. The previous surcharge of

Table 9.4 Tax brackets and rates of Colombian personal income tax

Net taxable income	Marginal tax rate	Average tax rats at mid-brackets
COP 0–21,800,000 (US$9,2506)	0	0
COP 21,800,000–34,000,0000 (US$14,400)	19	5.0
COP 34,000,000–82,000,000 (US$34,750)	28	15.5
Over COP 82,000,000 (US$34,750)	Lump-sum payment (COP 15,760,000) plus 33% of the excess over and above COP 82,000,000	27.7% as example for an income of COP 200,000,000 (US$84,750)

7 percent was abolished by the 2006 reform. Of particular interest is that dividends are exempt from NIT when they are taxed at the corporate level, or are taxed at 33 percent when untaxed at that level. Interest may be taxed at either 0 or 33 percent, depending on its source. All payments to a party of a jurisdiction defined as a tax haven are subject to the 33 percent rate.

Corporate tax – CIT

CT is levied on the following broad categories of taxpayer:

1   Colombian corporations or foreign corporations making profits in Colombia;
2   state-owned enterprises and mixed public/private companies;
3   investment funds, mutual investment funds, family compensation funds and so on;
4   cooperative and mutual societies, unions, non-profit-making foundations or associations.

Colombian citizens are taxed on their worldwide income, whereas foreigners on their Colombian earnings.[21] A broad income concept is applied in principle. Total income includes all receipts, unless specifically exempt. Once all proceeds and capital gains have been added up, net income is then given by subtracting cost and expenses from total revenue. Tax losses may be carried forward without any limitations, but no carry-back is allowed. A large number of exemptions are provided for, and their entity was further enlarged by the December 2007 reform. They include:

1   40 percent of the value of tangible fixed assets in the tax year the said assets were purchased;
2   all taxes paid as a consequence of the economic activity performed are fully deductible;
3   up to 25 percent of the tax levied on financial transaction;
4   placement or transfer to capital reserve of certain items;
5   those incentives granted to business enterprises operating in the free zones (FZS).

The CT tax base is deemed to be the higher of the taxable income, and a "minimum presumptive income" equal to 3 percent of a corporation's net worth.[22] Corporate income will be taxed at a flat rate of 33 percent from 2008 onwards (taxed at 34 percent in 2007).[23, 24]

Other direct taxes

FINANCIAL INCOME PAID TO RESIDENTS

Interest and capital gains received are included in taxable income, i.e. they are taxed under the ordinary rules, with the exception of a few items which are exempted/subject to special rules. Dividends paid to Colombian residents by Colombian corporations or Colombian branches of foreign companies are no longer taxable (they were taxed at 7 percent before the December 2006 reform).

NET WEALTH TAX AND OTHER TAXES ON CAPITAL AND PROPERTY

Up until the year 2010, net wealth tax will be levied on those taxpayers (individuals or enterprises) whose liquid net worth at 1 January of each year exceeds a given amount (COP3,000,000 in 2007). The tax rate is 1.2 percent (compared with 0.3 percent before the December 2006 reform), and the tax is levied on the net value of wealth excluding shareholdings in nationalized companies.[25] Real estate benefiting from works of local public interest may be subject to the payment of a battlement contribution. Inheritances, bequests and gifts are not taxed as such, but are considered and taxed as capital gains within the income tax framework.

FINANCIAL TRANSACTIONS TAX

This tax was originally conceived as a temporary measure when introduced in 1998: nevertheless, since the 2000 tax reform it has became a permanent feature of the tax system, and the revenue it produces now plays a sizeable role in Colombia's fiscal revenue. The tax is levied at the rate of 0.4 percent on those financial transactions regarding cashier's checks and savings account deposits. However, transactions between accounts belonging to the same person or company are exempt from financial transaction tax, and a 25 percent deduction from income tax is granted.

Indirect taxes

VALUE ADDED TAX – VAT

Since 1983, VAT has gradually emerged as a vital source of tax yield, taking the place of the then general sales tax. Certain of its present, important features have only emerged over the course of time, including the gradual increase in VAT rates, its extension to services, the deductibility of machinery, and its being credited against incoming VAT rather than against PIT or CT due (Shome 1995). VAT is levied on the supply and importation of all goods and services, unless those explicitly excluded by law. In the latter case, the goods may be either excluded (i.e. not subject to VAT) or exempted (zero-rated, i.e. subject to VAT at 0 percent). The former category of goods includes a basket of essential goods consumed by, among others, poor households. The latter category consists mainly of exports, financial and insurance services and some social services (health, public transport, education). Special rules apply to small taxpayers. A share of the yield is transferred to lower tiers. The standard VAT rate is 16 percent,[26] although certain goods and services are taxed at four different rates: 1.6 percent (in the case, for example, of cleaning and private security services); 10 percent (certain foods, health insurance, entertainments, cotton, tobacco, works of art, air freight); 20 percent (e.g. mobile telephone services, some vehicles and some alcoholic beverages); while other vehicles and alcoholic beverages may be subject to 25 and 35 percent VAT.

Other indirect taxes

STAMP DUTY

Stamp duty is payable on any public or private document concerning the creation, existence, changes or cancellation of obligations over and above a certain threshold. Pursuant to the 2006 reform, the tax is due to be gradually phased out. The current rate of 1.5 percent will be reduced to 1 percent as of 2008, then to 0.5 percent in 2009, before the tax is abolished altogether in 2010.

EXCISE DUTIES AND AGRICULTURAL PRODUCTS' TAXES

Excises duties are due on petrol, tobacco and alcoholic beverages. Tax rates vary, depending on both the characteristics and type of product in question, but most are relatively high, as they indeed are in other developing tax systems.[27] Exports are exempt from such duties. Other lesser taxes are levied on agricultural products (such as rice, cacao, wheat, barely, maize, sorghum and oats).

IMPORT AND EXPORT DUTIES

Certain custom duties are levied on foreign products. As a member of the Andean Group, Colombia must abide by a mutual plan regarding external tariffs. According to this plan, the rate levied on those raw materials either not produced in the member countries or scarce therein, is set at 0 percent. Intermediate goods are taxed at 5, 10, or 15 percent while a 20 percent rate is applied to final products. The duties on vehicles are the highest of all, and may even be as high as 35 percent. With the sole exception of coffee, which is subject to several duties, no taxes are levied on exports.

Local taxes

Taxes may be imposed by Colombia's parliament, although certain levies may also be introduced by departmental assemblies and municipal councils. However, the revenue from these taxes constitutes a very small part of the total tax burden and a very small share of the resources needed to finance local spending. If authorized to do so by parliament, the departments may establish taxes on alcoholic beverages, cigarettes or tobacco, gasoline, lottery tickets and horse race betting, together with registration duties and social security contributions. The *unified real estate tax*, together with the *industry and commerce tax*, represent the municipalities' main source of revenue. The basis used to assess the property tax is the national cadastre, while the rates are chosen locally from a range set by national law. Public establishments, government departments, state-run enterprises, mixed public/private companies, and companies belonging to departments, are not subject to the tax. Furthermore, municipalities may levy road, forestry, gambling and prize-winnings taxes, and benefit from contributions when real estate properties appreciate as a result of public works.

Social security contributions

Subsequent to the 1993 pension reform[28] (Clavijo 1998; Rudolph *et al.* 2006), and its following amendments, any public or private sector employee[29] has to contribute to the pension system at a rate of 15.5 percent of wages, approximately two-thirds of which was charged to the employer, while the rest to the employee. Subsidies are provided to those citizens who are not able themselves to contribute to social welfare funds. Only those taxpayers earning over and above a certain threshold income are asked to pay their social security contributions in full. The healthcare insurance charge is about 5 percent for employees and 7 percent for employers. Payroll taxes are due from employers to cover unemployment insurance, subsidies for families and poor children, occupational accident insurance and technical training, at rates varying from 2 to about 8 percent for any single item. Hence, the total burden of payroll taxes amounts to all of 47 percent, about 37 percent of which is charged to employers and about 10 percent to employees.

One may ask why such high rates do not give rise, as is the case in Brazil, to higher revenue from social security contributions than the present figure of 2.8 percent of GDP (see Table 9.2). One answer may lie in the fact that the present pension system is estimated to cover only about 25–30 percent of the entire labor force, and in the lengthy term of transition to the new pension system (completion is due in 2013).

The principal tax policy issues

The distribution of Colombia's fiscal burden

The increasing Colombian social expenditure over the last 20 years has not been very effective from the redistributive viewpoint. This has been due to the lack of a valid evaluation system, to the fragmentation of the welfare programs (Perotti 2000), and to the fact that these measures have mainly consisted in funding education and healthcare – expenditures which however appear to be progressive (Zapata and Ariza 2005) – while no attempt was made to implement a social security safety net. Colombia has merely adopted a targeted program of transfers to the poor (*Familias en acción*) like to those introduced in recent years in other Latin American countries (Clavijo 2005).[30]

It is thus worthwhile analyzing the redistributive effects of taxation. Over the last few years, Colombia's government has made efforts to expand progressive taxation. In particular, from 1998 onwards increasing importance was given to the financial transaction tax; however, it is difficult to assess the impact of this tax on the progressivity of the tax system.[31] At first sight it would seem that income tax has contributed towards the redistribution of income, given its system of progressive rates. In fact, the average value of the PIT quasi Gini coefficient[32] for 1993–2000 (Sanchez and Espinosa 2005) is quite high (0.64).[33] These values point to a huge concentration in the distribution of the tax burden, whereby the richer quantiles of the population pay the majority of the tax. However, this does not necessarily imply that the tax system significantly levels out the inequalities plaguing Colombian society. To check this effect we ought to look at the post-tax Gini Index. A good example is provided by Zapata and Ariza (2005), who calculate the Reynolds-Smolensky index[34] for 2003 and obtain a miniscule value (0.005). The weak redistributive power of the tax can be accounted for by two simple facts. The first is that the above-mentioned series of exemptions substantially narrows the tax base; second, we ought not to forget the massive effect of tax evasion in Colombia. To conclude then, even though the legal structure of Colombia's PIT is a progressive one, its equalizing power is quite weak since the incidence of the tax is extremely low.

Standard literature of public finance point out the negative equity effects of indirect taxation, due to taxpayers' decreasing consumption propensity. However, one must take into account the structure of Colombian VAT, whereby many basic goods are VAT-exempt, while certain luxury goods are taxed at higher rates. According to Ávila *et al.* (2001), the tax allows for income redistribution for the first 18 ventiles, whereas the situation differs in the case of the last two ventiles where the rates of saving are quite high. Other scholars, on the contrary, believe that the tax is fully capable of improving equity at any stage. Sanchez and Espinosa (2005), for example, consider the contribution of each decile towards the amount of VAT collected by the government. They show that the tax is a progressive one that is mainly paid by the rich people.

The decentralization of government layers

Over the last two decades, Colombia has made substantial efforts to define its fiscal decentralization model. The first step taken towards this goal was the 1991 Constitutional Reform, one aim of which was to assign greater control over welfare expenditure to the lower tiers of government. The process, however, failed to modify the allocation of tax revenue. While taxation remained centralized, a complex system of vertical transfers was set up to allow local governments to maintain high levels of spending (mainly on health and education; Lozano 2000). The transfers were granted as a share of central government revenues, and were calculated using revenue-sharing parameters. This way of financing the lower tiers produced a sharp rise in the flow of resources from central to the lower governments. During the second half of the 1990s, the quantity of transfers grew enormously, and this discouraged tax efforts at the local level (Jungito and Rincon 2004). The ensuing debate pointed out that the main weakness of the existing transfers' system was the imbalance between the revenue raised by local layers and their actual spending. Since local administrations were also able to borrow to finance their expenditure, and could rely on transfers from central government, the problem of the moral risk arose (Iregui *et al.* 2001). Local layers did not need to promote efficient spending, since they knew that central government could bail them out (Alesina *et al.* 2000). However, the entity of resources was not the only factor creating bad incentives. Transfers to municipalities were established as an average of various indicators, where the percentage of those people with "unsatisfied basic needs" accounted for more than 60 percent. While this scheme improved horizontal equity, it also contributed towards the "soft budget constraint" problem.

The inadequacy of Colombian fiscal decentralization was one of the main concerns analyzed by the "Alesina mission" (Alesina 2000), a study group whose aim was to suggest institutional reforms. The group's advisors recommended that a few simple changes be made as follows:

1   municipalities and departments should not be allowed to borrow;
2   allocation rules should be changed, not by eliminating transfers but allocating them using a rule ensuring that local tiers benefit from a share of the taxes collected in the local area;
3   greater flexibility and clarity with regard to spending decisions and responsibilities.

In line with these recommendations, and in an attempt to reverse the trend in public expenditure while at the same time preserving a decentralized system, Colombia witnessed a new reform in 2001 (Sanchez *et al.* 2002). This reform set up a new system for the period 2002–8. A limit was imposed on local tiers' spending. The link between the revenue of central government and transfers was removed, and transfers were converted into lump-sum grants. From 2002 to 2005, the upper limit yearly increases in transfers was set at 2 percent in real terms; from 2006 to 2008, it was due to rise to 2.5 percent. Finally, as of 2009, transfers will be allowed to rise at the same pace as central government's tax revenue. Hence, after 2009, funding to local layers will once again be linked to central government's revenue; the consequences of this will depend largely on the degree to which the transition scheme manages to recovery fiscal responsibility (IMF 2006).

The latest changes in the Colombian tax system: a lot of work resulting in a limited, unfair reform and an alternative proposal

Step one: the need for a broad, theoretically coherent tax reform

After the 1998–2001 adjustment plan, clear evidence emerged of the need for a broad reform of the Colombian tax system. A politically accountable, academically authoritative committee was appointed to identify the weaknesses of the existing system, to establish a coherent framework and to set directions for change: the *Misión de Ingreso Público* (2002), and it drew up these guidelines:

1 both vertical and horizontal equity, as well as efficiency, need to be improved;
2 the government has to create new taxes that are easy to handle;
3 a good working relationship between central and local governments needs to be built.

Consequently, the implementation of the following measures was suggested:

1 the widening of the PIT basis, by limiting some deductions and abating exemption thresholds;
2 the simplification of para-fiscal contributions, to be also divided according to payers incomes;
3 the strengthening of CIT by enlarging its basis and reducing the existing generous allowances;
4 the widening of the range of goods on which VAT is due, and the reduction of the number of VAT rates. The final proposal was to expand the base so as to cover one half of GDP, and to apply a single 10.4 percent rate[35] on all goods while preserving the same revenue as before. The negative effects on redistribution could be compensated for by keeping some essential goods tax-free, or by giving poorer households a VAT rebate. In this case the VAT rate should remain at 16 percent;
5 the reduction of the financial transactions tax;
6 the strengthening of local taxation.

Step two: the wide-ranging, ambitious program of reforms proposed in July 2006

In July 2006, the Colombian government submitted a program for a tax reform to broadly modify the existing system. The taxes due for change were as follows (Government of Colombia, 2006):

1 *CIT* – exempt incomes to be cut but not fully cancelled out; all fixed investments to become deductible. A rate of 34–32 percent to be applied from the first to the third and later years.
2 *PIT* – the level of exemption to be raised and marginal rates reduced. All allowances, barring the basic exemption, to be repealed.
3 *VAT* – rates to be greatly simplified (10, 16, 25 percent). Exemptions not to be completely abolished, but in the main replaced by zero rates. Rebates of COP236,000 (= US$100) to be introduced to in part compensate the poor for the lesser number of essential goods exempt.

4   *Financial transaction tax* to be kept in force at the rate of 0.4 percent, while
    stamp duty and *wealth tax* to be abolished.[36]

The tax reform package was not at all in keeping with the MIP's recommendations. The exemption thresholds not had to be reduced but raised to the point
where total allowances were extended rather than reduced. VAT should continue
to be levied at more than one rate, and a dual system of untaxed goods and
rebates to poor households established. A number of important issues were not
addressed: e.g. the question of decentralized government's revenue, and the
reform of para–fiscality. In terms of equity, the reform proposal greatly favored
the middle and upper classes, whose incomes were lightly taxed while their
wealth was now largely to escape taxation. Colombia's poor citizens, on the
other hand, were penalized when it came to taxation on consumption.

Step three: the minor, unfair 'reform' introduced in December 2006

We have mentioned the changes introduced by 27 December 2006 reform in
the previous description of the Colombian taxes, since these changes will
come into force from 1 January 2007. However, the overall picture shows that
once again the few real changes made are to the advantage of the country's
wealthier citizens and its large corporations. Income tax has remained almost
unchanged. While on the one hand, the lower limit of the top bracket has been
brought down, on the other hand no adjustments for inflation have been made
yet. The rate of wealth used to calculate "presumptive" personal and corporate
income has been halved. The wealth-tax rate has been increased, but the tax
will be abolished in 2010. A few goods have been exempted from VAT, but in
the case of a larger number of goods, the previous rates have been replaced by
a higher rate.

An alternative strategy for tax reform designed to benefit the poor rather than the rich

To counter social deprivation, any tax reform would need to be different from
the latest proposals and bills submitted. The cornerstones of such a reform
should be the extension of PIT to middle incomes at a reasonable mean rates,
together with a reduction in VAT charges. Wealth tax should be made permanent, and serious measures should be adopted to combat tax evasion and smug-
gling. In our opinion, political forces rather than economic factors are
preventing Colombia from substantially increasing both income and wealth
taxes. This potential revenue could be added to that recovered by extending
instruments such as presumptive assessments and minimum taxes. A surcharge
should be introduced on the rents of those large corporations operating within
the framework of a natural monopoly or exploiting natural resources, land
included. The revenue gathered in this manner could then be used to subsidize
the poor of this beautiful, culturally and historically wealthy country; those same

citizens who inhabit the shantytowns one sees when landing at Cartagena Airport, or who inhabit the impoverished villages of Colombia's interior.

Notes

1 The authors would like to thank J. Agudelo, A. Barreix, V. Tromben and J. Zapata for the contribution they made to this work. A. Rodriguez supplied us with a lot of updated material, and also carefully revised the text, correcting our mistakes and providing numerous useful suggestions. The usual disclaimer applies.

2 UN data show that about 100,000 people are at war in the mountains together with army forces and US "advisors." A large number of private police forces and government "informers" are at work. Kidnappings, assassinations and robberies – the so-called *violencia* – occur with alarming frequency. The official view (also IMF 2006), which is not shared by everyone in Colombia, is that the security situation has improved over the past few years, due the fact that some (right-wing) guerrilla groups have lain down their arms since 2005, benefiting from a full amnesty as a result thereof.

3 The question of the reliability of these forecasts remains open, however. The said IMF report defines them as "prudential," but subject to a series of structural reforms and to virtuous governmental behavior. In the long-run, the most critically important trend seems to be the one regarding pension expenditure, notwithstanding the 1993 reform (see below).

4 These aggregates are given in the ILPES-CEPAL data that constitute the main for this study. The *non-financial public sector* includes state, departments, municipalities, social security, *and* public enterprises. *General government* and *central government* correspond to their counterparts in OECD and EUROSTAT public accounts. Unfortunately, the ILPES data fully cover the NFPS and the central government, but just partially the general government.

5 The expansion in public spending was largely due to the new 1991 Constitution, which led to a process of expenditure decentralization. This rise in expenditure was also the result of pension reforms, interest payments on public debt, and the salaries paid to public employees. A further contribution to this process was made by the restriction imposed on the Central Bank's power to finance the government's budget deficit. (Lozano 2000; Jungito and Rincon 2004).

6 At a first guess (data are not given in IMF 2005) the three said sectors accounted for about GDP 15 percent by 2005 (education 5 percent; pensions 4 percent; health 6 percent). Military spending probably accounted for GDP 4 percent.

7 For example, the increase in oil prices pushed up the NFPS' current non-tax revenue from GDP 10.3 percent in 1998 to 18.8 percent in 2004 (ILPES-CEPAL).

8 The main reforms were based on studies by highly-qualified tax professionals, such as Musgrave and Gillis, Mc Lure, Bird, and Poterba. However, politicians repeatedly failed to follow the experts' recommendations.

9 Taken together, these reforms increased fiscal pressure by about 7 percent (Government of Colombia 2006).

10 The more theoretically consistent substantial recommendations, illustrated in Shome (1995), were largely ignored.

11 However, it has been pointed out that there were too many small, short-term reforms granting preferential treatments, and too many tax amnesties, which had the effect of reducing the tax base (MIP 2002).

12 It also introduced OECD-like transfer price rules.

13 The government believes that the removal of the wealth tax in 2007 will be compensated for by the increase of import taxes and VAT, while other observers maintain that the tax gap must be closed by tax reforms (Clavijo 2005).

14 Bolivia, Colombia, Ecuador, Peru and Venezuela.
15 It is not easy to properly evaluate Colombian fiscal pressure. Tax evasion is deemed to be high (Shome 1995; Ministerio de Hacienda 2006; Clavijo 2005), and yet remains underestimated since the potential tax bases are calculated from national accounts, which in turn allow for the large-scale exclusion of illegal business activities.
16 We lack figures for subsequent years.
17 According to CONFIS (2006), these included 515,000 corporations and shareholders who paid 85.9 percent of taxes on income and profits in 2005, and 830,000 individuals, comprised of 317,000 employees (accounting for 7.7 percent of total tax paid by withholdings) and 513,000 self-employed (6.4 percent of total tax paid by tax returns). These data pale when compared with the number of the employed, to about 16.2 million (according to UN data).
18 82.9 percent of total revenue went to central government, 6.6 percent to departments and 10.7 percent to municipalities in 2002 (Lozano *et al.* 2004).
19 Income originated in countries of the Andean Community is in general taxable only in the source country.
20 US$1 = COP2,360; €1 = COP3,013 (Forex, average 2006).
21 Foreign income tax paid by Colombian enterprises may be creditable under certain specific rules. Income from business activities located in the Andean Group countries is in general only taxable within the source country.
22 This presumption does not apply to enterprises subject to special regimes or to taxpayers operating mainly in financial markets and the public services.
23 Colombia's is the highest such rate among Latin American countries, and is on a par with that of Paraguay. The Latin American average is 28.3 percent, while the lowest rate – 15 percent – is that of Brazil (ILPES-CEPAL).
24 However, the taxpayers listed under four are entitled to pay at a lower rate of 20 percent. Enterprises operating in FZS are subject to a rate of 15 percent provided they qualify for it.
25 The value of the house in which a taxpayer usually resides is subject to taxation just for a part. Some non-profitable organizations are exempt from payment of this tax.
26 This rate is slightly higher than the Latin America average (14.7 in February 2006 (ILPES-CEPAL)
27 For instance 20 to 40 percent on alcoholic beverages; 48 percent on beer; 55 percent on tobacco.
28 The main change introduced by the reform was the establishment of a fully funded, privately administered defined contribution pension system running parallel to the existing defined benefit PAYG state scheme. Workers may choose *between* the two systems, but may *not combine* the two. Hence the system ought to be defined as a single pillar system, the main consequence of which being that the contribution rates are the same for both the systems.
29 Self-employed workers may join either system voluntarily, provided their contributions reach a minimum level.
30 "*Progresa*" in Mexico in 1997, "*Bolsa-Escola*" in Brazil in 1995.
31 This would require certain assumptions regarding the transactions carried out by the various strata of the population. Some attempts were made in this direction. Sanchez and Espinosa (2005) conclude that the FTT has a small redistributive effect, whereas Clavijo (2005) holds that it only affects users of bank markets, not the owners of financial capital.
32 This is the Gini Index calculated considering the distribution of tax on households' incomes or consumption.
33 The same index computed by Ariza and Zapata (Zapata and Ariza 2005) for 2003 is even higher at 0.89.
34 This index gives the reduction in inequality (Gini Index) after tax, which combines the quasi-Gini with the mean rate.

35 Apart from some presumed theoretical merits, the efficiency advantage of single-rate VAT is its greater administrative simplicity, ease and lower cists of compliance, especially given the resulting reduction in tax refunds; it may also help limit tax avoidance. Chile is the main example of a Latin American country with single-rate VAT.
36 According to the government's estimates, the PIT threshold exempted all tax payers within the first seven deciles, and the tax would also have been very light when it came to higher incomes. The situation regarding VAT was quite different however. A roughly flat rate of around 5.5 percent was to be levied on taxpayers within the first five deciles (those earning up to approximately COP16.5 million yearly – about US$7,000), above which the tax rate rose and burdened the tenth decile to the greatest degree. To sum up then, only those taxpayers with an annual income of at least COP104 million (about US$44,000) were to pay a combined (PIT + VAT) rate of just over 20 percent.

References

Alesina, A. (2000) "Institutional Reforms in Colombia?," documento de trabajo n. 001155, Bogotá, Fedesarollo.

Alesina, A., Carrasquilla, A. and Echavarrìa, J. J. (2000) "Decentralización in Colombia," in Alesina, A. (ed.) *Institutional Reforms in Colombia*, Cambridge, MA: The MIT Press.

Ávila, J., Cruz, A. and Orduña, R. (2001) "Progresividad de los impuestos a las ventas y renta de personas naturales," Cuadernos de Trabajo, Bogotá: DIAN.

Clavijo, S. (1998) "Fiscal Effects of the 1993 Colombian Pension Reform," IMF Working Paper no. 98/158, Washington, DC: IMF.

—— (2005) "Tributación, equidad y eficiencia en Colombia," *Borradores de economia*, Bogotà: Banco de la Repubblica.

Colombian Tax Flash vol. 1, n. 2, July 2004; vol. 2, n. 4, January 2005; vol. 3, n. 6, January 2006; vol. 4, n. 8, January 2007.

Congreso de Colombia (2006) "Ley Numero 1111 de 2006 por la cual se modifica el estatuto tributario de los impuestos administrados por la dirección de impuestos y aduanas nacionales," reported by *Colombian Tax Flash*, vol. 4, n. 8, January 2007.

Controleria fiscal – CONFIS (2006) *Plan financiero 2007*, Bogotà: Ministerio de Hacienda y Crédito Publico.

Government of Colombia (2006) "Proyecto de ley por medio del cual se sustituye el estatuto tributario de los impuestos administrados por la dirección de impuestos y aduanas nacionales. Exposición de motivos," http://www.minhacienda.gov.co.

IBFD (2006) *Latin America – Taxation & Investment: Colombia*, Amsterdam: IBDF CD ROM 1/2006.

IMF (2006) "Colombia: Second Review under the Stand-by Arrangement," IMF country report, n. 06/234, Washington, DC: IMF.

International Law Office (2006) *Tax Bill: Expected Changes for 2007*, Bogotá: Lewin & Willis Abogados.

Iregui, A. M., Ramos, J., Saavedra, L. A. (2001) "Análisis de la descentralización fiscal en Colombia," *Borradores de economía*, n. 001708, Bogotá: Banco de la República.

Jungito, R. and Rincon, H. (2004) "La política fiscal en el siglo XX en Colombia," *Borradores de economía*, n. 318, Bogotá: Banco de la Repubblica.

Lozano, I. E. (2000) "Colombia Public Finance in the 1990s: A Decade of Reforms, Fiscal Imbalance, and Debt," paper presented at the POE Structure Meeting On Fiscal Policy Issues, Osaka: September.

Lozano, I. E., Ramos, J. and Rincon, H. (2004) "Crisis fiscal actual: diagnostico y recomendaciones," *Borradores de economía*, Bogotá: Banco de la República.

Ministerio de Hacienda y Crédito Publico (2006) *Marco fiscal de mediano plazo*, Bogotá: June.

MIP (Misión del Ingreso Público) – (2002) *Informe – Consejo Directivo*, Bogotá, MIP.

Parra Escobar & Cia (2006) "Estudio sobra la riforma tributaria 2006–2007," http://www.apecia-law.com.

Perotti, R. (2000) "Public Spending on Social Protection in Colombia: Analysis and Proposals," Working Paper Series, n. 18, Bogotá: Fedesarrollo.

Rudolph, H., Cheikhrouhou, H., Rocha, R. and Thornbun, C. (2006) "Financial Sector Dimensions of the Colombian Pension System," Washington, DC: The World Bank.

Sanchez, F. and Espinosa, S. (2005) "Impuestos y reformas tributarias en Colombia," Document CEDE 2005–11.

Sanchez, F., Smart, M. and Zapata, J. G. (2002) "Intergovernmental Transfers and Municipal Finance in Colombia," documento de trabajo n. 001143, Bogotá: Fedesarollo.

Shome, P. (ed.) (1995) "Comprehensive Tax Reform. The Colombian Experience," IMF occasional paper n. 123, Washington, DC: IMF.

Zapata, J. G. and Ariza, N. (2005) "Eficiencia y equidad de la politica tributaria y su relacion con el gasto publico en la Comunidad Andina – El caso de Colombia," mimeo Comunidad Andina.

Websites

www.cia.gov/cia/publications/factbook/index.html – Cia-Factbook.

www.contaduria.gov.co – Colombian Government Budgetary Department.

www.dian.gov.co – Colombian Government Direction of National Taxes and Customs.

www.minhacienda.gov.co – Colombian Ministry of Public Finance and Public Credit.

www.dane.gov.co – Colombian National Statistics Department.

www.imf.org – International Monetary Fund.

www.eclac.cl/Ilpes/ – United Nations Economic Commission for Latin America – Latin American and Caribbean Institute of Economic and Social Planning.

www.worldbank.org – World Bank.

10 Costa Rica

*Jorge Cornick, Eric Thompson and
Adrian Torrealba*

Introduction and main conclusions

In the early 1990s, Costa Rica's tax system was characterized by its
complexity, consisting of a very high number of taxes, a broad use of tax
incentives that eroded the tax bases and a poor technical design of the taxes.
Tax administration was weak and lacked appropriate legal instruments to
enforce the tax code. Moreover, no interest accrued on tax debts. The Costa
Rican government was, in fact, a bank granting interest free loans to taxpayers
who did not pay their taxes on time. Since then, systematically but very
slowly, the tax administration has been strengthened and the tax code
improved and simplified; the use of tax incentives has diminished, the sales
tax's basis has been broadened while that of excise taxes has been narrowed –
conforming to best international practices – while the basis for the income tax
has also been expanded, modestly. The tax burden of the central government
has been increased from 11.3 percent of GDP in 1991 to 13.4 percent of GDP
in 2004 and is expected to reach 14 percent of GDP in 2007. Nevertheless, tax
revenue still falls short of the country's need for public investments and it is
well below the expected level in light of the country's income or the human
development level.

Both the income and the sales tax still have technical limitations: the income
tax is based on product-income concept (generically excludes capital gains taxation), a scheduler structure and has a significant rates' dispersion. The sales tax –
the name used in Costa Rica for VAT– excludes most services (Costa Rica's
fastest growing economic sector) and does not allow credit for goods or services
not physically incorporated into the final product.

Since 2002 the country has been discussing a tax reform bill that will
amend most of the deficiencies mentioned so far. When and whether there will
be a vote on this bill is uncertain. The pace of reform seems to have shifted
from slow to glacial and Congress's current top priority is ratification of the
free trade agreement between the Dominican Republic, Central America and
the US.

Structure of the tax system

The tax system in the early 1990s

The Costa Rican tax system, in the early 1990s, had such complexity that an IMF mission lead by Vito Tanzi,[1] stated:

> it will be difficult to find other countries, regardless of size or of economic development – with a more complex system. This complexity is the result of the extremely high number of taxes, the increase of special incentives, the vast number of public sector activities and the disintegration on the performance of those activities.

Deficiencies in the design of the principal taxes were summarized as follows.[2]

1   The sales tax basis was limited to goods, and only included certain listed services. The tax was based on the principles of invoice – credit of the value-added tax, but recognized credit only for the acquisition of goods and raw material physically incorporated into the final good. On the other hand, the selective consumption tax covered more than 1,000 tariff items, even though most of the revenue came from just a few goods.[3]
2   The personal income tax had a scheduler structure, with different rates for each schedule. Financial income was very lightly taxed. The corporate income tax had progressive rate structure based on gross income, with reasonable rates. Méndez (1991) summarized these features as follows:

> The income tax is characterized for imposing different rates on different types of income and on different legal persons. Thus, different rates exist for capital income and labor; for income of dependent employees and independent workers; for small businesses and for other companies, for cooperatives, for the agricultural sector; for the forest sector; for coffee and banana producing sectors.
>
> (Méndez 1991, p. 8)

3   Foreign trade taxes, in spite of tariff reductions in the 1980s, still represented 30 percent of central government revenue, or 3.4 percent of the GDP in 1991.
4   Many laws granted tax incentives to promote investment and exports: Tourism Incentives Law; Free Trade Zone Regime Law; Export Incentives Law; Industrial Production Incentives Law; and several laws to encourage the forest development. Thus:

> we created a system in which the success from the developing of the new model has a negative impact on the public finances. The development of non traditional exports, of tourism, of forest activities . . .

Table 10.1 Taxes as percentage of GDP, Costa Rica, 1991–5 per tax period

	1991	1992	1993	1994	1995
Tax revenue	11.3	11.9	11.9	11.6	12.3
Direct taxes*	2.2	2.2	2.7	2.8	3.1
Income taxes	*1.7*	*1.6*	*2.0*	*2.1*	*2.2*
Indirect taxes	9.1	9.7	9.2	8.8	9.2
General sales tax	*4.0*	*4.4*	*4.2*	*3.9*	*4.1*
Selective consumption tax/excises	*1.4*	*2.0*	*1.9*	*2.0*	*1.9*
Foreign trade taxes	*3.4*	*3.0*	*2.7*	*2.6*	*2.9*

Source: authors' elaboration based on Ministry of Finance and Central Bank of Costa Rica data.

Note
* It includes pension's contributions from the national budget.

requires public expenses and investments, but these sectors do not contribute to the revenue of the government.[4]

It is then not surprising that the tax burden of the country was relatively low and the direct taxes' contribution was very limited, as Table 10.1 shows.[5] Please note, however, that in 1995 the tax burden, for the first time in this period, is more than 12 percent of the GDP, which reflects changes in the tax structure and a better tax administration.

Regardless of these weaknesses, at the beginning of this period the fiscal deficit was reasonable, although it grew in 1994 and 1995, partly as a result of the shutdown of a state bank, since the costs were assumed by the government.

Tax reforms in the 1990s[6]

During the 1990s several reforms were proposed to increase tax revenue, improve tax design and strengthen tax administration. At the end of this section we will present some data which illustrate the effect of those reforms on the structure of public sector revenue. First, however, we will present a brief description of the reforms in this period.

Income tax

In 1992 almost all exemptions from the income tax were eliminated, except those for free-trade zones and cooperatives. The immediate effect, though, was limited since the "acquired rights" of the taxpayers who were enjoying the exemptions were maintained until the expiration of their contracts. In 1995, the "Tax Justice Law" tried to reduce income tax evasion by independent professionals through the increase of presumptive income standards and created a tax on fixed assets, creditable to the payment of corporate income tax, a type of minimum tax. In 1999 the Costa Rican Constitutional Court declared unconstitutional the main aspects of the law. In 1998 a tax was imposed on the Certificates of Tributary Credit (CAT), the main tax subsidy used as an incentive for exports. In 1991 a tax of 25 percent on CAT had been created, but only for those taxpayers who voluntarily elected to pay the tax and in exchange accepted an extension of the incentive period. In 1999 a new reform to the tax code modified one of the main deficiencies of the previous system. Tax debts resulting from tax assessments started to bear interest form the moment the debt was incurred in the first place; previously, interest charges started accruing only after the Administrative Tax Court had ruled on the debt, which usually happened several years after the tax assessment. In 2001, with the approval of the "Tax Efficiency and Simplification Law," the additional depreciation expenses caused by revaluation of fixed assets were abolished. This law also increased the applicable rate to certain types of income. Specifically, the income from remunerations, gratuities and salary in kind, previously subject to a 10 percent rate, increased to a 15 percent rate. In addition, private universities and "offshore" banking were included in the tax base. In this last case, a fixed annual tax was imposed, similar to an "operational license," and different from the obligation to pay tax on income as other companies. An 8 percent tax was imposed on revenue form repurchase of securities (*recompras y reportos*).

General sales tax

The tax rate was temporarily increased form 10 to 13 percent in 1991 and went back to 10 percent in 1994. In 1995 the rate was increased again, to 15 percent, for 18 months and then returned to 13 percent, its current rate. During the 1990s, the tax base was increased, but the list of exempt goods remained extensive, and included not only final consumption goods but also raw materials and other goods used in the agricultural production.

Selective consumption tax

The list of goods subject to selective consumption tax was extremely large in the early 1990s: 1,500 tariff items in 1995. In 1996 the number was reduced to 700 items. The executive's authority to increase the rate every six months without legislative approval was abolished in August 2001.

Foreign trade taxes

The average tariff level continued to decrease, as did tariff rates' dispersion. All taxes on exports were repealed, except those on coffee, bananas, meat and cattle.

Changes in the revenue structure of the central government

These changes resulted in a substantial modification of the revenue structure of the central government, as shown in Table 10.2, which includes also the first column from Table 10.1.

Table 10.2 Tax revenue as percentage of GDP, Costa Rica, 1991 and 1996–2004

	1991	1996	1997	1998	1999	2000	2001	2002	2003	2004
Tax revenue	11.3	12.7	12.5	12.6	11.9	12.3	13.3	13.2	13.3	13.4
Direct taxes*	2.2	3.0	3.0	3.2	3.6	3.5	3.9	3.9	4.1	4.1
Income taxes	*1.7*	*2.2*	*2.2*	*2.4*	*2.9*	*2.7*	*3.1*	*3.1*	*3.3*	*3.3*
Indirect taxes	9.1	9.8	9.5	9.3	8.3	9.1	9.4	9.3	9.2	9.3
General sales tax	*4.0*	*5.4*	*5.1*	*4.8*	*4.3*	*4.5*	*4.9*	*4.9*	*4.7*	*4.9*
Selective consumption tax and excises	*1.4*	*2.3*	*2.4*	*2.7*	*2.7*	*3.2*	*3.3*	*3.4*	*3.4*	*3.2*
Foreign trade taxes	*3.4*	*1.8*	*1.7*	*1.6*	*1.2*	*1.0*	*1.0*	*0.9*	*0.8*	*0.9*

Source: author's calculations based on Ministry of Finance and Central Bank data.

Notes
* It includes pension's contributions from the national budget.

Note that tax revenue of the central government increased by about two points of the GDP, from 11.3 to 13.4 percent, between 1991 and 2004. Of this increase, 1.9 percentage points were due to increased collection of direct taxes', while sales tax collection increased by 0.9 percentage points. In contrast, taxes on foreign trade, which in 1991 were equivalent to 3.4 percent of the GDP, barely reached 0.9 percent in 2004, as a result of the tariff reduction and the elimination of exports taxes. Overall, a slow but steady increase of the tax burden occurred during this period. Preliminary data suggests that this upward trend will continue from 2005 to 2007. However, is this rate of increase enough to satisfy the public expenditure needs of the country? Agosin *et al.* (2005a, 2005b) have argued persuasively that it is not: Costa Rica's tax burden is less than the expected,[7] either taking as a reference the level of income of the country or its level of human development.

Distribution of the tax burden

The incidence and allocation of the tax burden in Costa Rica has been analyzed in detail by Taylor (1997) and Bolaños (2002), works which updated the previous results and concluded that pre and post-tax income distribution is almost identical.[8] Nevertheless, the distribution of the tax burden showed a slight improvement between 1988 and 2000. The gross effective burden in 1998 increased from the first to the third income decile and it decreased from there on; however in 2000 it did oscillate. The change of the trend was characterized by the author as a movement from "solid regressiveness" to "moderate regressiveness." However, there are no great differences in the tax burden by income level: for the first decile the total is 21.9 percent of gross income, and for the tenth decile the total is 20.9 percent of gross income.

International comparisons

Considering the differences in terms of income levels and human development between Costa Rica and other Central American countries, perhaps it will be surprising that the tax revenue structure, without considering the social security charges, is very similar in all these countries. Naturally, if payroll taxes are included (by judicial fiction, payroll taxes, other than the income tax, are not considered taxes in Costa Rica) the Costa Rican tax burden is higher, but nevertheless the basic similarities remain. In Table 10.3 we compared the structure and level of tax revenue (as percentage of the GDP) of Costa Rica and the Central American average for the year 2002. It can be noticed, that the countries with higher tax burden are Nicaragua and Honduras but this information probably shows an underestimation of the GDP in the above-mentioned countries. In any case, the tax pressure in Costa Rica is closer to the Central American average and the structure of the tax revenue structure is also very similar, with low importance on direct taxes and a big burden on indirect taxes. In Table 10.3 we do not distinguish between income taxes paid by companies and by individuals, however further on we will disclose some information on this matter for the case of Costa Rica.

A comparison with the tax structure of MERCOSUR countries, on one hand, and with the average structure for the European countries, shows different results (Table 10.4).

Table 10.3 Central American countries tax pressure per type of tax on the year 2002 (% of the GDP)

Concept	Costa Rica	El Salvador	Guatemala	Honduras	Nicaragua	Central America
Total tax revenue	12.8	12.0	10.6	16.1	14.3	12.3
Direct taxes income	3.5	3.5	2.8	3.7	2.8	3.2
Income	3.1	3.4	2.8	3.5	2.8	3.1
Families	0.0	0.0	0.0	0.0	0.0	0.0
Companies	0.0	0.0	0.0	0.0	0.0	0.0
Properties	0.4	0.1	0.0	0.2	0.0	0.2
Other direct taxes	0.0	0.0	0.0	0.0	0.0	0.0
Indirect Tax income	9.3	8.5	7.8	12.3	11.4	9.1
Goods and services general tax	4.9	6.3	4.8	5.5	5.9	5.3
Domestic	n/d	3.0	1.9	n/d	n/d	2.3
Imported	n/d	3.3	2.9	n/d	n/d	3.0
Goods and services specific tax	1.1	1.1	1.5	1.9	3.7	1.5
Petroleum derivatives	S/d	0.6	0.9	0.7	2.5	0.9
Others	S/d	0.5	0.6	1.2	1.3	0.6
Trade and international transactions	0.9	1.1	1.2	2.0	1.1	1.2
Other indirect taxes	2.4	0.0	0.3	2.9	0.7	1.1

Table 10.4 Partial comparison of revenue of the central government: Europe 1997, MERCOSUR 2002, Costa Rica 2004 (% of GDP)

	Europe	MERCOSUR	Costa Rica
Tax revenue, from which	29.1	19.8	13.4
Sales tax	7.3	5.9	4.9
Income tax	14.5	4.2	3.3

Source: Costa Rica: Ministry of Finance; Mercosur: Barreix and Roca (2005); Europe: Bernardi and Profeta (2004).

The tax burden of the central government in Costa Rica is not only much lower than the European average, but also lower than the simple average of the countries of the MERCOSUR. On the other hand, in Europe the income tax collection almost duplicates VAT collection, in contrast, in both Costa Rica and the MERCOSUR sales tax collection is higher than the income tax collection.

Structure of the main taxes

Income taxes

It is customary to classify income taxes as either individual or corporate taxes, depending on who bears the burden of the tax. Due to Costa Rica's scheduler income tax structure, this allocation is not entirely possible. However, taxes on personal and corporate profits and on wages can be classified. This is done in Table 10.5. However, some clarifications are needed: salaried workers in Costa Rica do not file a tax return and the tax is withheld at source. Only independent workers must file a tax return. Therefore, in Table 10.5 the total contributed by individuals is the sum of the withholdings from the salary of employees and pensions of retirees more than income tax from independent individuals. In any case, it is clear that still adding the withholdings from employees and the income tax from individuals (the sum totals 25.9 percent of the collection related to this tax) the corporate income tax contribution is much higher, equivalent to 49.5 percent of the entire collection of personal direct taxes, or almost double the tax paid by individuals. The contrast with the European case, in which individuals pay almost three times more taxes than companies, is clearly remarkable. This scheduler income tax structure represents an important challenge to the tax reform currently in discussion and it will be described further on this chapter. The fact is that there is a strong internal and external pressure, in the sense of reducing the corporate income tax and compensating this revenue loss. This compensation requires a broader corporate income tax base and a constant raise on individual income tax collection, and both efforts are substantially challenging.

Income taxation in Costa Rica, ruled by Income Tax Law 7092, of 1988,

Table 10.5 Percentage distribution of the income tax collection, Costa Rica, 1998–2004

	1998	1999	2000	2001	2002	2003	2004
Salary and pension's contributions	25.6	23.1	27.8	24.4	27.6	26.6	23.8
Other withholdings[a]	25.0	21.1	23.5	22.3	27.3	24.8	23.4
Individual and Corporate contribution, from which:	45.0	45.1	46.4	40.3	43.8	45.5	51.6
Corporate	43.2	43.6	44.7	38.6	41.9	43.0	49.6
Individual	1.8	1.5	1.8	1.6	1.9	2.5	2.1
Others[b]	4.4	10.7	2.2	13.0	1.3	3.1	1.2

Notes
a It includes securities withholding.
b It includes non-domicile financial institutions tax.

has three main features: it is "scheduler" which means it is formed by several different income taxes; it is based on a territorial principle; it is based on the product-income concept. A "scheduler" system imposes different tax rates on different sources of income. The classification of the income is structured according to different criteria chosen by the legislator: for example, if income is obtained for personal services rendered in the capacity of dependent employee or independent worker; if it comes from labor or from capital and, related to this one, if it comes from regulated financial market transactions or not, etc. The so-called income tax, then, comprises several different taxes:

1   a tax on profits of both corporation and independent workers. These taxpayers file a tax return and pay their own taxes;
2   several withholding taxes on: dividend income; interest; salaries; pensions; payment remittances to non-residents.

On the other hand, the Costa Rican income tax system is based on territoriality: only income of Costa Rican sources is taxed. Finally, under "product-income," only income from capital or labor services is taxed, while capital gains generally are not taxed.

Profits (or net income) tax

This tax is imposed on some net income obtained by some individuals and corporations.[9] The types of taxable income are: income from services rendered by practicing professionals (since there is a specific tax in the law for the income from dependent labor) and corporate income; capital income from real estate and movable property, and from the disposition of capital, through secured financing transactions different from financial market transactions, since the law includes a scheduler tax on financial market profits under article 23. As a general rule, capital gains are not taxable. However, there are two exceptions to that rule:

1   habitual capital gains: defined under article 6 d);
2   depreciable assets: defined under article 8 f), when the taxpayer sells them
    for a price higher than their book value.

The tax is calculated on net income, defined as gross income minus all costs
and expenses necessary to produce said income. In general, depreciation of tangible assets is recognized, however, revaluation is not. In regards to amortization
of intangibles, it is recognized for software and invention patents, and it is not
authorized for a restrictive list that includes goodwill, trademarks, manufacturing procedures, copyrights, intellectual property rights, or formulas or other
similar intangible assets.
   The difference between the tax treatment for individuals and for corporations
gives the applicable rates. For individuals, marginal tax rates from 0 percent to
25 percent[10] apply as follows:

1   for income below and up to US$3,584[11] annually, 0 percent;
2   income between US$3,584 and US$5,313 annually, 10 percent;
3   income between US$5,313.01 and US$8,928 annually, 15 percent;
4   income between US$8,928.01 and US$17,890 annually, 20 percent;
5   income over US$17,890 annually, 25 percent.

Minor deductions for family charges are allowed.[12]
   The general corporate tax rate is 30 percent. However, businesses with up to
US$53,637 pay a 10 percent tax and those with gross income up to US$107,894
pay 20 percent. As shown in Table 10.5, most of the collection comes from corporations, while collection from independent workers is much smaller. Salaried
workers pay roughly half as much income tax as corporations.

Withholding taxes

1   Dividends for private corporations are taxed at 15 percent, but are exempt
    when paid in stock or to another corporation. The rate is 5 percent for pub-
    licly traded corporations, cooperatives and "*asociaciones solidaristas.*"
2   Interest bearing instruments are taxed at 15 percent, except those traded in
    the Stock Exchange, which are taxed at 8 percent. Securities issued in
    foreign currency are exempt when issued by the government or a state-
    owned bank. All securities issued by the "Banco Popular y de Desarrollo
    Comunal" and the National Housing Financial System are also exempt.
3   Salaries, wages and executive compensation. In case of the income of
    regular personnel (employees and officials) of the company and of the
    income from retirements and pensions of all regimens, the applicable rate is
    a progressive scale that starts at 0 percent for income up to US$809, then 10
    percent (from US$819 to US$1,213) and finally 15 percent (on the excess of
    US$1,213). On the other hand, the applicable rate to executives remunera-
    tions and income in kind is a flat 15 percent, without any exempt amount.

Minimal family allowances are permitted to be deducted from income to which the progressive rate is applicable: for children (US$0.89 monthly per each child) for the spouse (US$1.60 monthly). In the case of income received from periods longer than a month, a deduction from income is allowed for every month. The employer is the withholding agent.

4   Foreign remittances tax. Income from Costa Rican sources received by non-domiciled individuals or corporations is taxed at varying rates: 10 percent for wages, salaries and pensions; 15 percent for independent personal services; 25 percent for technical assistance, royalties, patents; 15 percent for interests and dividends, except for interest paid to a "first order entity," declared as such by the Central Bank; 5 percent for transportation services and communications; 5.5 percent for insurance; 20 percent for movies, recordings, discs and the like; 30 percent for the rest. If the income recipient cannot claim a credit for the remittance tax paid, Costa Rica exempts him. Also, it includes some exceptional cases of Costa Rican source: technical assistance, financial and other advisory services although clearly rendered in a foreign country in favor to a Costa Rican company.

Other income taxes

1   Special tax for non-domiciled banks and financial institutions controlled by or related to local banking or financial group. This tax substitutes the foreign remittances tax and it consists on a flat annual amount of US$125,000. The Costa Rican institution is the withholding agent.

2   Investment funds regime ruled by the Securities Market Law. Except for profits subject to the tax imposed on the financial market interests, all other incomes received by the funds is levied by a return-auto liquidation tax of 5 percent, including habitual and non-habitual capital gains.

3   The amount referred as "others" in Table 10.5, includes the collections from non-domiciled banks and financial institutions. However, the current information does not allow us to do a precise calculation of the collection in each situation.

General sales tax

The general sales tax is based on the value added tax model, consumption type, and allows a complete and immediate credit for the taxes paid for purchases of fixed assets. The sales tax in Costa Rica adopts the consumption tax method. Therefore, there is an exemption of the instrumental assets, only when the final destination is not consumption. Thus, in order to obtain the credit, it is enough to acquire a capital asset that will be used in an activity subject to tax, although it is exempt. Even if it is anticipated that in three months the tax credits will not be absorbed, it is possible to claim compensation or return. Hence it is not a requirement to hold the capital asset related to the activity until the end of the useful life in order to obtain the right to claim the total amount of the credit for the tax paid in the acquisition. In regards to the criteria applied to allow a credit, the Costa Rican tax does not follow the international trend, since it follows the "physical deduction" method and not the "financial deduction" method, due to an administrative and judicial interpretation. The tax credit is allowed only for inputs that are physically incorporated to the manufacturing process, as well as capital assets that are directly related to the production phase.

All goods are taxed, except those explicitly exempt. In contrast, all services are exempt, except those explicitly taxed. Consequently, the inclusion in the list determines if certain activity is subject to tax, or not. The Attorney General's Office has accepted this limited and restrictive characteristic. In contrast, the inclusion of goods is presumed. Consequently, according to the method, first you have to disregard the possibility that the good is excluded from the definition of "goods" stated in the law and regulations, and second you have to discard the possibility of an exemption listed under article 9 of the law or in some another legal norm. There are two basic forms of taxable events: imports and local operations and exports. In the first case, each isolated input is taxed. In the second case, each transaction is taxed but in the context of periodical tax returns. The taxpayer description follows the typical system in the value added tax based on the combination between a special type of taxpayer, the figure of the seller or service provided in each phase of the productive chain.

Although the general sales tax is technically characterized by its "multiphase" coverage, under the "Special System of determination and payment of the tax by factories and customs," taxes are assessed on the basis of estimated retail prices and collected from factories, wholesalers and customs. To apply this special system the tax administration must issue a resolution that sets the parameters to be applied and other information needed by the taxpayer. As the Costa Rican tax is based on the destination principle, exports are in practice "zero rated" even though this precise terminology is not used in the law, while imports under the free-trade zone regime, established by Law 7210, are exempt.

The current tax rate is 13 percent, except for the consumption of residential energy which is taxed at a 5 percent rate. The tax bases of the three basic forms of the taxable event (imports, sales of goods and rendering of some services) are the following:

1   In the selling of goods: the net selling price including the total of the consumption selective tax. There are deductions for the following items:

   • Discounts, whenever they are commonly used and are separated from the selling price in the invoice;
   • The value of the services rendered in the selling of goods, whenever they are provided by third parties, invoiced and taken into account separately. It refers to services which value is included in the price of the goods, and as a basic condition a third party has to render

the service and the financial expenses have to be invoiced and accounted separately. As special rule, in the case of leases with call option, the base will be the market value of the goods. Aside from this specific provision, the general sales tax does not contain any extensive rule related to market valuation between independent parties.

2   In rendering of services, the tax base is the sales net price, determined deducting the amounts described for the sale of goods.
3   In the case of imports, the sum of the Costa Rican customs – CIF value – and the amount effectively paid for tariffs, economic stabilization tax, consumption selective taxes or specific and any other tax that affects the imports, as well as other charges that appear in the insurance policy or in the customs form.

Credit card companies should withhold a sales tax advanced payment on electronic payment transactions. The processing company withholds a percentage with a ceiling of 6 percent on the total amount of the transaction, excluding that of the sales tax. These withholdings constitute an advance payment to the account of the taxpayer's monthly liquidation.

Selective consumption tax and other excise taxes

The consumption selective tax is generated either when a good is imported, or when the local manufacturer sells it. Different rates apply depending on the product and its basic features:

1   It is a one-phase tax: this means it taxes only the importation or the sale of product by its producer. Further sales are not taxable.
2   It taxes consumption products only. If an item is taxed and then used as an input in the production of taxable goods, a credit equal to the amount paid for taxes on the input is allowed. Therefore, this tax does not have "cascading" effects.

When the manufacturer produces by order of the distributor and the distributor supplies the raw material, the distributor, rather than the manufacturer, becomes the taxpayer. The tax administration can modify the tax base so that prices between related companies reflect "arms length" prices. Additionally, the following goods are subject to excise taxes:

1   Alcoholic beverages, based on alcoholic content;
2   Non-alcoholic beverages (except milk) by consumption unit. For tax purposes, consumption units for all beverages are defined 250 milliliters and for sodas 39,216 ml. For containers with different contents the tax will be imposed proportionally. The tax applies to national production and the imports.
3   Toilet soap: approximately US$0.00015 per gram at the current exchange

rate. The tax, in Costa Rican currency, is updated quarterly according to changes in the consumer price index.

4   Single tax on fuels (oil derived): tax established on fuel either of national production or imported. This tax excludes the application of the sales and consumption selective taxes. The taxable time occurs for the national production at the moment of the manufacture, distillation or refinement. For this purpose, national production means the moment in which a product is ready for sale (excluded the reprocessing), and for imports when the customs declaration is accepted. The taxpayer of this tax is Costa Rican Oil Refinery Corporation (RECOPE), either as producer or as importer. For each type of fuel, the update of this tax is also quarterly, in accordance with consumer index prices determined by National Institute of Statistics and Censuses (INEC). However, the quarterly adjustment cannot exceed 3 percent.

Recent tax reforms

Comprehensive tax reform

The ad hoc Committee of Former Secretaries of the Treasury was created with the mandate to design a fundamental fiscal reform including, naturally, tax reform. The committee's final report was presented on April 2002[13] and it recommended a substantial transformation of the income and value added taxes. The secretary of the Treasury issued instructions to the tax administration to prepare a bill based on the committee's recommendations. The bill, under the name "Fiscal Order Law" was introduced in Congress on April 10, 2002, discussed for almost four years, had its name changed to "Fiscal Pact Law" and was finally approved on its February 2006,[14] but the legislative procedure was declared unconstitutional by the Constitutional Court and the bill was sent back to Congress. A new government took office in May 2006 and it sent a separate bill for the VAT, two minor reforms comprising and excise on luxury homes and a fixed US$200 fee on registered corporations and has indicated that it will send other bills to Congress, including an income tax bill. In sum, four years of discussion and a project neither approved nor rejected, seem to indicate that Costa Rica lacks an agreement on the need of the reform and the technical characteristics that should guide it. Let's now discuss the reform proposed so far.

Income taxes

There are two major taxes for residents: one for individuals and one for corporations, but some sources of income are taxed separately (scheduler system) and only national source income is taxed. As a consequence:

1   The tax paid on a certain amount of income will be different depending on whether the income was made up from salaries, honoraries for independent professional services, bonds or stock.

2   Major loopholes leave certain sources of income untaxed:

- non-recurrent capital gains are not taxed;
- foreign source income or national source income "placed" abroad is not taxed at all;
- it does not tax all incomes of a resident in Costa Rica. This is contradictory to the idea that everyone pays taxes according to his financial capacity, since one is more or less wealthy according to the total of ones wealth.

The proposed income taxation imposes a burden on income from labor, professional activities, businesses and capital, either personal or real property, tangible or intangible obtained by a taxpayer on the tax year. Therefore, the project proposes a shift towards global income and unified taxation. This system accumulates all income in one tax basis; it establishes exemption thresholds for individuals and families; medical expenses, rents and residential mortgage interest payments are deductible. Tax rates range from 0 to 30 percent.

A special tax basis is created for capital gains and losses, which can be compensated and would pay at a 10 percent tax rate. This special treatment is justified by the economic capacity principle, due to the irregular characteristic of these gains that normally are generated during several tax periods. Hence, this special basis was created in order to avoid an excessive effect over the progressive scale during the realization year. No special base is retained in the corporate income tax, which becomes truly global. This is reasonable since at corporate level the capital gains are closely tied to the economic activity. In the case of family corporations whose sole purpose is the tenancy of real estate and values, a pass-through regimen is suggested, which means that the individual shareholders could file the tax returns, therefore allowing the special tax base.

Special treatment is give to income from the financial market and from Real Estate Investment Funds. In these cases, a withholding of 10 percent could be imposed. Nevertheless, the income will be included in the general basis in order to determine the average in the progressive rate, though it can be deducted by an amount resulting from multiplying the total income by the above-mentioned average, and not exceeding the total of US$55,000. It is a solution that wants to mitigate the concern of the easy reallocation of this type of income, justifying certain favorable treatment, compatible with a progressive system. At a corporate level, the basic rule applies. Nevertheless, the favorable treatment of 10 percent ends at the threshold of US$55,000, since the corporate rate is proportional and not progressive. This rule does not apply for financial intermediation institutions.

The proposal includes the worldwide income taxation model, including some features for the capital gains treatment, according to two distinctions.

1   The source of income, Costa Rican or foreign: if the source of income is Costa Rican it will be taxed on accrual basis. If it is foreign the income will

be taxed on cash basis, both for individuals and for corporations. The presumptive income regime provides that the income is presumed as being Costa Rican sourced, except if the taxpayer proves the opposite; it is not possible to defend and unjustified net worth increase with the foreign source income.

2 The registration and filing of offshore capital: its timely compliance allows an identical regime to the one applied to income from the financial market. The lack of compliance allows the general treatment in order to encourage the filing of income from foreign source. This regime applies also to the corporations, except in case of financial intermediation institutions, for which the general treatment applies. At a corporate tax level, in case of corporations that own other corporations with a trade or business (not portfolio income) in countries with a corporate income tax, double taxation is avoided by exempting the dividends received by local corporations from foreign corporations.

When dividends are distributed to individuals in Costa Rica, they pay income tax on them. Dividends to non-residents are exempt, unless they reside in a "tax haven." The exemption method is applicable to avoid international double taxation and includes a prior resignation of the resulting collection between the lower foreign rate and the higher local one, in contrast to the imposition method. In general worldwide income system is usually combined with the imposition method: Spain and Canada reserve it for business income; France reserves it for corporate income. In theory, this method promotes capital import neutrality, which means equal treatment to local and external investments in the internal market. If the country is a net capital importer, it will guarantee the avoidance of internal discriminations between foreign and local investment. Nevertheless, if the exporting country taxes capital based on residence, the source country cannot guarantee this neutrality. Due to this, if the country is a capital exporter, it might be interested in encouraging this neutrality so that its companies could compete with the local companies on equal conditions in the source country. If it is like that, worldwide income with the exemption method is the instrument to encourage this neutrality from the country of residency.

In regards to the integration between the income tax on individuals and corporations, as of today dividend income has double taxation, and imposes a 40.5 percent total rate: 30 percent at a corporate level; 15 percent on individuals. This generates a problem of horizontal equity for other incomes: for example, interests can be taxed at 8 percent or 15 percent. Also, capital gains from the non-habitual sales of stock are not taxed. It creates a strong incentive towards debt financing that has been criticized. The reform proposes that dividends received by individuals should be part of the global income in order to keep the applicable average in the progressive scale, and then it excludes them, since at corporate level the dividends already paid 30 percent. If the rate decreases to 25 percent, or in cases of a favorable treatment regime (pioneers, minor relative development zones, which would pay 15 percent), the payment at corporate level would have a credit in the individual income tax. In the same line, capital gains from the sale of stock would have the same treatment.

It is also important to mention the effect in equity of the potential reduction of the corporate income tax at a 25 percent rate. Due to this fact the comparison between the current situation is fundamental. The 30 percent of the income tax is applicable to a limited tax base: of the financial or accounting income of a company, one part is taxed at 8 percent and the other one at 0 percent (except for income from foreign source or non-taxable capital gains). With the proposal, the 25 percent would be applicable to a wide and uniform base including the income that as of today is excluded. Additionally, it is important to mention that the dividends distribution or the capital gains received by individual shareholder would be taxed in the progressive tax rate on their individual income.

In order to strengthen tax collection, and to compare the situation of the different types of taxpayers with regard to the effective application of the tax, the global imposition on income includes the withholdings on incomes, to guarantee the compliance control. Accordingly, the income payers have the obligation to withhold a tax percentage and then pay it to the tax administration. This percentage operates as a tax credit applicable to the taxpayer's obligation at the end of the period, either by compensation against the tax debt or by claiming a return, if the withholding was higher than the tax obligation. The current income tax legislation contains this system, limited to few hypotheses, such as governmental or other public entities suppliers, with a 2 percent rate of advance payment.

Value added tax

The proposed bill taxes goods and services unless specifically exempt, in contrast to the current system under which goods are generally taxed, but services are not. As for tax credits, the concept of "financial deduction" is substituted for "physical deduction," while only exports are zero rated. The most contentious issues under discussion are the list of exempted goods and services as well as the introduction of the preferential rate of 6 percent for certain goods and services. The tax rate, currently at 13 percent, is not modified.[15]

Tax administration

The proposed tax reform includes the creation of the National Tax Direction that would integrate, under a unique technical authority, customs, internal taxes and tax control police, allowing higher coherence in global the tax administration. In addition a special human resources regime for the tax administration is proposed.

Several amendments to the "tax code" are proposed: executive tax debt collection and precautionary measures would be transferred from the judiciary to the administration, to prevent the disappearance of assets while a company is being audited or tax assessments are being challenged. These reforms have created concern in the private sector over potential abuses of the tax administration. To allay theses concerns, a Taxpayer Bill of Rights has been included in the bill. In addition, the amendments to the main taxes facilitate and require sound improvements of tax management and collection. In this light, it is argued that the introduction of the worldwide income system reinforces the role of the presumptive income based on unjustified net worth increase included in the project. These combined mechanisms would facilitate the tax audits when the external signs of wealth of the taxpayer do not coincide with its tax returns amounts, lacking the plausible justification on the foreign sourced income. This line of argumentation points to the revenue potential of worldwide income taxation, a subject that has been questioned by other skeptical experts. Also it is argued that worldwide income taxation should be an obstacle to current tax planning that openly promotes the reallocation of territorial income in low tax jurisdictions in order to facilitate the future repatriation of tax free income. We reiterate that the arguments in favor of the residence or worldwide principle face questions and criticism on its effectiveness against the tax practices of sophisticated taxpayers, especially in light of the deferral system finally introduced in the bill. This debate is still open and it is safe to say that has been one of the tangible factors that have complicated the final approval of the comprehensive tax reform.

In contrast, there is a widespread consensus that the systematic effort by the tax administration on the implementation of transfer pricing audit techniques according to the international best practices should have an undeniable impact on the revenue, especially in the context of an economy with a growing weight on its export-oriented activities. Even the VAT, generally applicable to consumer goods and services, introduces a taxpayers' internal control network by promoting that they demand invoices among each other in order to be able to claim input tax credits. This simultaneously should strengthen the cross-control network for income tax purposes.

Notes

1 Tanzi *et al.* (1990) pp. 2–3.
2 This section is based on Cornick (1998), pp. 45 and ss.
3 See Méndez (1991).
4 Herrero (1994) p. 39.
5 See Cornick (1998 and 2002).
6 This section is based on Rodriguez-Clare and Angulo (2002).
7 In the econometric sense of the term: the value expected from the tax burden in Costa Rica, in an econometric exercise taking into consideration variables such as the level of income and the level of human development, is superior to the value actually observed.
8 Since it is predictable in this type of study, and to use the words of the author: "The results for low income groups are quite sensitive to the situations, particularity the matters related to the transfer of salary taxes."

9 A tax is imposed on permanent establishments and branches of non-domiciled entities. Additionally other collective entities with no legal personality.
10 Applicable rates for the period 2006, starting on October 1, 2005. Established by Executive Decree n. 32693-H from September 19, 2005. La Gaceta 198 from October 14, 2005.
11 Tax brackets are defined in colones (local currency). Currency conversion used was the official average as of September 5, 2006 (¢518.5 = $1).
12 $18 annually per dependant child. The credit is available only if the child is under age or can not attend his or her own necessities or is physically or mental disabled, or is studying and is not older than 25 years. If both spouses are taxpayers, only one can claim the credit. The credit for a depending spouse annually is $27. If the spouses are legally separate, the deduction can be applied only by the spouse that supports the other, according to the law. If both are taxpayers, only one will be able to credit it.
13 The report: *"Transformación Fiscal para el Desarrollo."* President of the Republic. Dr. Miguel Ángel Rodríguez Echeverría, San Jose, April 2002.
14 Under Costa Rican law, the bill has to be approved on two separate votes before it becomes law.
15 Nicaragua has 15 percent, Chile 18 percent, Iceland 22 percent, Spain 16 percent, Peru 17 percent, Mexico 15 percent.

References

Agosin, M. R., Barreix, A., Gomez Sabaini, J. C. and Machado, R. (2005a) *Panorama tributario de los países centroamericanos y opciones de reforma.*
—— (2005b) "Recaudar para crecer. Bases para la reforma tributaria en Centroamérica," Banco Interamericano de Desarrollo, Washington, DC.
Barreix, A. and Roca, J. (2005) "Sistemas tributarios y reformas tributarias en América Latina," mimeo.
Bernardi, L. and Profeta, P. (eds) (2004) *Tax Systems and Reforms in Europe*, London: Routledge.
Bolaños, R. (2002) "Eficiencia y equidad en el sistema tributario costarricense," in *El Sistema Tributario Costarricense. Contribuciones al Debate Nacional*, Contraloría General de la República, San José, Costa Rica.
Castro, S. and Conejo, C. (eds) (1994) *Un acuerdo nacional razonable. Por un camino económico seguro y sostenible*, Costa Rica: Editorial Fundación UNA, Heredia.
Contraloría General De La Republica (2002) *El sistema tributario costarricense: Contribuciones al debate nacional*, San José, Costa Rica.
Cornick, J. (1998) "La reforma del sistema tributario en Costa Rica, 1994–1997," Ministerio de Planificación y Política Económica, Gobierno de Costa Rica.
—— (2002) "Evaluación de la gestión tributaria," in Contraloría General De La Repùblica (2002) *El sistema tributario costarricense: Contribuciones al debate nacional*, San José, Costa Rica.
Herrero, F. (1994) *La Crisis Fiscal y la Necesidad de un Acuerdo Nacional*, in Castro, S. and Conejo, C. (eds) (1994) *Un acuerdo nacional razonable. Por un camino económico seguro y sostenible*, Costa Rica: Editorial Fundación UNA, Heredia.
Méndez, J. C. (1991) *Proposiciones de Reforma de la Estructura Tributaria en Costa Rica*, San José, Costa Rica.
Rodriguez-Clare, A. and Angulo, J. E. (2002) *El sistema tributario y aduanero: una visión de Conjunto*, in Contraloría General de la República (2002) *El sistema tributario costarricense: Contribuciones al debate nacional*, San José, Costa Rica.

Tanzi, V., Shome, P., Atchabahian, A. and Beytia, M. (1990) "Costa Rica, El Sistema Tributario," Fondo Monetario Internacional, Departamento de Finanzas Públicas.

Taylor, M. (1997) "Income Redistribution through the Fiscal System. A Study on the Incidence of Taxes and Public Expenditure in Costa Rica," Ph.D. dissertation, Carlton University, Ontario, Canada.

11 Mexico

Daniel Alvarez

Introduction and contents[1]

The current tax system prevailing in Mexico is the result of a long and unfinished process of reform. During the last 35 years, the tax system has been subject to substantial overhauls aimed at achieving efficiency, neutrality, competitiveness, and equity goals compatible with the development of the Mexican economy and the international economic setting. Even though some of these objectives have been accomplished, the tax ratio is still insufficient to meet the social and infrastructure needs at the onset of the twenty-first century. The purpose of this chapter is to present the underlining features of the tax reform process in Mexico during this period, the main components of the current tax system, and the reform agenda pending for the future. To give a broader perspective of this process, it will cover some of the main domestic and external circumstances surrounding each stage of the tax reform, and a comparative view with other Latin American countries.

The next section will be devoted to the structure of the tax system and its development from the 1970s. It will discuss the current tax structure of Mexico, its composition, an outlook of the macroeconomic framework, and some of the main features underlining the economic policy strategy followed by the current administration. It will go on to summarize the reform development path followed by the tax system in the 1970–2005 period, and the policymaking objectives pursued along the way. The third section will cover some of the quantitative and institutional features of the main taxes collected in Mexico: corporate and personal income tax, asset tax, value added tax and excise duties. Special sections are designed within this chapter to expose the tax treatment of income derived from financial capital, and property taxation. As a salient feature of the Mexican tax system, this section will also present a brief description of the *maquiladora* industry (inbound manufacturing) tax regime, designated to cost centers facilities built along the border with the US, and also some policy and administrative issues of the transfer pricing regime adopted by Mexico, following the OECD guidelines as a member country.

The fourth section will display information regarding Mexican fiscal federalism. The institutional features of it are presented, together with the financing tools existing for intermediate and loser layers. The main question which emerges is the fact that the main share of resources go to non-central level of government as transfers from this last. So that states and municipalities suffer because of a decoupling between financing sources (external) and expenditures' decisions (in their own power). Finally, the fifth section will present some of the tax reforms implemented in Mexico since the 1990s, an important period of efforts pursued to reconcile the tax legislation to an increasingly open and modern economy, and to the admission of Mexico to the OECD, introducing competitiveness, stability and predictability into the system. Also it will discuss the desirable features the Mexican tax system should adopt in the near future to overcome the revenue-insufficiency aspects still embedded in the main broad-based taxes, as a necessary condition to meet mid-term budget commitments.

The structure of the system and its development from the 1970s

The current structure of taxation

Notwithstanding the series of tax reform efforts carried out by the Mexican government geared towards modernizing its tax system and to adopt it to a more competitive economic scene, the overall level and structure of taxation in Mexico has not changed substantially over the last 25 years. In fact, total tax revenues have decreased in about half percentage points of GDP. VAT collection is the only tax source which has improved during this period, though at an insufficient pace compared with other Latin American nations (see below). Income taxes have been the most important revenue source in Mexico, with the corporate income tax holding steady at around 2.5 percent of GDP. Import taxes are low and declining due to NAFTA and, in general, to a wide trade liberalization economic strategy. From 1980 to 1994, total revenue as percentage of GDP showed a steady behavior. During this period, total tax revenue showed a slight increase, mainly as a result of the indirect taxation overhaul. Nevertheless, the slowly increasing trend was curbed by the sharp reduction of main tax sources as a result of the economic crisis of 1995. The pre-crisis tax revenue collection level, in terms of GDP, was not reached again until 1999.

Oil-related revenues contribute with a relatively large, though highly fluctuating, share of the government revenue. Oil fees paid by PEMEX contribute to total revenue from different sources:

1   duty on oil extraction, designed as a cash flow tax levied on total revenues accrued by PEMEX, and consisting of three components: ordinary, extraordinary, and additional;
2   gross revenue tax, levied on PEMEX from its gross revenues;
3   price cap, which applies whenever crude oil export prices exceed annual budget;

Table 11.1 Mexico: federal government revenue (% of GDP)

	1980	1990	1994	2000	2005
Total	14.9	16.2	15.5	15.8	16.9
Tax revenues	10.8	11.1	11.3	10.6	9.7
Income	5.5	4.9	5.1	4.7	4.6
VAT	2.7	3.5	2.7	3.4	3.8
Excises	1.0	1.3	2.0	1.5	0.6
Import	1.0	0.9	0.9	0.6	0.3
Others	0.5	0.5	0.6	0.3	0.4
Non-tax	4.5	5.1	4.2	5.2	7.2

Source: Ministry of Finance of Mexico.

4   excise tax on gasoline and diesel levied on consumers, calculated as the difference between the consumer price fixed by government, and the producer price equivalent to the spot price, plus transport costs and quality adjustment;
5   income tax, based upon a tax structure similar to that applicable to other corporations.

The oil-related component of non-tax sources have fluctuated sharply since 1980. However, higher international oil prices during the last years have resulted in a substantial increase of non-tax revenues. In 2005, the contribution of non-tax sources to the total federal government revenue has reached 42 percent, from less than 30 percent a decade ago. The overall oil revenue take, which includes excise tax on gasoline and diesel, has contributed annually to 25–35 percent of total revenue. The relatively high reliance on oil-related sources, especially during high oil-price periods, produces significant and undesired effects on macroeconomic policy, budget allocation, and on the sense of urgency for revenue-enhancing tax reform.

Developments of the system (from 1970 to 2000)

The current Mexican tax system barely resembles the structure that prevailed 40 years ago. Over the past four decades, developments of the tax system have been guided by the social and economic objectives pursued by the Mexican government in different development stages. Before 1970, taxation in Mexico followed a highly pragmatic view. In response to the need to raise revenue with the least administrative burden, the tax system was integrated by numerous levies on industrial production, natural resources and international trade. Yet, as a result of important tax efforts to streamline administration and the introduction of a more efficient scheme to tax gross income, tax collection increased from 6.5 to 10 percent of GDP during the 1940–70 period. This substantial increase on the tax burden also responded to a gradual move towards an economy based on manufacture and service sectors, from traditional non-mineral primary activities.

In order to keep up with the economic strategy prevailing at that time towards industrialization and internal-market orientation, a set of tax reforms were approved by Federal Congress during 1955–72. On the income taxation structure, a "cedular system" was replaced by general regimes for individuals and corporations based on "net global income." For corporations, an accelerated depreciation scheme applicable to equipment was introduced as a means to foster investment in key industrial sectors. The new tax regime also featured special tax regimes for small taxpayers in primary sectors, such as agriculture, livestock and fishing activities, in such a way that fiscal authorities collected fixed amounts of tax, without regard to income, cost, and investment performance. Also, these reforms included an overhaul of the indirect taxation structure. A number of production and sales taxes were substituted by a simpler scheme based on a single turnover tax. In the administrative sphere, a national taxpayers' registry was created for the first time.

Between 1978 and 1981, another important set of tax reforms was introduced, basically aimed at adapting to a rampant inflationary environment. Previously, during the 1971–5 period, public expenditure increased from 20.5 to 30 percent of GDP as a result of an significant expansion of state-owned enterprises. New oil field discoveries fed favorable expectations on oil revenues. As a result, the federal government decided to finance public expenditure with foreign credit resources and with inflationary taxation. In 1975 fiscal deficit reached 10 percent of GDP. As a result of the second oil price shock and concomitant increases on oil revenues extracted form *Petróleos Mexicanos*, or PEMEX – the national oil monopoly – President López-Portillo decided to further expand the number of state-owned enterprises under an ambitious program of public investment. Consequently, public expenditure reached 41.1 in of GDP by 1981, whereas inflation rose to almost 30 percent. Income tax reforms carried out during this time addressed the inflationary adjustment as one of the main objectives. The tax schedule for personal income tax was corrected for the effects of inflation to prevent undesirable distribution effects associated with "bracket-creeping." Also, the capital gains assessment mechanism was revised to allow cost adjustment for general price increases. Though partial and incomplete, inflation adjustments paved the way for further reforms intended to fully recognize the effect of inflation on tax bases. The indirect taxation structure was the object of a deep reform. In 1980, a value added tax replaced the turnover tax, 30 federal excise taxes, and about 400 local taxes, under the policy objective of reducing typical distortions, such as the "cascading effect," associated with a turnover tax system.

Starting in 1982, the administration of President De la Madrid faced a profound macroeconomic crisis as oil prices collapsed, and external credit lines were depleted. In spite of the implementation of an aggressive economic adjustment through drastic reduction on public expenditures and the privatization of several state-owned enterprises, the Mexican economy fell into deep recession and inflation rates reached three-digit levels. As part of the economic package, excises tax rates increased and the VAT was reformed to introduce a multi-rate structure. By the end of the 1980s, the tax system structure proved to be insufficient to address revenue, efficiency and equity concerns. At that time, the tax system contained a set of rules conceived for a different development strategy, such as uncompetitive tax rates, rampant tax credit allowances, and an uneven distribution of the tax burden among sectors. The new development strategy based on economic openness, deregulation, and privatization demanded a new tax structure compatible with the modernizing of the economic structure, to the adoption of the North American Free Trade Agreement (NAFTA) with the US and Canada, and to the entrance of Mexico in the OECD.

In due regard to these circumstances, the administration of President Salinas embarked on a profound overhaul of the tax system during the 1989–91 period. In perspective, the tax legislative initiatives approved by Congress in this short period of time are reckoned to be the most substantial effort undertaken by the Mexican government in modern times to streamline its tax system. As part of this set of reforms, income tax rates applicable to corporations were reduced to 35 from 45 percent, in an attempt to set a competitive level against trading partners: the US (38.3 percent) and Canada (43.3 percent). To facilitate international trade and investment by reducing the capital cost of firms increasingly doing business in Mexico, officials from the Ministry of Finance started negotiations with partner countries aimed at reaching income tax treaties.

The maximum personal income tax rate was brought down to 35 from 50 percent. Full integration between corporations and individuals was allowed. In an attempt to foster compliance and increase tax revenues the Congress approved a new 2 percent asset tax, totally creditable against corporate income tax. The CIT structure was adjusted to fully incorporate the effects of inflation. PIT brackets were also adjusted for inflationary purposes. For small enterprises, a new simplified tax system based on cash flow was devised to comply with tax obligations with fewer accounting records. An important element of this reform endeavor was the overhaul of some deductions and exemption items included into the tax codes supported by weak economic rationale. Some tax incentives were trimmed, such as the accelerated depreciation scheme for investment projects carried out outside the areas of Mexico City, Guadalajara, and Monterrey. In others, deductions linked with executive meals and automobiles were curbed. Finally, special tax bases applicable to firms and individuals engaged in primary sector and other activities which usually conveyed a small or nil tax base for taxpayers, were eliminated. Finally, VAT rates previously settled at 6.15 and 20 percent, were replaced by a single tax rate of 10 percent.

From a broad perspective, the tax reform effort carried out during the 1970–90 period showed mixed results. The reduction of tax rates; the elimination of some unjustified preferential regimes; full integration of income tax between individuals and corporations; the total recognition of inflation effects into tax bases; and rationalization of the indirect taxation structure, provided a more efficient, fair, and competitive tax system. Nevertheless, those reforms fell short of providing the Mexican government with an adequate source of non-oil tax revenues. By 1990, tax collection as a percentage of GDP of 11.1 percent compared unevenly with other Latin American countries such as Chile (18.6 percent), Brazil (17.6 percent), Argentina (14 percent), or Colombia (12.2 percent). The severe financial crisis underwent by the Mexican economy at the end of 1994 resulted in a substantial loss of tax revenues. In fact, this reduction turned out to be even more severe than the contraction of national income. The tax ratio decreased by 23 percent from 1994 to 1995. This effect was explained by the credit crunch experienced by economic agents, so that they financed short-term debt payments with tax withheld from income tax and VAT.

As part of the economic package put forward by President Zedillo's Administration, the VAT general rate increased to 15 from 10 percent along with a substantial increase of real prices of goods and services provided by public entities. At the same time, and in order to ease the effects of the financial crisis, the government announced a set of temporal tax incentives, such as the reduction of the tax on assets general rate for small and medium enterprises, the immediate expense of marginal investments carried out during 1996, and also tax credits to foster employment. The emergent tax policy measures probed to be efficient to achieve the desired effects. The Mexican economy activity resumed relatively fast. By 1996, real GDP grew by 5.1 percent. However tax collection increased by only 0.8 percent due to the effects of the corporate operating losses carried forward. The downward tendency was not reverted until 1997, when tax collection increased to 9.8 as a percentage of GDP, from 8.9 percent in 1996. During the post-crisis period of 1997–2000, the tax reform agenda addressed again some issues pending after the 1989–91 overhaul of the tax system. Clearly, its limited capacity to raise revenue scored high again in the government priorities. In 1999, the tax ratio reached only 11.3 percent of GDP, which turns out to be the same level of 1994 before the financial crisis. Yet, the plural composition of the Congress observed in 1997 for the first time in the modern history of Mexico, resulted in poor agreements to reach consensus upon a revenue-enhancing reform. This lack of agreement in Congress over one of the most pressing and unaccomplished issues in Mexico, still lingers as of today.

Some quantitative and institutional features of main taxes

The personal income tax (PIT)

The general regime for resident individuals is applicable on a global and world-wide income basis. Therefore, taxable income includes all kind of realized income, in cash or in kind, accrued from wages and salaries, personal services, business income (e.g. partnerships, sole proprietorship), capital gains, interest, exchange rate fluctuations gains, rents, dividends, or any other source. Non-residents are also subject to this regime for their personal income sourced in Mexico. An individual is resident of Mexico when she establishes her home or center of vital interest in the country. Following mainly economic and administrative reasons, the Mexican PIT regime excludes from its base items such as financial interest income, imputed income from owner-occupied housing, proceeds from house sales, gifts and bequests, gains from sale of stock exchange-listed shares, authorship rights income, and fringe benefits. Exclusion of fringe benefits from taxable income, stands out not only as a major base-erosion and a low revenue-elastic concept in the Mexican PIT regime, but also as a source of inequity among wage earners with the same income position, but different composition. Qualified fringe benefits granted under a very broad definition, and usually valued and apportioned on arbitrary basis, have traditionally been used by employers as a tax planning tool to reduce average tax rates. As a result, policymakers were forced to further push down tax rates, especially for mid-level income earners, causing concerns about the ability of the PIT to incentivize work, savings and human capital formation.

Individuals are allowed to deduct from taxable income the following personal itemized-deductions: medical, dental and funeral expenses (including dependents), charitable contributions, real mortgage interests, child school transport, contributions to qualified individual retirement accounts (up to the equivalent of five minimum wages, approximately Ps88,000 per year), and health insurance premiums for themselves and their dependents. Once taxable income is defined, the PIT regime establishes a system of marginal tax rate and subsidy schedules to compute for the individual income tax. Despite insufficiencies of efforts pursued to broaden the PIT base, the highest marginal rate has decreased from 40 percent in 2002 to 28 percent effective as of 2007, driven by the need to achieve efficiency goals and a more competitive tax environment in Mexico. For the 2006 fiscal year, the highest marginal tax rate arises to 29 percent (Table 11.2.)

Individuals are entitled to a marginal non-refundable subsidy up to 50 percent (Table 11.3) of the tax obtained from the application of the marginal tax rate schedule. Introduced into the PIT regime back in 1991, the subsidy mechanism is designed to overcome inequities among wage earners with the same level, but different kinds, of remuneration. The subsidy mechanism is designed to phase out as the proportion of exempt fringe benefits from total remuneration increases.

Further on, the PIT regime allows low wage earners to claim a tax credit as a relief measure aimed at increasing their disposable income. The wage tax credit varies from Ps2,611 to Ps4,884, depending on the level of wage income up to Ps88,588 annually.

The Mexican Income Tax Law (ITL) establishes individual rather than familiar filing unit. All resident taxpayers are required to file an annual tax return, except for those cases where salary is the only source of income and it does not

Table 11.2 Personal income tax, Mexico, 2006

Income brackets (Ps)			Tax rate (%)
0.01	–	5,952.84	3
5,952.85	–	50,524.92	10
50,524.93	–	88,793.04	17
88,793.05	–	103,218.00	25
	over 103,218.01		29

Table 11.3 Mexican PIT: subsidy schedule 2006

Income brackets (Ps)			% subsidy over marginal tax rate
0.01	–	5,952.84	50
5,952.85	–	50,524.92	50
50,524.93	–	88,793.04	50
88,793.05	–	103,218.00	50
103,218.01	–	123,580.20	50
123,580.21	–	249,243.48	40
249,243.49	–	392,841.96	30
over 392,841.97			0

exceed an annual threshold of Ps300,000. As of 2006, most individual taxpayers are required to file an annual tax return on electronic basis and pay the tax due through electronic transfer of funds. For non-resident individuals with sources of income in Mexico, the PIT regime establishes an almost uniform 25 percent flat rate, striving towards a more neutral and simple treatment for inbound operations. This rate is applicable to independent personal services, fees paid to members of boards of directors, lease of property, and most capital gains. Mexican residents or non-residents with a permanent establishment in Mexico are required to withhold the tax when payments are made to non-resident individuals. For wages sourced in Mexico and received by non-residents, the ITL sets marginal rates of 15–30 percent.

The corporate income tax (CIT) and the asset tax

Mexican corporations are taxed on their worldwide income. CIT statutory rate is as of 2007. Corporations are deemed to be residents if they are incorporated under the provisions of Mexican corporate law, or if the principal center of administration, or the effective place of management, is located in Mexico. Despite substantial decreases on inflationary levels during the last decade (3.3 percent in 2005, from 35 percent in 1995), mechanisms to adjust the CIT base for inflation still remain enacted as a means to enhance business income measurement. Yet, for simplification purposes, an annual adjustment has replaced an old one calculated on monthly basis. This adjustment was originally conceived to include taxable income, inflationary gains and losses accrued by corporations due to monetary liabilities and assets holdings. In terms of capital cost allowances, buildings generally depreciate at a rate of 5 percent, and automobiles at 25 percent, whereas other machinery and equipment depreciate according to the type of assets and the industry use, ranging from 5 to 50 percent. Immediate expensing is allowed for pollution abatement and control engineering assets, as well as for special adaptations to taxpayer facilities designed to allow the access for handicapped individuals. Only straight line depreciation method is allowed. An accelerated depreciation incentive is granted for corporate investments on assets located outside of the areas of Mexico City, Guadalajara and Monterrey, or within these regions, if corporations probe their operations are not water intensive, and comply with environmental standards.

As of 2005, the CIT law allows for deduction of inventory cost under standard accounting principles, using LIFO, FIFO, average cost, retail, and identified cost (when the value of merchandise sold exceeds Ps50,000) as valuation methods. Net operating losses are allowed to be carried forward to offset future tax liabilities over a ten year period, adjusted for inflation. Similar to other corporate income tax codes around the world, as of the 2005 financial year the Mexican CIT system contains a thin capitalization rule to restrain corporations from using excessive debt payments as a tax shelter mechanism. Thus, interest paid by taxpayers on certain debts deemed excessive to their equity (over a 3-to-1 ratio) are non-deductible. A tax credit is available for research and development (R&D) expenses. Taxpayers are required to submit an application to an ad hoc inter-institutional committee disclosing detailed information about each R&D project. Tax credit is granted only to qualifying investments on R&D expenses for approved projects. A fixed amount of tax credit is granted every year, as approved by Congress. For the 2006 financial year, an equivalent of Ps4,000 million is assigned for R&D approved projects.

CIT regime allows for a full integration system. Dividends distributed from after-tax earnings (previously recorded in the Net Tax Earnings Account, or CUFIN, by its initials in Spanish) have no further tax liability effect both at corporate and individual levels. Dividend paid from the CUFIN account is not subject to withholding tax when distributed. Individuals are required to include grossed-up dividends in their taxable income but, at the same time, they claim a credit for the income tax paid by the corporation. The Mexican CIT regime allows for group taxation. A single consolidated tax return may be filed on behalf of a group of Mexican resident corporations (holding and subsidiaries), under a detailed set of rules, consolidated corporations accrue mutual tax benefits such as full profit-losses offsetting, and tax deferral on inter-company flow of dividends. Following capital-export neutrality standards, Mexican CIT Law unilaterally grants a tax credit for taxes paid abroad in order to prevent, or ameliorate, double taxation effects. Normally, foreign source income is taxable until it is distributed as dividends to the Mexican resident holding corporation. However, the CIT regime sets forth an anti-deferral scheme based on effective tax rates, whereby foreign source income from investments in low-tax jurisdictions (preferred tax regimes), is includable into taxable income of the Mexican parent corporation at the time of realization, regardless of the time of distribution.

An asset tax (AT) is applicable in Mexico as a supplement minimum income tax. From its introduction in 1989, the AT scheme was designed as a control devise for those taxpayers that permanently reduce or eliminate their tax liability by engaging in accounting manipulation or aggressive tax planning. By assuring a tax payment based on a minimum presumptive return on assets, the AT has also embedded efficiency features as it is an incentive for corporations to allocate their fixed assets to their highest productivity use. AT is payable at a rate of

1.8 percent on the value of assets held by individuals or corporations engaged in business activities, except on their first four years of operations (preoperative, initial, and two subsequent periods), when it exceeds income tax liability. Some non-financial debts are allowed to be deducted from the asset tax base.

Taxation of income from financial capital

The Mexican ITL allows for different treatment on the disposition of shares of stock issued by corporations. Exemption is granted for residents and non-residents income from the disposition of shares listed and traded on authorized stock exchange market, regardless of whether the issuing corporation is Mexican resident. However, sale of unquoted shares, or quoted shares not traded through authorized market, is taxable under the PIT regime. For this purpose, an income averaging mechanism is set forth, along with a detailed procedure to determine the average cost of shares, which includes an adjustment for inflation and for changes in the CUFIN account computed by the issuing corporation (see section on CIT) through the stock holding period. Non-residents are subject to either a 25 percent gross withholding rate, or the PIT statutory rate applicable to net income, provided certain rules are complied with.

Real interest income received by individuals is taxable, except for interest paid by banking institutions originated from checking accounts or payroll accounts, pensions and retirement or savings, provided the average daily balance is less than the equivalent of Ps88,820. Domestic law provides for a general withholding rate of 0.05 percent (annual rate) on interest paid by financial institutions. In general interest payments to non-residents are subject to the following withholding rates: 4.9 percent to interest payments on debt instruments placed in recognized local markets or placed abroad through financial institutions resident in countries which Mexico has a signed treaty with; 10 percent to interest paid to foreign government financial institutions, or derived from debt instruments placed through financial institutions in countries with no treaty with Mexico; 15 percent to interest paid to reinsurance entities and 21 percent in some other cases. Interest payments to non-residents are exempt, provided they are derived from loans to the Mexican Federal Government, or to the Bank of Mexico.

As said below, the income tax regime in Mexico follows a full integration system, in such a way that dividends are usually free of tax liability to the recipient, provided they originate from the CUFIN account. Statutory withholding rates could be reduced, or even eliminated, by applying tax treaty provisions. Mexico has pursued an active policy to engage in treaties to prevent double taxation and allow free exchange of information. Currently, over 30 treaties have been enacted with countries from diverse geographic locations.

Property taxation

Taxation on land and property in Mexico is levied and administrated at the sub-national level of government and the revenue collected from this source accounts for the main tax income for municipalities. Property tax is levied through an *ad valorem* rate applied to the appraisal value of property. State Congress approves changes to base and taxes every fiscal year, upon proposals made by municipalities. Municipal authorities keep track of cadastre records on location, size and ownership of each parcel of land. However, municipalities usually lack adequate cadastre register, as well as administrative and enforcement capabilities. Part of these insufficiencies are explained by the relatively high rotation of personnel in charge of these duties, given the fact that the municipal government term in Mexico lasts only three years, with no re-election.

Property tax base tends to lag behind market values in most municipalities. In addition, preferential treatments are granted for some extensions of land, particularly to rural areas and some urban areas devoted to social needs. As a consequence, despite the clear advantages offered by this source of income in terms of revenue-raising capacity, as well as on efficiency and equity grounds, taxation of land and property is largely underdeveloped in Mexico. Municipalities collect only around 0.2 percent of GDP, well bellow OECD (1 percent), and Latin America (0.7 percent) averages. No bequest, inheritance or gift tax is imposed in Mexico.

Value added tax

The Mexican VAT system stands out for its low revenue yield capacity, complex structure, and high levels of evasion. The multiplicity of tax rates, along with broad preferential treatments granted to a variety of goods and services, not only undermines revenue collection, but also distorts relative prices and falls short of meeting the distribution objectives it is intended to pursue. A general 15 percent rate is applicable to most goods and services traded domestically, as well as imported. A reduced 10 percent rate is levied on the consumption of goods and services along the border with the US, to address undesirable distortion effects that could arise in the economic activity carried on in this region with a higher rate. As a result of the comprehensive zero-rating and exemption treatment (Table 11.4), VAT tax expenditures represent almost 2 percent of GDP, approximately one-third of total tax expenditure budget for 2005.[2] Yet, 50 percent of total benefit is received by the wealthiest decile of the Mexican population, whereas the lowest income families only receive 3 percent of total tax expenditure.[3] Thus, the application of a narrow-based VAT structure arises serious concerns for policymakers, and consequently scores high in the tax reform agenda for the near future.

A salient feature of the Mexican VAT is its cash flow basis time of supply rule. Introduced as a measure to alleviate the financial stand of small and medium firms suppliers of large corporations, as of 2002 a taxpayer is liable to VAT upon receipt of payments from customers, whereas input credits are claimed at the time of payment to suppliers of goods or services.

However, VAT imposed on interest payments by households on final consumption is still levied on accrued basis. Taxpayers are required to compute

Table 11.4 Mexican VAT preferential treatments

Zero rating	Exemptions
Exports, including in-bound *maquila* and *sub-maquila* exports	Medical and education services, residential construction, books, magazines, and newspapers published by third parties, public transportation, lease of residential property, shares, bank interest payments, life insurance, author copyright, sale of participation certificates on real estate investment trusts, temporal imports by a corporation endorsed by the *maquila* or similar export-oriented program, or by the automobile industry.
Food products, medicines, magazines and newspapers published by the taxpayer, gold and jewelry; farm and livestock products and services, sale or lease of agriculture machinery, and domestic water supply.	

VAT on a monthly basis. Excess of VAT input-credits is either fully refundable or carried forward to offset future liabilities.

Small businesses are eligible for simplified procedures to calculate tax liability on presumptive basis. Under this scheme, tax authorities pre-estimate the monthly value of turnover and input tax credits, based on a variety of parameters typical for each type of taxpayer, such as inventory levels, machinery and equipment, and overheads. Tax liability is obtained by applying the tax rate to the estimated output value, reduced by the estimated input credit. Corporations are required to withhold VAT paid to individuals performing professional activities, ground transportation of goods services, lease of tangible property, as well as to commissioners. VAT withholding is also required on payments to non-residents with no permanent establishment in Mexico, for the sale or lease of tangible assets. Finally, in-bound *Maquiladoras*, Temporal Import Program for Export companies (*PITEX*, by its initials in Spanish), and automobile industry firms with bonded warehouse facilities are required likewise for their payments to domestic suppliers.

Excise duties

The special tax on products and services (IEPS, by its initials in Spanish) is levied on the sale or import of selected products such as gasoline, diesel, tobacco, soft drinks, concentrate syrups, beer and spirits, as well as services related to the commission, mediation, agency, and distribution activities of these products. Generally, IEPS tax liability calculation follows a credit mechanism similar to VAT, so it is collected at the import, producer, and wholesale levels. Retail sales of IEPS products are usually exempt, so the IEPS levied at the wholesale level is usually passed on to final consumers. Tax withholding is required on taxable sales from producers or importers to taxpayers engaged in mediation or distribution activities. A differentiated *ad valorem* rate schedule is applicable to taxable sales. Beers and sprits are taxed at rates ranging from 25 to 50 percent, depending on the alcoholic content.

A 20 percent rate is levied on soft drinks and concentrate syrups, 11 percent to cigarettes, and 20.9 percent to cigars. Taxation on the sale of gasoline and diesel products follows special rules. According to the IEPS Law, tax rates levied on these items are calculated monthly through a detailed mechanism based on international prices. Monthly rates are assessed and published by the Secretariat of Treasury and Public Credit on the Federal Official Gazette. IEPS tax on gasoline and diesel is collected on a single stage basis at each *Petróleos Mexicanos* (PEMEX, by its initials in Spanish) sale point. For the 2006 financial year, the Federal Congress approved amendments to the IEPS Law to introduce an environmental incentive. A new ruling allows beer producers, importers and bottling companies to apply a tax credit when using recyclable containers.

Maquiladoras *tax regime and transfer pricing issues*

Maquiladoras, or inbound cost centers, are Mexican assembly plants capable of maintaining equipment, machinery and inventories provided by their foreign-owner corporation, for their transformation into semi-finished and finished goods destined for export to the US market. Parent corporations also grant *maquiladoras* free use of patents and technology to carry out the manufacturing process. Ever since its initial stages dated back in the late 1960s, the *maquiladora* industry has contributed to the expansion of Mexican manufacturing exports. However, this contribution reached meaningful levels in the decade of the 1990, especially since the adoption of the North American Free Trade Agreement (NAFTA) with the US and Canada in 1994. The contribution of the *maquiladora* industry to the Mexican economy has been substantial. For 2005, the value of total *maquiladora* exports was US$96.75 billion, equivalent to 55 percent of total manufacturing exports, and 45 percent of total exports, mainly to the US market. The number of *maquiladora* plants has risen to 2,811, from 1,703 in 1990, mainly located along the border zone with the US. Currently the industry employs 1.17 million. Part of the expansion of this export sector is explained by the tax incentives granted by the Mexican government to assembly plants carrying on *maquiladora* activities, as defined and recognized by the Secretariat of Economy. Capital required to perform *maquiladora* activities in Mexico is considered in-bound for their export. Therefore, duty free and VAT exemption to the temporary imports of machinery, equipment, parts and material are granted, provided they are designated to be transformed into export products, according to the *maquiladora* program regulations. Also, inventories considered to be in-bound for export are exempt from AT.

The income tax treatment to the *maquiladora* activities has spurred special attention to policymakers and members of the industry for the last decade, especially since 1995 when Mexico joined the Organization for Economic Co-operation and Development (OECD). The continuous set of reforms introduced to the *maquiladora* regime since then, has responded to the changing economic conditions surrounding their activity, in Mexico and abroad, and also to the develop of the transfer pricing practice in Mexico. The continuous coordination and mutual agreement between tax authorities from Mexico and the US has played a key role in shaping the *maquiladora* tax regime. Before 1995, the Mexican Income Tax Law offered no special treatment to the *maquiladora* activity. Thus, *maquiladoras* constituted a permanent establishment of foreign residents, subject to the general regime of corporate income tax in regard to their business activities carried out in Mexico. Also, the income tax legislation required *maquiladoras* to charge foreign corporations a profit-margin from 2 to 5 percent above operation costs as a transfer price.

By the mid-1990s, as a response to the need to enlarge the income tax base for the *maquiladora* industry, the Mexican tax legislation developed for the first time special rules applicable to their activities. The key issue was the exemption of the permanent establishment status for the foreign-resident owners of Mexican-based *maquiladoras*, provided that they comply with income tax requirements, either by adopting a *safe harbor* rule of 5 percent on all assets, or by abiding to an Advance Price Agreement (APA) ruling. However, the economic dynamism shown by the sector during the past decade, threatened the ability of these transfer pricing rules to adequately reach the tax base originated by the *maquiladoras* activity in Mexico. To address this concern, *maquiladora* rules were modified as of the 2000 financial year following the Mexico-US Mutual Agreement on the Tax Regime applicable to Maquiladoras (MAP agreement), reached in October 1999, allowing the exemption of permanent establishment status to *maquiladoras* owned by foreign residents, when satisfying one of the following requirements:

1 Adopt a safe harbor rule, whereby *maquiladoras* consider a taxable income by the amount greater between 6.5 percent of total cost and expenses, or 6.9 percent of total assets used in connection with their operation, or

2 Apply and obtain an APA, following procedures set forth by the Mexican Fiscal Code. By 2003, the Mexican Congress approved reforms to the Income Tax Law, including some additions to the rules applicable to the *maquiladora* activity. This reform was important for two reasons. First, the addition of the applicable tax rules, including the permanent establishment exemption assumption, into the text of the law provided a sense of certainty to the business community. Previously, those rules were subject to annual confirmation. Secondly, a wider set of methods was offered for the *maquiladora* industry to comply with Mexican transfer pricing regulations, in accordance with OECD Transfer Pricing Guidelines (Table 11.5).

In an effort to reconcile the *maquiladora* tax rules to a relatively recessive economic period in the export market, by the end of 2003 President Fox signed a tax relief decree granting *maquiladoras* a partial exemption, equivalent to 50 percent of the taxable income assessed upon the current rules. This tax benefit has been enacted without a time limit.

Table 11.5 Current options for *maquiladoras* to comply with transfer pricing requirements

---

I. Arm's length principle, plus fixed assets net value
Declare income and deductions according to prices determined by arm's length methods described by the Income Tax Law, in accordance to OECD Guidelines, plus 1 percent of the net value of the machinery and equipment owned by foreign residents, devoted to the *maquila* activity (APA is not mandatory, but transfer pricing study records should be kept).

II. Safe harbor
Declare as taxable profit the greater of:
    a) 6.5 percent of total cost and expenses;
    b) 6.9 percent of total assets used in the *maquila* operation.

III. TPM predetermined methodology
Declare taxable income as resulted from arm's length prices obtained following the Transactional Profit Margin (TPM) Method, considered within the transfer pricing methods allowed by the Income Tax Code, in accordance to OECD TP Guidelines, accounting for the machinery and equipment transferred by the foreign resident to the *maquiladora* to carry out assembly activities. (APA is not mandatory but transfer pricing study records should be kept).

Source: OECD Transfer Pricing Guidelines.

Taxation by levels of government and fiscal federalism

The Mexican United States is organized as a federal and democratic republic consisting of 31 free and sovereign states, unified by a federal government rested in the capital city sited in the federal district (a.k.a. *Mexico, D.F. or Mexico City*). The federal government is divided in three autonomous powers: executive, judicial and legislative. This scheme is replicated in every state government. Further on, each state is conformed by a number of municipal governments ruled by an autonomous executive branch, but without legislative powers. Fiscal relationships among the three level of government is ruled out by the Fiscal Coordination National System (FCNS). The FCNS Law was enacted in 1980, jointly with the introduction of the VAT, in response to the need to harmonize vertical and horizontal distortions caused by the existence of multiple local turnover and excise taxes. Under the FCNS arrangement, the federal government is exclusively empowered to impose broad-based taxes, meanwhile state governments share part of a pull of federal revenue collection, formally denominated Revenue-Sharing Fund (RSF), according to a distribution formulae constructed upon two elements: population and tax capacity.

Also, state governments share total collection from both sales taxes for new cars (*ISAN*) and the annual automobile registration fee (*tenencia*), both imposed at the federal level, but collected and enforced locally. By disposition of the FCNS Law, part of the revenue-sharing transfers received by each state is passed on to municipalities. Besides the revenue-sharing mechanism, the FCNS also defines rules to transfer spending responsibilities to state and municipal governments on itemized areas, such as education, health, and local infrastructure. For this purpose the FCNS establishes seven appropriate funds for earmarked expenditure, transferred every fiscal year to local authorities. As a result of the FCNS revenue-sharing and spending decentralization mechanisms, the Mexican federal government transfers up to 60 percent of federal revenue collection to local governments, compared to an average of 22 percent in OECD and Latin American countries. Due to an increase in the bulk of federal revenue integrated into the RSF, transfers to sub-national governments have increased from 2.8 percent of GDP in 1990, to 3.3 percent in 2006.

In terms of local revenue sources, the Mexican Constitution grants limited taxation powers to states and municipalities. Indeed, state governments rely on the local payroll tax as their major tax source. Additionally, states raise revenue from some additional sources such as the real estate transfer tax, tax on motor vehicles older than ten years, and some fees and licenses for public services. At the municipal level, property tax is the single most important source of revenue, followed by local fees and licenses, water fees and real estate transfer tax. The combination of limited local taxation powers with a vast transfer of fiscal resources originating from the FCNS revenue-share mechanism, has created an undesirable local dependency on federal transfers. On average, federal transfers currently account for 90 percent of total state revenue. As a result, local governments find few incentives to enhance local tax effort. Property tax is a case on its own, as municipalities collect only 0.2 percent of GDP, compared to an average of 0.7 percent in Latin America countries or 1 percent in other OECD countries.

The high centralization of taxation in Mexico, combined with a substantial decentralization of spending responsibilities, induces distortions in the efficient provision of public goods. Lack of correspondence between the level of government in charge of collection and that responsible for spending, results in a sub-optimal allocation of resources. Furthermore, unbalanced fiscal responsibilities means local governments are not adequately held accountable for their tax and spending decisions. During recent years, the Mexican Congress approved reforms geared towards correcting some of the distortions induced by the FCNS fiscal arrangement. As of 2004, state governments are empowered to legislate and implement low-rate cellular taxes on individual income obtained from the following sources: professional services, lease of fixed property, disposal of property, and business activity. Nevertheless, by 2006 only three state governments – Chihuahua, Guanajuato, and Oaxaca – have already implemented some form of local cellular tax. Arguably, unless deep reforms on the Mexican fiscal federalism system are carried out, local governments would perceive it cost-ineffective, both from economic and political perspectives, to incur new tax responsibilities or to enhance current sources of revenue collection.

Table 11.6 Mexico: revenue sharing fund, RSF (% of GDP)

	1995–2000	*2001–4*
Average	11.9	13.2

Source: Ministry of Finance and Public Credit.

Tax reforms in the 2000s and those currently planned

The fiscal policy during the 2001–5 period contributed to achieve the public finance objectives estimated by the Mexican government. The public deficit as a percentage of GDP decreased from 1.1 in 2000 to 0.2 in 2005. Also, the Public Sector Borrowing Requirements (PSBR), a broader measure of the amount of money needed by the government to cover any deficit in financing its own activities, followed suit reducing from 3.3 to 2.3 in the same period (see Table 11.7).

As a result of the combination of tax administration efficiency gains and a reorientation of public expenditures, the public sector has increased capabilities to mobilize resources towards social needs. Public expenditure allocated to social development increased to an average of 10.1 percent of GDP during the 2001–5 period, from 9.3 percent registered in 1998–2000.

Tax reforms already passed

Tax reforms approved by the Mexican Congress are geared towards a more efficient and competitive system. In general terms, the reforms pursued four basic objectives: competitiveness, simplicity, revenue capacity enhancement, and fiscal federalism.

Competitiveness

Similar to other small and increasingly open economies, globalization and international tax competition poses challenges to the Mexican tax system. Consequently, the new Income Tax Law recently enacted introduced reforms to attain a competitive framework for individuals and corporations in Mexico. During the last few years, the CIT rate has been reduced by 30 percent to reach 28 percent effectively from 2007, increasing the competitive stance of the tax system. Effective CIT tax rate is reduced even further as of 2005 considering the new deduction of the employee profit-sharing item (*Participación a los Trabajadores en las Utilidades de las empresas, PTU*), which is expected to reduce CIT rates by 4.4 percentage points. In order to foster investment and employment, an immediate deduction applicable to fixed assets was introduced into the Income Tax Law. This tax incentive was restricted for investment in new fixed assets utilized outside the metropolitan areas of Mexico City, Guadalajara, and Monterrey, unless corporations prove the employment of a

Table 11.7 Public finance 1997–2005, Mexico (% of GDP)

	1997	1998	1999	2000	2001	2002	2003	2004	2005
Public deficit	0.7	1.2	1.1	1.1	0.7	0.6	0.4	0.2	0.2
PSBR	4.5	5.9	5.9	3.3	3.0	2.6	2.5	1.8	2.3

Source: Ministry of Finance and Public Credit.

sizeable labor force, the utilization of clean technologies with respect to the emission of pollutants, or engage in production processes not reliant on the use of water. Also, a 30 percent tax credit on R&D investments and expenses was enacted for corporations.

Aimed at promoting the Mexican real estate market, a tax incentive was granted to real estate investment trusts by allowing investors a tax deferral scheme. For the *maquiladora* industry, a 50 percent reduction of the CIT base was granted as a response to short-term economic impacts, such as US economy contractions and strong competition from China. Congress also approved measures for individuals to deduct medical insurance premiums supplementary to or separate from health services furnished by social insurance institutions, and also to deduct real interest paid on home mortgage loans granted by a bank or auxiliary credit organization. On a move to introduce equal competing conditions for domestic corporations seeking funds in the domestic financial markets to finance investment projects, PIT reforms were introduced to tax previously exempt interest government bonds. Parallel to the CIT rate reduction, the maximum marginal tax rate applicable to individuals gradually reduced from 40 to 28 percent, effective from 2007, introducing incentives to work, save and invest. As a measure to promote the tourism industry, Congress introduced discretionary changes to the VAT consisting of expanding the 0 percent export rate to tourism services rendered to international tourists in connection to their attendance of seminars, congresses, or any other similar events taking place in Mexico.

Simplicity

During the last five years, several simplicity measures were introduced into the tax system. As part of a major effort to modernize and enhance operations, the Tax Administration Service (SAT) has implemented IT solutions aimed at encouraging voluntary compliance and lower compliance costs. One of the salient features of the recent reform efforts has been the widespread introduction of electronic means to file returns, pay taxes, and comply with information requirements. Nowadays, more than half of total taxpayer obligations are fulfilled through the Internet, accounting for the total universe of corporate return filing. The SAT website registered 115 million visits/transactions in 2005, from 1.1 million in 2000. Besides administration efficiency gains, several tax policy initiatives were taken in order to simplify calculations and reduce compliance costs. The corporate income tax was reformed to eliminate the tax differential scheme previously introduced to account for the reinvested profits, and the mid-year adjustment of installment payments. Also, the calculation for inflation adjustment to real interest was greatly simplified, by introducing an annual mechanism to adjust for monetary position (assets and liabilities), combined with a nominal deduction and inclusion of interests.

The most important reform of the PIT regime towards simplicity was the implementation of cash flow regime to individuals engaged in trade and business, and professional activities. This new regime allows individuals to include taxable income and deduct expenses on cash flow basis, to wave inflationary adjustment calculations, and also to keep a single and simple accounting record. For taxpayers with limited administrative capacity, a new *intermediate regime* was also designed. Under this new scheme, individuals and corporations with annual incomes below a four million pesos threshold, are allowed immediate expense of investment on fixed assets, following a simpler set of rules to comply with the Income Tax Law. The VAT law was reformed accordingly. A new supply rule was introduced in such a way that the tax levied upon the sale, rendering of services and the temporary use or enjoyment of property is due at the time of collection. Also, tax credit is allowed at the time of payment. Accordingly, in those cases where an obligation to withhold arises, tax is collected on the amount actually paid. In terms of administration ease, it has eliminated the obligation for taxpayers to file an annual VAT return, leaving only monthly tax returns. Towards simplification of the withholding tax rate structure devised for non-residents with sources of income in Mexico, Congress approved reforms to levy a single general withholding rate of 25 percent applicable to almost all sources of income.

Fiscal federalism

During the last few years, initiatives towards increasing the availability of revenue sources to sub-national governments were approved by Congress, in two different ways: share of federal tax bases and new local taxing powers. Considering the relatively less mobility of individuals engaged in small business activities, reforms were introduced to allow state governments to share with the federal government part of the income tax collection sourced in their territory. The same sharing arrangement was established for the proceeds of the sale of immobile property. Operation and administrative rules were needed for local governments to expand capacities in order to receive tax returns, collect part of the provisional installments paid by taxpayers every month, and to grant tax credits against federal tax due. Besides administration and collection duties, inspection powers were granted for sub-national tax authorities to oversee the appropriate compliance behavior of small taxpayers operating locally. As discussed above, in terms of new taxing responsibilities for local governments, the federal congress approved legislation to empower state governments to implement cellular taxes on income obtained by individuals from independent professional services, lease and disposal of fixed property, and business activities. To avoid distortions on location decisions, state congresses are constrained to impose tax rates beyond an interval of 2 to 5 percent.

Tax reforms underway and planned

During the last 25 years, the Mexican tax system has been subject to a permanent reform process geared towards providing a more competitive fiscal environment to economic agents. As a result, the tax legislation includes some salient efficiency features, such as full integration of dividends, recognition of inflationary impacts, and relatively competitive statutory tax rates. Facing the need to adapt to an increasingly open and modern economy, the tax system has successfully adopted international best practices, such as standard transfer pricing guidelines. Also, the Mexican tax system has adopted a wide network of tax treaties to avoid double taxation and exchange of information, with more than 30 partner countries. The membership of Mexico to the OECD and NAFTA has greatly contributed to the tax system modernization process. Nevertheless, the pursuit of a more competitive and efficient tax system has not gone together with parallel reforms to strength its revenue capacity. The tax system is currently limited by its own structure to yield adequate collection levels. Therefore, the key issue on the reform agenda is to bridge the gap between actual and potential tax capacities, primarily by broadening tax bases while keeping tax rates to competitive levels. By doing so, it is expected not only to attain revenue targets, but also to alleviate horizontal inequities currently caused by unjustified preferential treatments, as well as to ease compliance and the administrative costs.

Several attempts have been made recently to overcome some of the revenue insufficiencies embedded into the tax code. The executive branch of the Mexican government has recurrently sent to Congress diverse reform initiatives with the explicit objective of closing loopholes and to level the playing field for all economic sectors and productive activities. The Integral Fiscal Reform Bill (IFR) introduced to Congress in the early stages of President Fox's term stands out for its depth and potential consequences to attain revenue collection goals. Though some of the proposals contained in the IFR were actually approved and implemented, the core part of it, which basically included a broad-based new VAT structure, is still pending. Given the immediate and unavoidable fiscal pressures faced by the Mexican government in the short term, it is expected that new tax reform initiatives, covering similar issues proposed by the IFR, will be introduced again to Congress by newly elected federal government authorities. In this section, some of the main IFR proposals pending, along with some considerations about efforts underway to modernize the SAT operational system, are laid out.

Value added tax

As discussed in the present chapter, the wide and numerous exemption and zero-rated goods and services items considered in the VAT law, have resulted in a significant reduction of the potential consumption base. The narrow-based structure has also contributed to low compliance levels, as taxpayers have found the way to arrange transactions in such a way that they appear either exempt or zero-rated. The IFR proposed a new VAT legislation, though keeping intact a substantial part of the current law articles in order to facilitate compliance. The zero rate was only granted for export activities, under destination principle considerations. For control purposes, the initiative required taxpayers to engage in electronic transfer of funds when arranging for the export transaction payment, to be eligible for VAT refund. The proposed VAT base included most items currently zero-rated or exempt, such as food, medicine, books, magazine, education, and transport. Exempt treatment was only granted to those transactions that, by their intrinsic nature, do not represent consumption expenditure, or entail difficult-to-tax goods and services, such as the sale of land, hard currency, stocks, gold, jewelry, art objects, and financial services, except for interest paid on individual final consumption. Lease or sale of housing construction was also proposed to be exempt from VAT.

The general tax rate proposed by IFR was equal to the current 15 percent, maintaining the reduced 10 percent rate for transaction of goods and services along the border with the US. The rationale behind proposing to leave the dual tax rate system was to avoid market price distortions in the referred area, given the considerable influence of the US southern economy over residents living in the Mexican border states. However, the reform proposal maintained the current exclusion of the reduced border rate to the taxable sale of fixed property. Some of the IFR original proposals for VAT reform were adopted in an effort to streamline the current structure. The obligation for taxpayers to fulfill an annual tax return, besides provisional monthly payments, was repealed. Nowadays, a monthly taxable period prevails, easing tax administration and compliance costs. Also, in an attempt to simplify tax assessment, facilitate inspections, and allow neutrality with respect to the decision of firms to handle commerce practices with suppliers and clients, the VAT time of supply rules switched to pure cash flow basis.

Personal income tax

Besides low revenue-yield capacity, the Mexican PIT structure shows serious deficiencies in terms of efficiency, equity and simplicity. The adoption of broad exemptions grounded on poor social or economic justifications, promotes low personal saving rates and productive investment disincentives. Consequently, the PIT system has unnecessary adapted relative high marginal tax rates to medium level income individuals, along with arbitrage opportunities to evade the tax burden. The IFR addressed most of these insufficiencies by followed a basic approach: to broaden the tax base and reduce marginal tax rates. To achieve these objectives, the IFR tried to widen the tax base, along with a decrease of marginal tax rates which included the introduction of the zero percent marginal tax rate for the lowest income end.

One of the top priorities of the PIT in the future reform agenda is the tax treatment of fringe benefits into the wage-earners' tax base. As discussed before, the exclusion of this item from taxable income, which accounts for an estimate of one-third of total wage remuneration, biases the distribution of the tax burden among individuals at the same level of wage income, but with different composition. Full taxation of fringe benefits would not only bring revenue and equity benefits to the PIT structure, but also simplicity. The inclusion of this item into the wage-earners' taxable income makes no longer necessary to sustain the fiscal subsidy system, arranged for those individuals receiving a smaller portion of their salary by fringe benefits. By applying a single marginal tax schedule,

instead of two, the PIT regime will get rid of one of its most complex administrative features. Therefore, a single effective rate could be applicable to each
level of income. Part of the extra revenue collection expected form the inclusion
of fringe benefits could be used to reduce marginal tax rates to medium income
level individuals, and so effectively increasing incentives for work and capital
formation. The reform agenda should not only streamline the PIT structure,
widen its tax base and further contribute to achieve horizontal and vertical
equity, but also eliminate the exemption granted to authorship rights.

Corporate income tax

The current CIT structure allows preferential treatment for taxpayers in specific
economic activities, regardless of their size, ability to pay, or administrative capabilities. Through a combination of tax incentives granted by the *simplified
regime*, such as immediate expense of investments, partial exemption of tax liability (about 45 percent for agriculture), and administrative facilities to fulfill deduction requirements, taxpayers carrying out land transport and agriculture activities
afford comparatively lower effective CIT tax rates. As a result, medium and large-
sized corporations dedicated to agriculture and transport activities, pay little or no
CIT. Preferential regimes granted in an indiscriminate way to a broad range of
sectors in Mexico not only seriously erodes the tax base, but also promotes economic inefficiency, horizontal and vertical inequity among taxpayers, evasion and
elusion opportunities, as well as complications to the tax administration. The limi-
tation of non-neutralities within the CIT structure represents a necessary condition
towards a more transparent and efficient system. Thus, the reform agenda should
consider canceling the *simplified regime* as a means to eliminate preferential treatment for medium and large firms engaged in transport and agriculture activities.
As for small-scale taxpayers, it is desirable to allow them to comply with the
income tax either through the *small taxpayer's regime* or the *intermediate regime*,
already applicable to individuals engaged in small business activities.

Reform on tax administration

A profound reform on the SAT's operation and infrastructure is currently underway. The drive to change is oriented towards increasing tax compliance through a
comprehensive broadening of the taxpayer universe, and a thorough simplification
of payments and tax filing processes. One of the basic components of the ongoing
reform effort is the redesign and computerization of key processes. In the recent
past, SAT operations relied on fragmented information systems, excessive procedures and lack of integration between operating areas. SAT reforms aim at shifting
from an organization based on functions towards a different one operating by
processes. To achieve this goal, an improved IT platform is currently under design
in order to support newly designed tax administration operating processes, either
in substantive areas such as taxpayer services, auditing and collection, or support
functions such as human, financial and material resources management.

Also, some different efforts to improve tax administration are currently underway, such as a comprehensive fiscal census geared towards improving registration
and control of individuals and enterprises engaged in trade or business, the
Advanced Electronic Firm which allows taxpayers to fulfill obligations and file tax
returns by electronic means, and the implementation of the risk management
program. Looking to the future, important steps should be taken to grant autonomy
status to the SAT agency. The wave of autonomy reforms undertaken by tax
administrations of different countries during the last decade, have proven to be
relatively successful in providing an institutional framework capable of enhancing
operation in developing countries. Besides improving corporate governing and
allowing mid and long-term strategic planning scenarios, an autonomous SAT
would empower managers with greater control over personnel, funding and budgeting to achieve highest standards of efficiency and quality. A constitutional
reform should be passed by Federal Congress for SAT to achieve autonomy.

Notes

1 The author would like to thank Mr. Julio C. Aguilar, Chief of the Revenue Policy Unit,
   for his support on this endeavor, and also Mr. Alfredo Gutiérrez Ortiz Mena, Chief of
   the Large Taxpayers Unit, Tax Administration Service (SAT by its initials in Spanish),
   for his valuable comments and insights.
2 Tax Expenditure Budget, SHCP (2005).
3 Integral Fiscal Reform Project, Fiscal Research, n.1, 3rd stage, SHCP (2001).

Bibliography

Aspe, P. (1993) *Economic Transformation: The Mexican Way*, Cambridge, MA.: The
    MIT Press.
Banco de México (2003) "Un comparativo internacional de la recaudación tributaria,"
    México: DF, mimeo.
Chávez, J. and Gabriel, M. (2000) "Logros y retos de las finanzas públicas en México,"
    Serie de política fiscal, n. 112, Santiago de Chile: División de desarrollo económico de
    CEPAL.
Gil Díaz, F. (1987) "Some Lessons from Mexico's Tax Reform," in Stern, N. and
    Newbery, D. (eds.) *The Theory of Taxation for Developing Countries*, Oxford: Oxford
    University Press, pp. 333–56.
—— (2002) "La prolongada reforma fiscal de México," *Gaceta de Economía del ITAM*,
    vol. 5, n. 9, pp. 7–62
Giugale, M., Lafourcade, O. and Nguyen, V. (2001) *Mexico, a comprehensive Develop-
    ment Agenda for the New Era*, Washington, DC: World Bank.
Instituto Tecnológico Autónomo de México (2001) "Una agenda para las finanzas públi-
    cas de México," *Gaceta de Economía del ITAM*, México, DF.
OECD (2003) "Peer Review of Mexican Transfer Pricing. Legislation and Practices,"
    working party 6 of the Committee on Fiscal Affairs, Centre for Tax Policy and Admin-
    istration, Paris: OECD.
SHCP (Secretaría de Hacienda y Crédito Público), various years, *Informes sobre la
    situación económica, las finanzas públicas y la deuda pública*, México, DF.

12 Paraguay

Caterina Ferrario

Introduction and contents[1]

Paraguay is one of the smallest South American countries, both in terms of area and population. This landlocked country covers an area of about 407 million km^2 and has a population of about 5.5 million people. The Republic of Paraguay's political history, beginning with independence from Spain in 1811, has been shaped by three postcolonial dictatorships (from 1814 to 1870), followed by a period of high political instability, which ended in 1954, when General Alfredo Stroessner assumed the presidency after a military coup. Mr. Stroessner's authoritarian and corrupt regime lasted until 1989. In June 1992 a new democratic constitution was adopted, establishing Paraguay as a Presidential Republic, which is divided into 17 departments and 231 municipalities. Since 1989 all presidents have come from the Colorado Party, the most powerful party, which has ruled uninterruptedly since 1947. In 2003 Nicanor Duarte Frutos, leader of the reformist faction within the Colorado Party, was elected president with an ambitious program of state reform. Among the actions taken, with encouragement from international organizations (primarily the IMF), was a major tax reform approved in 2004, but with implementation partially delayed to 2006.

This chapter analyzes Paraguay's tax system and its recent reforms. After a brief introduction to the economy contained in the remainder of this section, the second section presents basic data on public finances and compares the Paraguayan tax system with the other Latin American systems. The third section details the main taxes and their features. The fourth section evaluates recent tax reforms. The chapter closes with a critical evaluation of the initiatives taken and those still needed to improve the country's social and economic conditions.

From an economic perspective,[2] Paraguay lags behind the other Latin American countries in many respects. It is one of the poorest and most uneven countries, both in terms of income and land distribution; it is also one of the least developed and least industrialized countries in the region. The informal economy is large (Nickson 2004b) and the perceived corruption index is one of the highest registered (TI 2005). Paraguay is a middle-income country. In 2004 GDP per head was US$1,205, approximately one-quarter of that of Argentina and Brazil, and below the Latin American average of US$3,815. Furthermore, income distribution is very unequal, as measured by the Gini Index (0.58 in 2002, the third highest value in Latin America, after Brazil and Guatemala; UN 2005), and 16.4 percent of the population lives on less than US$1 a day (1990–2003 average), in a country where unemployment and underemployment are high (EIU 2006). Inequality extends also to land ownership. Most of the land is owned by a few large landowners, through which a traditional elite retains significant economic power. In 2002, 62 percent of total agricultural production came from as little as 1 percent of total landholdings (EIU 2006). Economic activity is also unequally distributed on the national territory and is centered around Asunción and Ciudad del Este (EIU 2006). Official figures are biased by the existence of a large informal sector, comprising up to 24 percent of GDP according to recent estimates (IMF 2000). It occupies approximately half of the urban labor force, and includes both illegal and unregistered legal activities (Sohn 2005; EIU 2006).[3]

Within this framework, economic growth is strongly hindered. Over the last 15 years the economy has gone through a few years of growth followed by years of stagnation and recession (in 1998–2002 GDP growth was negative or zero). The export-led growth driven by agricultural products is encountering serious difficulties, due to extreme vulnerability to the effect of weather conditions on agricultural output and to international price fluctuations. Exports have also suffered as a consequence of the recent economic downturns of Paraguay's main trading partners, Argentina and Brazil. In addition, since 1995 the economy has been plagued by repeated banking crises and political uncertainty has discouraged private investment. Since 2003 the economy slowly recovered, thanks to improved macroeconomic management. In 2004, GDP grew by 4.1 percent and per capita income by 2.8 percent, levels not reached since 1995. However, per capita income in 2004 was still slightly lower than in 1991 and remains among the lowest in Latin America.

The poor economic performance has been accompanied by minimal structural changes. The economy still relies primarily on agriculture, whose contribution to total GDP grew from 27 percent in 1990 to 31 percent in 2003. The industrial sector is underdeveloped. Its contribution to total GDP is limited and declining (from 16 percent in 1991 to 14 percent in 2003) and is mainly limited to the processing of agricultural products and to the production of basic consumer goods for the internal market. In addition, the major companies remain in public sector ownership, despite repeated attempts to privatize state assets (EIU 2006).[4]

A general overview of the tax system and its development since the early 1990s

A first view of budgetary, revenue and expenditure features

Since 1989, economic policy has focused on monetary and fiscal stabilization and on regional integration to boost economic growth. The high inflation rates of the late 1980s and early 1990s have been brought under control since 1995.[5] Balanced budgets have been pursued throughout the 1990s, but in the late 1990s the fiscal deficit widened. Public finances are negatively affected by economic stagnation and the significant extent of informal economy, illegal trade, and corruption. Furthermore, tax collection is deemed inefficient and tax evasion is widespread (Villela *et al.* 2005). Finally, the low level of industrialization limits the extent of the tax bases.

During 2003 a large fiscal imbalance had led to weeks-long arrears in salary payments to public sector workers, and Paraguay was at the brink of external default when the first repayments on a US$400 million loan from Taiwan became due. In December 2003 the IMF approved a US$73 million stand-by arrangement, giving the government access to loan disbursements from the World Bank and the Inter-American Development Bank, to be used to regularize external debt servicing. In 2005[6] the non-financial public sector total revenues were 34.9 percent of GDP,[7] while total expenditures were 33.3 percent of GDP, of which 28.3 made up by current expenditures. The year closed with a budget surplus of 1.5 percent of GDP, lower than in 2004 (2.3 percent) but confirming a reversal from the repeated deficit registered until 2003 (Table 12.1).

Due to the lack of disaggregated data, a detailed analysis of public sector finances is possible only with reference to central government,[8] which, in 2005 amounted to approximately 85 percent of general government revenues and expenditures. Central government revenue (Table 12.2) in 2005 amounted to 18.3 percent of GDP, the main sources being tax revenues (11.9 percent of GDP), non-tax revenues – primarily revenues from the bi-national hydroelectric plant Itaipú (4.7 percent of GDP) and social security contributions (1.2 percent of GDP). Tax revenues are mainly revenues from indirect taxes, which yield 82 percent of total tax revenues (9.8 percent of GDP), primarily made up by VAT (5.2 percent of GDP), excise duties and custom duties (respectively 2.2 percent and 1.8 percent of GDP). The direct tax yield is significantly lower, at 2.1 percent of GDP, comprising almost entirely revenues from the corporate income tax (99.5 percent of total direct tax revenues).

In 2005 current expenditure was 12.3 percent of GDP, mainly salary payments, which grew from 3.4 percent of GDP in 1990 to 7.2 percent in 2005, due to increased public employment in education and health services (Nickson 2004a).[9] Capital expenditure was not very limited (4.1 percent of GDP in 2005) but Paraguay still lacks significant public infrastructures (EIU 2006). In 2005, interest payments on public debt were 1.2 percent of GDP, mainly repayments to external sources (90 percent of total financing). Due also to the country's low credit rating and to its limited access to international capital markets (Sohn 2005), Paraguay debt stock is one of the lowest among Latin American countries and has been reduced in recent years (from 41.7 percent of GDP in 2004 to 34.7 percent in 2005).

Tax system and its structure since the 1990s and a comparison with that of other countries

Paraguay's current tax system was established in 1992 (Law 125/91, approved January 9, 1992). The 1992 fiscal reform aimed to rationalize and modernize an

Table 12.1 Structure and development of operation in the non-financial public sector, Paraguay, 1990–2005, percentage of GDP

	1990	1991	1992	1993	1994	1995	1996	1997	1998	1999	2000	2001	2002	2003	2004	2005
Total revenues, of which:	27.2	25.7	27.0	27.8	30.0	28.5	29.6	32.6	33.6	33.0	34.4	35.7	32.7	31.9	33.9	34.9
Current revenues	26.4	25.4	26.6	27.1	29.5	27.7	28.9	31.6	32.9	32.2	33.1	35.0	32.6	31.8	33.9	34.7
Capital revenues	0.7	0.3	0.3	0.7	0.6	0.8	0.6	1.0	0.7	0.8	1.2	0.8	0.1	0.0	0.1	0.1
Total expenditures, of which:	21.3	23.7	26.8	26.1	26.8	27.4	28.5	33.5	33.2	36.1	38.4	35.9	34.6	30.8	31.6	33.3
Current expenditure	18.1	19.0	21.3	21.0	22.2	21.2	23.1	23.9	24.5	23.6	30.5	29.3	28.9	26.2	26.6	28.3
Capital expenditure	3.2	4.7	5.6	5.1	4.6	6.2	5.4	9.6	8.7	12.5	7.9	6.5	5.8	4.9	5.2	4.9
Budget balance	5.8	2.0	0.1	1.7	3.2	1.2	1.0	-1.0	0.4	-3.1	-4.0	-0.1	-1.9	1.1	2.3	1.5
Total public debt of NFPS	30.3	25.7	18.2	19.0	15.1	17.6	16.5	23.2	23.5	33.5	35.3	44.0	63.0	46.9	41.7	34.7
Total public debt of central gov.	14.0	12.8	9.5	11.1	8.3	13.4	11.9	20.3	20.5	30.4	32.6	41.1	59.2	44.4	38.0	31.4
Total debt of public sector	34.7	29.2	22.5	20.9	18.1	18.4	17.3	23.9	24.3	34.2	35.9	44.7	63.9	47.4	42.1	35.0

Source: ILPES-CEPAL 2006.

Note
The figures for 2005 are provisional.

Table 12.2 Structure and development of central government fiscal revenues and expenditures, Paraguay, 1990–2005, percentage of GDP

	1990	1991	1992	1993	1994	1995	1996	1997	1998	1999	2000	2001	2002	2003	2004	2005
Total revenues	13.3	12.7	14.3	14.9	17.0	17.5	16.5	17.1	17.6	18.0	17.2	18.8	17.5	17.0	18.4	18.3
Total fiscal revenues, of which:	*9.9*	*9.8*	*9.9*	*10.2*	*12.0*	*13.6*	*12.7*	*12.7*	*12.6*	*11.8*	*12.0*	*12.0*	*11.2*	*11.3*	*12.9*	*13.0*
Total tax revenues	*9.4*	*9.1*	*9.1*	*9.3*	*11.0*	*12.5*	*11.5*	*11.6*	*11.5*	*10.5*	*10.8*	*10.8*	*10.0*	*10.3*	*11.9*	*11.9*
Direct taxes	1.5	1.5	1.8	1.6	2.3	2.6	2.5	2.2	2.2	2.4	2.0	1.8	2.0	1.8	2.1	2.1
Income and profits	1.2	1.2	1.5	1.6	2.3	2.5	2.4	2.2	2.2	2.4	2.0	1.7	2.0	1.7	2.1	2.1
Individuals	–	–	–	–	–	–	–	–	–	–	–	–	–	–	–	–
Corporations	1.2	1.2	1.5	1.6	2.3	2.5	2.4	2.2	2.2	2.4	2.0	1.7	2.0	1.7	2.1	2.1
Property	0.3	0.3	0.3	0.0	0.0	0.0	0.0	0.0	0.0	0.0	0.0	0.0	0.0	0.0	0.0	0.0
Other	0.0	0.0	0.0	0.0	0.0	0.0	0.0	0.0	0.0	0.0	0.0	0.0	0.0	0.0	0.0	0.0
Indirect taxes	7.9	7.6	7.3	7.6	8.8	9.9	9.1	9.3	9.3	8.1	8.8	9.0	8.0	8.5	9.8	9.8
General sales (VAT)	0.0	0.0	1.4	3.7	4.5	4.9	4.5	4.9	4.9	4.6	4.7	4.6	4.3	4.4	4.7	5.2
Excises	1.1	1.1	1.3	1.2	1.3	1.3	1.5	1.4	1.4	1.4	1.8	2.2	1.8	2.0	2.4	2.2
Custom duties	2.3	2.1	1.8	1.9	2.2	3.1	2.5	2.5	2.4	1.8	2.0	1.9	1.7	1.9	2.2	1.8
Other	4.6	4.4	2.7	0.8	0.7	0.6	0.5	0.5	0.5	0.4	0.4	0.4	0.2	0.3	0.5	0.6
Social security contributions	*0.5*	*0.6*	*0.8*	*0.9*	*1.0*	*1.1*	*1.2*	*1.2*	*1.1*	*1.3*	*1.2*	*1.2*	*1.2*	*1.0*	*1.1*	*1.2*
Total expenditures, of which:	10.1	12.9	15.0	14.4	15.8	17.9	17.8	18.6	18.6	21.8	21.7	20.0	20.7	17.4	16.8	17.5
Current primary expenditure	7.3	9.0	11.1	11.3	12.1	12.7	13.7	13.3	14.0	14.7	15.5	15.2	14.8	12.6	11.8	12.3
Interest on public debt	1.6	1.0	1.0	0.9	0.8	0.8	0.6	0.5	0.8	0.8	1.2	1.4	1.5	1.3	1.1	1.2
Capital expenditure	1.2	2.9	2.9	2.3	2.9	4.4	3.5	4.8	3.8	6.2	4.5	3.5	4.4	3.7	4.0	4.1
Primary surplus	*4.8*	*0.9*	*0.4*	*1.3*	*2.0*	*0.4*	*-0.6*	*-1.0*	*-0.3*	*-3.0*	*-3.3*	*0.2*	*-1.7*	*0.9*	*2.7*	*2.0*
Budget balance	*3.2*	*-0.2*	*-0.6*	*0.4*	*1.3*	*-0.4*	*-1.2*	*-1.6*	*-1.1*	*-3.8*	*-4.6*	*-1.2*	*-3.2*	*-0.4*	*1.6*	*0.8*

Source: ILPES-CEPAL.

Note
The figures for 2005 are provisional.

obsolete system, based on about 150 specific taxes with widespread exemptions. The resulting tax system was based on nine main taxes and rested primarily on indirect taxation. Since its approval, numerous incentives, deductions and exemptions were introduced, eroding the tax bases and tax revenues (Alarcón 2004). This system lacked a net wealth tax and an inheritance and gift tax and, until recently, it was characterized by the absence of a personal income tax (a feature that Paraguay shared with Bolivia and Uruguay). The Administrative Reform and Fiscal Adjustment Law approved in June 2004 (Law 2421/04) introduced some amendments to the system: it broadened the tax basis of VAT and of the corporate income tax; introduced a more effective tax regime to large producers; eliminated some large exemptions; and, finally, it brought in a new personal income tax. However, after heated protests, the application of this law was partially postponed to 2006.

In 2004 central government fiscal pressure, as a percentage of GDP, was the sixth lowest among 19 Latin American countries (12.9 percent), below the regional average of 15.5 percent (Table 12.3). However if we exclude social contributions and take into account tax revenue only, Paraguay is the country with the ninth lowest Latin American level of revenue (11.9 percent of GDP against a regional average of 12.9 percent).

When compared to other Latin American countries (Martner and Tromben 2004), the Paraguayan tax system displays a number of similar features, but also some peculiar traits. First, similar to other Latin American countries, central government tax revenue as a percentage of GDP increased since the early 1990s (+26.3 percent from 9.4 percent of GDP in 1990 to 11.9 percent in 2004). However Paraguay tax performance was weak in relative terms: its growth rate was lower than the regional average of 34.6 percent, and its ranking decreased up to 2003, to recover in 2004. In addition, Paraguay well reflects the regional trends as regards the contribution of different taxes to this increase: VAT revenues grew significantly (+25 percent from 3.7 percent of GDP in 1993 to 4.7 percent in 2004), and revenues from indirect taxes increased by 23.5 percent over the same period (Table 12.2). Second, similarly to other Latin American countries, the revenues from income taxes are very low, 2.1 percent of GDP in 2004, and this is the lowest recorded value, half of the regional average of 4.2 percent of GDP (Table 12.3), while indirect tax revenues (9.8 percent of GDP) are slightly above the regional average of 8.6 percent (Table 12.3). Furthermore, Paraguay displays a peculiar performance over the period 1990–2004: both the direct and indirect tax revenues' growth was below the mean Latin American value. Indirect tax revenues grew by 23.5 percent against an average of 25.7 percent, the growth in revenues from direct taxes was 41 percent against an average of 57 percent. In conclusion, Paraguay has not managed to increase its tax revenues, in particular those from direct taxes, as much as many other Latin American countries. Economic stagnation and decline in foreign trade, the extent of the informal and illegal economy, the inadequacy and inefficiency of tax administration, and the diffuse corruption all may have contributed to this outcome.

Table 12.3 Central government revenues in Paraguay compared with the Latin American average (19 countries)

	Paraguay					Latin America		
	1990		2004		1990–2004	1990	2004	1990–2004
	%GDP	Rank*	%GDP	Rank*	% increase	%GDP	%GDP	% increase
Total fiscal pressure	9.9	8th	12.9	6th	30.9	11.6	15.5	33.5
Tax revenues, of which	9.4	*10th*	*11.9*	*9th*	*26.3*	9.6	12.9	34.6
Direct taxes	1.5	3rd	2.1	1st	41.1	2.7	4.2	57
Indirect taxes	7.9	15th	9.8	13th	23.5	6.9	8.6	25.7
Social security contributions	0.5	*5th*	*1.1*	*5th*	*121.8*	2.1	2.7	28.5

Source: ILPES-CEPAL.

Notes

* For each type of revenue, the lower the country rank, the lower its revenues. Thus a country ranking first, has the lowest level of revenues.

Institutional characteristics of main taxes

The Paraguayan tax system partially reflects the three-tier government structure (central government, departments and local governments). Central government has the power to levy the main taxes and duties, such as: corporate income tax (*IRACIS – impuestos a la renta de actividades comerciales industriales o de seguros*); single tax (*Tributo Unico*); farming and cattle-ranching income tax (*IMAGRO – impuesto a la renta agropecuaria*); value added tax (*IVA – impuesto al valor agregado*); excise duties (*impuesto selectivo al consumo*), custom duties (*impuesto al comercio exterior*); registration and stamp duties (*impuesto a los actos y documentos*); and, from the year 2006, the personal income tax (*impuesto a la renta personal*). Local governments levy taxes on immovable property (*impuesto immobiliario*) and other minor taxes, while departments may charge fees for the licenses, concessions and other services they offer. According to the constitution, the power to introduce, abolish or change fiscal laws rests only with the central government. Local governments may only set local tax rates (except for the municipality of Asunción, which may apply some surcharges). The following sections describe the most important institutional features of the main taxes as they were in 2004, this is followed by the description of the main innovations introduced by the 2004 reform, where applicable.

Direct taxes

Corporate income tax

IRACIS, the corporate income tax, is an annual levy on income of resident[10] legal bodies. A specific category of business, that of individual entrepreneurs, are chargeable when their total revenues exceeds a maximum limit defined each year[11] (otherwise they are subject to the single tax). Taxation is based on the source principle and taxable income is made of all incomes of Paraguayan source. A flat tax rate of 30 percent applies to total yearly gross revenues, net of allowed deductions, but exemption is granted to a wide number of heads. Tax exemption is also granted to a selected group of companies and to free zone activities located in the international free zone near Ciudad del Este, which include trade (introduction of goods from abroad or from national custom areas), industry (manufacturing and processing of goods for export) and services.

The 2004 tax reform (Law 2421/04) introduced some significant changes to this tax, both with regard to the tax rate and the tax basis. First, in order to reduce incentives to tax evasion and promote a higher "formalization" of the economy, it lowered the tax rate from 30 percent to 20 percent during its first year of application (2005) and to 10 percent from the second year onwards (2006). An additional rate of 5 percent is charged on dividends distributed to residents, a higher rate of 15 percent applies to dividends distributed abroad. Second, the law extended the tax basis by limiting exempted heads, by reducing allowed deductions, by constraining the list of exempted bodies and by abolishing special regimes. Finally, it extended the definition of taxable income, and interests from capital investments abroad are included as revenues of Paraguayan origin.

Single tax/small business tax

The single tax is charged on individual entrepreneurs, resident in Paraguay, whose revenues are below the IRACIS threshold. Those chargeable by the single tax are exempted from the value added tax. The tax basis is made up by the revenues from commercial, industrial or service activities. The tax is levied at a rate of 4 percent, and the taxable income is either gross revenues or an imputed gross income given by the sum of: salaries and wages; rent; utility bills; purchases of goods, raw materials and other expenses, excluding financial expenditures (these expenditures are increased by a 30 percent profit mark-up, according to the concept of a presumptive profit). A tax credit of 50 percent of documented VAT paid during the fiscal year is allowed up to the taxpayers' single tax liability. The 2004 reform abolished this tax from 2007 and substituted it with a small business tax (*impuesto a la renta del pequeño contribuyente – IRPC*), that differs from the single tax in three main respects: the tax rate; the definition of the tax basis; and the threshold for its application. The small business tax is charged at a rate of 10 percent, the same of the IRACIS. The taxable basis is the net income, calculated as the difference between revenues and expenses, or an imputed income equal to 30 percent of gross revenues. Compared to the single tax, this tax is charged upon a wider range of businesses: the upper limit for its application was raised up to 100 million guaranis (approximately US$16,738 in 2004). Furthermore, the tax credit for VAT paid does not apply anymore. The small business tax has the potential to reduce the distortions favored by the previous regime, primarily the incentives for tax evasion by large companies due to the existence of two different tax rates for small and big businesses.

Farming and cattle-ranching income tax

IMAGRO, the farming and cattle-ranching income tax, is an annual tax on income from farming and cattle-ranching activities carried out in the national territory. The tax is charged at the flat rate of 25 percent on the landowner, unless a written contract proves that the land is used by third parties. The taxable income is the imputed gross income from the land, equal to 12 percent of the fiscal value of the land defined by the National Land Register Service (*Servicio Nacional del Catastro*), which is notoriously way below the commercial value of land, and this partly explains the tiny tax yield from IMAGRO. Exemption is granted to the first 20 hectares of any landholding of less than 100 hectares and to those parts of landholdings occupied by forests and permanent lagoons. The basis for taxation is the gross income after deduction of selected allowable deductions. The 2004 reform overhauled this tax, with effect from 2005.

It reduced the allowed deductions and introduced a distinction between large and medium-sized landholders,[12] both with regard to the taxable income and to the tax rate. While large landholders, are taxed on their net income (total revenues net of expenditures linked to the activity), except when less than 30 percent of their property is used for farming activity, medium-sized ones are taxed on presumptive income, calculated on the basis of productivity coefficients defined by law. Similarly to the previous regime, small landholders are exempted. The reform reduces the tax rate, from 25 percent to 10 percent for large landholders and to 2.5 percent for medium-sized landholders.

Personal income tax

The 2004 reform introduced a personal income tax (*impuesto a la renta personal*), to take effect from 2006. The tax is charged at a rate of 10 percent on individuals whose annual income exceeds 120 minimum monthly wages.[13] The taxable basis is the gross income from Paraguayan sources, defined as: employment income; 50 percent of dividends and profits distributed to shareholders of companies subject to IRACIS; capital gains from the transfer of buildings or land; interest payments received. The basis of taxation is gross income net of deductions: social security contributions; donations to the state or other bodies; expenditures and investments related to the contributor's job or profession, as well as personal and family expenses supported by VAT receipts. This latter provision aims to reduce tax evasion. However it significantly cuts potential revenues and will likely increase the costs of administering the tax (IMF 2006).

Indirect taxes

Value added tax

In 1993 Paraguay was one of the last Latin American countries to introduce a value added tax. However the VAT is now the pillar of the fiscal systems, generating more than 40 percent of total tax revenues. The tax follows the consumption type and it applies the destination principle. The value added tax is levied at a rate of 10 percent on the sale of goods and services and on the import of goods. The tax is charged on professional activities, on resident individual entrepreneurs with an income above the IRACIS threshold, and on all other legal bodies and importers, regardless of their income. Exports are not liable to VAT and exporters can recover the VAT paid on inputs through a system of fiscal credits against any kind of tax. Originally a tax characterized by a wide basis, the VAT basis (and therefore tax revenues) has been eroded by the introduction of preferential regimes and exceptions for some types of transactions (e.g. tourism and transport) and of various exemptions of selected goods or bodies. The 2004 reform broadened the VAT base and partially revised the tax rate as to January 1, 2005. First, the reform eliminated exemptions under special regimes and introduced the tax on services, rentals, transports and on previously exempted goods (such as basic foods and oil products). Second, basic goods are subject to a maximum tax rate of 5 percent, pharmaceuticals and financial services are charged at 5 percent for a transition period of two years, afterwards the tax rate will increase each year by one percentage point, up to 10 percent.

Excise taxes

A single stage excise tax is levied on some selected goods: fuel, beverages, alcohol, oil and tobacco, either produced in Paraguay or imported. Domestic goods are charged at the first stage of the distribution process, while foreign goods are charged when imported. Tax rates vary depending on the type of good charged, and increased in recent years due to the deterioration of the national fiscal scenario and the consequent need to easily and quickly increase fiscal revenues. The 2004 reform set new maximum rates, in some cases higher, in other lower, than the existing ones. It also introduced a rate of 5 percent on luxury goods and of 1 percent on electronic items. With the exceptions of fuels, the maximum rate is fixed at 12 percent.

Custom duties

Custom duties are levied according to the Custom Code and the MERCOSUR common external tariffs (in effect since January 1, 2005). With few exceptions, goods originating from MERCOSUR countries[14] are exempted, and common external tariffs are applied to imports originating from outside the area. Depending on the type of imports, the tax is levied according to four different systems: general system; tourism (the tax is calculated on a reduced value of goods); minor imports (applied by taxpayers, only up to a maximum amount and with immediate cashing); limited value goods (applied to the introduction of personal goods, up to a maximum amount and with immediate cashing); franchises.

Registration and stamp duty

The registration and stamp duty is applied to transactions and contracts completed or fulfilled through the production of written documents, such as financial intermediation activities. Many exemptions apply, in particular transactions subject to value added tax are exempted from stamp duty. Tax rates differ widely according to the nature of the transaction.

Local taxes

Property tax

The property tax is the main tax levied by municipalities, and there are two surcharges: on not built-up sites and on empty urban buildings. It is charged upon the owner or tenant of the property as of the start of the fiscal year. The tax base is the value of buildings within the national territory, according to the National Land Register Service.[15] The tax rate of 1 percent is reduced to 0.5 percent for rural landholdings of less than five hectares used for farming activities. Total or temporal exemptions apply to buildings owned by selected bodies or used for special purposes. In case of natural calamities, partial exemptions up to 50 percent of the tax amount may be allowed. Assessment and collection are autonomously regulated by each municipality, which retains 70 percent of total revenues and transfers the rest, on a 50–50 basis, to their departments and to less resourced local governments. No data are available on revenues from this source, which are estimated to be extremely low (Martner and Tromben 2004) due to limited local tax administration competencies and efficiency and to obsolete and incomplete cadastral data. In addition, fiscal values on which the tax is levied are way below the market value.

Social contributions

A compulsory social security system covers all hired workers and their families. The general social security system is administered by the Social Security Institute (*Instituto de Previsión Social*) and covers illnesses, maternity, disability and industrial accidents for everyone under 60 whose only mean of subsistence is the wage. In addition, six institutes provide social security to employees of selected bodies. Social security is financed by employers, employees and the state. Employees' monthly contributions range between 2.5 percent and 9 percent of net monthly wage – excluding family allowances and 13 month's payment. Employers' monthly social contribution ranges between 2.5 percent and 16.5 percent of gross wage.

Tax reform

Paraguay is generally regarded as a country that lags behind other Latin American countries in terms of modernization of the public sector and of the economy in general. Sohn (2005), referring to the situation in 2001, notes that: 'as we enter the XXI century, Paraguay, a country of 5.2 million people, is only reluctantly and at glacial speed making tentative moves to put in place the necessary ingredients to promote sustained growth and development.'

This comment is also true with regard to tax reform: compared to other Latin American countries, Paraguay was a late mover and introduced reforms only after the fall of the Stroessner's regime, the main ones being those contained in Law 125/1992 and Law 2421/2004.

The 1992 reform pursued the simplification of the tax system by reducing the number of taxes, rearranging tax legislation and introducing a value added tax. However, it failed to tackle the problem of tax administration efficiency and disregarded the introduction of a personal income tax, limiting income taxation to legal bodies. In 2003, the incoming government of President Duarte Frutos faced a fiscal crisis and tried to fight against it through an ambitious program of state reforms addressing the long-term weaknesses of Paraguay's public sector and private economy, and aiming to place the country on a path of sustainable growth. This program included the modernization of the public administration and the establishment of a favorable economic environment for foreign investors (Duarte Frutos 2003). A number of initiatives in fiscal policy were taken to address the problems highlighted above. In 2003 arrears on public debt were cleared, the custom code and the social security system were reformed, new public procurement procedures were introduced and a reform of tax administration began. In 2004 a stand-by arrangement with the IMF was signed and the tax reform was approved under Law 2421/04 (Duarte Frutos 2004,–2005). Improvements include a substantial broadening of the tax basis of VAT and of corporate income tax, the introduction of a new personal income tax for high earners, the elimination of numerous exemptions and a more effective tax regime to large farmers.

Overall, these measures have the potential to increase fiscal revenues and reduce public sector expenditures. They may have already impacted on the 2004 and 2005 (provisional) public sector budget, which show a reversal of the previous years' trends of increasing expenditures and declining revenues. However, the reform impact on the equity of the system is limited, due to the over-reliance on regressive indirect taxation and the restricted number of citizens chargeable under the personal income tax (which, in addition, allows significant deductions and is proportional). Furthermore, total revenues are still below their potential (Villela *et al.* 2005) due to corruption, tax evasion and the informal economy. Therefore, if fiscal policy is to be effective, these "corollary" problems have to be tackled with determination, through additional initiatives, some already approved by the government (Nickson 2004b). One main issue still to be tackled is the improvement of the tax administration, to make it more honest and efficient. A long due civil service reform would favor this change, but it seems far from happening, especially after the failure to implement the civil service reform approved in 2001. This is a worrying sign of the persistence of widespread interests protecting patronage in public administration and maintaining a "privatized" clientelist and politicized public sector, which for many years has provided both an opportunity of employment for activists of the Colorado Party and also a source for party funding (Nickson and Lambert 2002; Nickson 2004b).

Conclusions

Paraguay lags in Latin America for its limited industrialization, widespread poverty, high unemployment and underemployment, income and land distribution inequality, as well as for its delay in implementing needed policy reforms. The weight of the Paraguayan public sector has been traditionally limited and public finances inadequate to tackle the social and economic problems of the country. Taxation relies extensively on indirect taxes, which are easier to collect, but are regressive. Recent tax reforms have the potential to increase available resources. Surely these reforms may be improved, however the major challenge for this country is not the design of a better tax reform, rather the full implementation of the existing one. In addition, only if Paraguay is able to reduce tax evasion and erosion of the tax base, can the approved tax reform become fully effective, with regard to both the increase of tax revenues and the reduction of income inequality. In order to fight tax evasion, tax administration has to be improved and the competencies and commitment of tax inspectors have to be strengthened, through a long overdue civil service reform. Furthermore, the corruption that affects the Paraguayan economy and society, as well as its public sector, has to be tackled. Under the presidency of Nicanor Duarte Frutos, a number of initiatives have been approved since 2003 and more are planned, which should help Paraguay to move towards the directions outlined above. It is not an easy task, especially as the problems of the country are not limited to the tax system and the civil service, nor solely to corruption, but they extend to a wide array of social and economic issues. In addition a main obstacle to any reform is the strong and powerful opposition of the rich and the limited political mobilization and representation of the mass of impoverished and underemployed citizens – two factors that have meant that until now the pressure for reform has come almost exclusively from external sources.

Notes

1 I wish to acknowledge very helpful comments from Andrew Nickson, even though I remain solely responsible for the contents of this chapter.
2 Economic and public finance data are from Banco Central del Paraguay (2006); CEPAL (various years); DGEEC (2003, 2004a, 2004b); IMF (2001, 2005a, 2005b); IBFD (2006) and World Bank (1992, 2006).
3 It is estimated that half of Paraguayan imports are illegally re-exported to Brazil and Argentina. Attempts to fight these phenomena have been carried out in recent years, but laws are often weakly enforced or not applied (Nickson and Lambert 2002). For example, with reference to the public sector, the 1970 and 2001 civil service reform (Law 200/70 and Law 1626/01) were approved but not implemented. The 2001 law compelling government to propose balanced budget is generally ignored. In addition, a 1997 anti-money-laundering law is not rigorously enforced (EIU 2006).
4 Limited industrialization dates back to the Stroessner regime, but it is also due to the landlocked geographical position, the lack of significant mineral resources and might have been influenced by the two powerful neighbors, Argentina and Brazil, with an interest in Paraguay as a market for their products and as a cheap energy supplier from its enormous bi-national hydroelectric power plants (Itaipú with Brazil and Yacyretá with Argentina), which provide Paraguay with the world's second highest per capita energy resource availability after Nepal. The output from the power plants is almost entirely exported to Brazil and Argentina, although Nickson (2004a) highlights that a viable economic development strategy would be to use this enormous energy endowment to become a regional hub for energy-intensive industries.
5 The national currency is the Guaraní (PYG), since 1989 under a single free-floating exchange rate. In 2005 the average exchange rate was US$1=6,178PYG (IMF, International Financial Statistics).
6 2005 data are provisional.
7 The non-financial public sector (NFPS) budget reflects the relevant weight of state

companies on the overall economy, due also to the very limited privatizations undertaken. State companies make up nearly half of the NFPS revenue/expenditure.

8 Detailed official statistics by the National Statistic Institute (DGEEC), by the Treasury (Ministero de Hacienda) and by the Economic Commission for Latin America and the Caribbean (CEPAL) exist only for the central government, less detailed data are provided for general government, no data for decentralized governments.

9 Public sector employment grew by 50 percent between 1989 and 2004 (Nickson 2004b). This trend is the opposite of that registered in most Latin American countries, but it is due to the relatively limited number of public officials, especially in the health and education services, which were understaffed during the Stroessner years.

10 An individual has the status of "resident" if s/he stayed in Paraguay for a minimum of 180 days during the previous 12 months. A company is "resident" if established in Paraguay according to Paraguayan law (excluding its branches or agencies abroad) or if it is a branch, agency or plant owned by non residents but established in Paraguay.

11 The 20,400,000 guaranis (approximately US$15,394) threshold, set by Law 125/91, was to be adjusted every year according to the variation of the Consumers' Price Index published by the Paraguay Central Bank. In 2004 this threshold reached 52,389,833 guaranis (approximately US$8,805).

12 Large landholders are those with a property larger than 300 hectares in the eastern region and larger than 1.500 hectares in the western region. Medium-sized ones are those between 20 and 300 hectares in the former region and between 100 and 1500 hectares in the latter one. Small landholders are those whose property is smaller than 20 hectares in the eastern region and smaller than 100 hectares in the western region.

13 In 2006 120 minimum wages amounted to 130 million guaranis (approximately US$23,000).

14 Argentina, Brazil, Paraguay and Uruguay.

15 The National Land Register fiscal values were revised by decree n. 1267/03, in effect from the 2004.

References

Alarcón Säfstrand, M. (2004) "Impuestos Indirectos e Incentivos en el Paraguay," paper prepared for the Inter American Development Bank seminar on Dialogo Regional de Política – Seminario sobre Tributación para la Integración del MERCOSUR.

Banco Central del Paraguay (2006) *Sistema de Cuentas Nacionales del Paraguay, Año base 1994, Serie 1991–2004*, Asunción: Banco Central del Paraguay.

CEPAL (various years) *Economic Survey of Latin America and the Caribbean*, Economic Commission for Latin America and the Caribbean.

DGEEC (2003) *Principales Resultados del Censo 2002. Vivienda y Población*, Asunción: Dirección General de Estadística, Encuestas y Censos.

—— (2004a) *Situación del Empleo en Paraguay: Encuesta Permanente de Hogares, 2003*, Asunción: Dirección General de Estadística, Encuestas y Censos.

—— (2004b) *Anuario Estadistico 2004*, Asunción: Dirección General de Estadística, Encuestas y Censos.

Duarte Frutos (2003) *Por un País Mejor: Primer Informe de Gestión de Gobierno*, Asunción: Presidencia de la República.

—— (2004) *Informe Presidencial al Congreso de la Nación*, Asunción: Presidencia de la República.

—— (2005) *Informe Presidencial al Congreso de la Nación*, Asunción: Presidencia de la República.

EIU (2006) *Paraguay – Country Profile 2006*, London: The Economist Intelligence Unit.

IBFD (2006) *Latin America: Taxation and Investment*, Amsterdam: IBFD.

IMF (2000) "Paraguay: Selected Issues and Statistical Appendix," Staff Country Report n. 00/51, Washington, DC: IMF.

—— (2001) *Government Finance Statistics Yearbook*, Washington, DC: IMF.

—— (2005a) *Government Finance Statistics Yearbook*, Washington, DC: IMF.

—— (2005b) "Paraguay: 2004 Article IV Consultation and Second Review Under the Stand-By Arrangement and Requests for Waiver and Modifications of Performance Criteria," IMF country report n. 05/59, Washington, DC: IMF.

Martner R. and Tromben V. (2004) "Tax Reforms and Fiscal Stabilisation in Latin American Countries," CEPAL Series – Gestion Publica n.45, Santiago, Chile.

Nickson, R. A. (2004a) "Development Prospects for Paraguay under the Government of President Duarte Frutos," Madrid: Real Instituto Elcano de Estudios Internacionles y Estratégicos (www.realinstitutoelcano.org).

—— (2004b) "Reforming the State in Paraguay," presented at the International Conference Una Mirada al Paraguay y la Región, Universidad Autónoma de Asunción, 18–19 November 2004.

Nickson, R. A. and Lambert, P. (2002) "State Reform and the Privatised State in Paraguay," *Public Administration and Development*, vol. 22, 2, 163–74.

Sohn, I. (2005) "With All Deliberate Delay: Economic and Financial Reform in Paraguay," International Trade and Finance Association Conference Paper, 51/2005.

TI – (Transparency International) (2005) *Corruption Perception Index 2005*, Berlin: Transparency International.

UN (2005) *Human Development Report 2005*, New York: United Nations.

Villela L., Roca J. and Barreix A. (2005) "El desafío fiscal del MERCOSUR," Inter American Development Bank, INTAL-ITD Working Paper n. 19.

World Bank (1992) *Paraguay: Country Economic Memorandum*, Washington, DC: The World Bank.

—— (2006) *World Development Indicators*, Washington, DC: The World Bank.

13 Uruguay

Alberto Barreix and Jerónimo Roca

Introduction, content and main conclusions

Uruguay is one of the oldest democracies in the world. Since its independence, in 1830, it has been a democracy for 138 years. Situated between Argentina and Brazil, the country has a total land area of 180,000 km² and a population of 3.4 million inhabitants, of which 15 percent is older than 65 years old. The Uruguayan GDP per capita is approximately US$5,200 (US$9,050 at parity of purchasing power). The domestic economic structure is based on its agriculture (12 percent of the GDP and more than 50 percent of exports); manufacturing – basically agricultural related (18 percent of the GDP); tourism services (6 percent of the GDP); and the rest is composed of public and private services.

Uruguay has a difficult fiscal stance characterized by a public debt of 2.5 times its GDP – 180 percent of GDP of pension liabilities and 75 percent on foreign denominated bonds – a tax burden slightly above 30 percent of GDP but has more than 60 percent affected to pensions and interest payments – 5 percent corresponds to interest payment and 14 percent of GDP on pensions – that leaves a small margin (11 percent of GDP) to provide for all public services. Additionally, in spite of an extraordinarily positive phase of the cycle – low rates and weak dollar, quite favorable terms of trade and booming trade partners – it still runs fiscal deficits.

The second section of this chapter is dedicated to the brief summary of the economic and fiscal evolution since 1970, with special emphasis on the tax reform of 1974 – the only one of the last 30 years – and the tax system's evolution in the 1990s.

The third section presents a description of the characteristics of the main taxes of the current tax system, including its main problems. Finally, this chapter describes the tax reform recently approved. It analyzes the macroeconomic frame of the tax changes; the proposal for dual taxation *"Uruguayan style"* and its impact on equity; the new tax secrecy to fight evasion; the abolition of the employer's contributions to social security; and the simplification of the tax system proposed by the elimination of 11 low-revenue taxes and/or those with a high cost of administration and compliance.

General view of the tax system and its development since the 1970s

Brief review of the economic and budgetary evolution

In 1973, after 50 years of uninterrupted democratic rule, there was institutional break-up in Uruguay, resulting in a military dictatorship. The economic changes were also significant, led by abandoning the substitution model of imports, strictly speaking useless since 1955, opting for an export promotion model. Since 1974, this was translated in a deep financial liberation, followed by a progressive commercial opening that was accompanied by a monetary and fiscal reform.

The fiscal reform of 1974, the only tax reform of the last 30 years, was design for a combined strategy of export promotion model and a financial center. Its main features were:

1   the introduction of a VAT abolishing a traditional sales tax;
2   the abolition of the personal income tax (PIT), which had been pioneered in Latin America in the early 1960s, with a cedular design too complex for the level of the tax administration, thus, it never ended up collecting more than 0.3 percent of the GDP;
3   the simplification of the system, eliminating a slew of minor taxes, including those of estate and inheritance.

The period from 1975 to 1985, the year when democracy was recovered, was marked by the exchange rate crisis of 1982. This crisis was the result of the incompatibility between an expansive fiscal policy and an overvalued domestic currency. In terms of spending, the dictatorship reduced the salaries and public loans, but invested in large infrastructure projects of doubtful social profitability, which concluded in high deficits (see Table 13.1).

The first democratic administration, 1985–90, increased public spending, including high debt services, a by-product of the debt crisis of the early 1980s. To

Table 13.1 Uruguay – evolution of revenue and spending of public sector (% of GDP)

	1975	1980	1985	1990	1995	2000	2004
Total expenditures, separated in:	23.5	20.9	27.0	31.1	32.7	34.0	29.6
Current expenditures	13.2	6.8	6.7	17.4	15.1	15.1	11.9
Interests	0.9	0.5	6.5	1.7	1.4	2.0	4.9
Public investment	1.8	5.3	3.5	1.8	2.1	1.8	1.5
Social security	7.5	8.1	10.0	10.2	13.8	15.0	11.2
Total taxes	19.5	22.0	20.4	28.2	30.2	29.8	27.7
Total taxes	13.8	17.5	15.4	17.9	19.0	21.0	22.1
Social security contributions	5.7	4.5	5.0	10.3	11.2	8.8	5.6
Total deficit	–4.0	1.1	–6.6	–2.9	–2.5	–4.2	–1.9

Sources: IMF, Vallarino (2005), De Haedo *et al.* (1987), BCU, BPS and CGN.

Table 13.2 Uruguay – tax burden (% of GDP)

	1975	1980	1985	1990	1995	2000	2004
Direct taxes	2.4	3.2	1.9	2.7	4.0	5.7	5.8
Corporate income tax	*1.1*	*2.4*	*1.1*	*0.9*	*1.8*	*2.3*	*2.5*
Personal income tax (Shedular)	*0.0*	*0.0*	*0.0*	*0.6*	*1.1*	*2.1*	*1.4*
Net wealth and property taxes	*0.4*	*0.8*	*0.8*	*0.3*	*0.4*	*0.7*	*1.0*
Indirect taxes	8.6	12.7	11.9	13.0	12.1	12.3	13.0
VAT	*4.0*	*6.2*	*5.7*	*6.7*	*7.8*	*8.2*	*9.1*
Excises	*3.5*	*3.4*	*3.6*	*4.0*	*3.3*	*3.4*	*3.1*
Trade taxes	*0.7*	*2.4*	*1.8*	*2.3*	*1.0*	*0.8*	*1.3*
Local taxes	2.9	1.6	1.6	2.1	2.9	3.0	3.3
Total taxes	13.8	17.5	15.4	17.9	19.0	21.0	22.1
Social security	5.7	4.5	5.0	10.3	11.2	8.8	5.6
Total taxes	19.5	22.0	20.4	28.2	30.2	29.8	27.7

Sources: De Haedo *et al.* (1987), Vallarino (2005), DGI and CGN.

finance this, the government implemented extremely harsh and continuous tax adjustments[1] with the subsequent upsurge in the tax burden, which jumped from 20.4 percent to 28.2 percent of the GDP between 1985 and 1990 (see Table 13.2).[2]

The tax system and its structure from the 1990s

As it had happened in the late 1970s, Uruguay fell again, 20 years later, in an inconsistency between the foreign exchange regime and the fiscal policy. In the 1990s decade, the country made two interrelated errors:

1 it created a large deficit to finance the growing public spending on social security – doubling total public debt which includes transfers to the unfunded pension system and the foreign denominated long-term debt;
2 it allowed an overvaluation of the domestic currency that exacerbated the loss of competitiveness as Uruguay's productivity lagged behind that of its trade partners.

During this period an explosive growth in spending was verified in social security that went from 10 percent to 15 percent of the GDP between 1990 and 2000 (Table 13.1). In the same period, the deficit of the social security system went from 4.5 percent to 10.8 percent of the GDP. As a result of the abuse of the mechanism of indexing retirement pensions by less than the inflation rate during the dictatorship, through a referendum in 1989, it was established in the Constitution the obligation of adjusting them in function of the index of the last evolution of wages. Therefore, through the increase of public wages independently from their productivity, the Uruguayan government "creates" productivity by decree, and the Constitution multiplies it.

Also, the continuous growth of public spending forced a great fiscal effort larger than the revenue capacity to cover it,[3] moving the tax system away as the instrument for the integration and development strategy, for which it was designed. Therefore, in the last decade a "tax spiral" – continuous tax adjustments as answers to the growing expense – has ensued, with two main consequences:

1   It "muddied" the tax system with the creation of several distortionary taxes, which affected competitiveness, but, at the same time, relatively easy to collect.[4] Indeed, at least 13 new taxes were created in Uruguay, exactly at a rate of one per year.[5]

2   It increased the regressivity of the system. Since it is difficult to tax the mobile factor – the capital – the load should necessarily fall upon consumption and/or salaries. Between June 1984 and May 1995, the general rate of the VAT ("basic rate") increased almost 30 percent, moving from 18 percent to 23 percent, which is the current rate. Additionally, in May 2001 the COFIS was created, a wholesale VAT, with a rate of 3 percent. Added together, VAT and COFIS impose a tax of more than 26 percent on consumption.

Features of the (current) main taxes

Direct taxes

Personal income tax (PIT)

Contrary to what is usually claimed, Uruguay has a personal income tax. It is an incomplete cedular system, a variety of taxes that burden some sources of income at different rates but exempting others. For example, the tax to the personal retributions (IRP) is imposed on wages and pensions, the tax to the commissions reaches a great number of non-professional services (custom and currency exchange brokers, salesmen, etc.), sole proprietors are burdened by the corporate income tax, but other types of income – such as interests, real estate rents, capital gains and professional services – are not taxed.

Next, we describe the main characteristics of the different taxes of this incomplete cedular system.

Tax on personal retributions – wages, salaries, and pensions – (IRP)

The IRP taxes wages, salaries, and pensions on a monthly basis. The nominal income of each of the three categories[6] is taxed according to the quantity of *Bases de Prestación y Contribución* (BPC).[7] The IRP, which collected 1.2 percent of GDP in 2004, is applied on the whole income, not on the margin, but the income obtained from different jobs is not cumulative, on the contrary, it is taxed separately.

Additionally, there is a tax on commissions that levies on the income of commissions and brokerage services, which collected in 2004 some 0.10 percent of GDP.

Corporate income tax (CIT)

The corporate income tax – CIT – collected US$274 million in 2004, approximately 2 percent of the GDP, 9.5 percent of the total tax revenue.[8] The nominal rate of the tax is 30 percent and the income is determined in the traditional form, on real basis (inflation adjusted) and with the accrual method.[9] Although the nominal rate of the corporate income tax in Uruguay is 30 percent, the effective rate is significantly smaller. The country does not escape to the traditional *"dichotomic model"* in which numerous incentives are granted without a development strategy. This makes the effective rate significantly smaller to the nominal one.[10] Also, at a macro level, from the total collection of the corporate income tax (2.5 percent of the GDP) 48 percent was paid by state-owned corporations in 2004. Consequently, the burden of the Uruguayan private sector by CIT is the lowest in Latin America, except for Haiti.

Tax on small enterprises

The firm or individual, who carries out economic activities and whose sales are not higher than certain annual limit should not pay the corporate tax – IRIC – but the tax on small enterprises which is a fixed sum to be paid monthly. In the year 2004, this tax collected US$12.2 millions, approximately 0.09 percent of the GDP.

Taxing non-residents

Currently, the following rents are taxed:

1   income derived from the lease, use, or alienation of trademarks, patents, etc. carried out by taxpayers subject to the corporate tax – IRIC – to non-residents;
2   technical assistance paid by firms subject to the CIT to non-residents;
3   dividends credited by firms subject to CIT to non-residents, when they are taxed in the home country and it is entitled to tax credit;
4   income derived from the lease, use, or alienation of the copyright on literary, artistic or scientific works carried out by taxpayers subject to CIT to non-residents.

In 2004, for these items US$14.6 millions, approximately 0.11 percent of the GDP were obtained in revenues.

Net wealth tax

Uruguay is one of the few countries in the world that levies on net wealth. The collection of the net wealth tax at company level was of US$124 million, almost 1 percent of the GDP, in 2004 and the one on individuals reached only 0.1 percent of GDP. Approximately half of this revenue comes from state-owned enterprises. The tax burdens the assets located in the country, it is allowed to deduct bank debt and the credit from suppliers. As there is no intention to burden the investments on productive assets, it presents a great deal of exemptions – for example, the land and livestock in agriculture and 50 percent of the fiscal value of the manufacturing equipment – which determines that the tax burdens almost exclusively on the personal goods. The general rate is 1.5 percent, 2 percent for financial institutions and 2 percent for withholding on the principal of non-resident's loans.

Additionally, the net wealth tax can be credited to the corporate income tax with a limit of 50 percent of the former. On the other hand, the collection of the net wealth tax levied on individuals is insignificant: in 2004 it was only US$8 million, 0.06 percent of the GDP. The tax burdens the local assets disregarding the national bank liabilities, with a minimum exempt of US$85.000 progressively, with rates that go from 0.7 percent to 3 percent. In the same pattern as in the case of the net wealth tax levied on corporations, practically only the real estate is taxed.

Indirect taxes

Value added tax (VAT)

As it was stated, Uruguay was one of the first countries in Latin America on introducing the VAT, in 1974. Their revenue was US$1.200 million in 2004, 9.1 percent of the GDP, more than 40 percent of the total tax revenue. Approximately 40 percent is captured in customs (VAT on imports). The productivity of the VAT in the last three years, amid a very favorable economic cycle, has been lowered to 0.40 if it is estimated according to the GDP and it is slightly higher than 0.40 if the consumption is considered. According to estimates carried out for 1999, VAT tax expenditures were 4.5 percent of GDP, almost 80 percent of the total tax expenditures (Rossa and Roca 2001). Also, Cobas *et al.* (2004) estimated that VAT evasion reached 25 percent of the real revenue. Nevertheless, if we exclude the calculation of the state-owned enterprises, which are not supposed to avoid taxes, evasion would reach 38.5 percent.

The Uruguayan VAT is consumption-based using the indirect method (all taxes on purchases are credited) and applies the destination principle. The general rate ("basic rate") is 23 percent, however, certain goods and services are taxed at a reduced rate ("minimum rate") of 14 percent – medicines and goods of the basic needs basket. The main exemptions are health and education services; real estate leases; fuels – diesel oil is taxed; food staples of the basic needs basket; and books, magazines and newspapers. Tobacco and cigarettes and the sale of real estate, currently exempted, will be burdened by the proposed reform.

Regarding the financial transactions, the VAT only taxes interests of loans that finance consumption. It is distinctive of the Uruguayan VAT, the regime in "suspense" for the sales of the agricultural sector, similar to that of the internal community operations in the European Union.

Problems of the VAT

Uruguay has the highest VAT rate in the world: 26.1 percent (including the cumulative effect) – 23 percent of basic rate plus 3 percent of COFIS, which has also cumulative effect on services. Broadening the base would allow a substantial discount of the rate of the VAT, strongly diminishing the reward of evasion. According to Barreix and Roca (2006b), a uniform VAT at 17 percent with only five exemptions (education, financial intermediation, and health services, real estate lease and gasoline) would obtain the same revenue. However, in the tax reform the government resisted the inclusion of this proposal for fairness purposes, and decided to reduce the rates of VAT to 22 percent and 10 percent and to eliminate COFIS.[11]

Excise taxes

The excise taxes – IMESI – collects 3.1 percent of the GDP, approximately 15 percent of the total tax revenue, of which the tax on gasoline, diesel, and fuel oil represents 38 percent of the total.

The excises in Uruguay reach the traditionally taxed goods, that is:

1   goods with negative externalities: tobacco products and cigarettes, alcoholic beverages;
2   as substitutes of user charges: fuels,[12] oils and lubricants, and automobiles;
3   other luxury goods, as non-alcoholic beverages, cosmetics, and perfumes.

Table 13.3 shows the specific tax per unit on selected products.

Table 13.3 Excise taxes on selected products in Uruguay

Type of product	Tax
Cigarettes	US$0.50p/20cigarettes
Gasolines	US$0.64 per liter
Diesel	US$0.06 per liter
Whiskies	US$4.00 per liter
Beer	US$18 per liter

Source: Government Decrees.

Trade taxes

Trade taxes mainly charge on imports since export levies were practically eliminated since the mid-1980s. The revenue was 1.3 percent of the GDP, nearly 6 percent of the total tax revenue in 2004. This fall was accentuated with the advances of MERCOSUR.

Local taxes

Uruguay is a unitary state constituted by 19 departments, of which the capital, Montevideo, concentrates 42 percent of the population. Property taxes, user charges and automobiles licenses constitute 80 percent of the local revenue.

The rate of the rural property levy is fixed by the national government, which is collected for and by the departmental governments. Municipalities have a high autonomy in the determination of the taxable base and in the arrears collection on this local tax.

In 1990, the central government's transfers hardly represented 11 percent of total revenue of the municipalities, growing to 17 percent in 2000. These transfers as a share of local revenues are quite low comparing not only for the region but also contrasting with developed countries. The types of transfers are:

1   revenue sharing of selected national taxes;
2   reimbursement of specific infrastructure investment costs;
3   subsidies to transportation infrastructure.[13]

The transfers of shared taxes represent approximately 36 percent of the total resources transferred to local governments.[14]

Social security contributions

In 1996, Uruguay implemented a pension reform adopting a mixed system with two pillars:

1   the one of "intergenerational solidarity" (pay-as-you-go), of allotment, obligatory, with defined benefits which is administered by a public decentralized entity, social security administration – BPS;
2   the "individual savings," financed by an obligatory contribution after certain wage threshold (approximately US$1,000 per month to a limit of approximately US$3,000), based on individual capitalization, and managed by four funds – of which the state-owned fund represents 50 percent of the market.[15]

Finally, the employers only contribute to the allotted pillar – employer's social security.

Table 13.4 Social security contributions in Uruguay (% of gross wages and salaries)

	Total	*Workers*	*Employers*
Commerce and industry	21.04	15.00	6.04
Construction	17.77	15.00	2.77
Civil	31.53	15.00	16.53
Rural	15.00	15.00	0.00
Domestic services	27.50	15.00	12.50
Total	24.38	15.00	9.38

Source: BPS (Social Security Administration).

Issues on the employer's social security contributions

As can be seen in Table 13.4, the employer's social security contributions – approximately 2 percent of the GDP – present a great and unjustified scattering among the different sectors. In the tax reform, the government has proposed a 7.5 percent uniform rate that is revenue neutral. It must be pointed out that a country with high unemployment – stabilized near 10 percent for more than 30 years – sub-employment estimated at more than 15 percent, a weak employment to GDP elasticity (0.33), and a public workforce of more than 20 percent of total employment, there are no doubts that these "employer's" social security contributions truly fall on workers, reducing wages and/or employment.[16]

Tax reform

Economic and tax perspectives

Revenue collection in Uruguay surpasses its tax capacity and, therefore, taxes should not be increased. The current tax burden is slightly above 30 percent of the GDP.[17] On the other hand, Uruguay cannot diminish it because of the high level of welfare (mainly pensions) that the country has enjoyed for the last 40 years. Assessing the level of the government's degrees of freedom to provide public services, Villela *et al.* (2005) have defined the *disposable fiscal income* as the tax revenue minus the social security spending and the interest payment of the public debt – the committed spending.

Therefore, the *disposable fiscal income* is the residual flow after paying social security benefits and debt interests, that is to say, before paying any public services or employees.

This will be the government's budgetary restriction to assign resources to the remaining public spending categories.[18]

In Table 13.5, it can be observed that the *disposable fiscal income* for Uruguay was only 10.2 percent of the GDP for the year 2003. Of the 31.2 percent of GDP, approximately 15 percent were destined to the payments of social security benefits and 6 percent to the public debt interest payment. This *disposable fiscal income* is lower to the Central American average (11.2 percent)

Table 13.5 MERCOSUR: disposable fiscal income 1994 and 2003

| | 1994 | | | | 2003 | | | |
	Total revenues[1]	Public debt interests	Social security expense	Disposable fiscal income*	Total revenues[1]	Public debt interests[2]	Social security expense	Disposable fiscal income*
Argentina	21.60	1.40	5.40	14.80	24.40	3.50	6.80	14.10
Brazil	28.70	2.90	4.70	21.10	35.50	9.30	11.20	15.00
Paraguay	17.50	0.70	2.40	14.40	16.40	1.70	5.90	8.80
Uruguay	30.80	1.20	16.30	13.30	31.20	6.20	14.80	10.20
Average	*24.70*	*1.60*	*7.20*	*15.90*	*26.90*	*5.70*	*9.70*	*12.00*

Notes

* It is not considered the possibility of incurring in deficit.

1 It includes net results of public companies, sales of assets and donations. For Paraguay, the net estimated result of Itaipú and Yaciretá is included.

2 For Argentina, the interests of the public debt were estimated considering the exchange offer.

and less than half of that of the OECD (23.6 percent). The reduction of the *disposable fiscal income* – fell 30 percent between 1994 and 2003 – is explained by the increase of the interest payment of the public debt, which more than compensates the slight drop on social security spending and the increase of the fiscal income.

Some consequences could be drawn, which have been included when designing the current tax reform:

1   The need to maintain a tax burden of approximately 30 percent of the GDP determines that the indirect taxation (approximately 15 percent of the GDP) will continue to play a high role in the tax structure. This is highly regressive and thus makes it necessary to introduce a global personal income tax to counteract the negative effects on equity.[19]

2   There is consensus that the most suitable instrument for income redistribution is social public spending. Nevertheless, the fiscal situation of Uruguay determines that close to 10 percent of GDP are available, once benefits of the social security and interests of the public debt have been paid. This fact, again, shows the need of introducing a personal income tax that will help to correct the inequality of the income distribution.

   Furthermore, it must be established that, according to several studies, the public spending in social security is regressive and pro-rich, i.e. is it concentrates on the strata of higher income.[20] The reason is that such a spending has certain co-lending character for the contributions during the working lifespan of those whose activity was developed in the formal sector of the economy, but it doesn't reach those who have worked in the informal economy, who obviously are the poorest.

3   Finally, a very low *disposable fiscal income* to finance low quality public services, coupled with a high tax burden, incentives the informal sector and weakens voluntary compliance, increases the risks on fiscal sustainability, and hinders the level of services of physical and social infrastructure necessary for economic development.

The tax reform[21]

The Uruguayan dual income tax

The dual income tax *Uruguayan style* takes from the Nordic dual the central idea of levying personal income – at progressive rates – and the capital income – at a proportional rate – separately. On the other hand, it establishes a lower tax rate for capital income (interests, dividends and profits, rents, capital gains), that is almost the same as the lowest marginal rate that taxes the labor income. These rates constitute the "anchors" of the income tax system, the minimum rate at which you begin to tax. Besides, the highest marginal rate which taxes labor income is very close to the rate levied on the (net) corporate income.

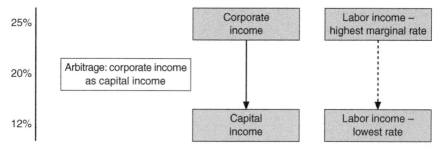

Figure 13.1 Dual Uruguayan style.

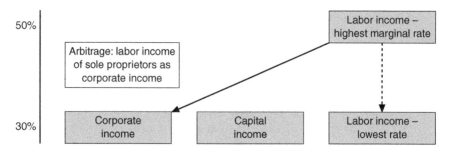

Figure 13.2 Nordic dual.

Therefore, the main difference with the Nordic dual, which is reflected in the Figure 13.1, is that it "anchors" at the rate that taxes both the corporate income and the capital income (close to 30 percent), which in turn is the lowest rate to labor income that is levied progressively until rates reach close to 50 percent. Thus, the Nordic dual provides an arbitrage opportunity for the income of sole proprietors disguising it as corporate income.

Many experts consider this as its "Achilles' heel." Something similar occurs in Chile – which applies a synthetic PIT – where CIT's rate is 17 percent and the marginal highest rate that taxes the labor income reaches 40 percent.[22] On the contrary, the dual *Uruguayan style* limits the possibility of arbitration to the point that the taxpayer can choose to pay corporate or individual income tax. However, it does not solve the possible arbitrage between corporate income and capital income. This can be solved through ordinary rules of the corporate income tax, of much easier implementation than the controls the Nordic dual imposes. For example, the arbitrage in the dual *Uruguayan style* between interests – taxed, as it will be seen, at 12 percent – which are deducted from the CIT at the rate of 25 percent can be solved adjusting the deduction to the proportion between the capital income tax rate and that of corporate income (12/25 in this case).[23]

It is interesting to point out that the new Spanish PIT follows a dual model closer to the "Uruguayan" than to the "Nordic" dual. Indeed, capital income is levied at a uniform rate of 18 percent, labor income is taxed from 24 percent to 43 percent, and CIT reaches a 30 percent rate.

Additionally, the dual *Uruguayan style* takes from the uniform (*flat*) income tax:[24]

1   it limits the number of deductions and credits that erode the base of the PIT, especially in Latin America;
2   it sets a high non-taxable minimum threshold in order to leave out of PIT almost 60 percent of the population.

Personal income tax (PIT)

The new PIT levies capital income at 10 percent and, in turn, the labor income in five brackets, with a lower marginal rate of 10 percent and a highest marginal rate of 25 percent. The proposed rate design has four characteristics.

1   It avoids the arbitrage between the different types of income and/or the taxpayers' juridical nature. Therefore, the incentives for avoidance decrease, and also do not alter taxpayer's choice of portfolio.
2   Moderate taxes – marginal highest rate is 25 percent – assure that, given the high contributions to the social security in Uruguay (approximately 25 percent of the labor cost[25] on average), the PIT does not diminish the disposable income of the middle class significantly and, with it, does not affect private saving and/or the labor supply and does not incentive evasion.
3   There is an administrative reason to apply a reduced rate to the capital income: it avoids "delocalization" of savings in a financially integrated world. In general, the richest individuals are those that have capital returns and they are captured by the highest marginal rate when applying the integral method.[26] Therefore, it generates an incentive to avoid it, mobilizing the savings to jurisdictions where they are not taxed and not exchanging information with other jurisdictions.[27]
4   Finally, the most relevant argument, that is efficiency, which prescribes that the capital returns should be taxed at lower rates than those from labor (or even not to be taxed at all).[28] In theory, to tax the capital income with reduced rate is equivalent to apply different weights between the current and future consumption (Boadway 2005).[29] Actually, almost all legislations that apply the integral type of income tax protect savings by exempting:

    •   pension contributions, which are usually taxed at retirement (pensions);
    •   the income (consumption) provided by durable goods;
    •   the deduction of the mortgage interests and, simultaneously, not taxing the imputed income generated by the consumption of the individual's own home.

Equity in the PIT

Some observations related to the progressivity and redistributional incidence of the new dual PIT, in particular comparing it with the current IRP, should be made.[30] In Table 13.6 the average effective rate for the IRP (currently applied) and the proposed PIT for each decile. As it can be observed, the highest Kakwani index in the PIT (0.3887) in connection to the IRP (0.1973) shows the higher progressivity of the former.

A first evidence of the superior redistributional capacity of the PIT (in connection to the IRP) is appreciated in the previous table: the five poorer deciles are better off with the introduction of the PIT, the situation of the sixth decile remains practically unchanged, the seventh decile will pay slightly more PIT that IRP, and the significant collection increase is on the population's three richer deciles (in particular the 20 percent richer), the losers of the reform.[31]

The highly superior progressivity of the PIT over the IRP can be shown comparing the collection by decile.[32] In turn, the 20 percent richer population will contribute with 60.4 percent of the IRP and they would pay 80.5 percent of the PIT. It should be stressed that while the IRP collects 0.87 percent of the GDP while the PIT will collect 2.5 percent approximately.

Finally, more technically, the Reynolds-Smolensky (RS) index has to be considered as global indicator of the redistributional capacity. The highest RS associated to the PIT (0.0222) in connection with the RS associated to the IRP (0.0047) shows that the PIT causes an improvement in the distribution of income of more than two points of the Gini, superior to the one of the IRP, of half a point of the Gini, which would allow the IRP to be identified as (almost) neutral. From a different viewpoint, the introduction of the PIT determines a

Table 13.6 Uruguay: PIT versus IRP – progressiveness and redistribution

	Average effective rates by decile			Percentage paid by each decile		
	IRP	IRPF	IRPF–IRP		IRP	IRPF
Decile 1	0.23%	0.10%	–0.13%	Decile 1	0.27%	0.05%
Decile 2	0.70%	0.22%	–0.48%	Decile 2	1.27%	0.18%
Decile 3	1.05%	0.48%	–0.58%	Decile 3	2.37%	0.47%
Decile 4	1.36%	0.91%	–0.45%	Decile 4	3.50%	1.02%
Decile 5	1.60%	1.31%	–0.28%	Decile 5	4.72%	1.69%
Decile 6	1.84%	1.89%	0.04%	Decile 6	6.36%	2.82%
Decile 7	2.13%	2.73%	0.60%	Decile 7	8.55%	4.76%
Decile 8	2.51%	3.94%	1.42%	Decile 8	12.53%	8.53%
Decile 9	2.89%	6.22%	3.33%	Decile 9	19.13%	17.80%
Decile 10	3.21%	11.23%	8.03%	Decile 10	41.28%	62.69%
Kakwani	*0.1973*	*0.3887*		*20% + vs 40%*	*8.1*	*46.9*
Reynolds-Srr	*0.0047*	*0.0222*		*40% –*	*7.4%*	*1.7%*
				20% +	*60.4%*	*80.5%*

Source: Barreix and Roca (2006).

transfer of 2.2 percent of the total income (after the PIT) of 20 percent of the richest households to the poorest 80 percent.

Corporate and international income

The reform introduces international taxation in Uruguay levying with a uniform final withholding[33] on interests, royalties, technical assistance, and capital gains remitted or credited abroad at 12 percent. Dividends, including those paid to residents, will be taxed at 7 percent. Also, a battery of traditional instruments is introduced such as transfer prices, definition of permanent establishment, tax haven regulations, etc., as key elements of the fiscal pyramid.[34]

Finally, the territorial approach will be applied until the administration improves, a network of information exchange agreements will be in place, and MERCOSUR consolidates as a common market. Fulfilling those conditions, the country will be able to compete for investments and, then, to implement world-wide income taxation.

New tax secrecy

The dual system allows the country to maintain tax secrecy on financial savings instruments and, at the same time, to tax the capital returns by final withholding (12 percent). Consequently, the country cannot be considered a tax haven[35] according to the regulatory scheme of the OECD. Indeed, for a jurisdiction to be considered a tax haven by the OECD the country must have low or no taxation on capital income. Uruguay would not fulfill the criterion as it taxed at least at a 12 percent rate through a similar system to the one defined by EU Saving Directive.[36]

Nevertheless, to fight evasion there is a proposal to lift the tax secrecy only on the banking operations for "transaction motive" – current and savings accounts – and to maintain it for "accumulative motive" (savings) – bank deposits, bonds, etc. (Barreix and Roca 2006a).

Tax simplification

The revenue of the dual PIT can substitute 11 taxes that compose the current incomplete cedular income tax and so, simplifying the tax structure. There are two main reasons to abolish these taxes:

1   eliminate taxes which compete with the new income tax system and collect 1.26 percent of the GDP – IRP, Tax on Commissions, IMABA (tax on bank assets) and Tax to the Granting of Sportsmen;
2   remove seven taxes of high administration and compliance costs and/or low yield (0.84 percent of GDP in 2004) in order to simplify the system – COFIS (wholesale VAT), ITEL (excise on telecommunications), ICOSIFI on some bank transactions, tax on the forced auctions, tax on credit cards, tax on lotteries, tax to the sales in public auctions.

Notes

1 Those "adjustments" included, among other measures:

 1 the increase of the general VAT rate from 20 to 22 percent;
 2 the rise of the corporate income tax rate (CIT) from the 30 to 35 percent;
 3 the implementation of the Taxes on Bank Assets (IMABA) – which burdens bank loans at differential rates according to length of the credit, similar to the debit tax but on loans;
 4 strong rise of the excise tax on petroleum products, which collected almost 2 percent of the GDP;
 5 a significant increase of the employer's contributions to social security;
 6 a jump of almost 2 percent of the GDP in the property and net wealth taxation – punishing the agricultural sector with a fivefold increase in the assessment value of the land.

2 This increase on the fiscal burden was complemented with heavy price hikes that increased the surpluses of state-owned energy, water and telecommunications monopolies to more than 2.5 percent of GDP.
3 This point will be carried out later on.
4 Rezende (2005) complained on the emergence of a new tributary principle based on the easiness to collect by the tax administrators.
5 Actually, the tax on sales of agricultural goods (IMEBA January 1996) and the tax on insurance companies (February 2001), were also created.
6 In fact, four income categories are considered, as towards the inside of the public sector the income of the employees of the judicial power taxed to a minimum rate is considered as a separate category.
7 The current value of BPC is UR$1,482, approximately US$63. Until December 2005 the tax fringes were determined in minimum wages (SMN). The expressed intent of the government raising gradually the SMN has taken the same to use the BPC to determine the tax brackets and thus not to lose revenues.
8 The revenue of the tax on farming income – IRA – did not reach one million dollars. The producers with a volume of sales lower to a certain limit can choose to pay the IMEBA, a tax on the sales of farming goods at differential rates. This tax collected US$42 million, 0.3 percent of the GDP in 2004.
9 It is important to point out that in Uruguay, like in most Latin American jurisdictions, the entrepreneurial income carried out in personal societies, including the sole proprietors and the limited liabilities partnerships, are taxed with the same tax as the corporations.
10 For example, for the period between 1993–7, a sample of 2.368 companies that represented more than 30 percent of the total output, paid an effective rate average of 21 percent.
11 Nevertheless, with the broad-base VAT at 17 percent, the poorest decile – the only loser – could be easily compensated with targeted public expenditures. A 17 percent flat VAT implies a reduction of 35 percent of the rate and is highly superior in competitiveness, neutrality, political enforcement and administrative simplicity. This is even more relevant regarding the global impact of the reform determines that the seven poorest deciles end up the winners.
12 By a recent modification, the excises on fuel in Uruguay – and their uses – became a fixed amount per liter. A fraction of the excise revenues are transferred to municipal governments.
13 Approximately, 3.5 percent of the excises collection (IMESI) on gasolines and fuels, and 5 percent of the IMESI on tobacco products are transferred to the municipalities and distributed among them according to their area and population – distributive

approach. Furthermore, 20 percent of the IMESI on the diesel oil is transferred to the local governments and the distribution criterium takes into consideration the origin of the revenue – devolution approach.

14 Finally, the central government pays the employer contribution to the social security for municipalities' employees, except for the capital – Montevideo.

15 The personal contributions to the first pillar are 15 percent of the salaries up to the aforementioned limit (US$1,000) and to the pillar of individual capitalization the same rate to the income between this figure and a new. The contribution for the wage surplus is optional.

16 Additionally, regarding coverage, estimates of Bucheli *et al.* (2006), only 28 percent of the active workers would receive pensions at the age of 65 (minimum age of retirement for both men and women). Within this percentage, the public employees represent 57 percent, which reinforces the hypothesis of a very informal labor market as well as the high protection offered by the immobility – cannot be fired – of public employees. In fact, 85 percent of the public servants will fulfil the condition (35 years of work) to get a pension at 65 years old.

17 There are three estimates to be considered:

1 Piancastelli, M. (2001). He considers a sample of 75 countries, in the period 1985–95 and the income of central government. The coefficient of tax effort estimated for Uruguay is 1.411.

2 Teera, J. M. (2001). This sample is of 122 countries, developed and underdeveloped, in the period 1975–98. The resulting coefficient for Uruguay is 1.236.

3 Cobas, P., Perelmuter, N., and Tedesco, P. (2004) "Evasion in Uruguay: a study on VAT," Research paper, FCEA – UDELAR, Unpublished. They work with the income of central government with a sample of 17 Latin American countries, in the period 1990–2000. The estimated coefficient for Uruguay is 1.707.

18 Uruguay has a stock of total public debt of more than two and a half times its GDP (it includes social security and financial public debt, not including contingencies). The conditionings imposed on its flow but not performing a sustainability analysis are considered.

19 The regressivity of the overall tax system in Uruguay, and in particular of the consumption taxes, are presented in Barreix and Roca (2006a, 2006b).

20 Planning and Budget Office (OPP 2003).

21 In July 2005, the government formed a Tax Reform Commission. The authors were members (pro bono) of the Commission, which worked until January, 2006. In August 2005, they presented a report to the government, which was considered the "Base Report" of the reform, which introduced the dual income tax *Uruguayan style.*

22 For this reason, Chile has a tax expenditure – individual income disguised as corporate income – of more than 100 percent of what is received as revenue. Indeed, the tax expenditure originated in the CIT is estimated 2 percent of the GDP when it is revenues for PIT are slightly less than 2 percent of the GDP.

23 Another more complex way to avoid this arbitrage is using the paid credit of the retained capital income and simultaneously applying thin capitalization rules for interests or limitations of other kind of capital income in the determination of the company's profits.

24 A modified model of the theoretical version developed by Hall and Rabushka (1995) was enforced recently in more than a dozen countries, especially in ex Soviet bloc economies.

25 It includes all the social security charges (health insurance, unemployment, employers and workers contributions, etc.).

26 In Barreix and Roca (2006b), it is argued about the inconvenience of introducing an income tax of the integral type in Uruguay.

27 Contrasting with our proposal, the new dual income tax approved in Spain, considers that lease are less prone to *delocalize* and, consequently, are taxed in the labor income basket at progressive marginal rates. Two observations become relevant:

1   as it will be seen, our proposal to tax all capital rents at a lower rate does not only take into account the possible delocalization but also its efficiency;
2   it is worth noting that the Spanish CIT taxes real estate capital gains (and loses), at the capital income rate (18 percent) while including rental income in the labor basket.

28 Although academics tend to recognize that income derived from savings must be taxed at lower rates due to efficiency, there are opposing viewpoints. For example, King (1980), answering the Meade Report (UK, 1978) conclusions, proposed that the income tax is similar to levy on individual consumption and sustained that there is little difference in efficiency between both systems.

29 Boadway summarizes the following arguments favoring preferential treatment on capital income:

1   the positive externality of investment linked to the innovation on the literature about endogenous growth;
2   the systematic tendency to save below optimum, which seems irrational (in practice, it can be that individuals act strategically anticipating the government or a philanthropist will help them when in need);
3   that the capital income at an individual level will discourage innovative projects as being inherently risky (the disadvantages of these market investments are originated in significant externalities developed in asymmetric information);
4   to tax the capital income discriminates against households whose income fluctuates, thus savings operate as a way of "smoothing" their consumption.

30 Actually, a correct comparison should consider, besides the IRP, the taxes which the PIT will substitute and which are paid by individuals (for example, certain percentage of the tax on commissions), but have not been taken into account in this estimate.

31 Another way of determining the winners and losers is to compare the participation in income of each decile before and after the reform.

32 Indeed, currently 40 percent of the poorer households pay 7.4 percent of IRP, and they would contribute only 1.7 percent of the dual PIT revenues.

33 The effective withholding in the source has a definitive character and it is not necessary to fill and identify the taxpayer.

34 In Barreix and Roca (2003), it is argued that the tax system must be organized in a *pyramidal way*, the tip of the pyramid being the international taxation, to which the most specialized actions correspond.

35 Null or insignificant taxation is the first criterion for which a country can be considered a tax haven. Uruguay levies at 12 percent on all capital income, however, it has great difficulties to fulfill the three subsidiary criteria for which a tax haven is defined: transparency, exchange of information and deadlock.

36 The EU directive on savings is compatible with tax secrecy regime proposed by Barreix and Roca (2006b).

References

Barreix, A and Roca, J. (2003) "Un nuevo modelo de Administración Tributaria," *Revista de la Facultad de Ciencias Económicas*, Universidad Católica del Uruguay. Available

online: www.ucu.edu.uy/Facultades/CienciasEmpresariales/RevistaFCE/articulos/
setiembre2003/
—— (2005) "Propuestas para la reforma tributaria de Uruguay 2005," Universidad
Católica del Uruguay. Available online: www.ucu.edu.uy/Facultades/Ciencias
Empresariales/ref_tributaria.htm.
—— (2006a) "Arquitectura de una propuesta de reforma tributaria," Universidad
Católica del Uruguay. Available online: www.ucu.edu.uy/Facultades/Ciencias
Empresariales/ref_tributaria.htm.
—— (2006b) "Siete Pilares para sostener la Reforma de Uruguay 2005," Universidad
Católica del Uruguay. Available online: www.ucu.edu.uy/Facultades/Ciencias
Empresariales/ref_tributaria.htm.
Boadway, R. (2005) "Income Tax Reform for a Globalized World: The Case for a Dual
Income Tax," *Journal of Asian Economics* 16.
Bucheli, M., Ferreira-Coimbra, N., Forteza, A. and Rossi, I. (2006) "El acceso a la jubi-
lación o pensión en Uruguay: ¿cuántos y quiénes lo lograrían?," Departamento de
Economía. Facultad de Ciencias Sociales, Universidad de la República.
Cobas, P., Perelmuter, N. and Tedesco, P. (2004) "Evasión fiscal en el Uruguay: un
estudio sobre el Impuesto al Valor Agregado," Trabajo de investigación monográfica,
FCEA-UDELAR mimeo.
De Haedo, J., Vegh, A. and Sapelli, C. (1987) *Las Finanzas Públicas en Uruguay*, Mon-
tevideo: Banco Central del Uruguay.
Hall, R. and Rabushka, A. (1995) *The Flat Tax*, Second Edition, Stanford: Hoover Insti-
tution Press.
King, M. (1980) "Savings and Taxation," in Hughes, G. and Heal, G. *Public Policy and
the Tax System*, London: George Allen & Unwin.
Piancastelli, M. (2001) "Measuring the Tax Effort of Developed and Developing Coun-
tries, Cross Country Panel Data Analysis – 1985/95," IPEA, TD n. 818, Rio de Janeiro.
Rezende, F. (2005) "Integracao Regional e Harmonicao tributaria: A Perspectiva
Brasileira," in Tanzi, V., Barreix A. and Villela, L. (eds.) *Tributación para la Inte-
gración del MERCOSUR*, Diálogo Regional de Política, BID.
Rossa, A. and Roca, J. (2001) "Estimación del costo de las exoneraciones fiscales de la
Dirección General Impositivia," Asesoría Económica, Ministerio de Economía y
Finanzas, mimeo.
Teera, J. M. (2001) "Tax Performance. A Comparative Study," University of Bath,
Department of Economics.
Vallarino, H. (2005) "Breve historia fiscal de Uruguay. 1990–2003," in Tanzi, V.,
Barreix, A. and Villela, L. (eds.) *Tributación para la Integración del MERCOSUR*,
Diálogo Regional de Política, BID. Available online: www.iadb.org/INT/Trade/
2_spanish/2_QueHacemos/1d_TaxDocumentos.htm
Villela, L., Roca, J. and Barreix, A. (2005) "O Desafío Fiscal do MERCOSUR," Caderno
de Finanças Públicas da Escola Superior de Administracao Fazandaria, Brasilia.

Index

T - #0017 - 160425 - C0 - 234/156/18 [20] - CB - 9780415443364 - Gloss Lamination